Bryan Talbot's

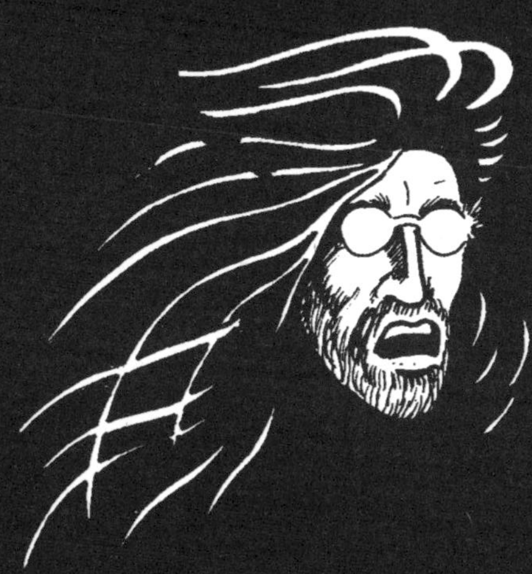

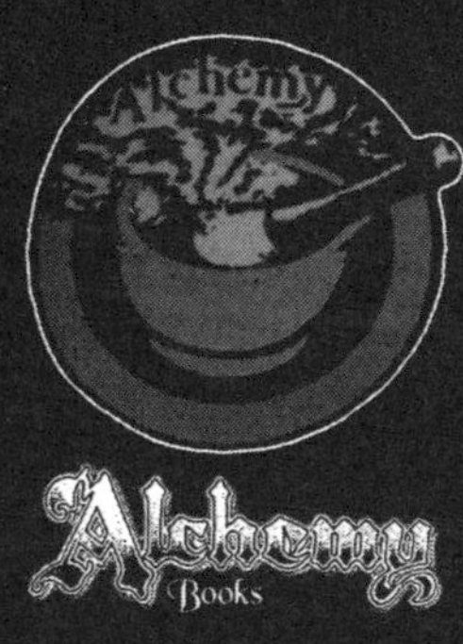

Alchemy Books

"Dedicated with great affection to Lee Harris, without whom ..."

Bryan Talbot

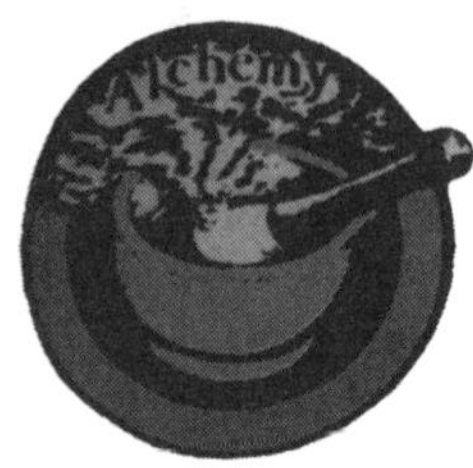

Published by
Alchemy
261 Portobello Road, London W11 1LR, UK
tel: 020 7792 0166
email: openmind@FSBDial.co.uk
www.euro.net/mark-space/shopAlchemy

Design and production by the Graveyard Shift, London

Printed in Canada

Publisher: Lee Harris

 ISBN 0-9508487-1-9. British Library Cataloguing in Publication Data. A catalogue record of this book is available from the British Library.

Additional Credits:
Bryan signing session photos (1982) by Steve Percival.
Flyover graffitti in introduction section (1975) by Tony Allen.
Lee & Brigitte Harris' wedding photo (1975) by Bryan Talbot.
Extracted illustrations: (page 73)
Hackenbush with Russell by Pete Loveday
Hawkwind: Ledge of Darkness by Bob Walker.

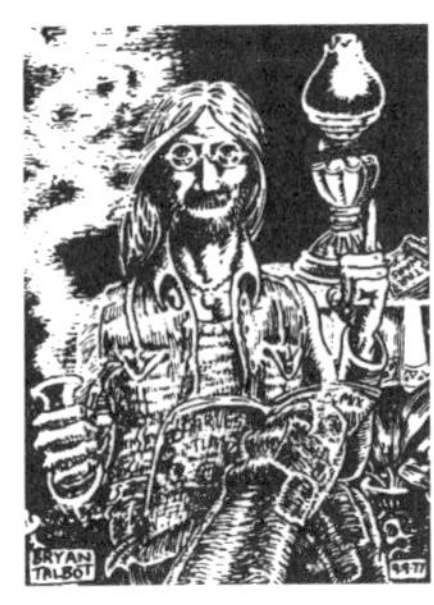

CONTENTS

INTRODUCTION

'WOTTA FREAKOUT! LEARY NEVER SAID ANYTHIN' ABOUT THIS!'
- Chester P. Hackenbush, Brainstorm No. 1.

Portobello Road, London, in 1975. Freaks and Heads everywhere. Hanging out at the Mountain Grill cafe, discussing the latest 'sides' from Hawkwind, the Pink Fairies and the Deviants - all local outfits, all habituees of the cafe. Fry-ups are devoured, stories exchanged, drug deals done. Spliffs are smoked and shared with black hipsters, when the Bill aren't watching. Within view of the cafe, somebody's graffitied 'Nuclear Waste Fades Your Genes' in huge letters on the Westway bridge. It's a serious message. But not today. There's too much giggling going on....

Enter Brainstorm Comix no.1. A new psychedelic comic, published by a Portobello headshop (Alchemy), and looking for all the world like it's the perfect product of its environment. The fact that it's been created and drawn by a lad from Lancashire - an unknown artist called Bryan Talbot - has nought to do with it. One look at the cover tells you it fits: the central image is of what appears to be a cosmic Hell's Angel on a rocket-powered bike hurtling through space; to his left, a joint with wings flies by; to his right, in the corner, there's a long-haired hippy called Chester Hackenbush muttering 'far out'.

If this didn't go down a (brain)storm among the denizens of the Mountain Grill, nothing would. Even the comic's title was shared with a Hawkwind song (indeed, the band were happy to advertise inside).

There had been other British underground comix before this date. But Cyclops, Nasty Tales and the Cozmic Comics line (all of which heavily featured American material), had had their day, and there seemed to be a hiatus in activity around 1974-5. Brainstorm broke the silence, and was immediately different because it included no US strips at all: the cover legend 'Made in Britain' promised a new start. Not only this, but the art was better than most undergrounds (despite Bryan's self-deprecating comments in his own introduction to this volume), and though you could see elements of Crumb, and perhaps of Dave Sheridan, in the end the style was somehow very British. This went for the writing, too: the star of the comic, the aforementioned Mr Hackenbush, even went round saying 'Ey up!'. (Was he based on Bryan himself? Draw your own conclusions.)

Indeed, Chester Hackenbush was to become something of a counter-cultural hero. His raison d'etre, in case you couldn't guess, was to consume vast amounts of drugs: '...essence of Fly Agaric and Peyote buttons... Qat...', he'd intone, mixing up his medicine, 'plus a dash of ole Lysergic - just to be on the safe side...'. Instead of killing him outright, such concoctions would catapult him into 'Euphoria' ('FLASH!'), where he'd meet various tripped-out characters, and try to discover the secret of the universe. Bryan has since referred to him as an Alice in Wonderland figure: 'He goes up, and he comes down - it's as simple as that'. But, to be fair, Alice in Wonderland never had this many laffs.

There was a serious side to the drugs content, too. It's clear from the Hackenbush stories, for example, that the counter-culture saw pharmaceuticals not just as a source of recreation, but also as a possible pathway to spiritual enlightenment - a way of 'opening the doors of perception', in Aldous Huxley's famous words. Brainstorm mainly featured LSD and dope (the latter was emphasised in later issues), and these two drugs were sometimes held in almost sacred regard. No wonder, then, that attempts by the authorities to clamp down on their use were met with such passionate resistance. By the mid-70s, Bryan was running a headshop in Preston, and both he and the publisher of Brainstorm, Alchemy's Lee Harris, had seen at first hand the brutal way in which the anti-drugs campaign was being waged (Portobello Road was a site of frequent busts). It was, as they say, a heavy time, and Bryan's dedication in issue 1 to 'all those freaks serving sentences for dope offences and paying off stupid fines' was heartfelt indeed.

It didn't take long for Brainstorm to garner a following. Hippies were its obvious constituency, but it also found fans among older members of the comics fraternity. Denis Gifford - cartoonist, author of numerous comics histories and publisher of Ally Sloper - was one. So, too, was Alfred Bestall, octegenarian creator of Rupert the Bear, who had met Lee Harris at a book fair. He signed a copy of Brainstorm for Bryan with the words: 'Am very intrigued!' (as no doubt he would have been): Bryan has kept the issue till this day. This anecdote explains why, in later issues of Brainstorm, Rupert makes numerous guest appearances.

Of course, due to its content, Brainstorm could not be sold from newsagents like regular comics: but on the headshop circuit it did remarkably well. (The main headshops in the UK at the time appear on a map drawn by Bryan in issue 1.) It was distributed by a variety of companies, including one that dealt in Sufi literature, and by a publisher of alternative sex publications, and eventually ended up with the much bigger Moore Harness, who were able to capitalise on its word-of-mouth success. At its peak, Brainstorm was selling a very respectable 10,000 per issue. It didn't make Bryan rich - he had a wife and two kids to support, after all. But the figures were pretty cool by underground standards.

But just when it seemed that everything was going so well, there came a challenge from an unforeseen source. It was 1977, and punk had arrived. All that mellowness, all that good Karma (man) that had come with Brainstorm's success was suddenly blasted away by the new youth revolution. Punk was a different kind of counter-culture - more a howl of

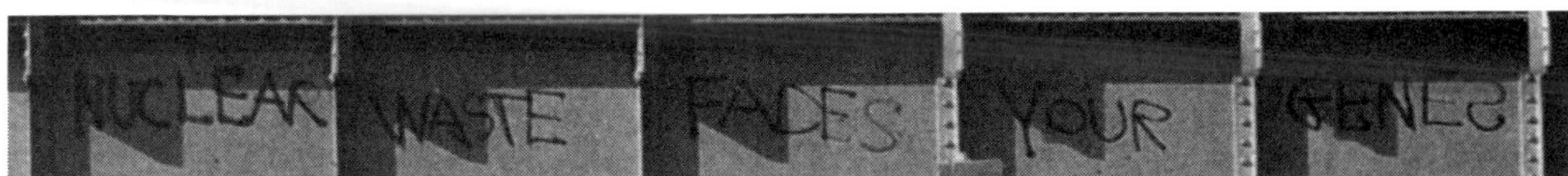

outrage than a movement with an agenda - which decreed, among other things, that hippies were the enemy. Long hair was out, dope was out, 'dinosaur bands' were out, and - yup - comix were out. If you were associated with any of these things, you were a Boring Old Fart, dadd-io, and you'd better either leave town or kill yourself. (Curiously, Portobello Road remained a centre for punkdom, just as it had been for the hippie scene.)

One punk convert was especially vocal in his dismissal of the underground. Cartoonist Andy Johnson, a.k.a. 'Andy Dog' (an old mate of Bryan's) complained in a series of articles (in Graphixus magazine, Kidz Stuff and a letter to the NME) that the hippy comix were just 'the same old drivel', and implied that Brainstorm was as out of date as Hawkwind. He went on to call for a 'new wave' in comics to take over, reflecting what he saw as the new spirit of the age. Bryan was obviously hurt by the broadside, and responded by producing a strip for Street Quomix in which he depicted Johnson as a mewling infant, the punk safety pin now being used for its proper purpose - to hold up his nappy. (In fact, Bryan patched up his relationship with Johnson to the point where they were going to collaborate on a new wave strip: but it came to nothing. Bryan's response to punk per se was 'The Omega Report' - again republished here - which came with the subtitle@ 'Flabbergasting Punk Rock SF!'.)

In retrospect we can see that the punk and hippie movements were not really that far apart - after all, Johnny Rotten claimed that Hawkwind were one of his favourite bands. But at the time, it seemed as if something had changed forever, and that the underground could not continue in the same vein. Johnson's 'new wave' of comics never materialised in the form he'd envisaged, but after the punk period the old-style sex-'n'-drugs comix did start to disappear - Brainstorm included. Henceforward the term 'alternative comics' would become much more common to describe anything that did not fit into the mainstream.

But Bryan was already ahead of the game. By 1977, he had sown the seeds of his future career in comics by moving away from doper material, and towards more involved science fiction subject-matter. In the third issue of Brainstorm (subititled: 'Mixed Bunch'), he debuted a new character - the remarkable Luther Arkwright. This seven-page strip revealed a new side to his art - more Richard Corben line-and-wash than Robert Crumb cross-hatching - and also to his storytelling. For this was a relatively complex yarn, set in a parallel universe in which England was a Catholic dictatorship where 'Henry IX was a tyrant, a religious fanatic...', and where Arkwright, a 'mercenary and infidel', is the only hope of 'maintaining the equilibrium of the parallels'.

The humour was still there: a group of sexy biker nuns play a starring role, and there is an amusing cameo from a Nazi bishop ('Herr Arkwright! I might haff known you vere in on dis.'). But beyond this the strip exhibits the influence of two more sober sources: Michael Moorcock's 'Jerry Cornelius' sagas, with their 'intra-dimensional realities'; and French bandes dessinees, which at this time were a cult in the headshops. In particular, Bryan had seen copies of Metal Hurlant (later Americanised as Heavy Metal), and he had been 'knocked out' by the ways in which artists like Moebius and Bilal had taken the science fiction genre in comics and reinvented it in adult form. Now it was his turn to do the same, and in the late 1970s and early 1980s, he set about expanding the Arkwright story to the point where it became a pioneering series of (serious) graphic novels.

The Adventures of Luther Arkwright books remain one of Bryans's outstanding achievements - though here is not the place to discuss them. Quite rightly, they opened the door for more commercial projects: Bryan went on to work for Britain's Fleetway on 2000AD, and for America's DC Comics on titles such as Batman, The Nazz and Hellblazer. After producing another award-winning graphic novel, One Bad Rat (1996), he returned to Arkwright, and the new series of adventures 'Heart of Empire', is currently available in the shops. In short, in the years since his underground days, Bryan has become one of the most in-demand creators in the industry. (Don't take my word for it: have a look at the excellent website that has been created to chart his progress: www.bryan-talbot.com.)

And as for Brainstorm itself? Well, it finally went under in 1978 after six issues. With hindsight, the comic has the aura of the last gasp of the British underground - though its influence has been significant (Alan Moore, Neil Gaiman and Grant Morrison have all attested to the effect it had on them - especially Moore, who paid homage to Hackenbush with his character 'Chester Williams' in Swamp Thing). Of course, Portobello Road is still there, but it doesn't have the same atmosphere that it did. The Mountain Grill is long gone, the graffiti has been cleaned up, and the area has become so yuppified that it was recently used as the location for the grim Hugh Grant comedy 'Notting Hill'. On the bright side, Alchemy continues to ply its dodgy trade, and for the price of a cup of herbal tea Lee Harris can even now be found ready to discuss ye good ole days. As Hawkwind might have sang: 'Brainstorm, here I go...'

***Roger Sabin** is a renowned comics historian and the author of Comics, Comix and Graphic Novels (Phaidon) and Adult Comics: An Introduction (Routledge).*

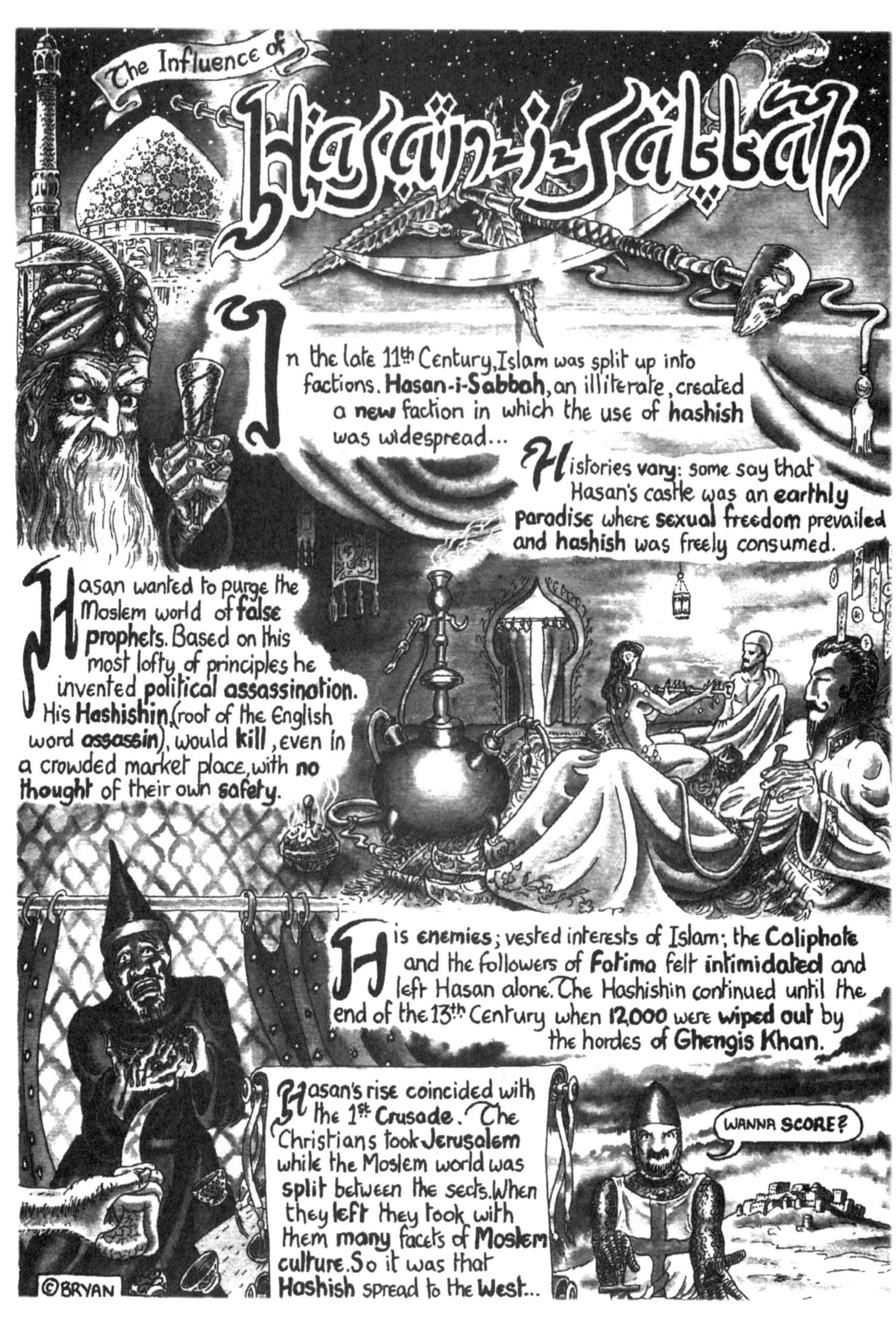
The Influence of
Hasan-i-Sabbah
In the late 11th Century, Islam was split up into factions. Hasan-i-Sabbah, an illiterate, created a new faction in which the use of hashish was widespread...
Histories vary: some say that Hasan's castle was an earthly paradise where sexual freedom prevailed and hashish was freely consumed.
Hasan wanted to purge the Moslem world of false prophets. Based on this most lofty of principles he invented political assassination. His Hashishin, (root of the English word assassin), would kill, even in a crowded market place, with no thought of their own safety.
His enemies; vested interests of Islam; the Caliphate and the followers of Fatima felt intimidated and left Hasan alone. The Hashishin continued until the end of the 13th Century when 12,000 were wiped out by the hordes of Ghengis Khan.
Hasan's rise coincided with the 1st Crusade. The Christians took Jerusalem while the Moslem world was split between the sects. When they left they took with them many facets of Moslem culture. So it was that Hashish spread to the West...
WANNA SCORE?
©BRYAN

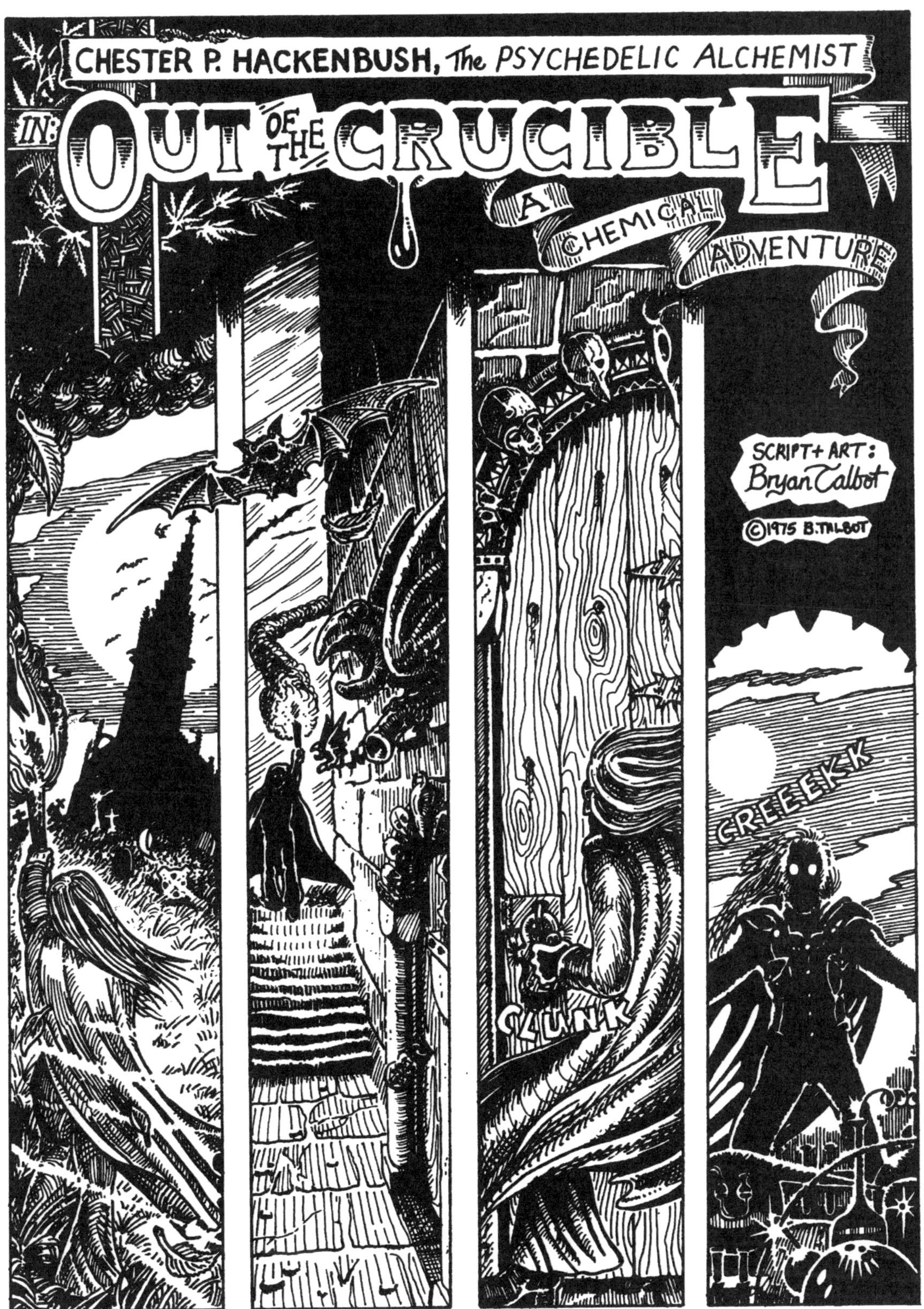
CHESTER P. HACKENBUSH, The PSYCHEDELIC ALCHEMIST
IN: OUT OF THE CRUCIBLE
A CHEMICAL ADVENTURE
SCRIPT+ART: Bryan Talbot
©1975 B.TALBOT
CLUNK
CREEEKK

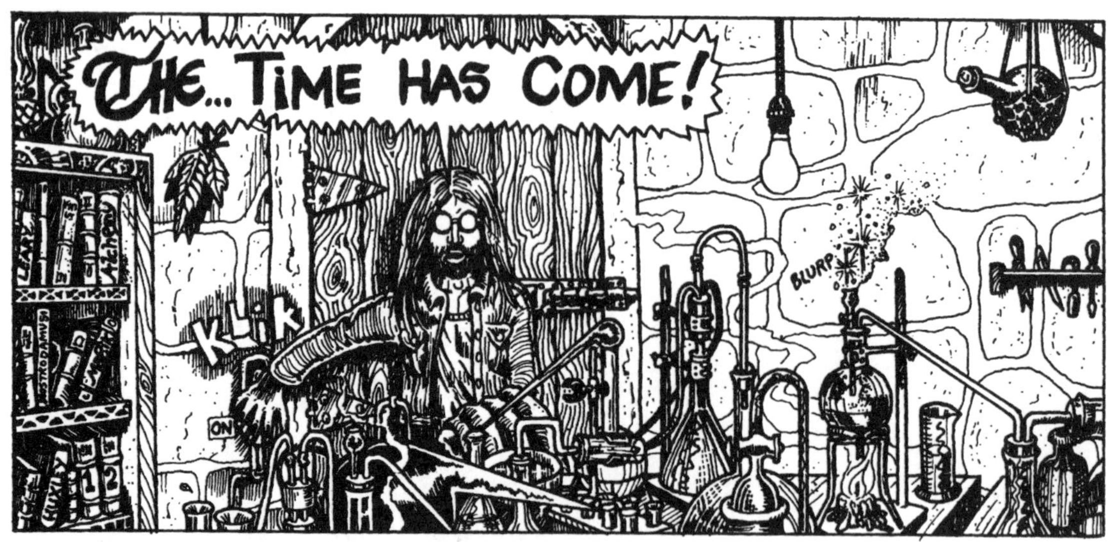
THE... TIME HAS COME!
KLIK
ON
BLURP
LEARY
NOSTRODAMUS
HUXLEY

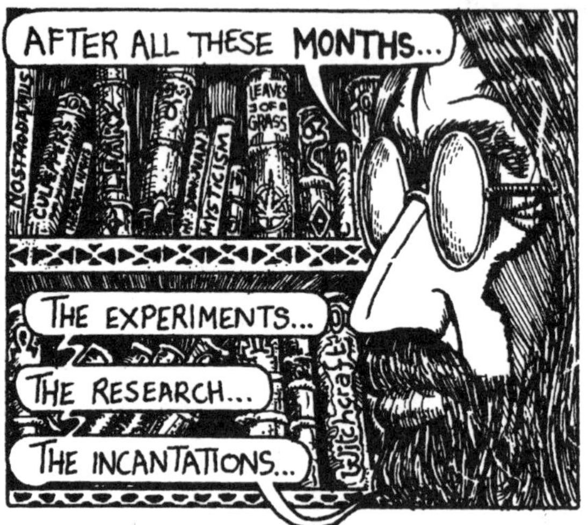
AFTER ALL THESE MONTHS...
THE EXPERIMENTS...
THE RESEARCH...
THE INCANTATIONS...
NOSTRODAMUS
LEAVES OF GRASS
MYSTICISM
WITCHCRAFT

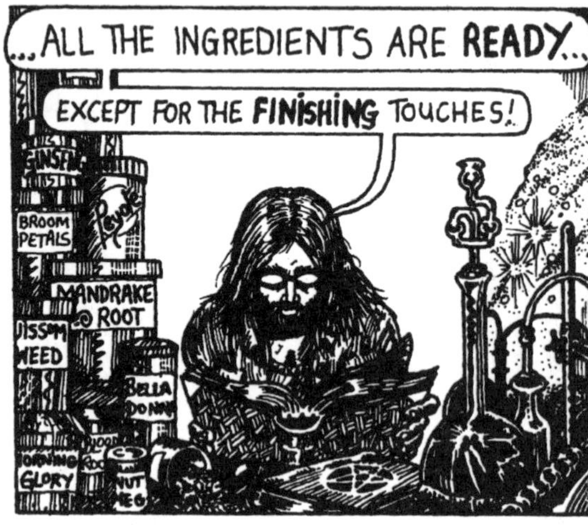
...ALL THE INGREDIENTS ARE READY...
EXCEPT FOR THE FINISHING TOUCHES!
BROOM PETALS
PEYOTE
MANDRAKE ROOT
BELLA DONNA
MORNING GLORY
NUTMEG

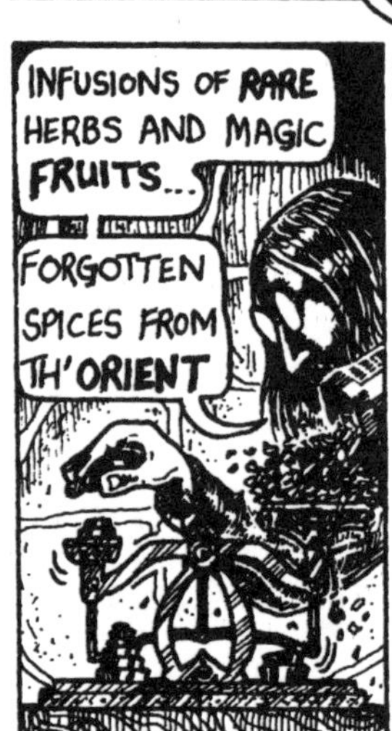
INFUSIONS OF RARE HERBS AND MAGIC FRUITS...
FORGOTTEN SPICES FROM TH' ORIENT

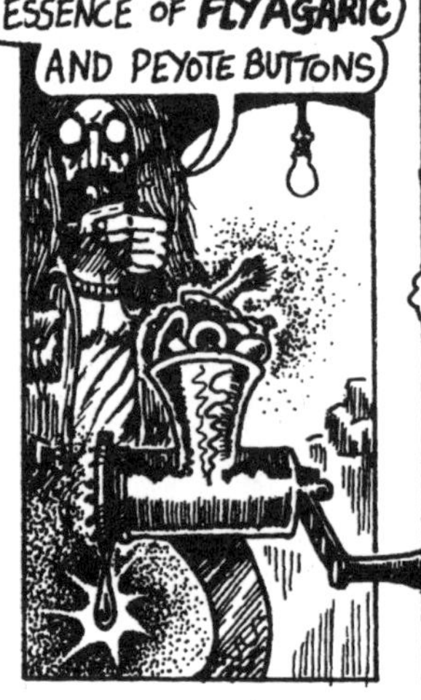
ESSENCE OF FLY AGARIC AND PEYOTE BUTTONS

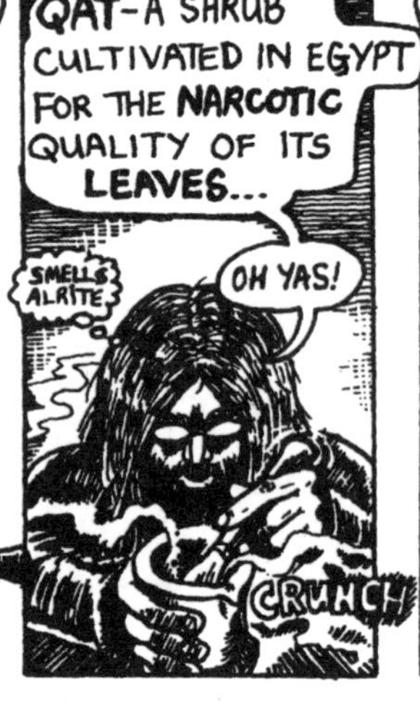
QAT—A SHRUB CULTIVATED IN EGYPT FOR THE NARCOTIC QUALITY OF ITS LEAVES...
SMELLS ALRITE
OH YAS!
CRUNCH

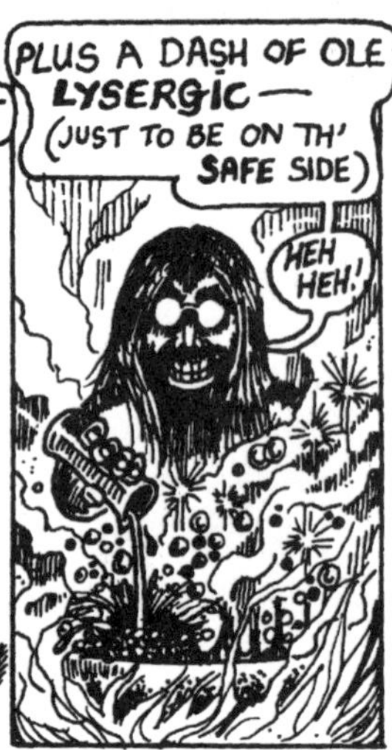
PLUS A DASH OF OLE LYSERGIC— (JUST TO BE ON TH' SAFE SIDE)
HEH HEH!

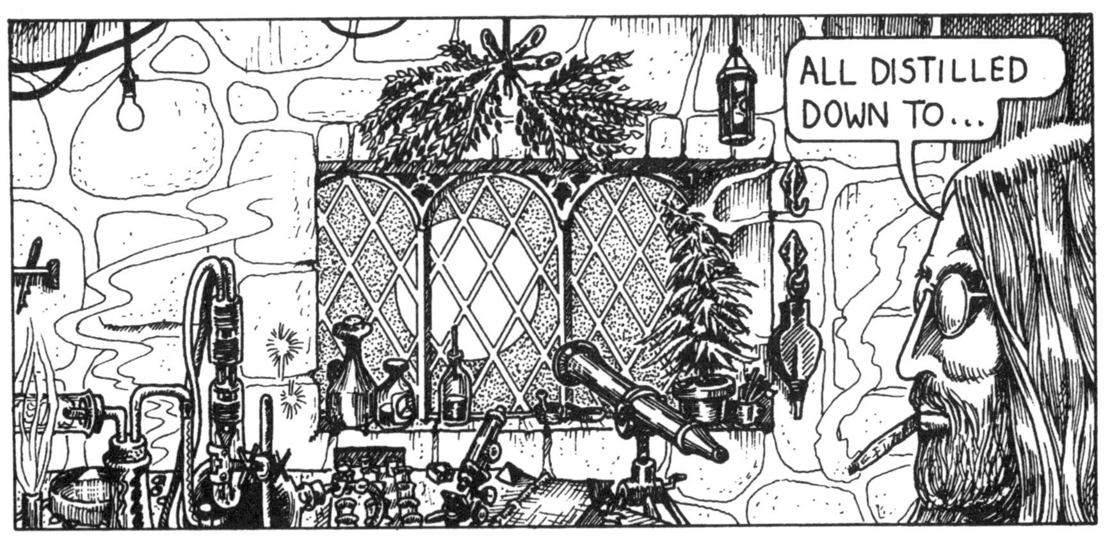
ALL DISTILLED DOWN TO...
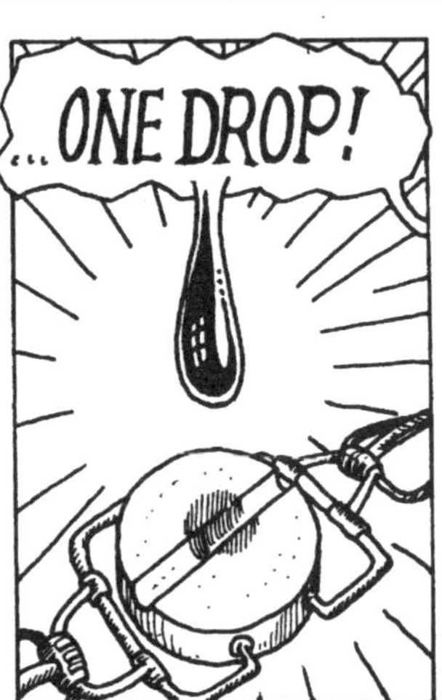
...ONE DROP!
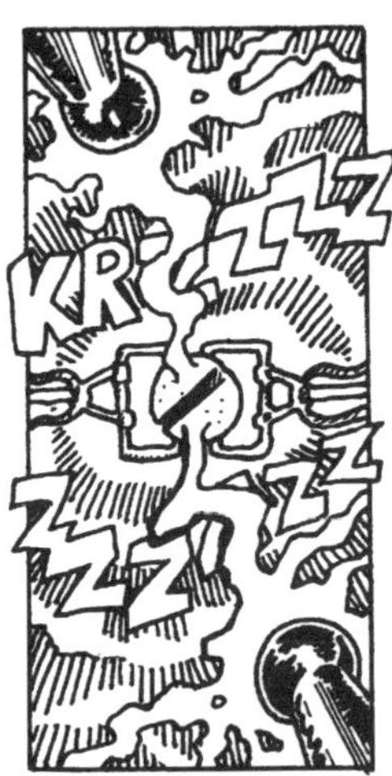
KR
ZZZ
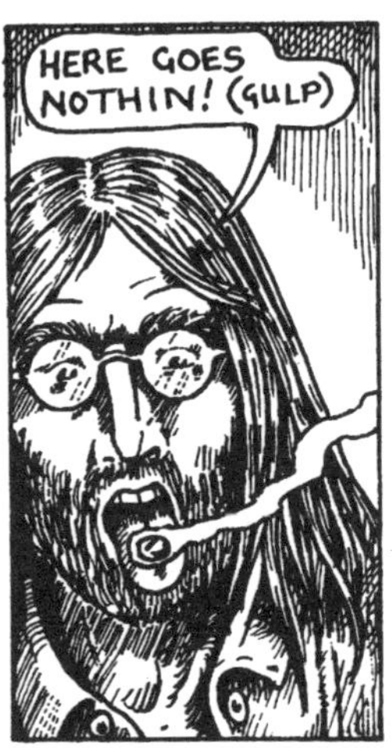
HERE GOES NOTHIN! (GULP)
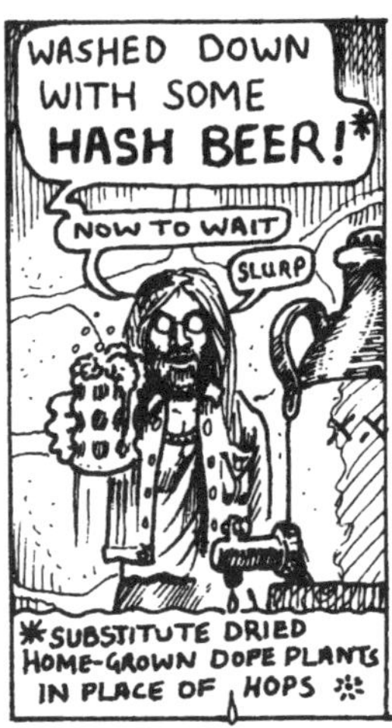
WASHED DOWN WITH SOME HASH BEER!*
NOW TO WAIT
SLURP
*SUBSTITUTE DRIED HOME-GROWN DOPE PLANTS IN PLACE OF HOPS
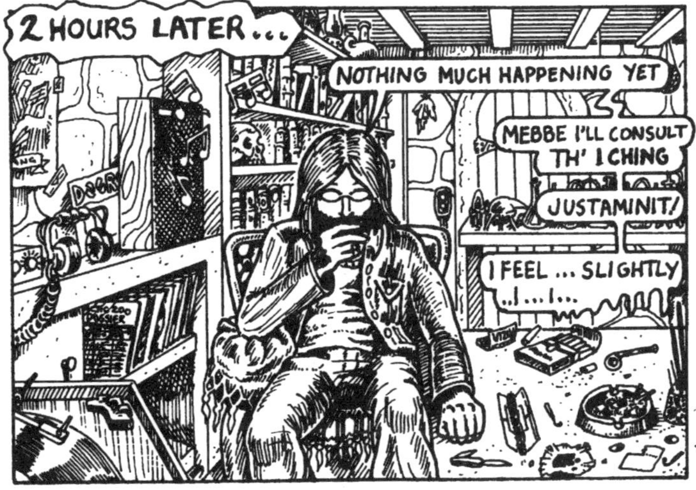
2 HOURS LATER...
NOTHING MUCH HAPPENING YET
MEBBE I'LL CONSULT TH' I CHING
JUSTAMINIT!
I FEEL ... SLIGHTLY ..I...I...
DOOR
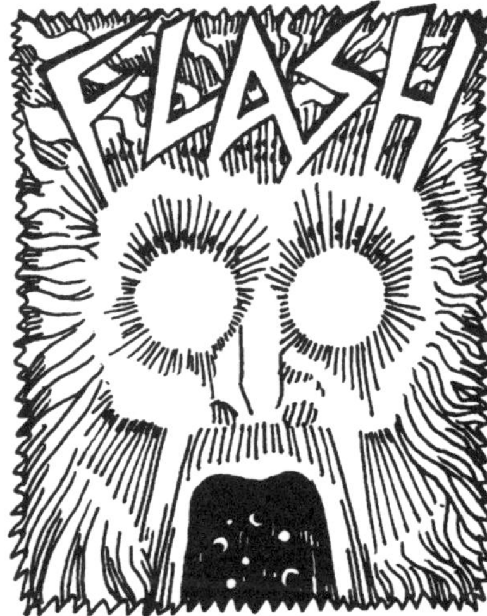
FLASH

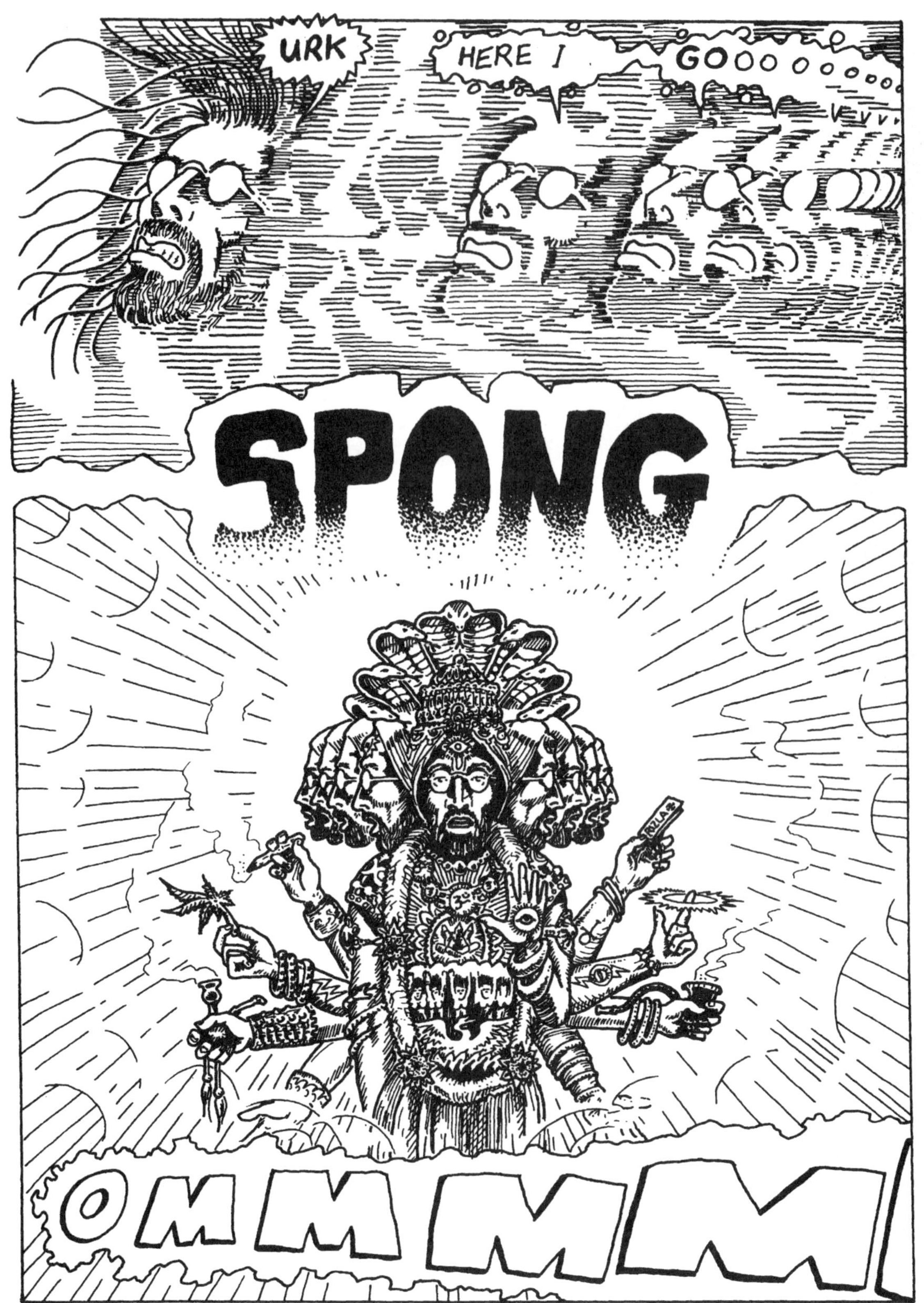
URK
HERE I
GOooo oooooo
SPONG
OMMMM

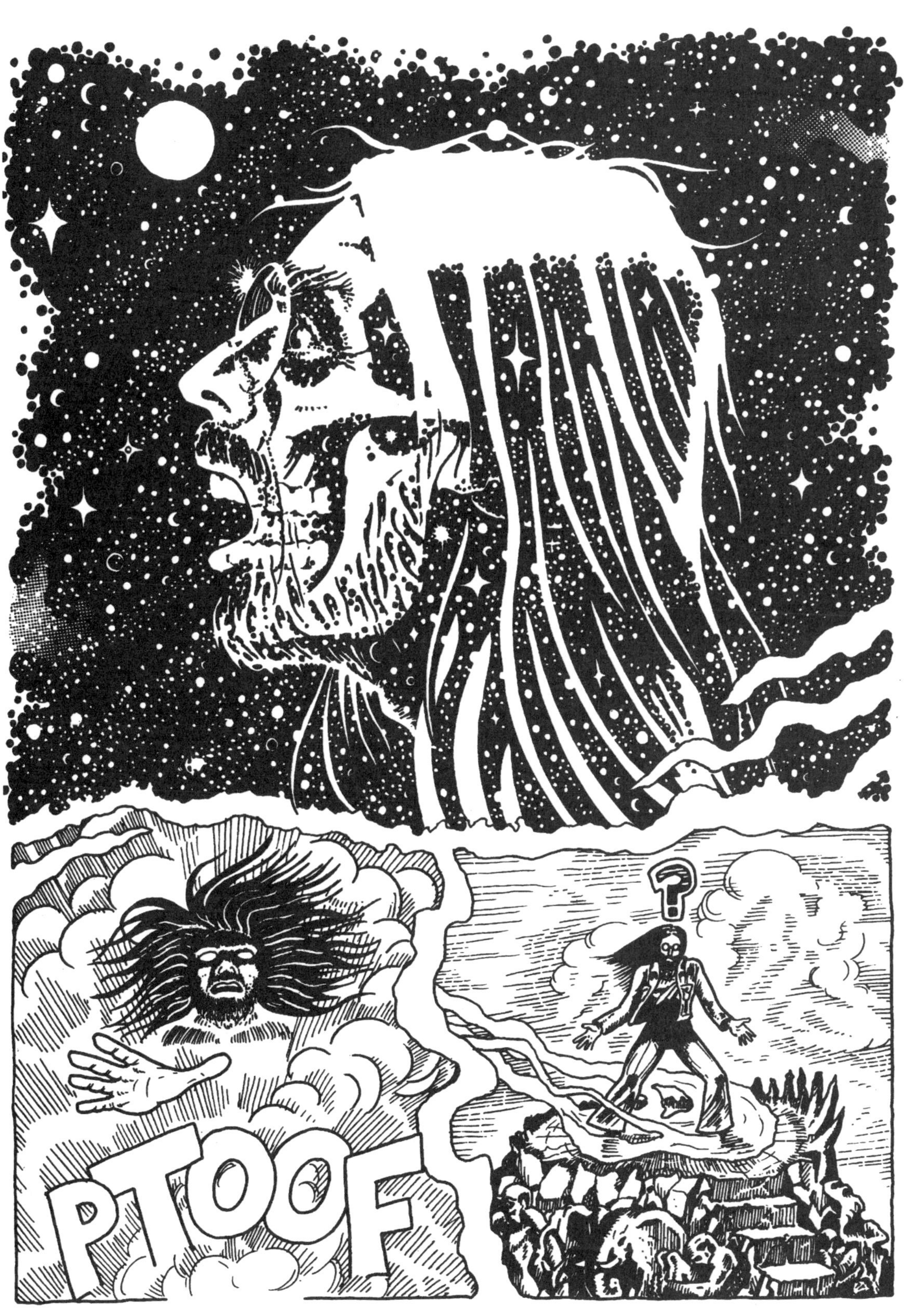
?
PTOOF

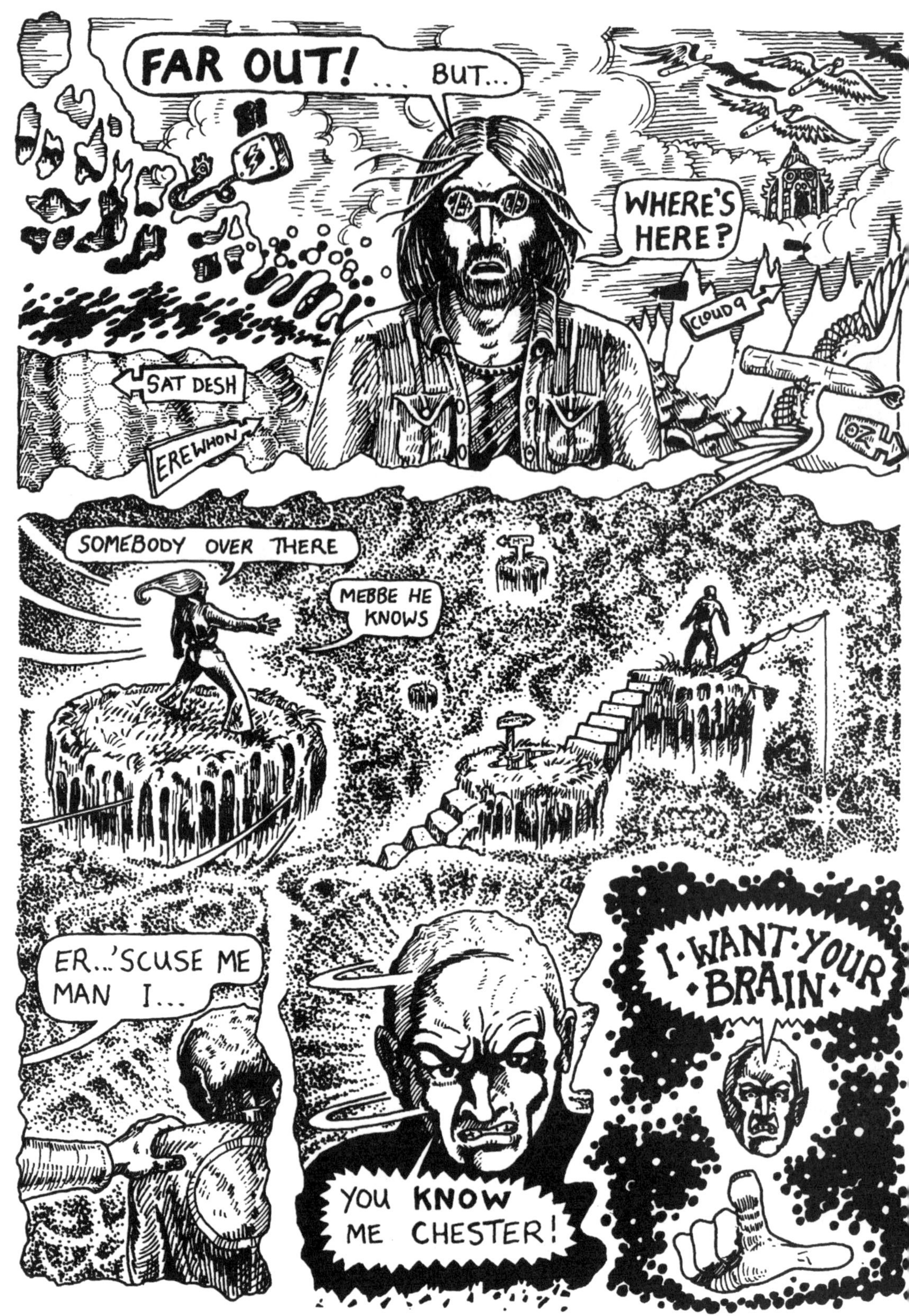
FAR OUT! ... BUT...
WHERE'S HERE?
CLOUD 9
SAT DESH
EREWHON
OZ
SOMEBODY OVER THERE
MEBBE HE KNOWS
ER...'SCUSE ME MAN I...
YOU KNOW ME CHESTER!
I·WANT·YOUR ·BRAIN·

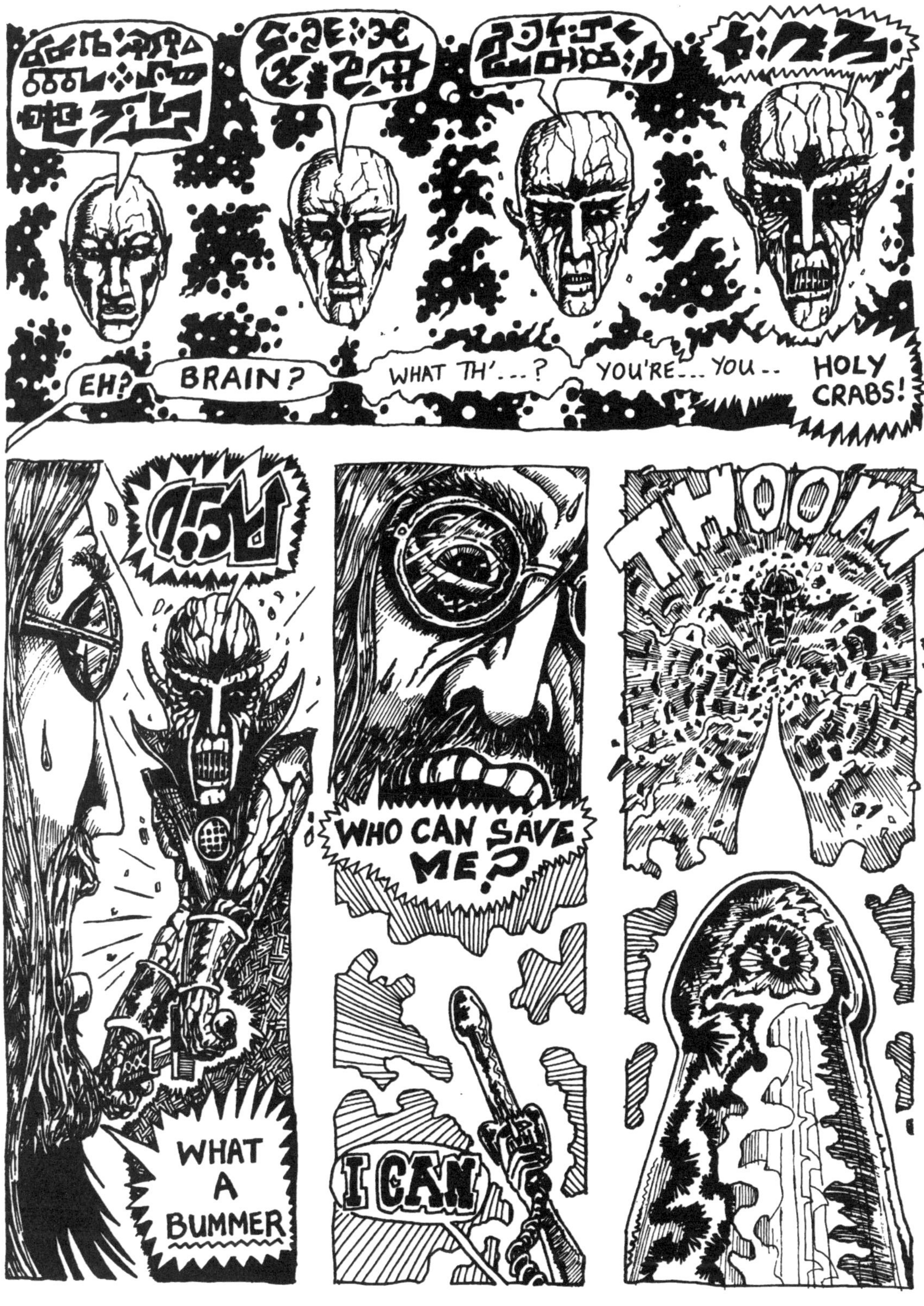

EH?
BRAIN?
WHAT TH'...?
YOU'RE... YOU..
HOLY CRABS!
WHAT A BUMMER
WHO CAN SAVE ME?
THOOM
I CAN

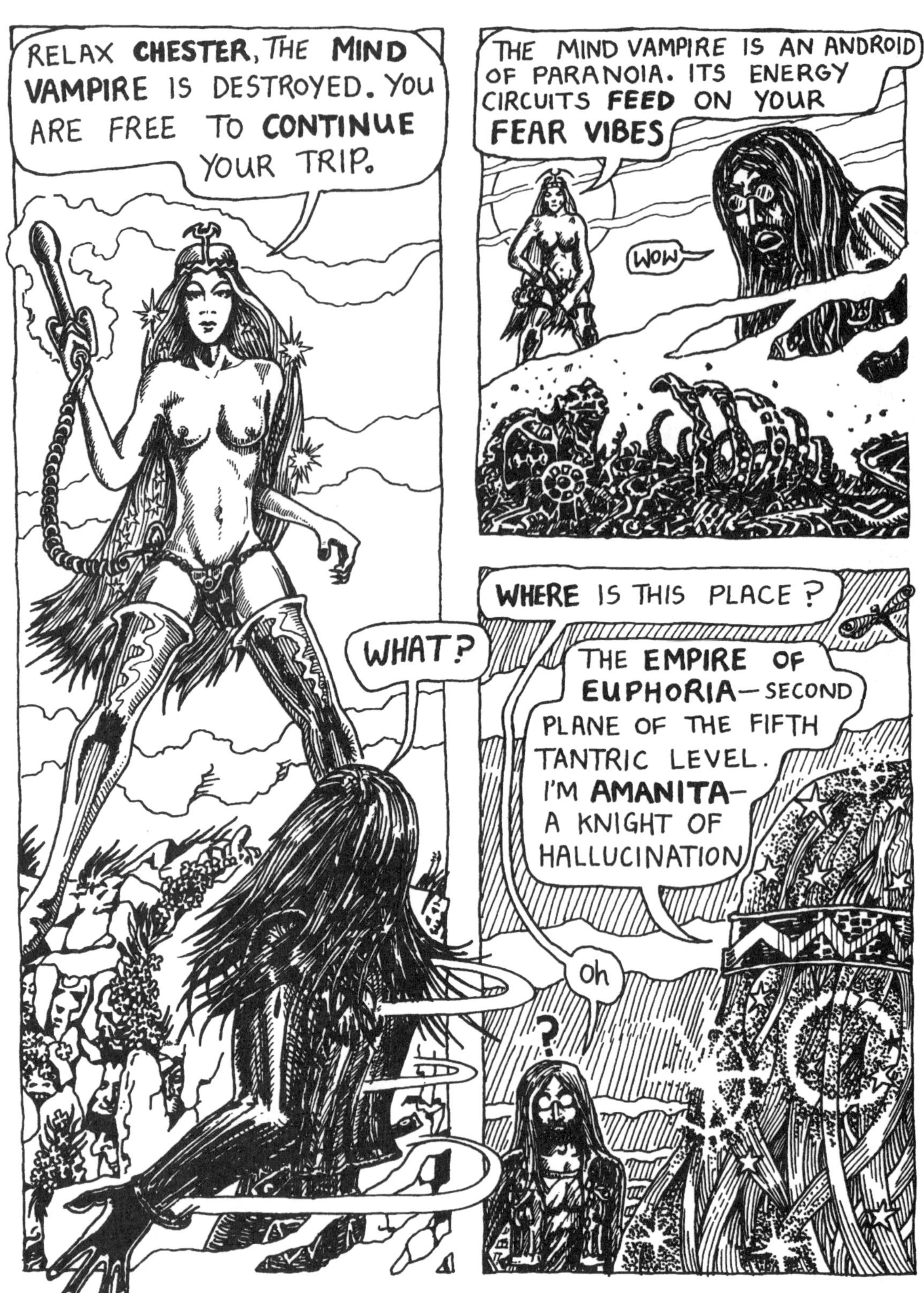
RELAX CHESTER, THE MIND VAMPIRE IS DESTROYED. YOU ARE FREE TO CONTINUE YOUR TRIP.
WHAT?
THE MIND VAMPIRE IS AN ANDROID OF PARANOIA. ITS ENERGY CIRCUITS FEED ON YOUR FEAR VIBES
WOW
WHERE IS THIS PLACE?
THE EMPIRE OF EUPHORIA—SECOND PLANE OF THE FIFTH TANTRIC LEVEL. I'M AMANITA—A KNIGHT OF HALLUCINATION
oh
?

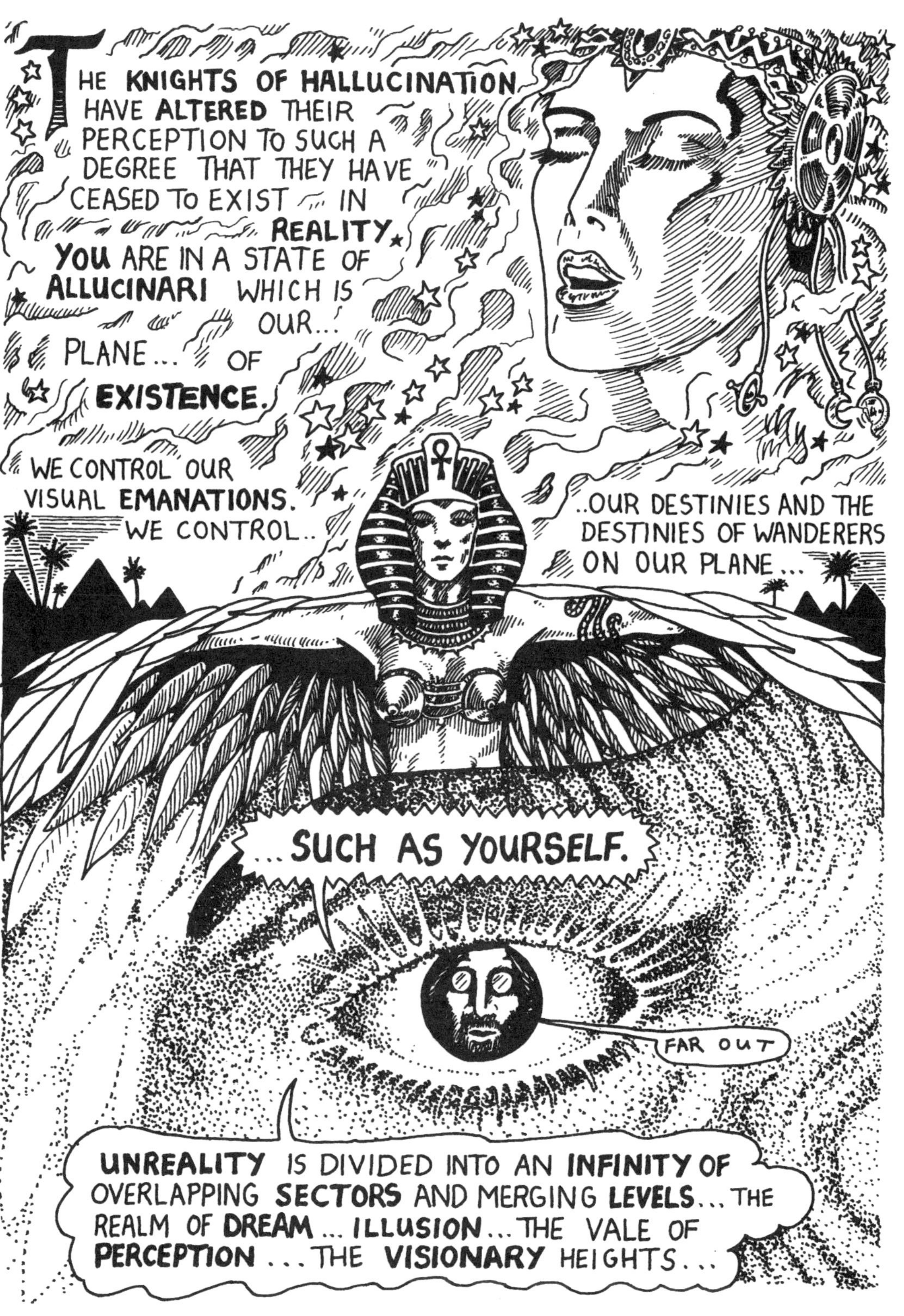
THE KNIGHTS OF HALLUCINATION HAVE ALTERED THEIR PERCEPTION TO SUCH A DEGREE THAT THEY HAVE CEASED TO EXIST IN REALITY.
YOU ARE IN A STATE OF ALLUCINARI WHICH IS OUR... PLANE... OF EXISTENCE.
WE CONTROL OUR VISUAL EMANATIONS. WE CONTROL..
..OUR DESTINIES AND THE DESTINIES OF WANDERERS ON OUR PLANE...
...SUCH AS YOURSELF.
FAR OUT
UNREALITY IS DIVIDED INTO AN INFINITY OF OVERLAPPING SECTORS AND MERGING LEVELS... THE REALM OF DREAM ... ILLUSION... THE VALE OF PERCEPTION ... THE VISIONARY HEIGHTS...

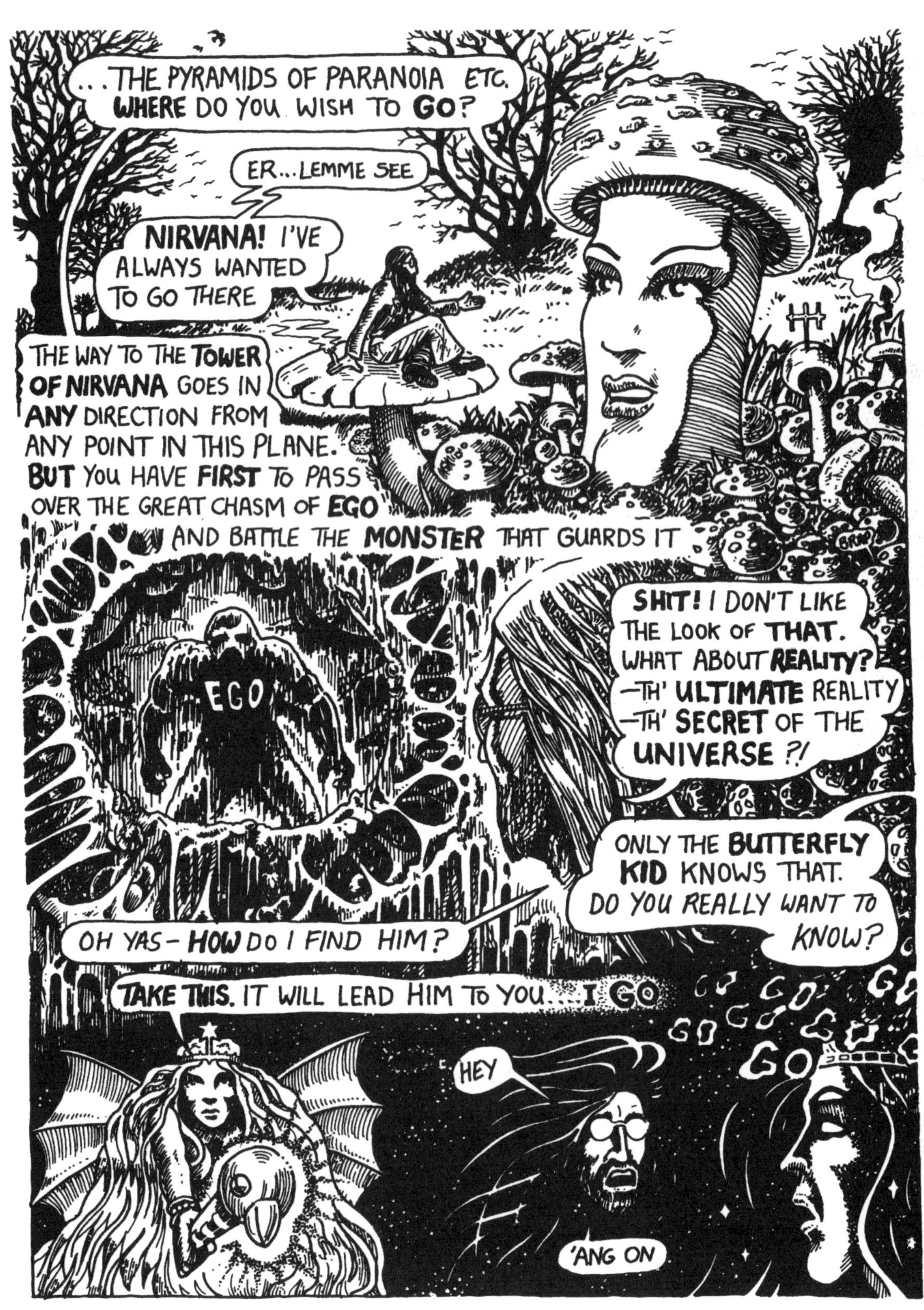
...THE PYRAMIDS OF PARANOIA ETC. WHERE DO YOU WISH TO GO?
ER...LEMME SEE
NIRVANA! I'VE ALWAYS WANTED TO GO THERE
THE WAY TO THE TOWER OF NIRVANA GOES IN ANY DIRECTION FROM ANY POINT IN THIS PLANE. BUT YOU HAVE FIRST TO PASS OVER THE GREAT CHASM OF EGO AND BATTLE THE MONSTER THAT GUARDS IT
EGO
SHIT! I DON'T LIKE THE LOOK OF THAT. WHAT ABOUT REALITY? —TH' ULTIMATE REALITY —TH' SECRET OF THE UNIVERSE ?!
ONLY THE BUTTERFLY KID KNOWS THAT. DO YOU REALLY WANT TO KNOW?
OH YAS- HOW DO I FIND HIM?
TAKE THIS. IT WILL LEAD HIM TO YOU...I GO
GO GO GO GO GO GO
HEY
'ANG ON

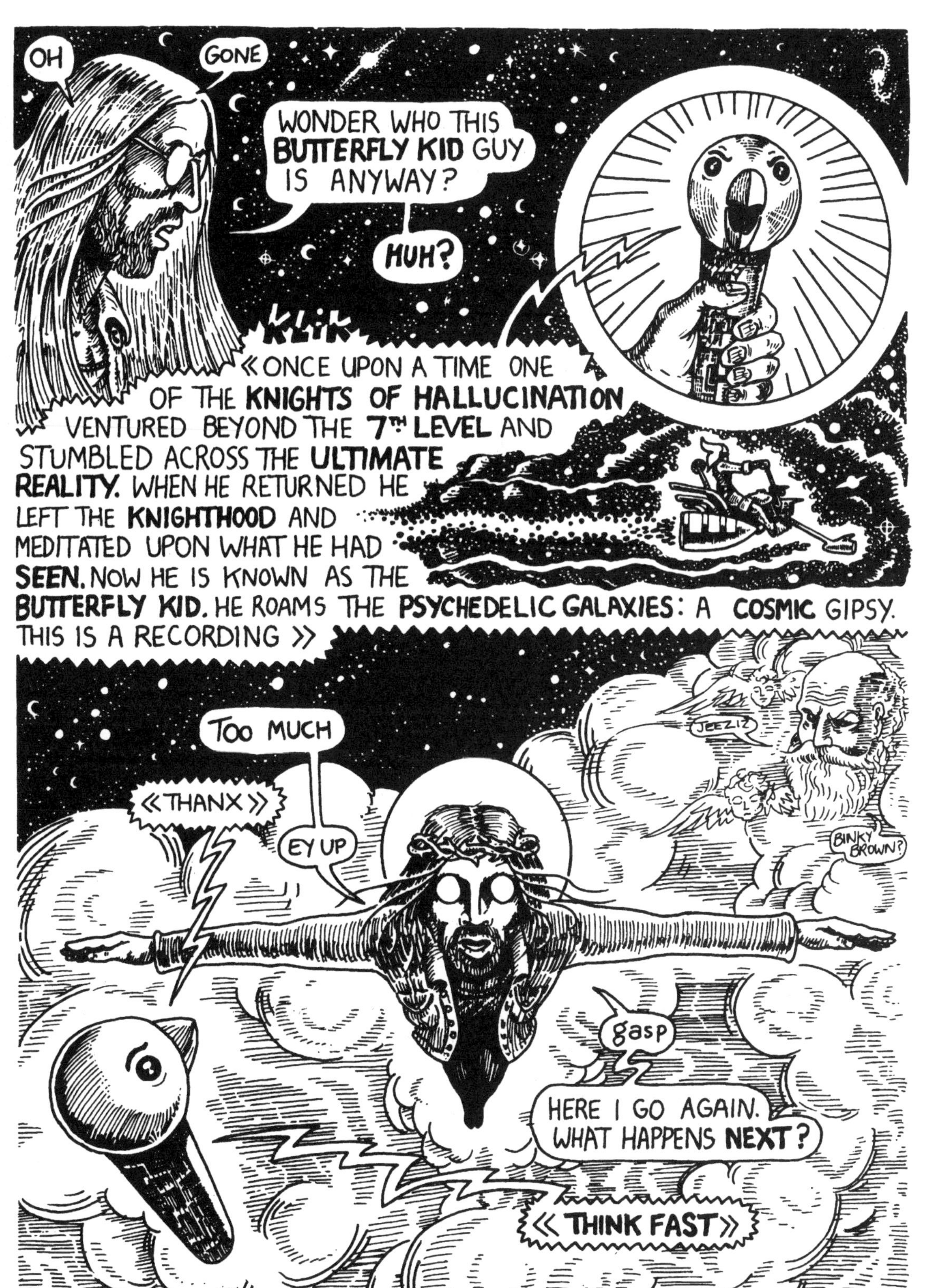
OH
GONE
WONDER WHO THIS BUTTERFLY KID GUY IS ANYWAY?
HUH?
KLIK
«ONCE UPON A TIME ONE OF THE KNIGHTS OF HALLUCINATION VENTURED BEYOND THE 7TH LEVEL AND STUMBLED ACROSS THE ULTIMATE REALITY. WHEN HE RETURNED HE LEFT THE KNIGHTHOOD AND MEDITATED UPON WHAT HE HAD SEEN. NOW HE IS KNOWN AS THE BUTTERFLY KID. HE ROAMS THE PSYCHEDELIC GALAXIES: A COSMIC GIPSY. THIS IS A RECORDING»
TOO MUCH
«THANX»
EY UP
JEEZIZ
BINKY BROWN?
gasp
HERE I GO AGAIN. WHAT HAPPENS NEXT?
«THINK FAST»

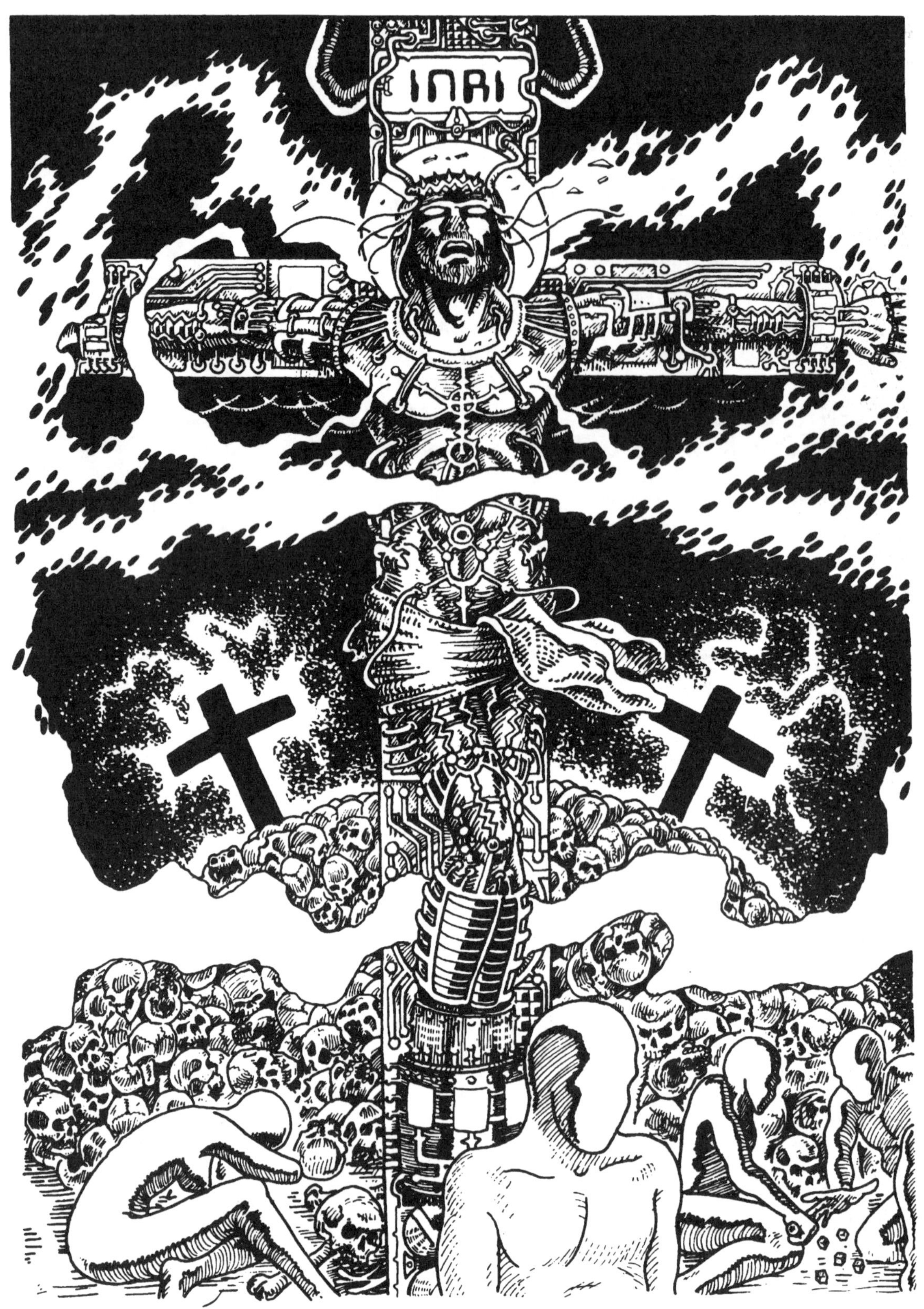
INRI

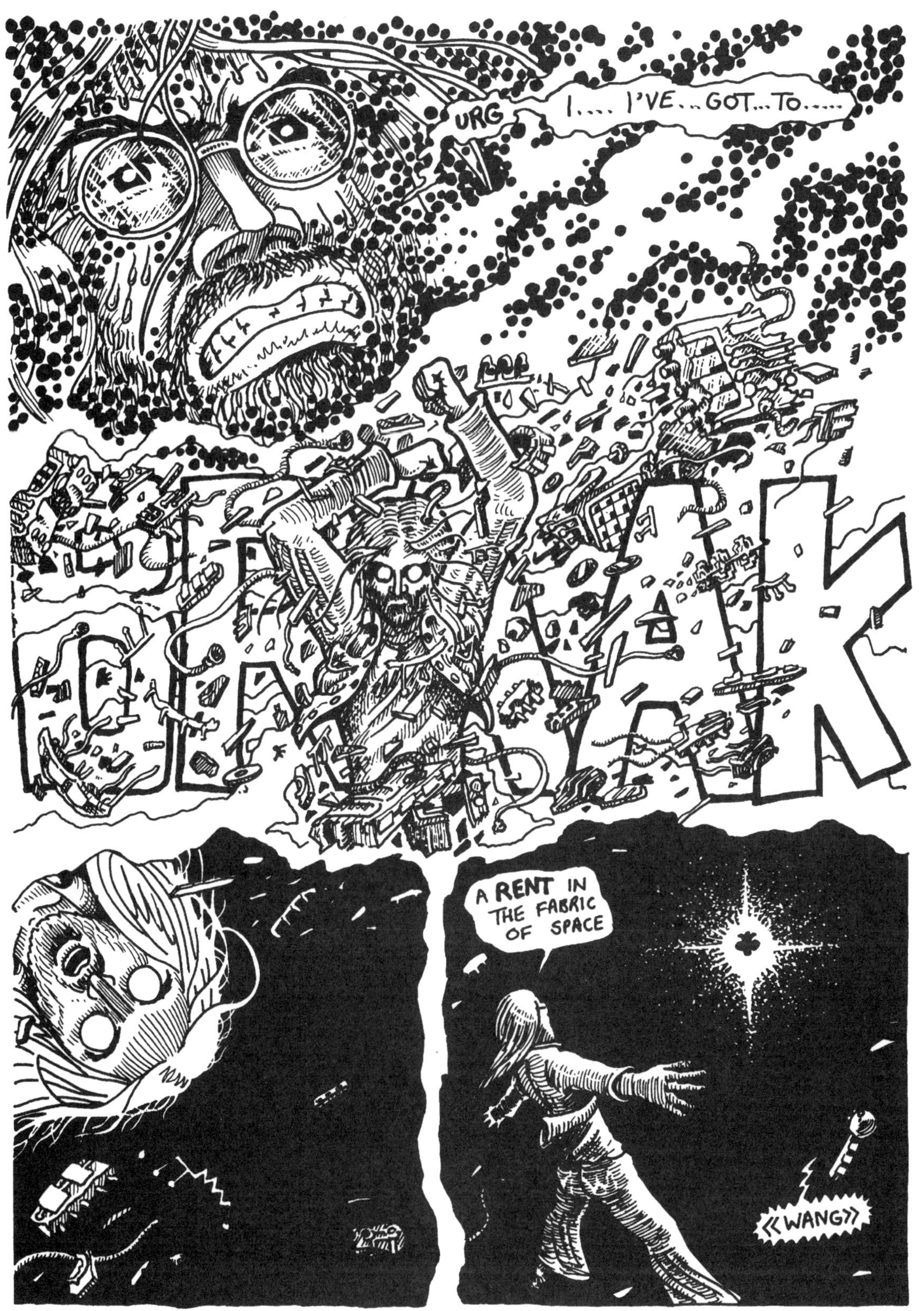
URG
I.... I'VE...GOT...TO.....
A RENT IN THE FABRIC OF SPACE
«WANG»

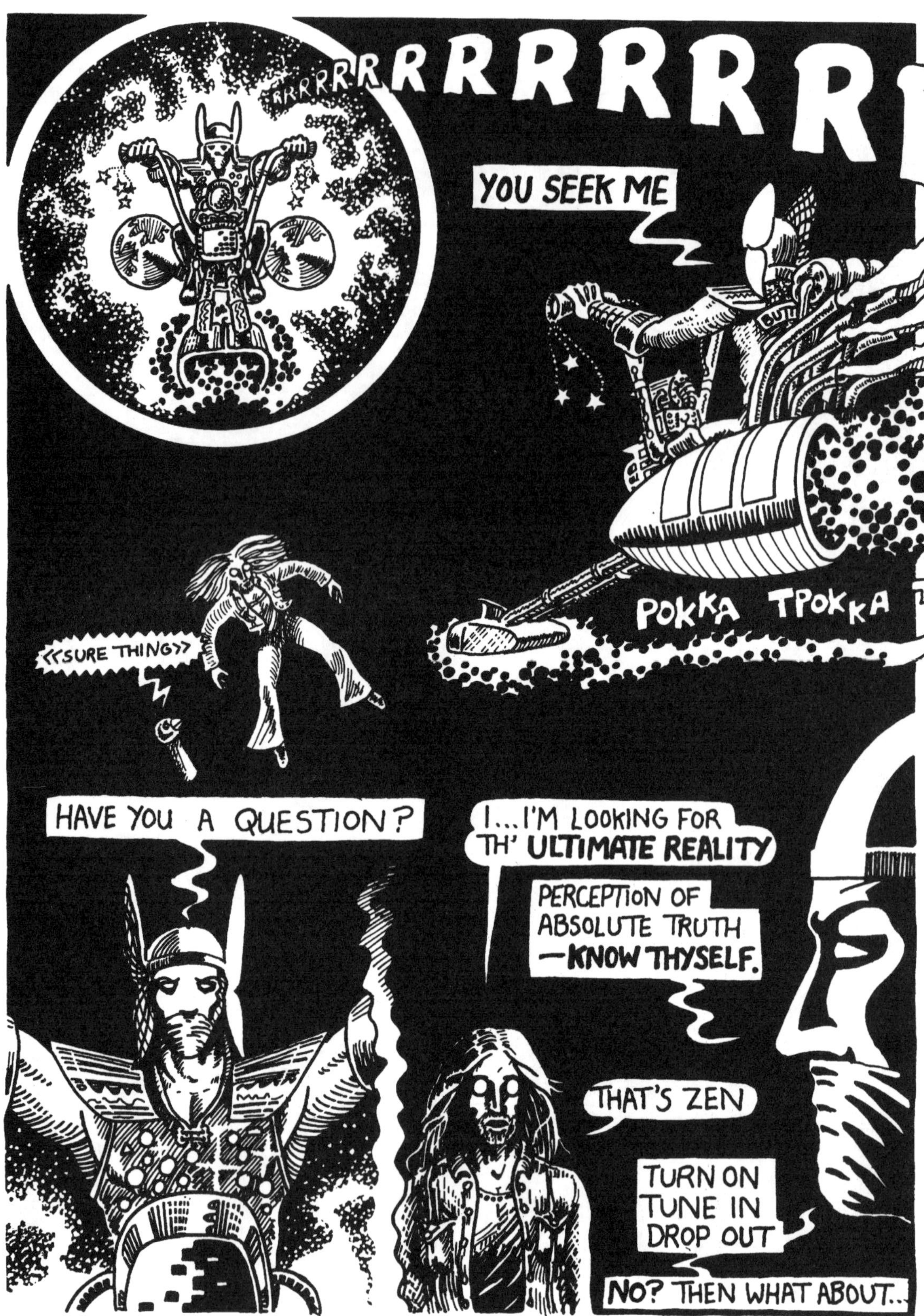
RRRRRRRRRRRRRR
YOU SEEK ME
POKKA TPOKKA
<<SURE THING>>
HAVE YOU A QUESTION?
I...I'M LOOKING FOR TH' ULTIMATE REALITY
PERCEPTION OF ABSOLUTE TRUTH —KNOW THYSELF.
THAT'S ZEN
TURN ON TUNE IN DROP OUT
NO? THEN WHAT ABOUT..

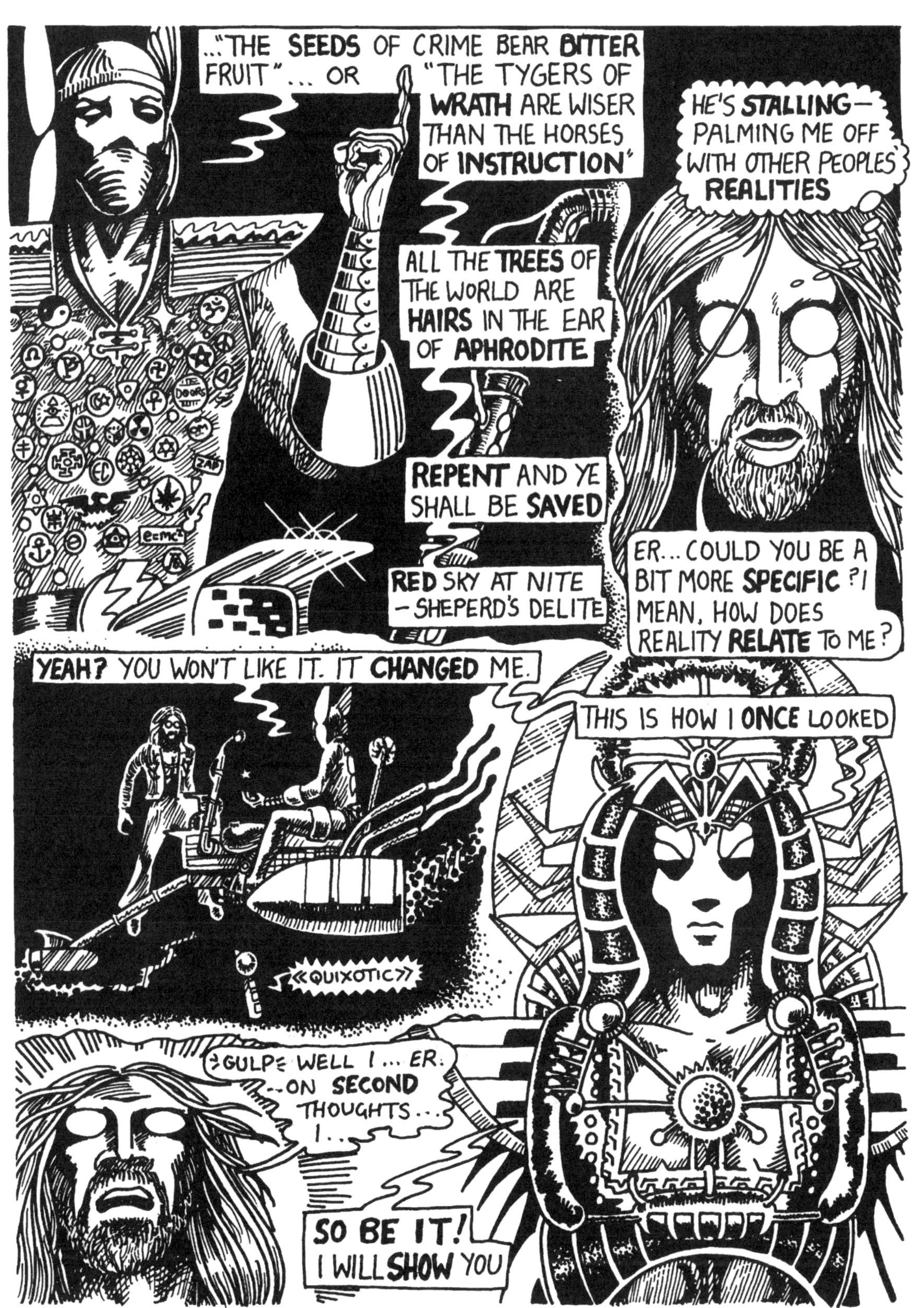
..."THE SEEDS OF CRIME BEAR BITTER FRUIT"... OR
"THE TYGERS OF WRATH ARE WISER THAN THE HORSES OF INSTRUCTION'
HE'S STALLING— PALMING ME OFF WITH OTHER PEOPLES' REALITIES
ALL THE TREES OF THE WORLD ARE HAIRS IN THE EAR OF APHRODITE
REPENT AND YE SHALL BE SAVED
RED SKY AT NITE —SHEPERD'S DELITE
ER... COULD YOU BE A BIT MORE SPECIFIC ? I MEAN, HOW DOES REALITY RELATE TO ME?
YEAH? YOU WON'T LIKE IT. IT CHANGED ME.
THIS IS HOW I ONCE LOOKED
«QUIXOTIC»
≥GULP≤ WELL I ... ER. ..ON SECOND THOUGHTS... I..
SO BE IT! I WILL SHOW YOU

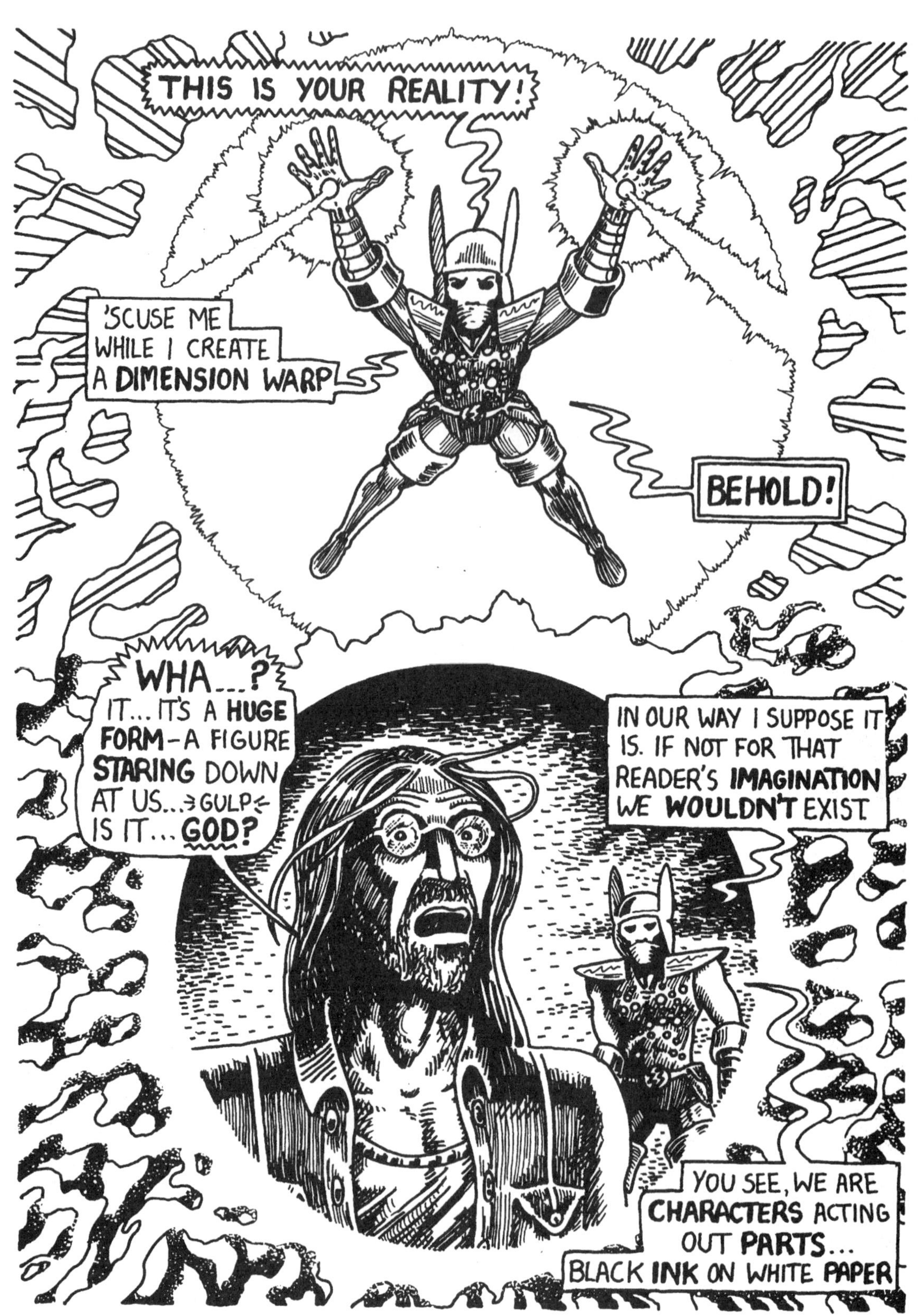
THIS IS YOUR REALITY!
'SCUSE ME WHILE I CREATE A DIMENSION WARP
BEHOLD!
WHA...? IT... IT'S A HUGE FORM - A FIGURE STARING DOWN AT US... GULP IS IT... GOD?
IN OUR WAY I SUPPOSE IT IS. IF NOT FOR THAT READER'S IMAGINATION WE WOULDN'T EXIST.
YOU SEE, WE ARE CHARACTERS ACTING OUT PARTS... BLACK INK ON WHITE PAPER

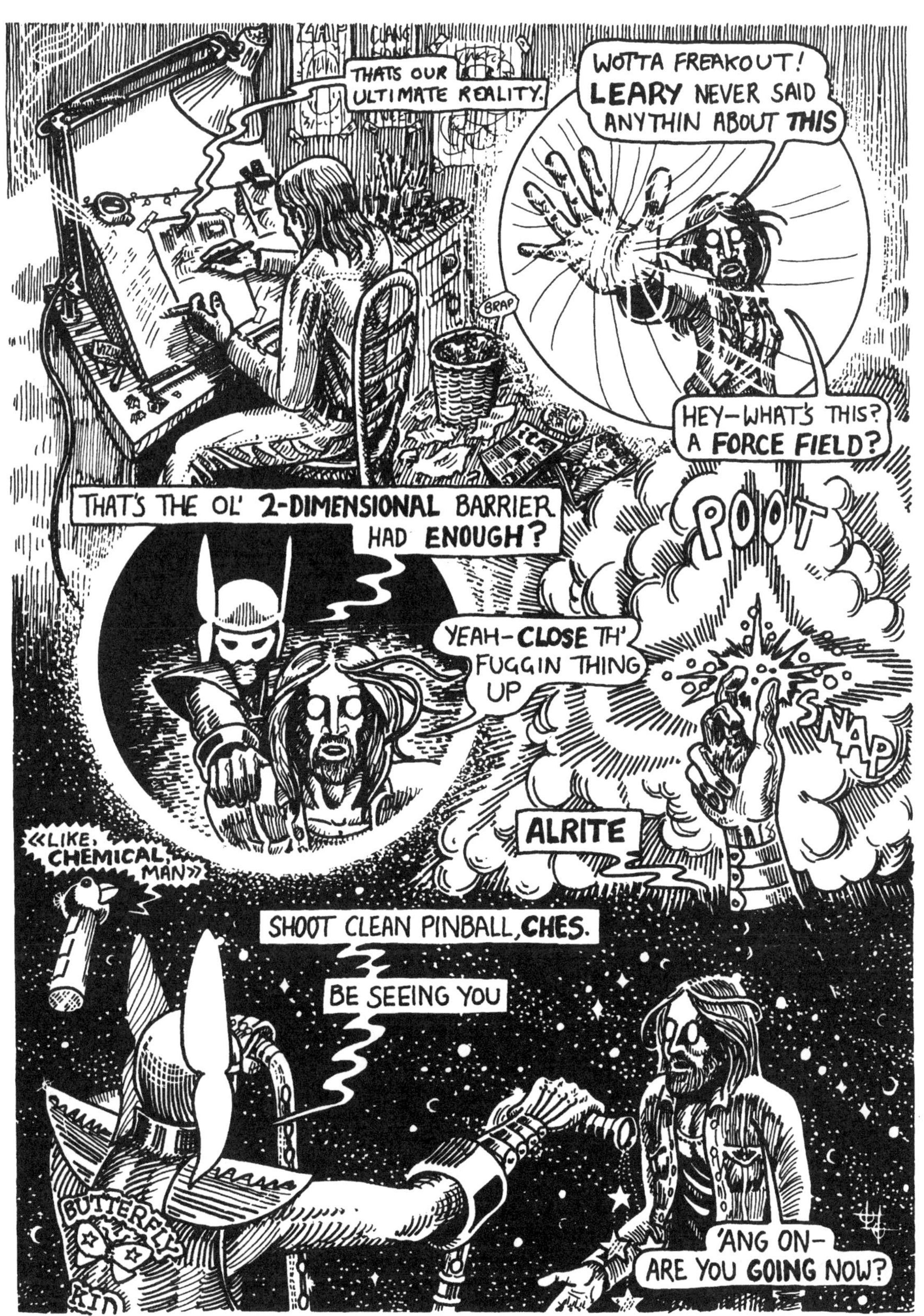
THATS OUR ULTIMATE REALITY.
WOTTA FREAKOUT! LEARY NEVER SAID ANYTHIN ABOUT THIS
BRAP
HEY-WHAT'S THIS? A FORCE FIELD?
THAT'S THE OL' 2-DIMENSIONAL BARRIER HAD ENOUGH?
POOT
YEAH-CLOSE TH' FUGGIN THING UP
SNAP
ALRITE
«LIKE, CHEMICAL, MAN»
SHOOT CLEAN PINBALL, CHES.
BE SEEING YOU
BUTTERFLY KID
'ANG ON- ARE YOU GOING NOW?

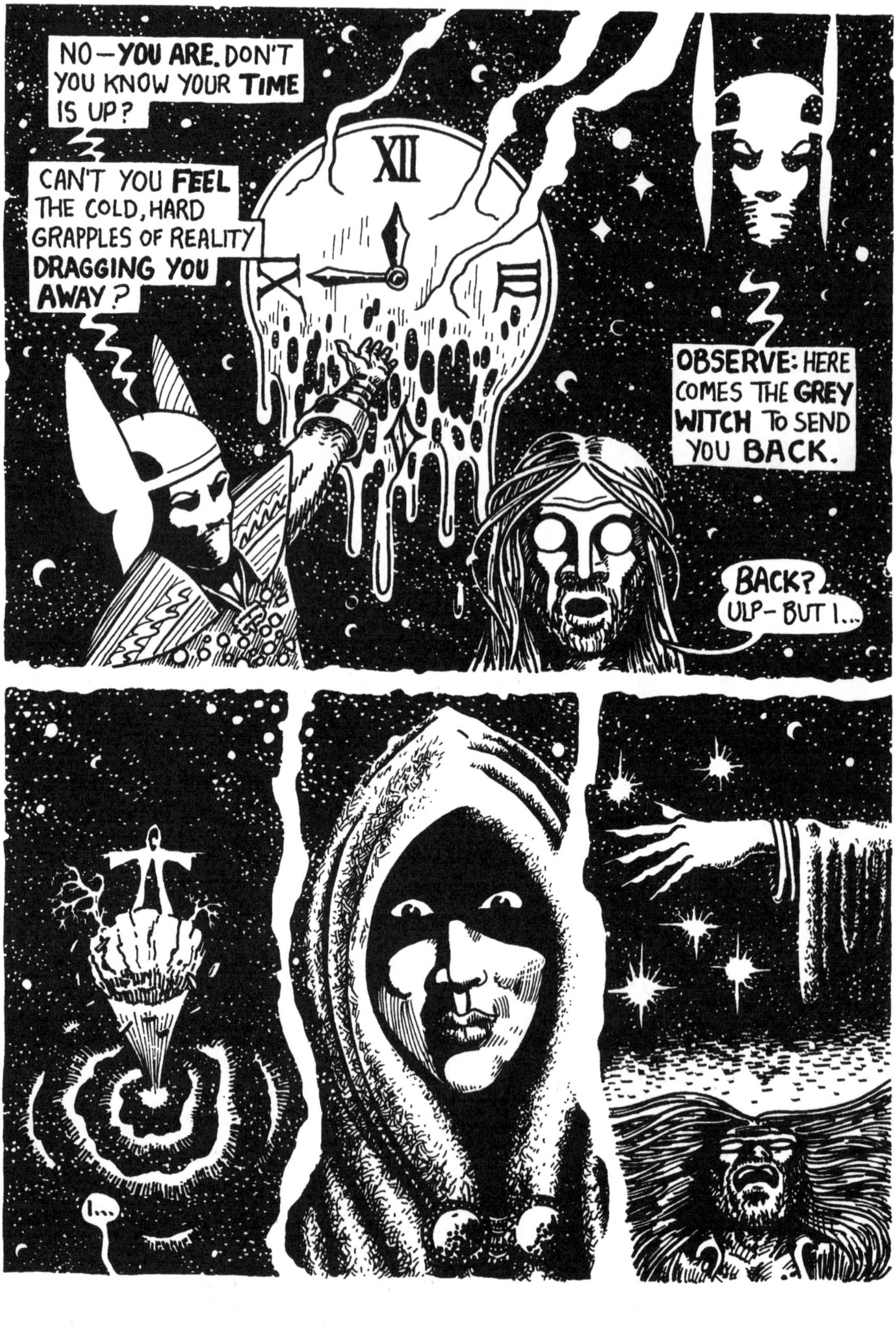

NO—**YOU ARE.** DON'T YOU KNOW YOUR **TIME** IS UP?

CAN'T YOU **FEEL** THE COLD, HARD GRAPPLES OF REALITY **DRAGGING YOU AWAY?**

OBSERVE: HERE COMES THE **GREY WITCH** TO SEND YOU **BACK.**

BACK? ULP—BUT I...

I...

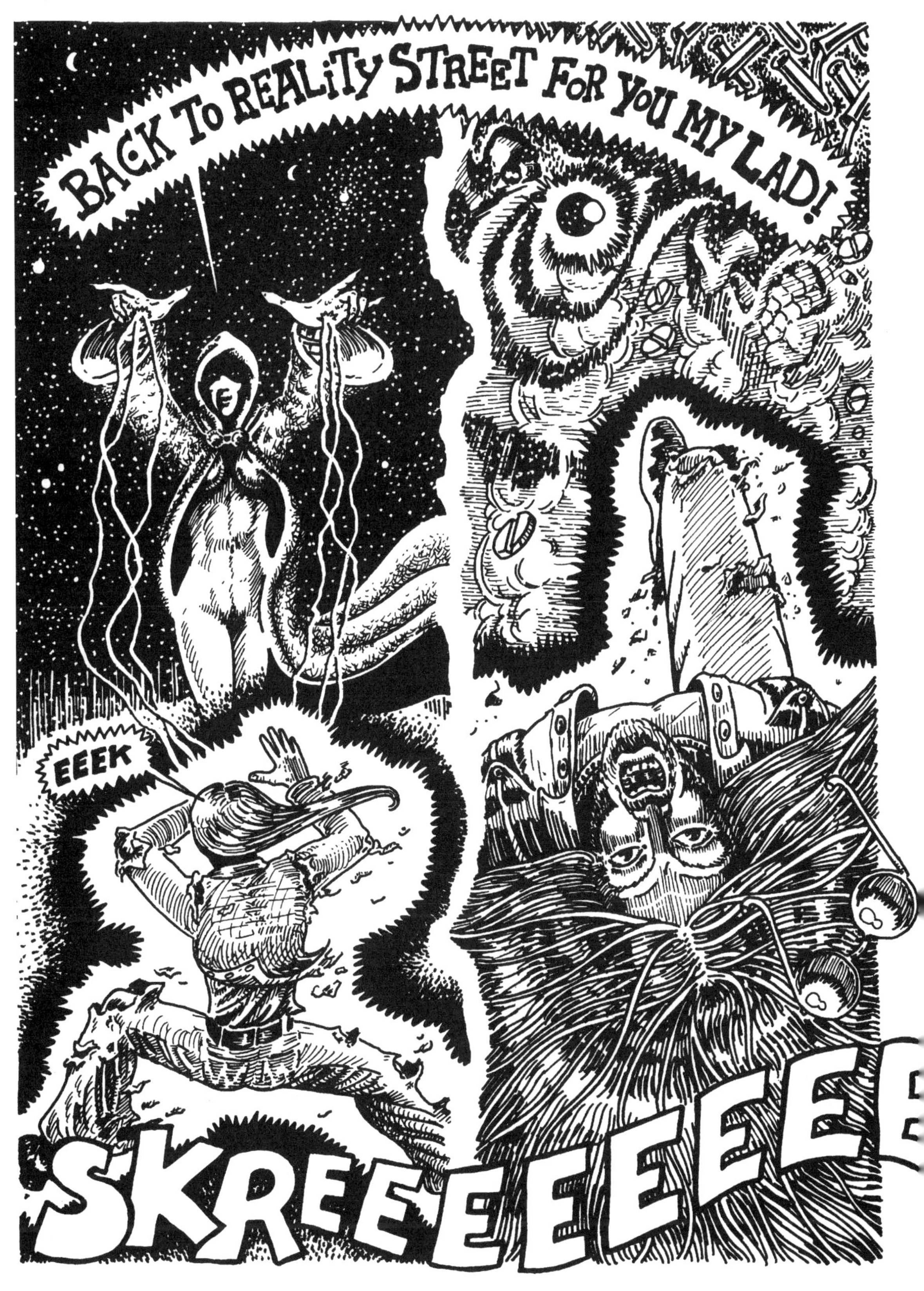

BACK TO REALITY STREET FOR YOU MY LAD!
EEEK
SKREEEEEEEE

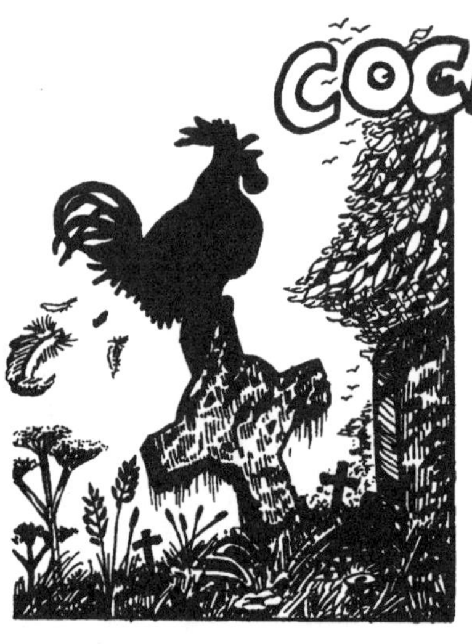
COCKADOODLEDOOOOOO
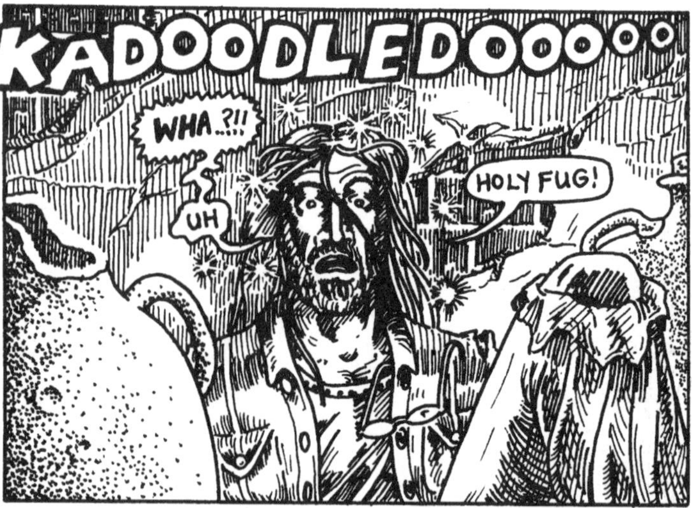
WHA?!!
UH
HOLY FUG!
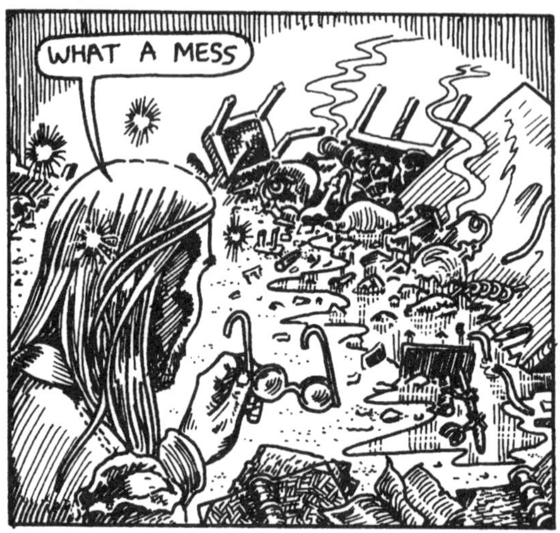
WHAT A MESS
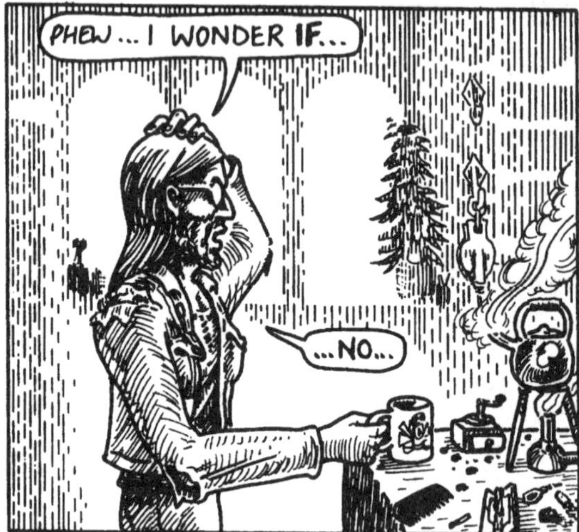
PHEW... I WONDER IF...
...NO...
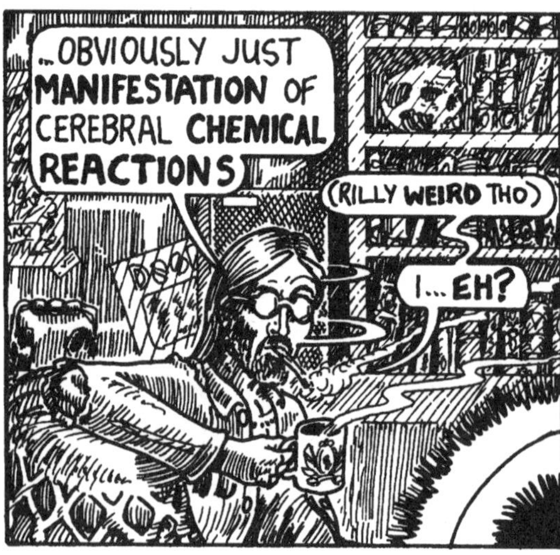
...OBVIOUSLY JUST MANIFESTATION OF CEREBRAL CHEMICAL REACTIONS
(RILLY WEIRD THO)
I...EH?
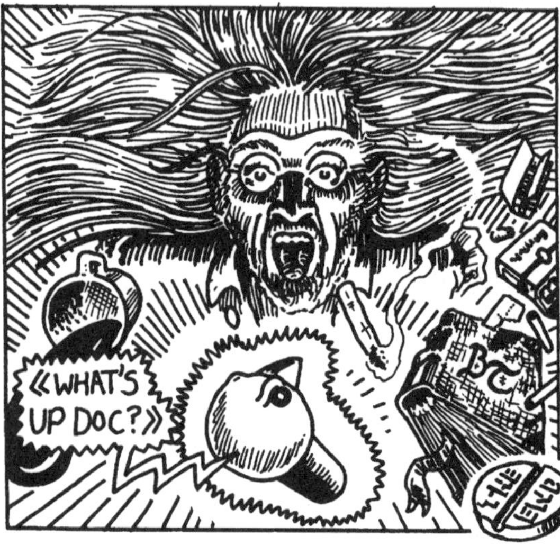
«WHAT'S UP DOC?»
THE END

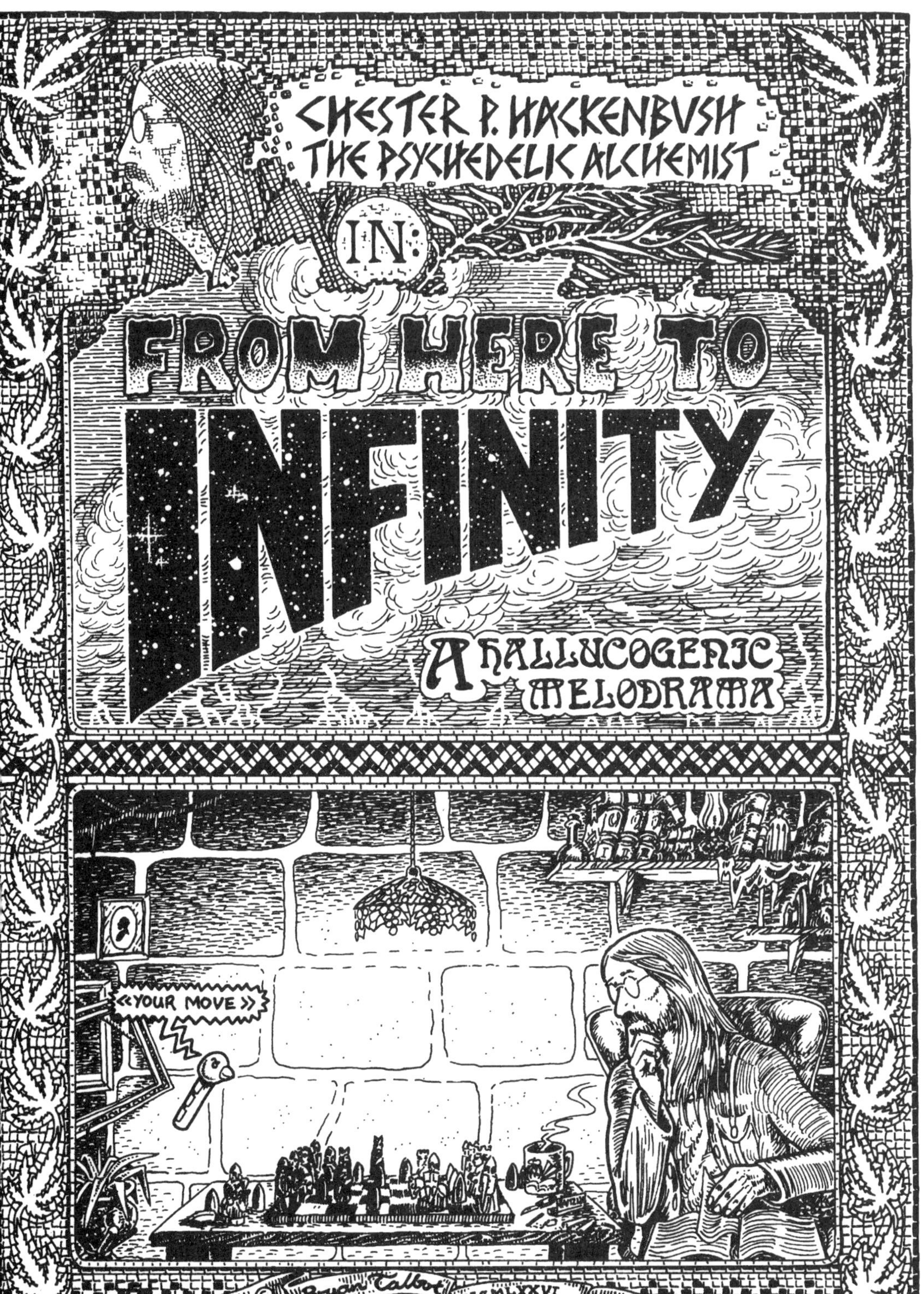
CHESTER P. HACKENBUSH
THE PSYCHEDELIC ALCHEMIST
IN:
FROM HERE TO
INFINITY
A HALLUCOGENIC MELODRAMA
«YOUR MOVE»
© Bryan Talbot MCMLXXVI

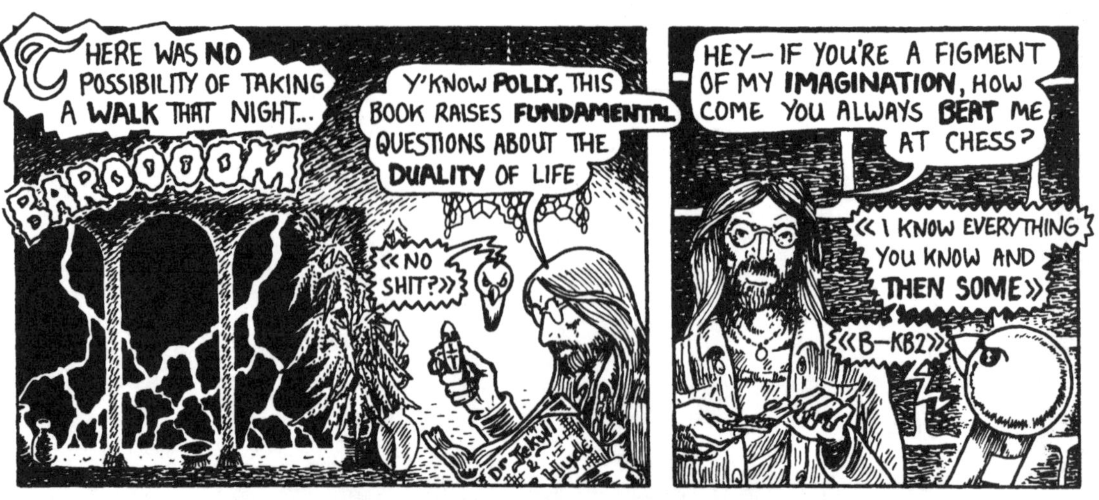
THERE WAS NO POSSIBILITY OF TAKING A WALK THAT NIGHT...
BAROOOOM
Y'KNOW POLLY, THIS BOOK RAISES FUNDAMENTAL QUESTIONS ABOUT THE DUALITY OF LIFE
«NO SHIT?»
Dr Jekyll & Hyde
HEY— IF YOU'RE A FIGMENT OF MY IMAGINATION, HOW COME YOU ALWAYS BEAT ME AT CHESS?
«I KNOW EVERYTHING YOU KNOW AND THEN SOME»
«B—KB2»
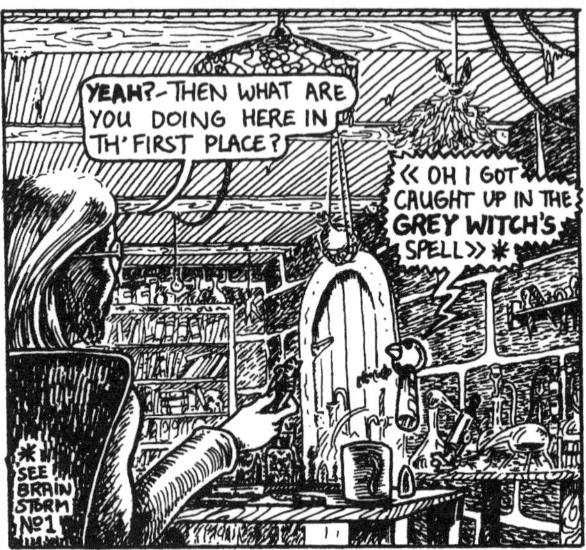
YEAH?-THEN WHAT ARE YOU DOING HERE IN TH' FIRST PLACE?
«OH I GOT CAUGHT UP IN THE GREY WITCH'S SPELL» *
* SEE BRAIN STORM No1
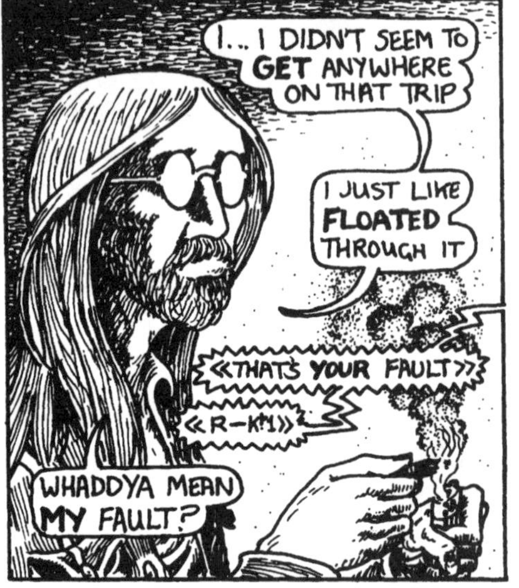
I... I DIDN'T SEEM TO GET ANYWHERE ON THAT TRIP
I JUST LIKE FLOATED THROUGH IT
«THAT'S YOUR FAULT»
«R—K1»
WHADDYA MEAN MY FAULT?
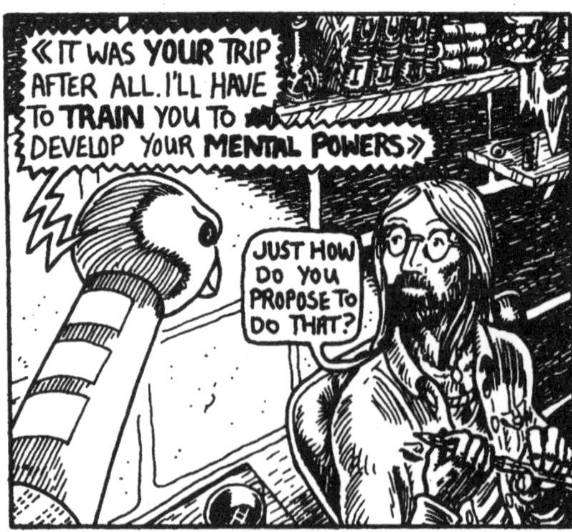
«IT WAS YOUR TRIP AFTER ALL. I'LL HAVE TO TRAIN YOU TO DEVELOP YOUR MENTAL POWERS»
JUST HOW DO YOU PROPOSE TO DO THAT?
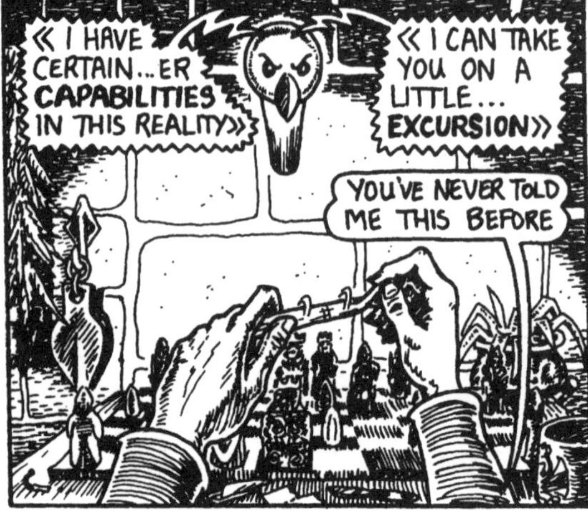
«I HAVE CERTAIN...ER CAPABILITIES IN THIS REALITY»
«I CAN TAKE YOU ON A LITTLE... EXCURSION»
YOU'VE NEVER TOLD ME THIS BEFORE

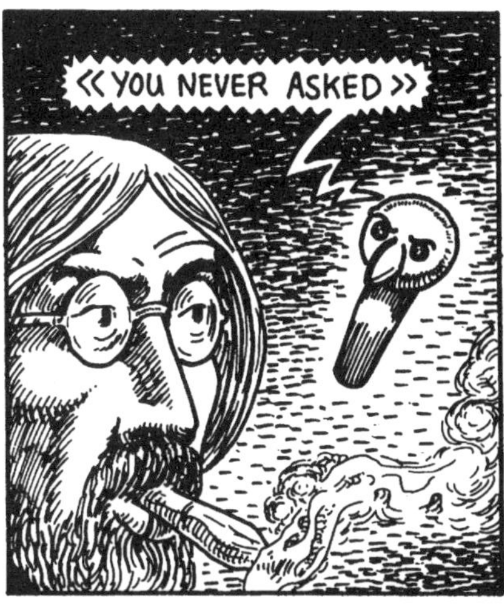
«YOU NEVER ASKED»

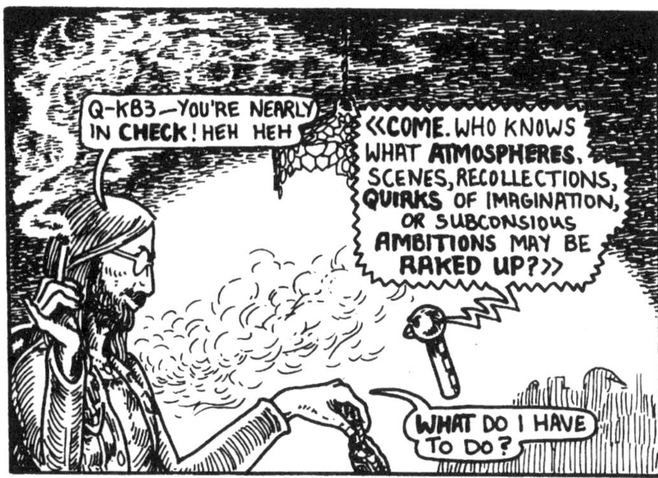
Q-KB3—YOU'RE NEARLY IN **CHECK**! HEH HEH
«**COME**. WHO KNOWS WHAT **ATMOSPHERES**, SCENES, RECOLLECTIONS, **QUIRKS** OF IMAGINATION, OR SUBCONSIOUS **AMBITIONS** MAY BE **RAKED UP**?»
WHAT DO I HAVE TO DO?

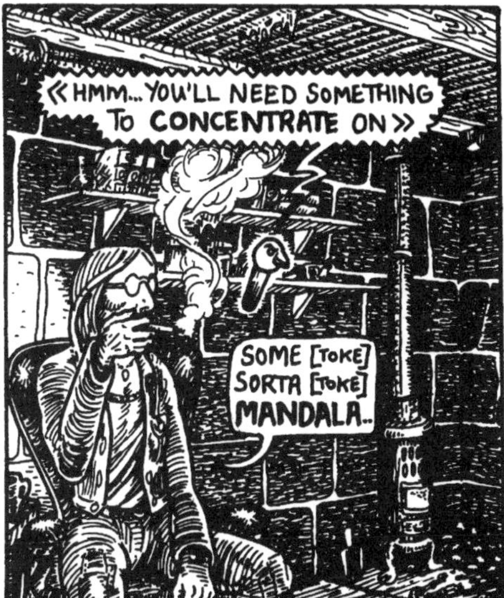
«HMM... YOU'LL NEED SOMETHING TO **CONCENTRATE** ON»
SOME [TOKE] SORTA [TOKE] **MANDALA**..

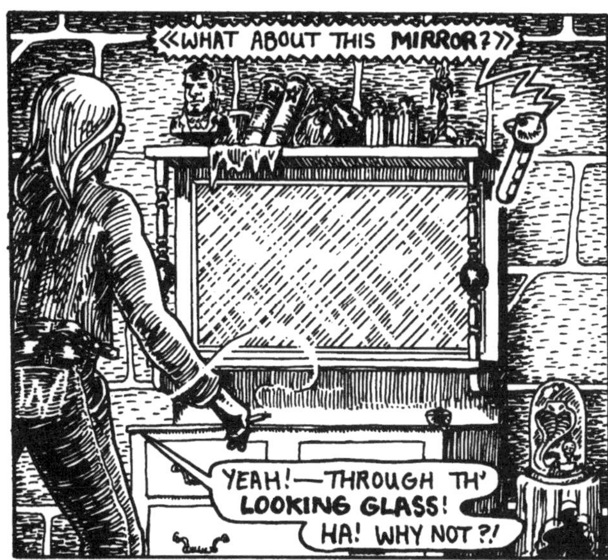
«WHAT ABOUT THIS **MIRROR**?»
YEAH!—THROUGH TH' **LOOKING GLASS**! HA! WHY NOT?!

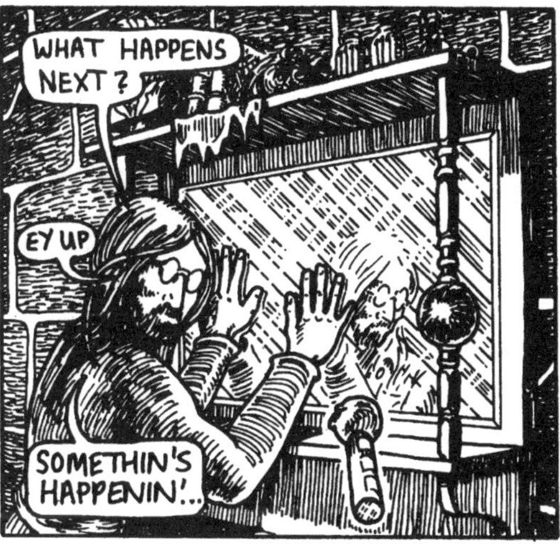
WHAT HAPPENS NEXT?
EY UP
SOMETHIN'S HAPPENIN'..

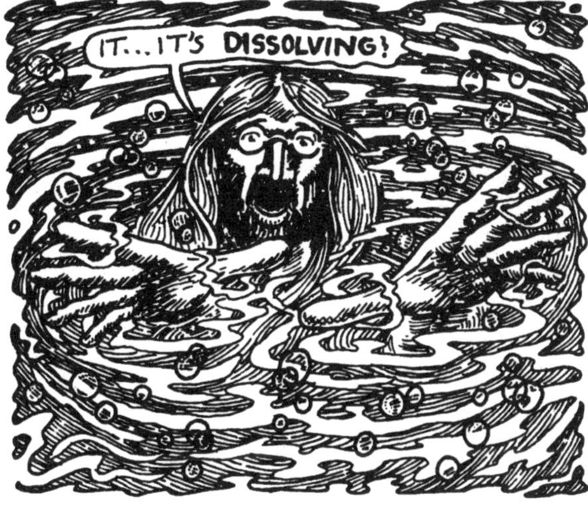
IT... IT'S **DISSOLVING**!

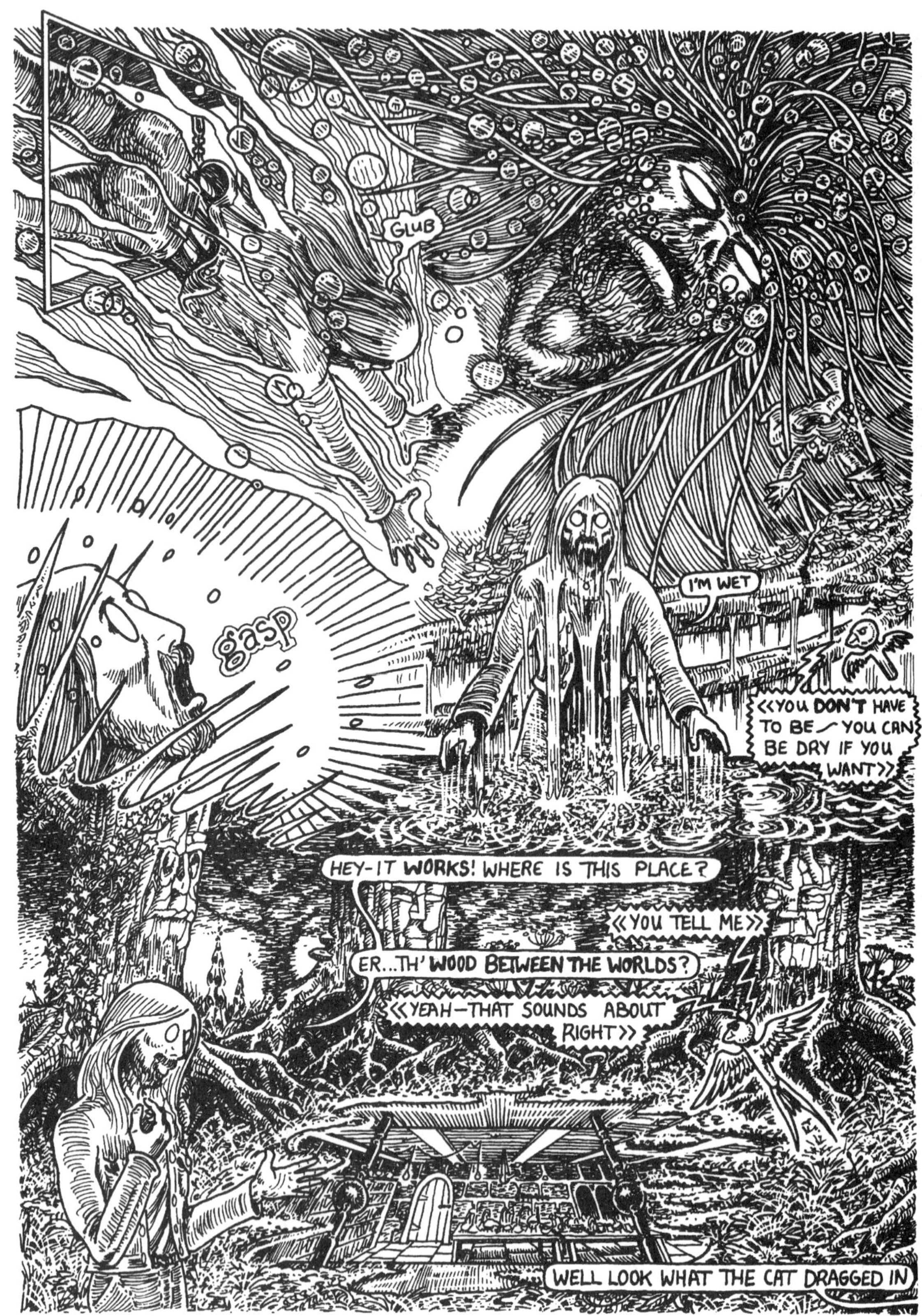
GLUB
gasp
I'M WET
«YOU DON'T HAVE TO BE — YOU CAN BE DRY IF YOU WANT»
HEY-IT WORKS! WHERE IS THIS PLACE?
«YOU TELL ME»
ER...TH' WOOD BETWEEN THE WORLDS?
«YEAH—THAT SOUNDS ABOUT RIGHT»
WELL LOOK WHAT THE CAT DRAGGED IN

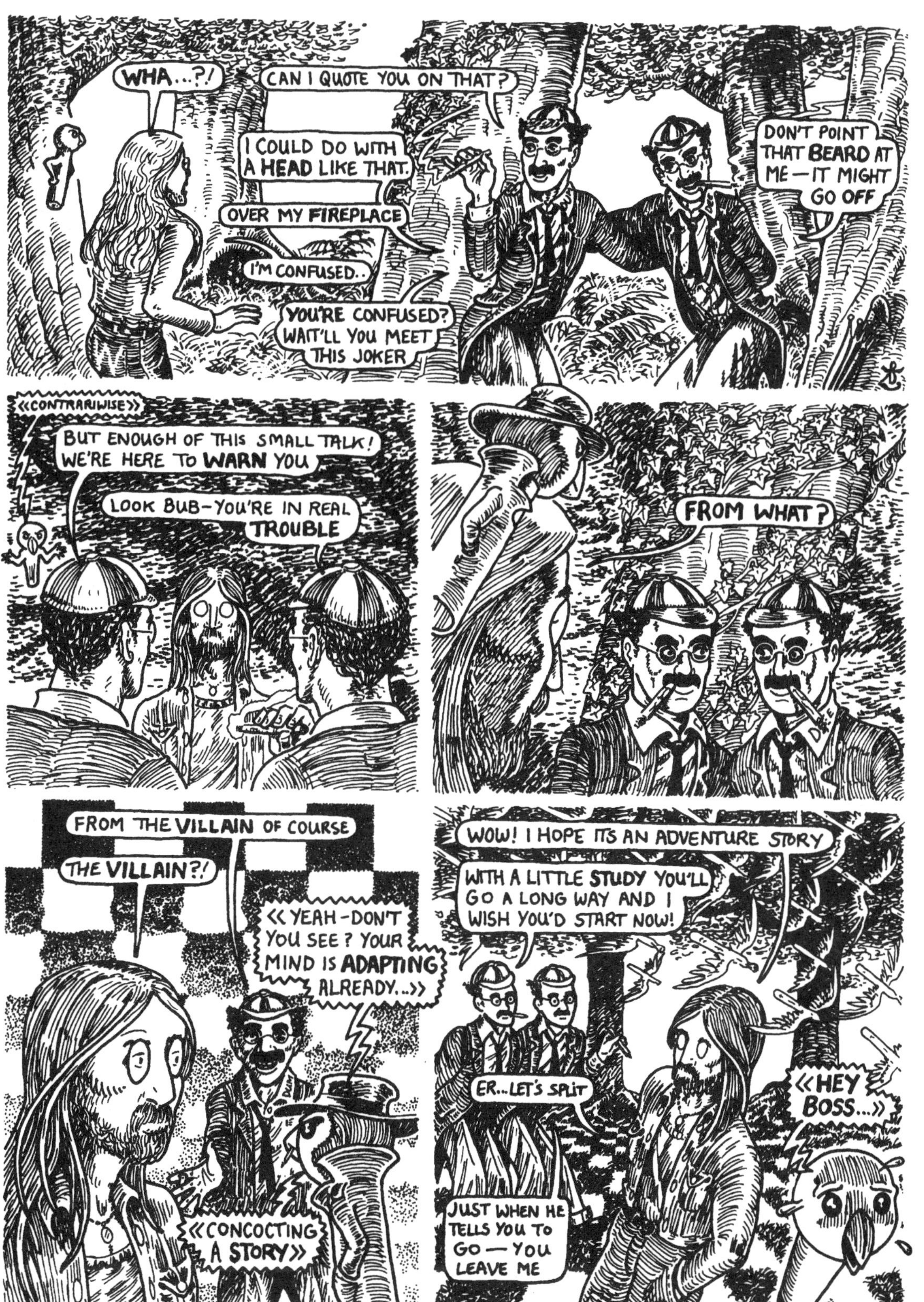
WHA...?!
CAN I QUOTE YOU ON THAT?
I COULD DO WITH A HEAD LIKE THAT.
OVER MY FIREPLACE
I'M CONFUSED..
YOU'RE CONFUSED? WAIT'LL YOU MEET THIS JOKER
DON'T POINT THAT BEARD AT ME — IT MIGHT GO OFF
«CONTRARIWISE»
BUT ENOUGH OF THIS SMALL TALK! WE'RE HERE TO WARN YOU
LOOK BUB—YOU'RE IN REAL TROUBLE
FROM WHAT?
FROM THE VILLAIN OF COURSE
THE VILLAIN?!
«YEAH-DON'T YOU SEE? YOUR MIND IS ADAPTING ALREADY...»
«CONCOCTING A STORY»
WOW! I HOPE ITS AN ADVENTURE STORY
WITH A LITTLE STUDY YOU'LL GO A LONG WAY AND I WISH YOU'D START NOW!
ER...LET'S SPLIT
JUST WHEN HE TELLS YOU TO GO — YOU LEAVE ME
«HEY BOSS...»

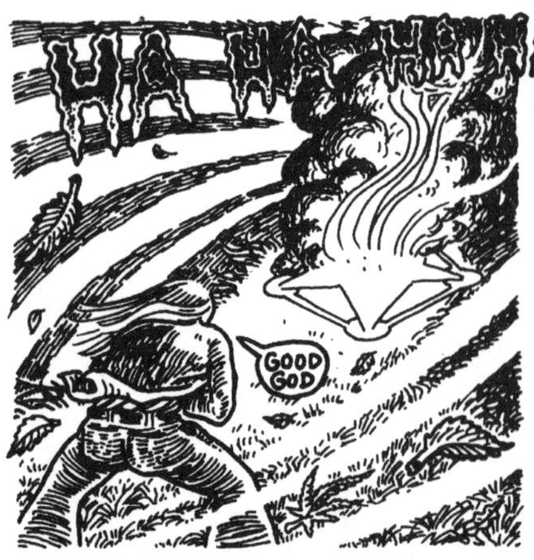
HA HA
GOOD GOD

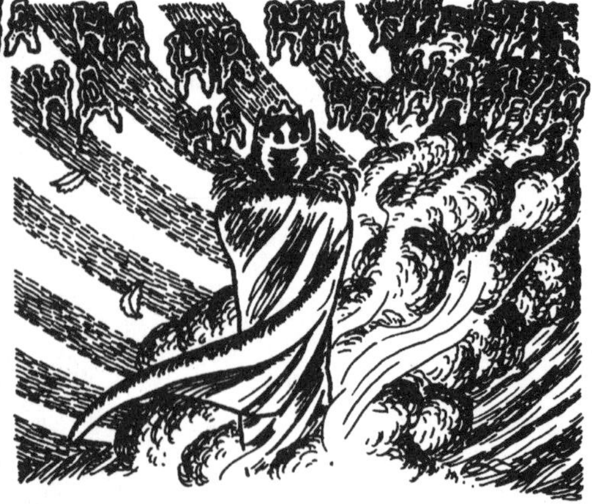

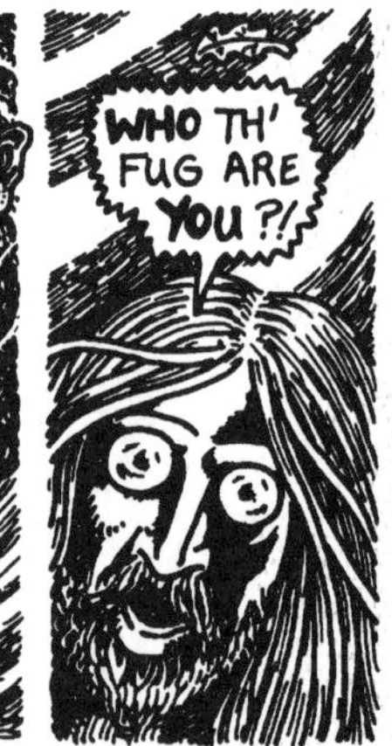
WHO TH' FUG ARE YOU ?!

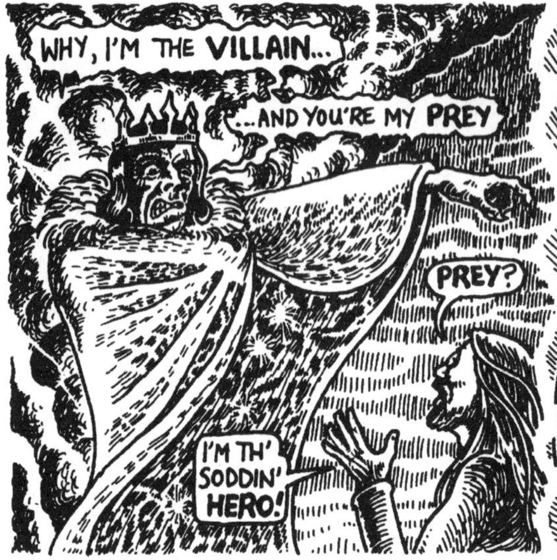
WHY, I'M THE VILLAIN...
...AND YOU'RE MY PREY
PREY?
I'M TH' SODDIN' HERO!

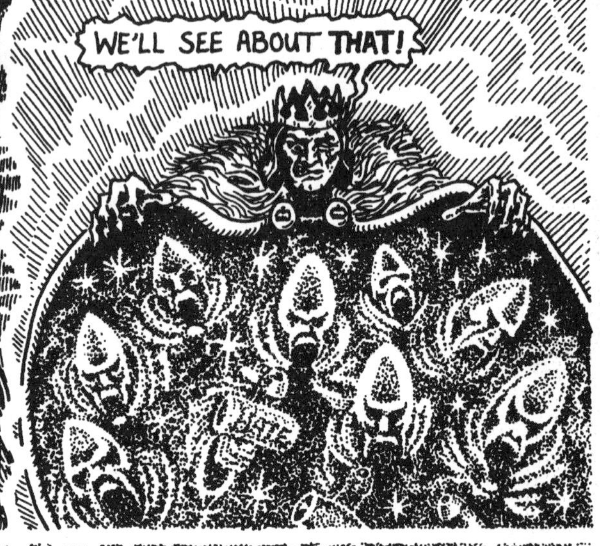
WE'LL SEE ABOUT THAT!

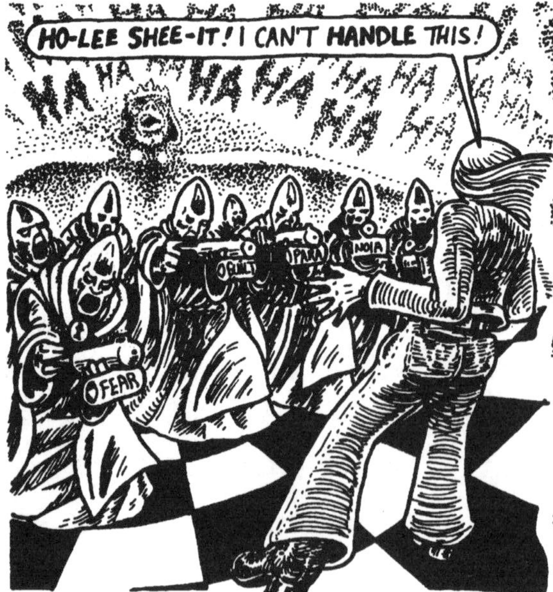
HO-LEE SHEE-IT! I CAN'T HANDLE THIS!
HA HA HA HA HA HA HA
PARA
NOIA
FEAR

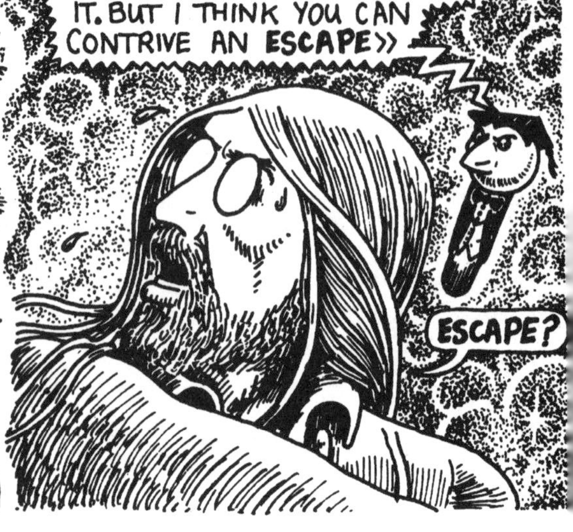
«A BIT TOO EARLY IN YOUR TRAINING FOR YOU TO MANAGE IT. BUT I THINK YOU CAN CONTRIVE AN ESCAPE»
ESCAPE?

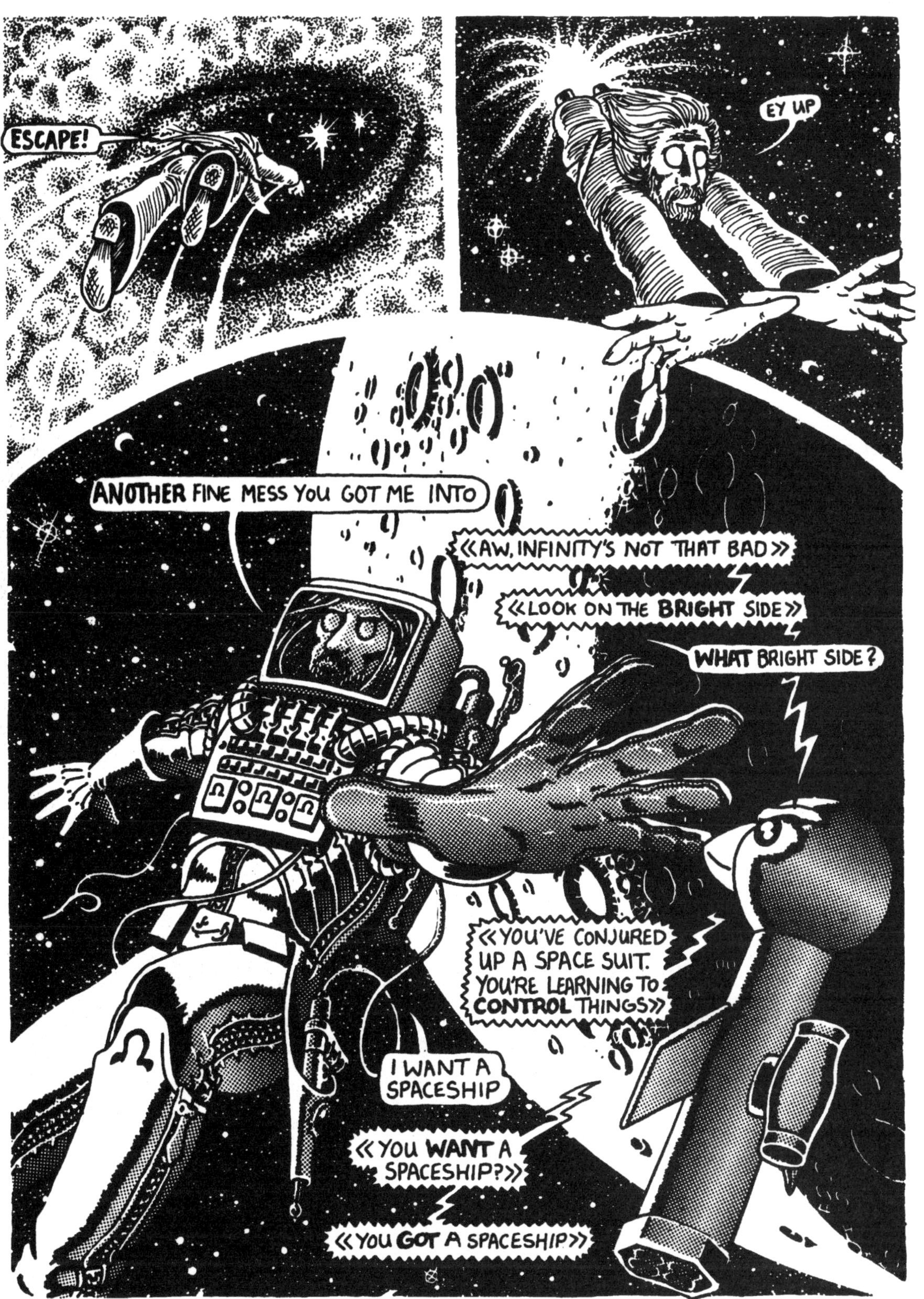
ESCAPE!
EY UP
ANOTHER FINE MESS YOU GOT ME INTO
«AW, INFINITY'S NOT THAT BAD»
«LOOK ON THE BRIGHT SIDE»
WHAT BRIGHT SIDE?
«YOU'VE CONJURED UP A SPACE SUIT. YOU'RE LEARNING TO CONTROL THINGS»
I WANT A SPACESHIP
«YOU WANT A SPACESHIP?»
«YOU GOT A SPACESHIP»

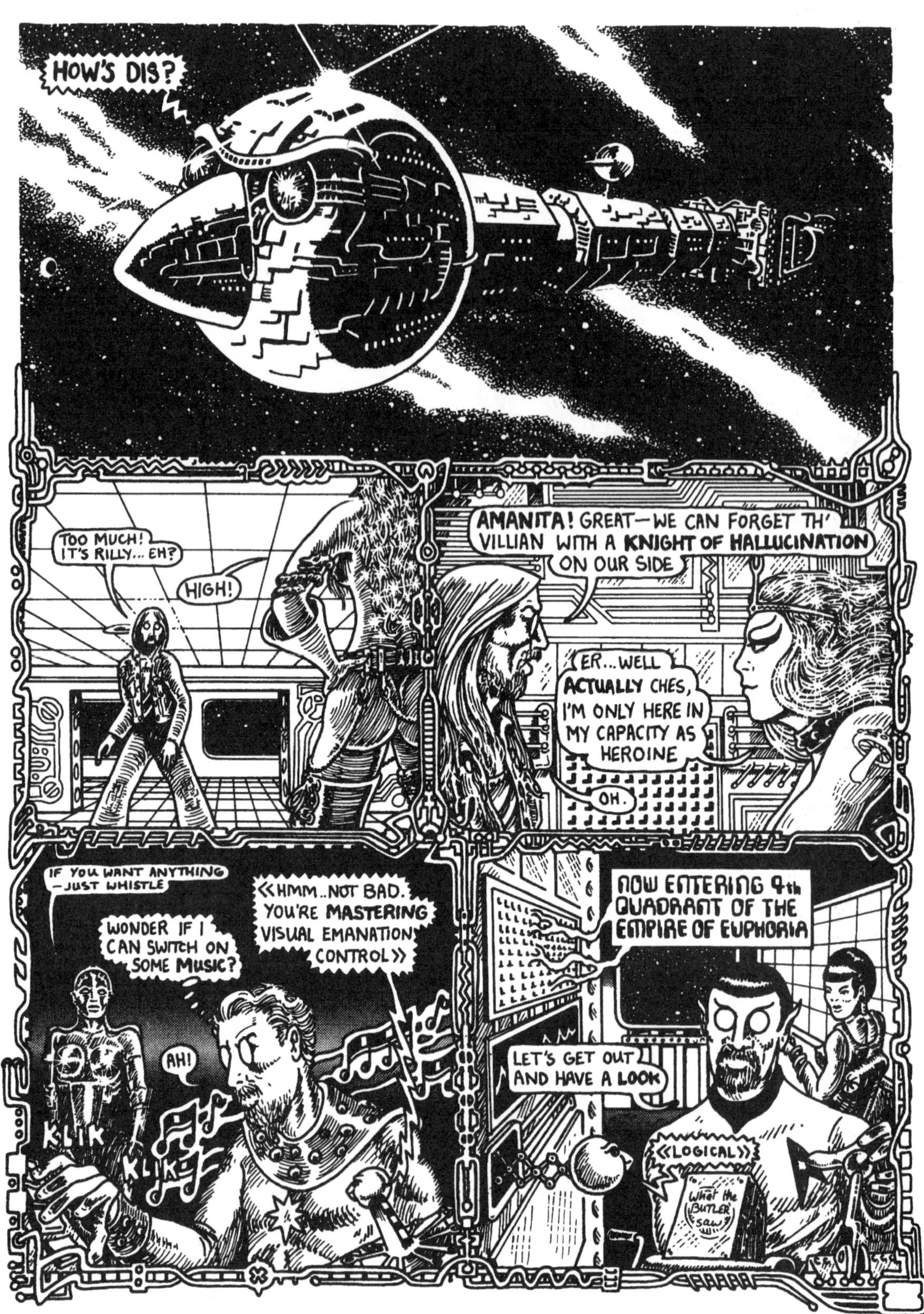
HOW'S DIS?
TOO MUCH! IT'S RILLY... EH?
HIGH!
AMANITA! GREAT—WE CAN FORGET TH' VILLIAN WITH A KNIGHT OF HALLUCINATION ON OUR SIDE
ER...WELL ACTUALLY CHES, I'M ONLY HERE IN MY CAPACITY AS HEROINE
OH.
IF YOU WANT ANYTHING —JUST WHISTLE
WONDER IF I CAN SWITCH ON SOME MUSIC?
«HMM..NOT BAD. YOU'RE MASTERING VISUAL EMANATION CONTROL»
AH!
KLIK
KLIK
NOW ENTERING 4th QUADRANT OF THE EMPIRE OF EUPHORIA
LET'S GET OUT AND HAVE A LOOK
«LOGICAL»
What the BUTLER Saw

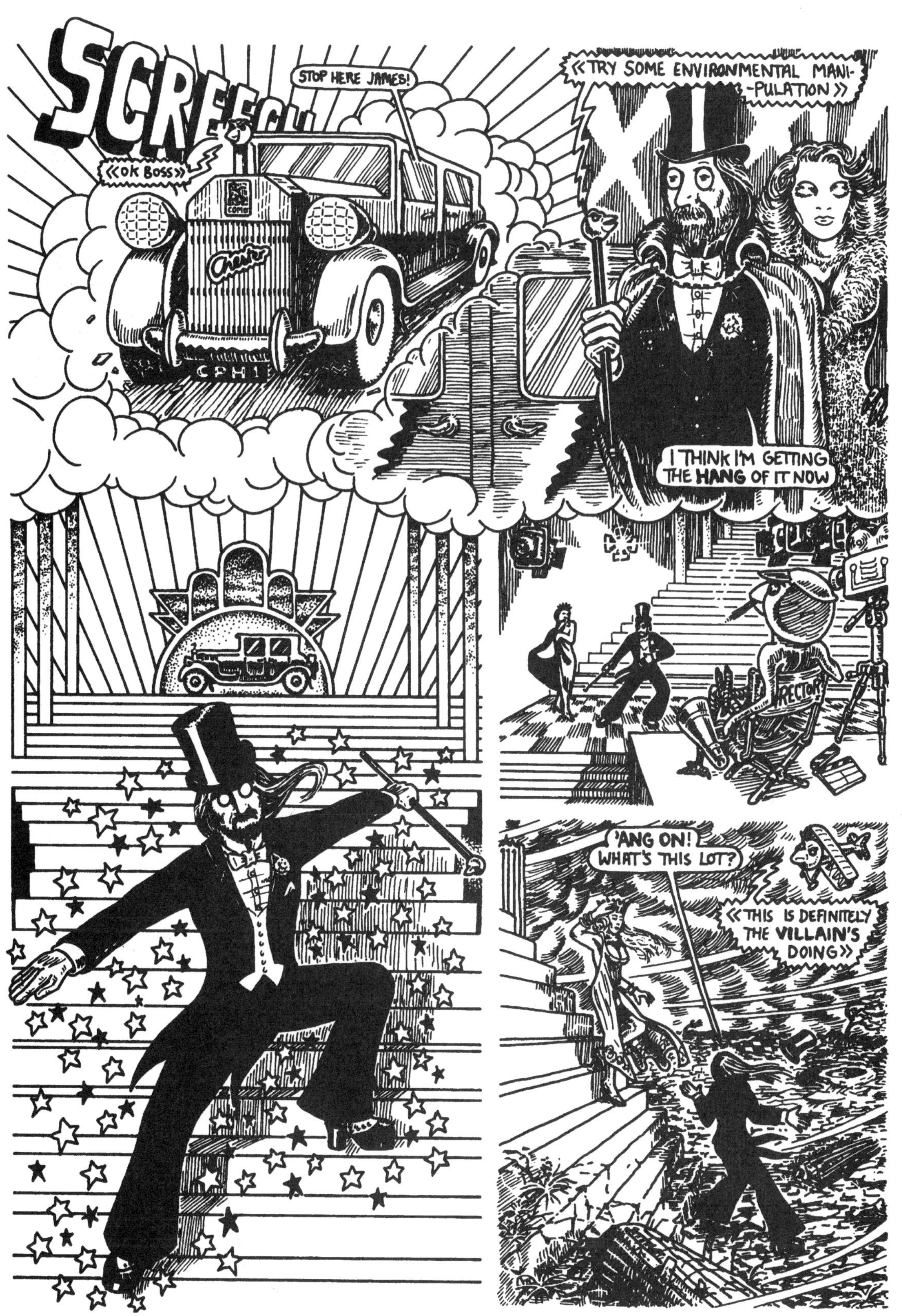
SCREECH
STOP HERE JAMES!
«OK BOSS»
«TRY SOME ENVIRONMENTAL MANI--PULATION»
I THINK I'M GETTING THE HANG OF IT NOW
'ANG ON! WHAT'S THIS LOT?
«THIS IS DEFINITELY THE VILLAIN'S DOING»

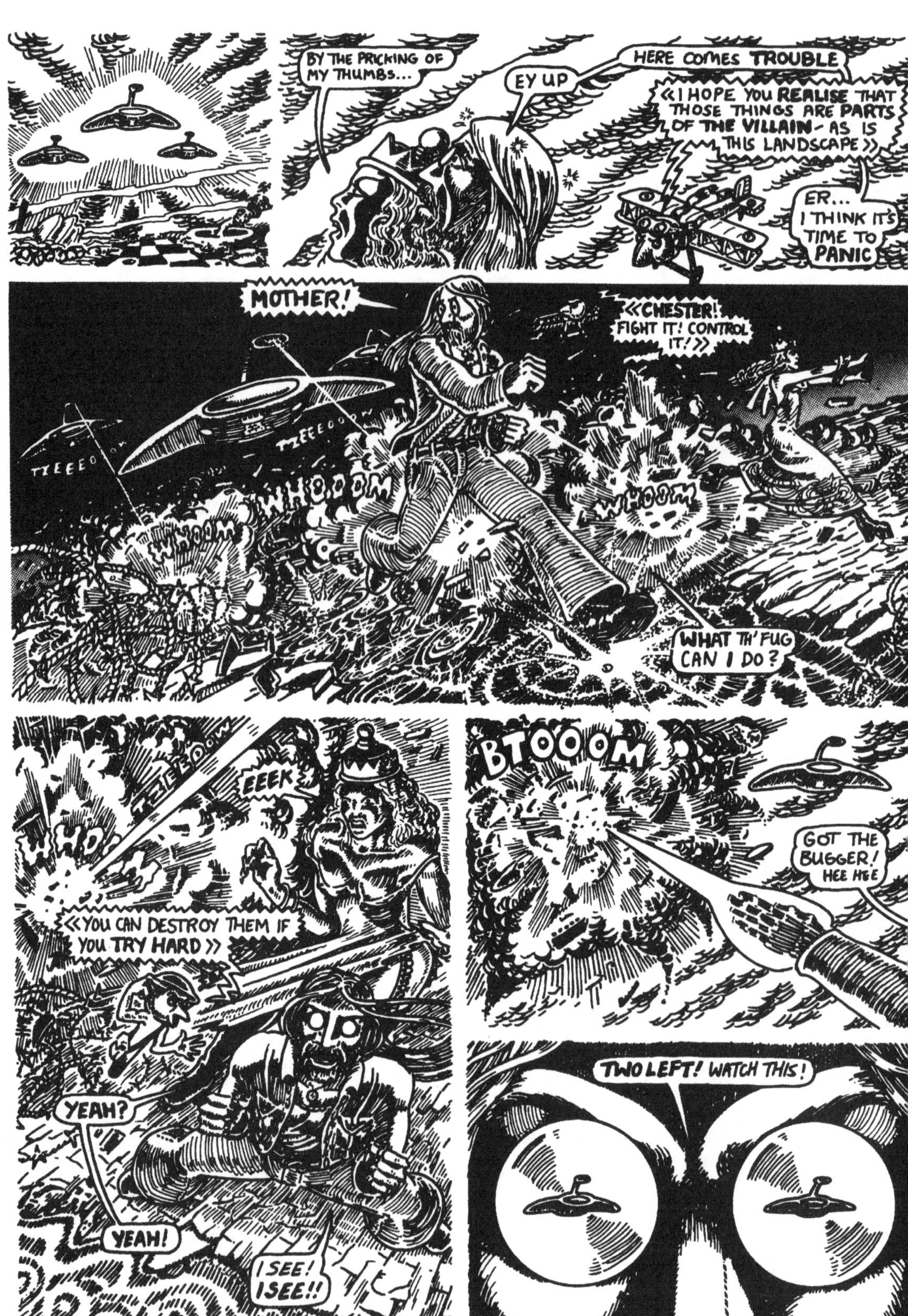
BY THE PRICKING OF MY THUMBS...
EY UP
HERE COMES TROUBLE
«I HOPE YOU REALISE THAT THOSE THINGS ARE PARTS OF THE VILLAIN - AS IS THIS LANDSCAPE»
ER... I THINK IT'S TIME TO PANIC
MOTHER!
«CHESTER! FIGHT IT! CONTROL IT!»
TZEEEO
TZEEEOOOW
WHOOOM
WHOOM
WHOOM
WHAT TH'FUG CAN I DO?
EEEK
«YOU CAN DESTROY THEM IF YOU TRY HARD»
YEAH?
YEAH!
I SEE! I SEE!!
BTOOOM
GOT THE BUGGER! HEE HEE
TWO LEFT! WATCH THIS!

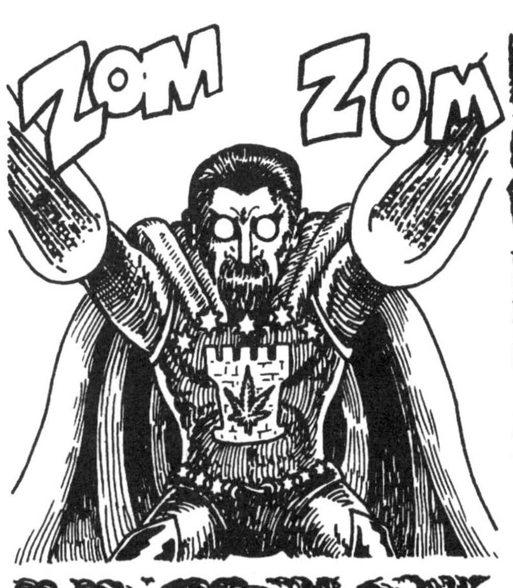
ZOM ZOM

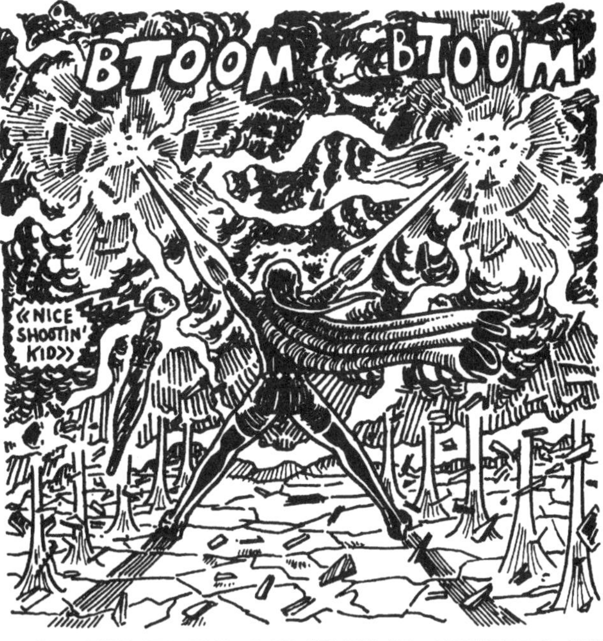
BTOOM BTOOM
«NICE SHOOTIN' KID»

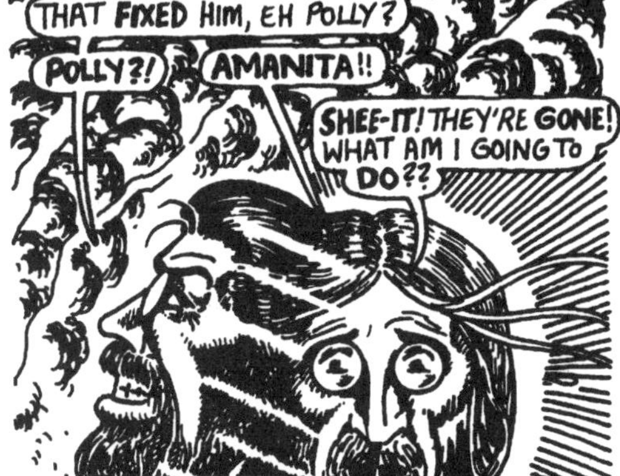
THAT FIXED HIM, EH POLLY?
POLLY?!
AMANITA!!
SHEE-IT! THEY'RE GONE! WHAT AM I GOING TO DO??

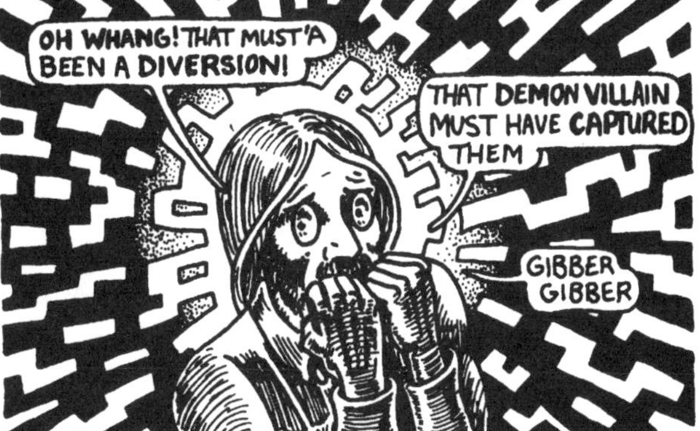
OH WHANG! THAT MUST'A BEEN A DIVERSION!
THAT DEMON VILLAIN MUST HAVE CAPTURED THEM
GIBBER GIBBER

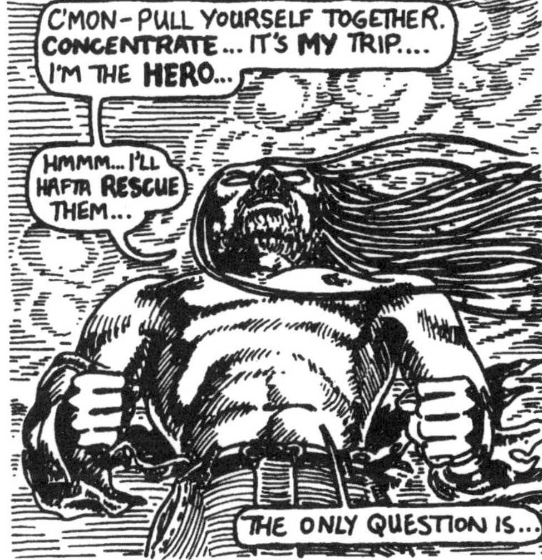
C'MON - PULL YOURSELF TOGETHER. CONCENTRATE... IT'S MY TRIP.... I'M THE HERO...
HMMM... I'LL HAFTA RESCUE THEM...
THE ONLY QUESTION IS...

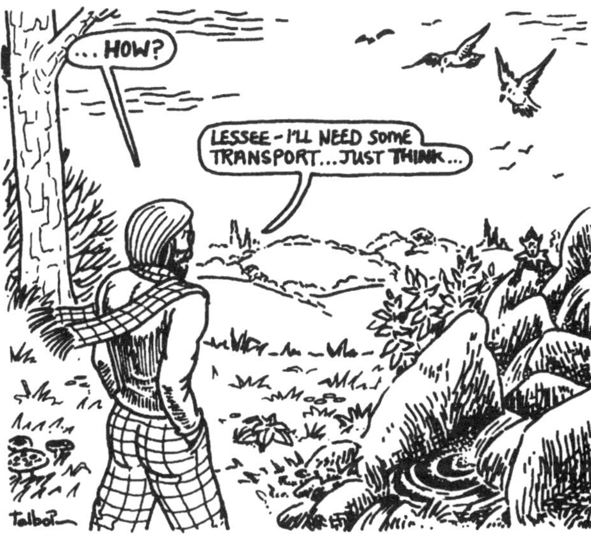
... HOW?
LESSEE - I'LL NEED SOME TRANSPORT... JUST THINK...
Talbot

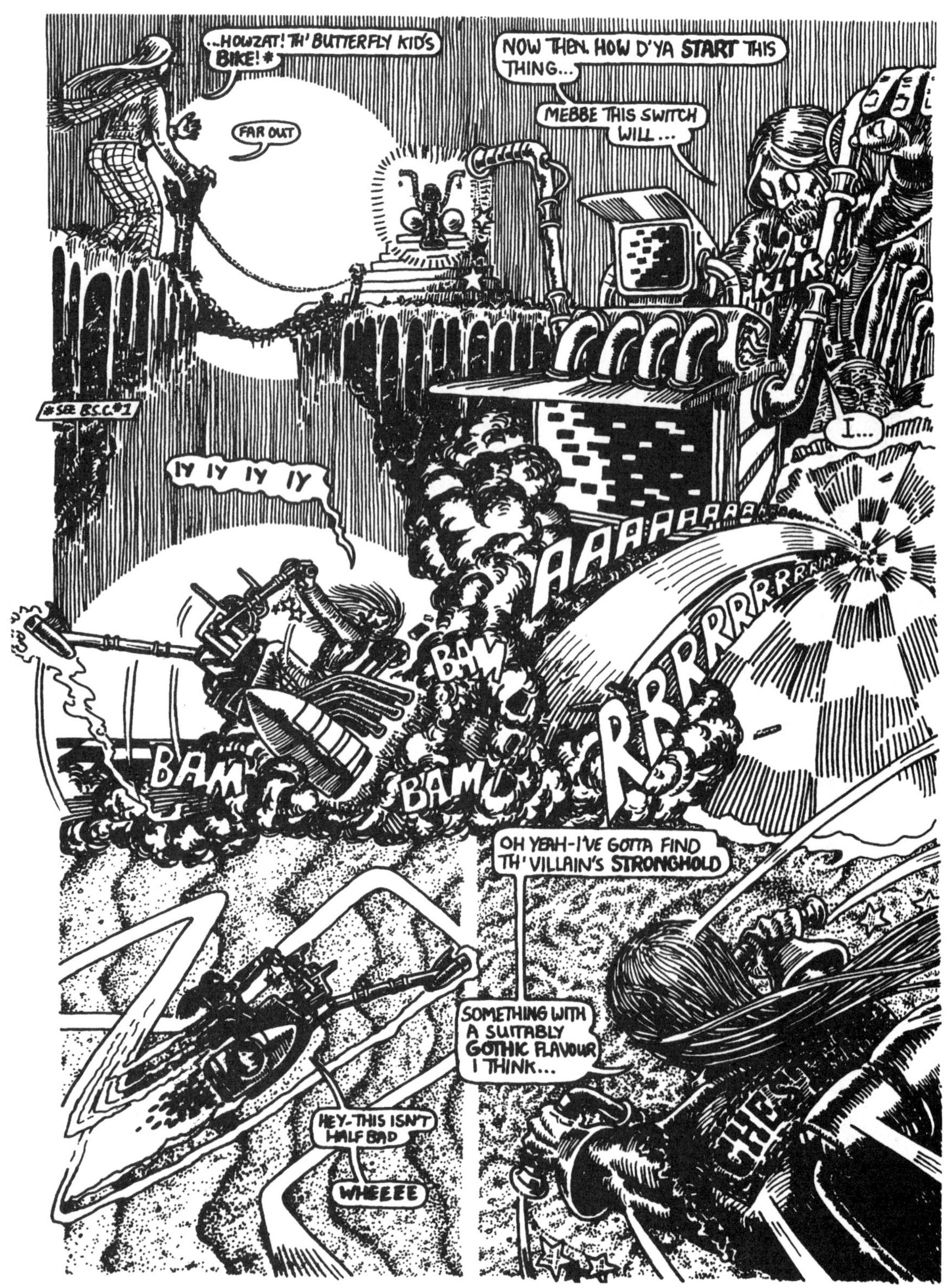
..HOWZAT! TH' BUTTERFLY KID'S BIKE! *
FAR OUT
NOW THEN. HOW D'YA START THIS THING...
MEBBE THIS SWITCH WILL...
KLIK
I...
* SEE B.S.C.#1
IY IY IY IY
AAAAAAAAA
RRRRRRRRRRR
BAM
BAM
BAM
OH YEAH-I'VE GOTTA FIND TH' VILLAIN'S STRONGHOLD
SOMETHING WITH A SUITABLY GOTHIC FLAVOUR I THINK...
HEY-THIS ISN'T HALF BAD
WHEEEE

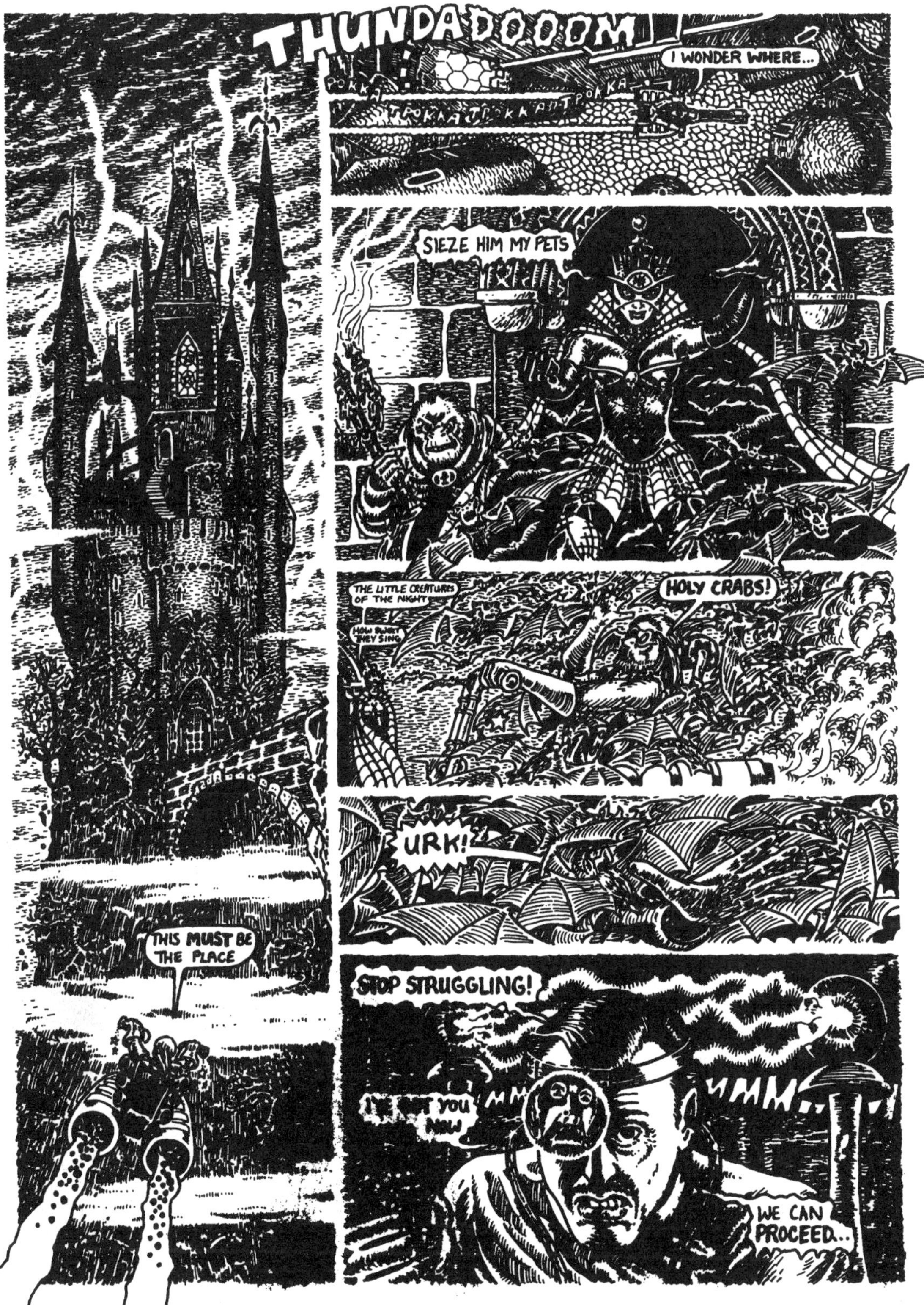
THUNDADOOOM
I WONDER WHERE...
SIEZE HIM MY PETS
THE LITTLE CREATURES OF THE NIGHT
HOW SWEET THEY SING
HOLY CRABS!
URK!
THIS MUST BE THE PLACE
STOP STRUGGLING!
YOU NOW
WE CAN PROCEED...

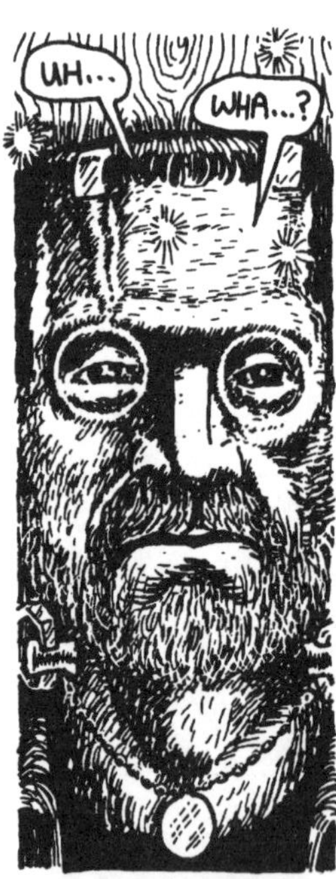
UH...
WHA...?

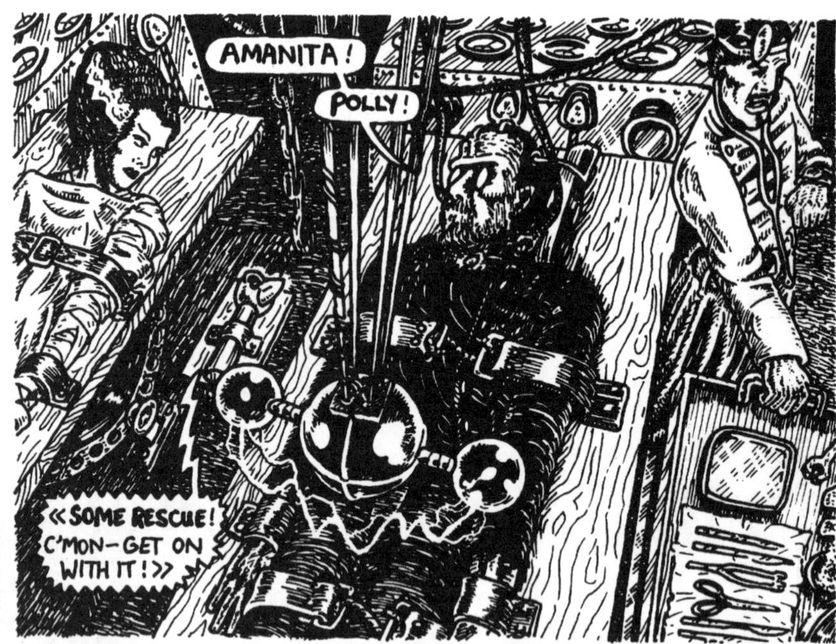
AMANITA!
POLLY!
«SOME RESCUE! C'MON—GET ON WITH IT!»

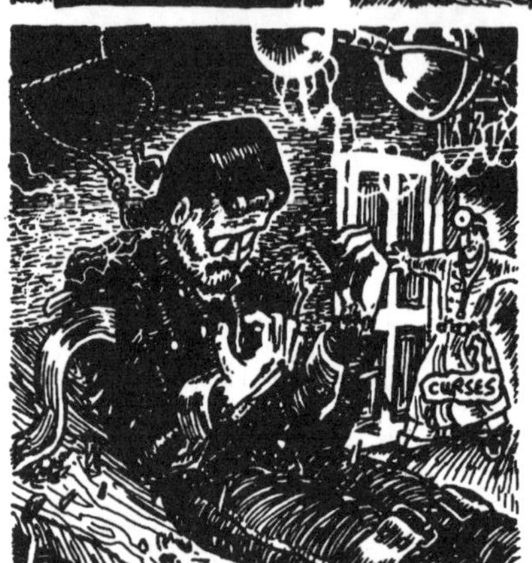
CURSES

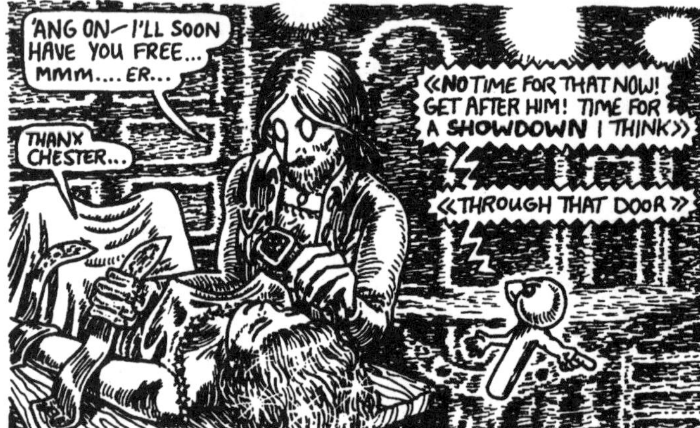
'ANG ON—I'LL SOON HAVE YOU FREE... MMM.... ER...
THANX CHESTER...
«NO TIME FOR THAT NOW! GET AFTER HIM! TIME FOR A SHOWDOWN I THINK»
«THROUGH THAT DOOR»

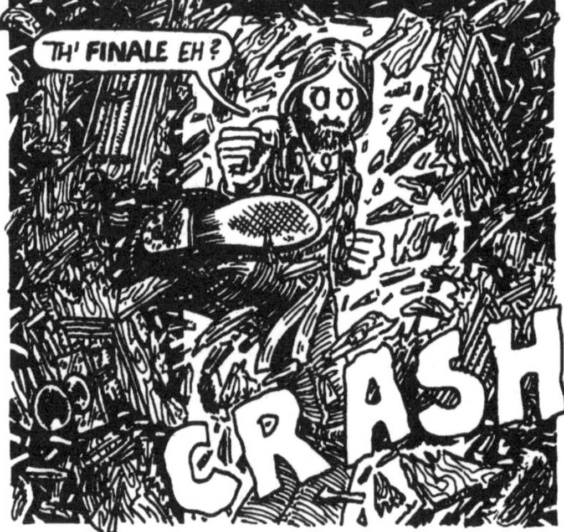
TH' FINALE EH?
CRASH

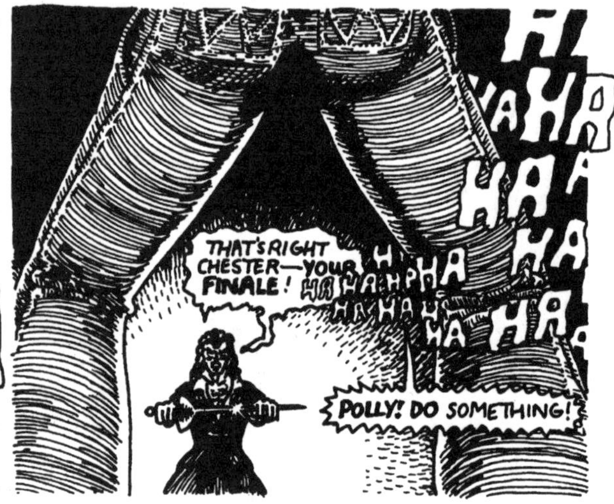
HA HA HA HA
THAT'S RIGHT CHESTER—YOUR FINALE!
POLLY! DO SOMETHING!

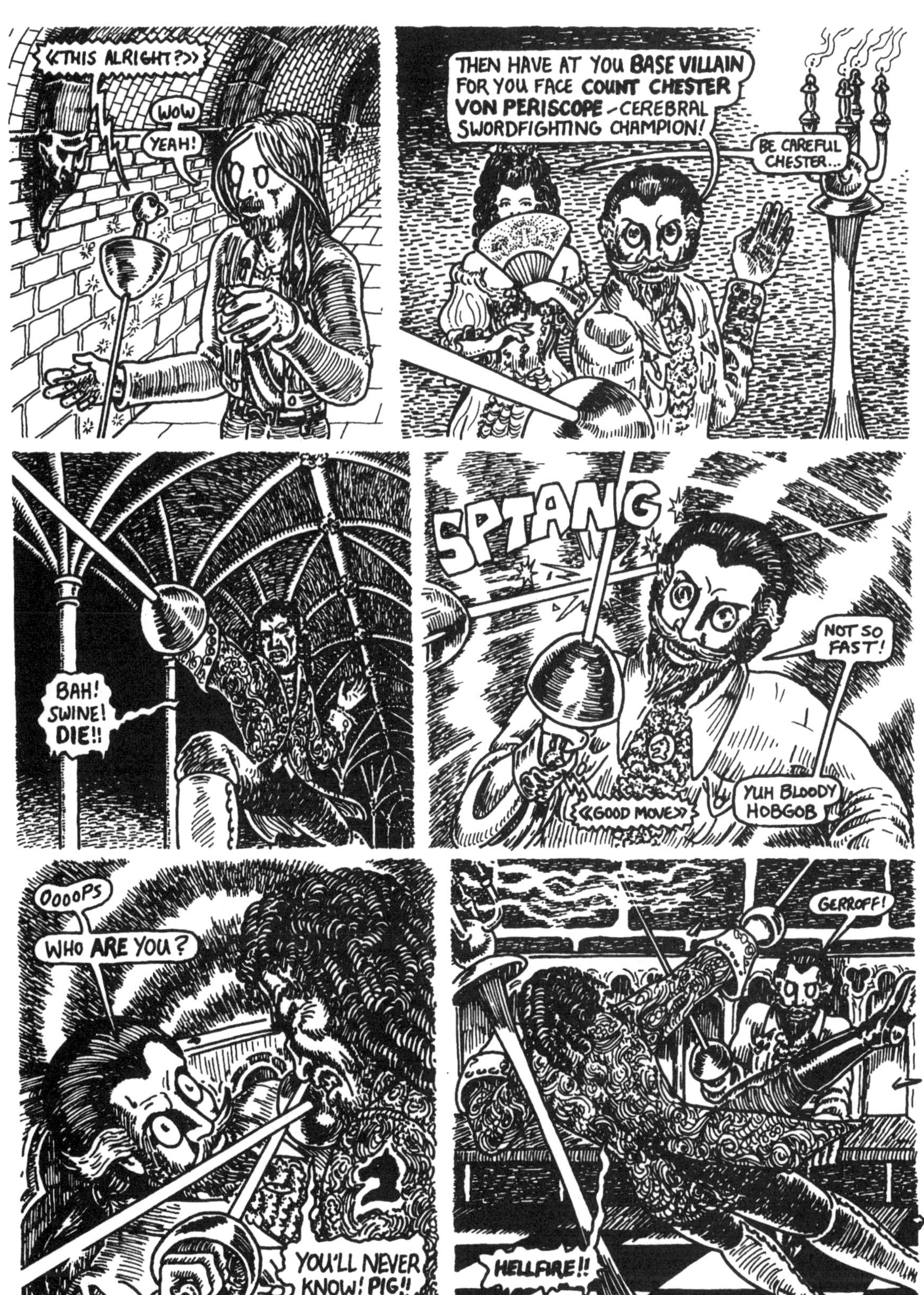
«THIS ALRIGHT?»
WOW
YEAH!
THEN HAVE AT YOU BASE VILLAIN FOR YOU FACE COUNT CHESTER VON PERISCOPE - CEREBRAL SWORDFIGHTING CHAMPION!
BE CAREFUL CHESTER...
BAH! SWINE! DIE!!
SPTANG
NOT SO FAST!
«GOOD MOVE»
YUH BLOODY HOBGOB
OOOOPS
WHO ARE YOU?
YOU'LL NEVER KNOW! PIG!!
GERROFF!
HELLFIRE!!

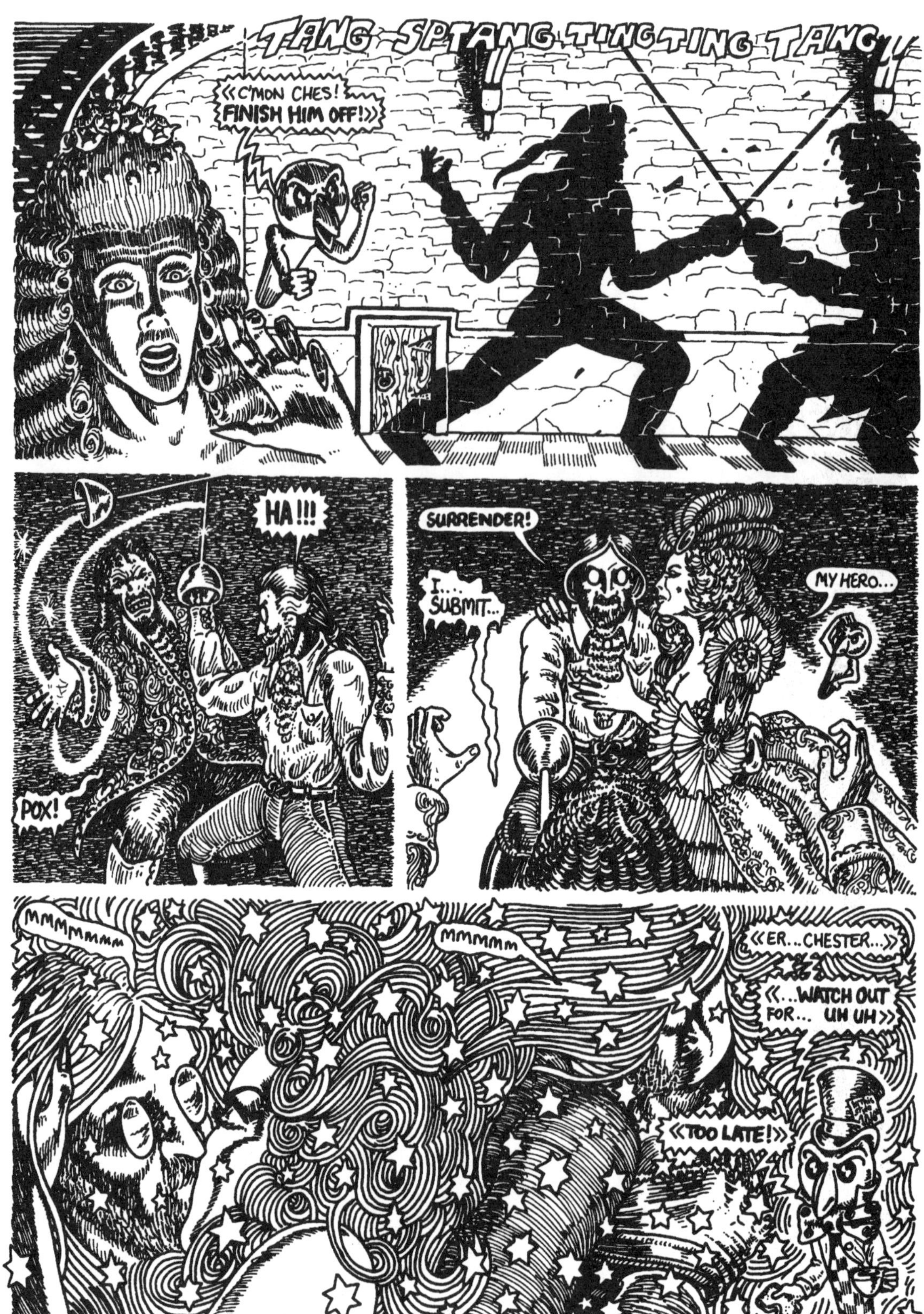
TANG SPTANG TINGTING TANG!!
«C'MON CHES! FINISH HIM OFF!»
HA!!!
POX!
SURRENDER!
I.... SUBMIT...
MY HERO...
MMMMMMM
MMMMM
«ER...CHESTER...»
«...WATCH OUT FOR... UH UH»
«TOO LATE!»

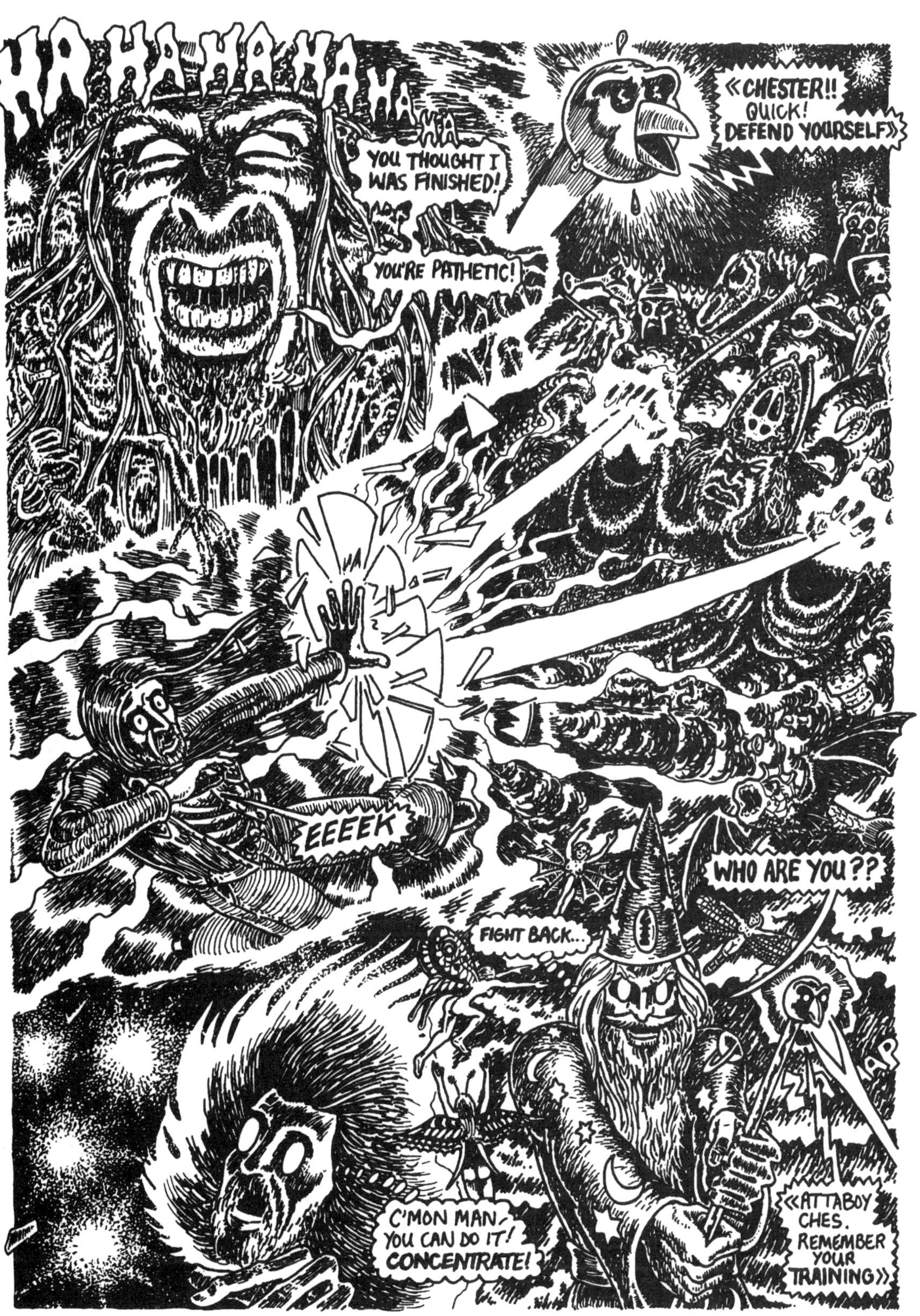
HA HA HA HA HA HA HA
YOU THOUGHT I WAS FINISHED!
YOU'RE PATHETIC!
«CHESTER!! QUICK! DEFEND YOURSELF»
EEEEK
WHO ARE YOU??
FIGHT BACK...
C'MON MAN, YOU CAN DO IT! CONCENTRATE!
«ATTABOY CHES. REMEMBER YOUR TRAINING»

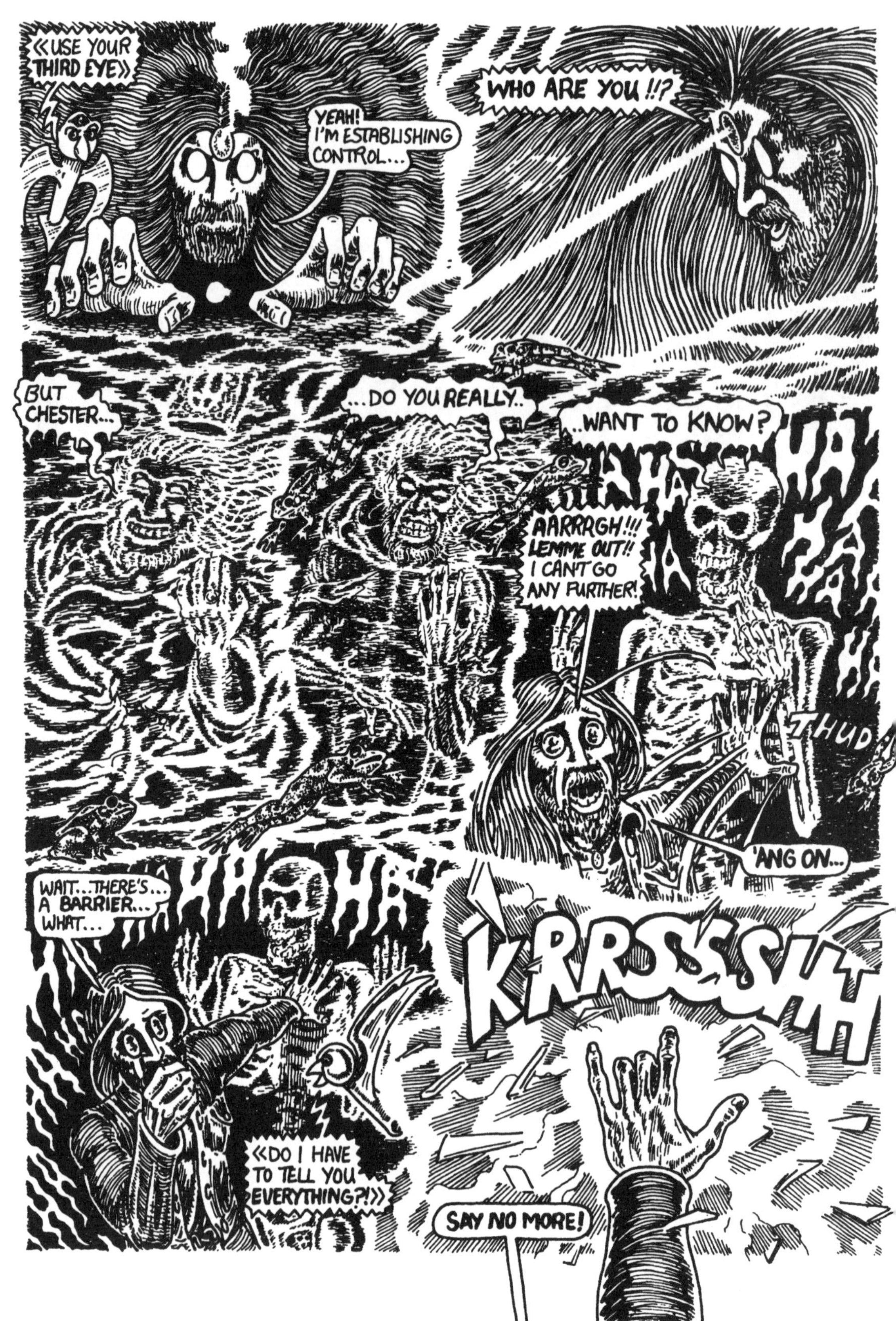
«USE YOUR THIRD EYE»
YEAH! I'M ESTABLISHING CONTROL...
WHO ARE YOU !!?
BUT CHESTER...
...DO YOU REALLY..
..WANT TO KNOW?
HA HA HA HA HA HA HA
AARRRGH!!! LEMME OUT!! I CAN'T GO ANY FURTHER!
THUD
'ANG ON...
WAIT...THERE'S... A BARRIER... WHAT...
HA HA
«DO I HAVE TO TELL YOU EVERYTHING?!»
KRRSSSSH
SAY NO MORE!

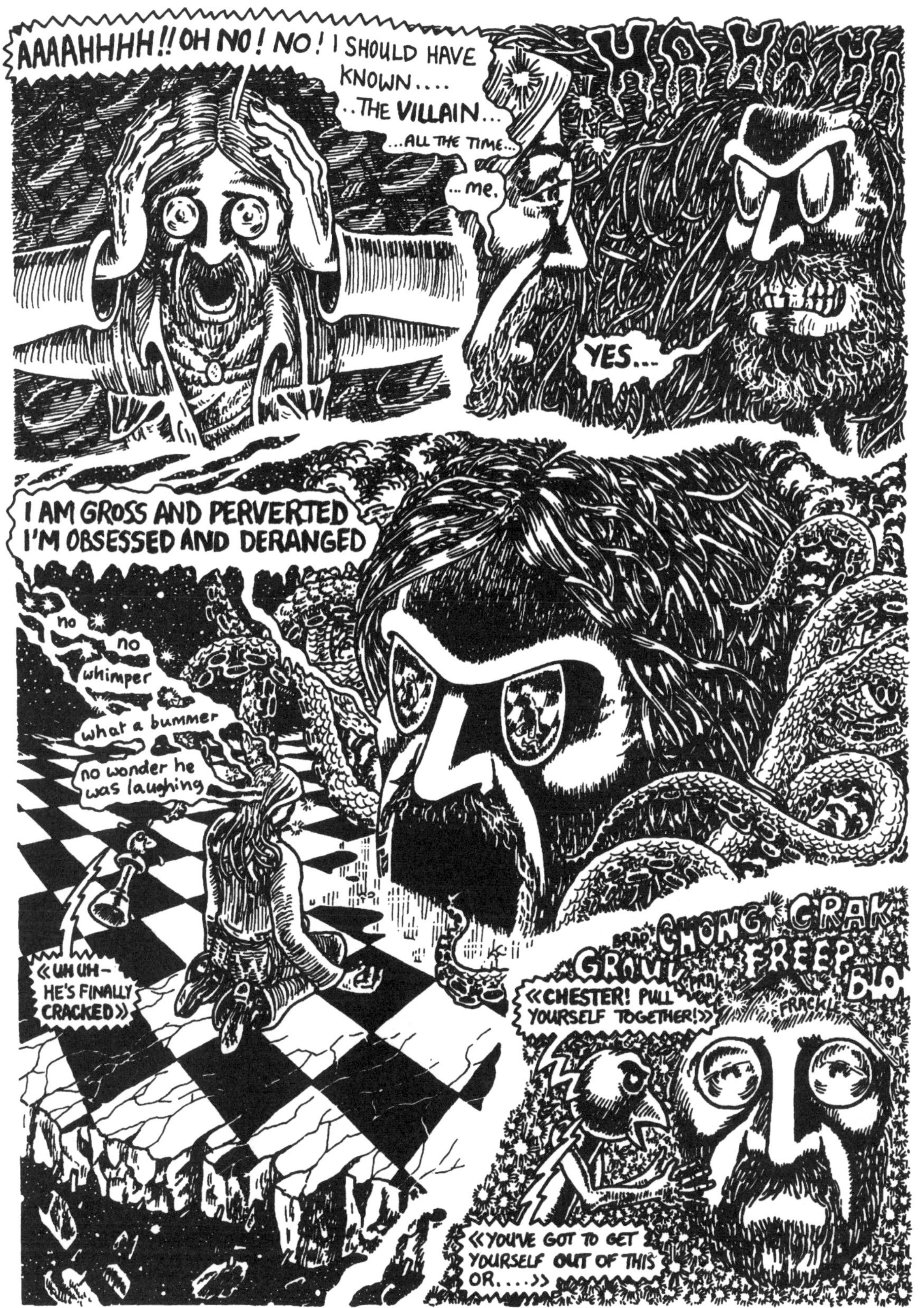

AAAAHHHH!! OH NO! NO! I SHOULD HAVE KNOWN....
..THE VILLAIN...
...ALL THE TIME...
...me.
HA HA HA HA
YES...
I AM GROSS AND PERVERTED
I'M OBSESSED AND DERANGED
no
no
whimper
what a bummer
no wonder he was laughing
«UH UH- HE'S FINALLY CRACKED»
CHONG CRAK
GRAVL
FREEP
BLO
FRACKLE
«CHESTER! PULL YOURSELF TOGETHER!»
«YOU'VE GOT TO GET YOURSELF OUT OF THIS OR....»

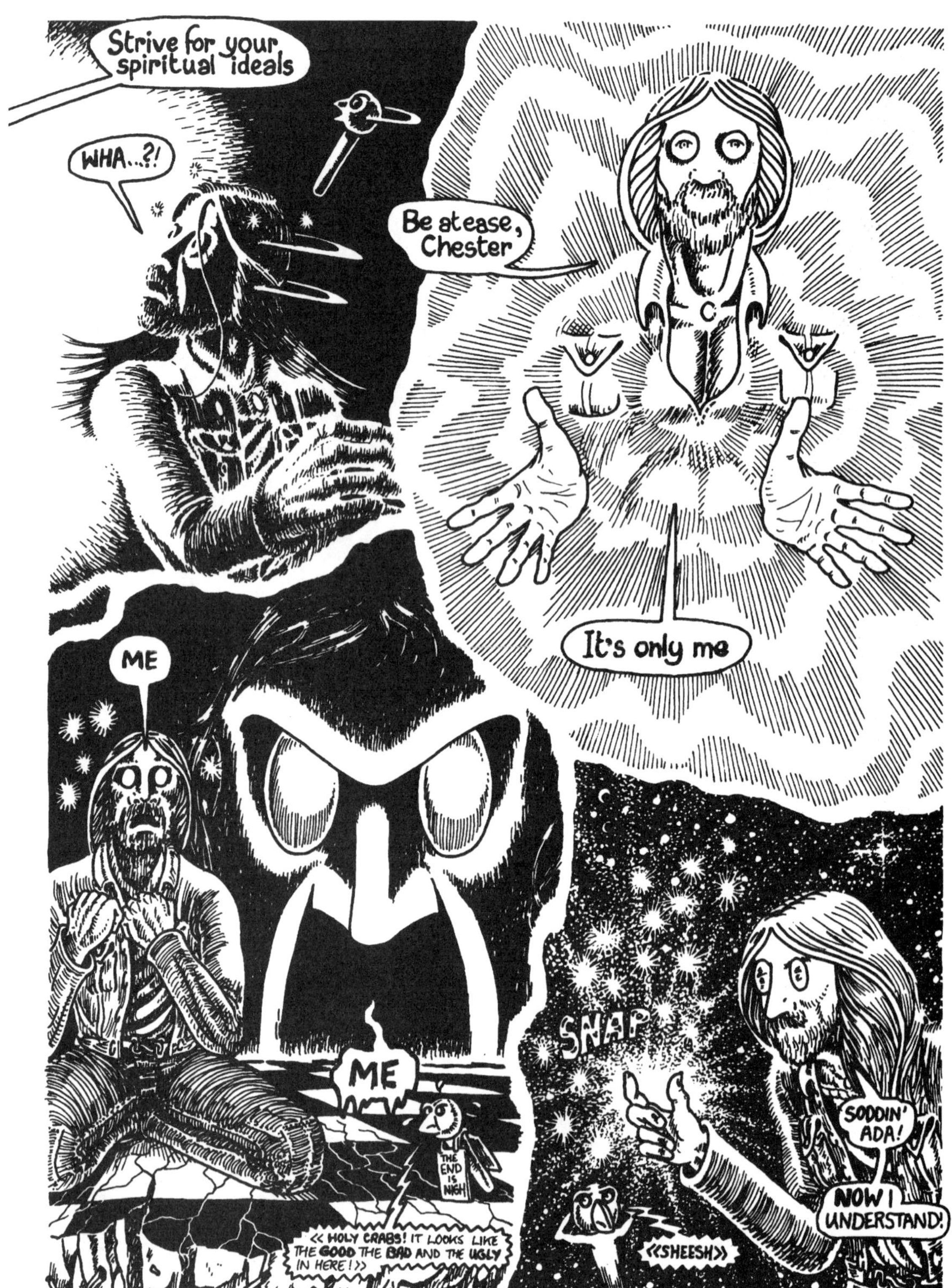
Strive for your spiritual ideals
WHA...?!
Be at ease, Chester
It's only me
ME
ME
THE END IS NIGH
<< HOLY CRABS! IT LOOKS LIKE THE GOOD THE BAD AND THE UGLY IN HERE! >>
SNAP
SODDIN' ADA!
NOW I UNDERSTAND!
<<SHEESH>>

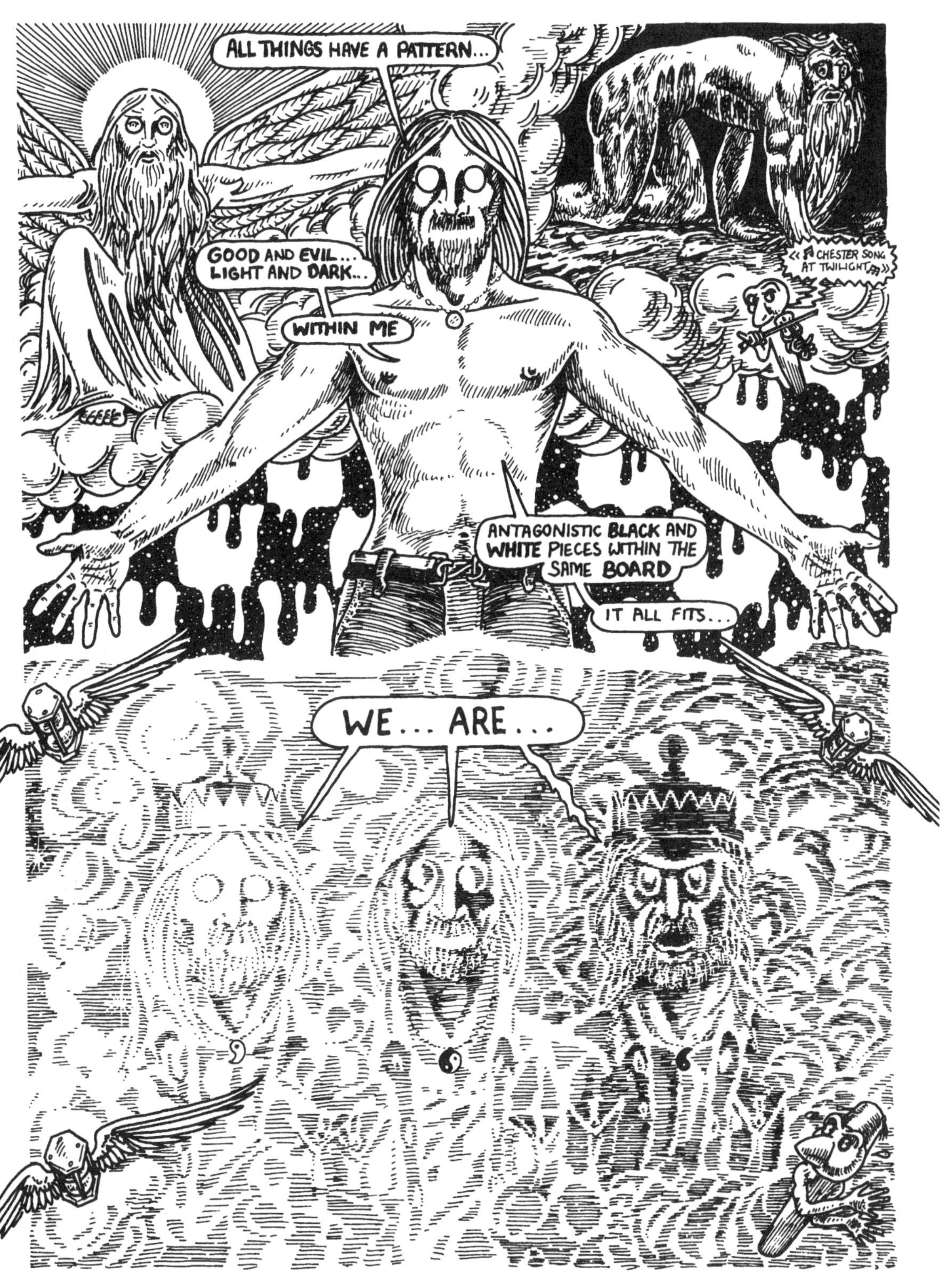
ALL THINGS HAVE A PATTERN...
GOOD AND EVIL... LIGHT AND DARK...
WITHIN ME
«♫ CHESTER SONG AT TWILIGHT♫»
ANTAGONISTIC BLACK AND WHITE PIECES WITHIN THE SAME BOARD
IT ALL FITS...
WE... ARE...

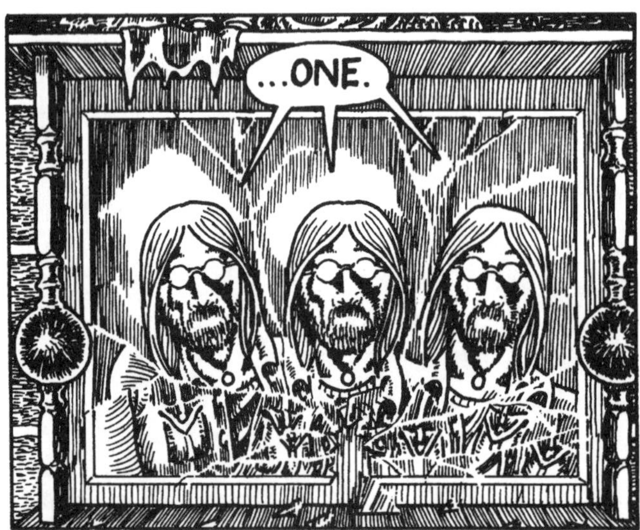
...ONE.

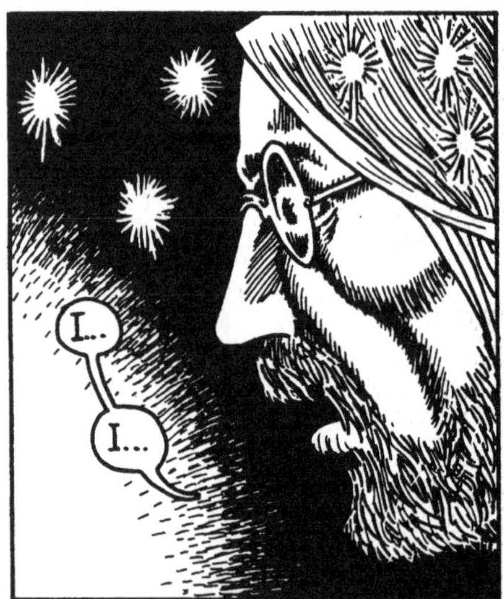
I...
I...

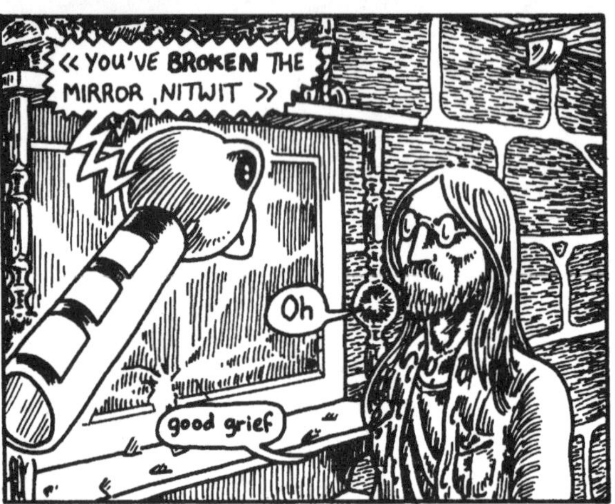
«YOU'VE BROKEN THE MIRROR, NITWIT»
Oh
good grief

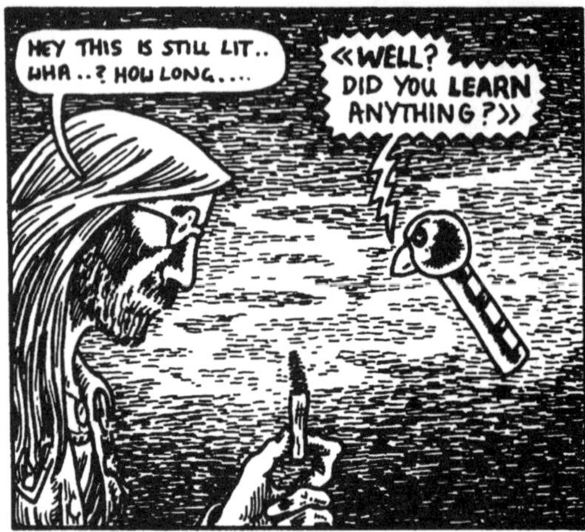
HEY THIS IS STILL LIT.. WHA..? HOW LONG....
«WELL? DID YOU LEARN ANYTHING?»

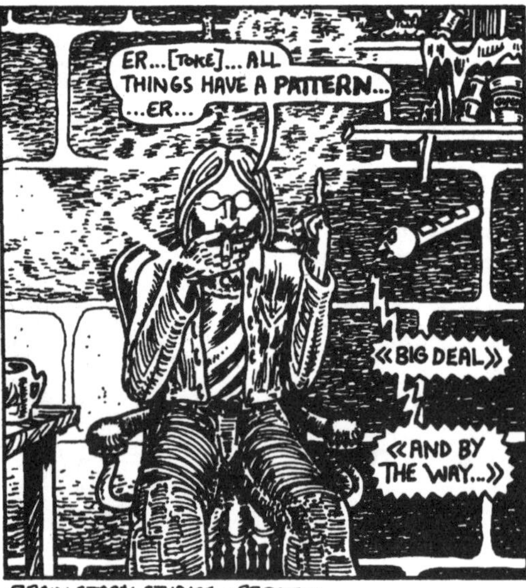
ER...[TOKE]...ALL THINGS HAVE A PATTERN... ...ER...
«BIG DEAL»
«AND BY THE WAY...»
BRAIN STORM STUDIOS — PRESTON

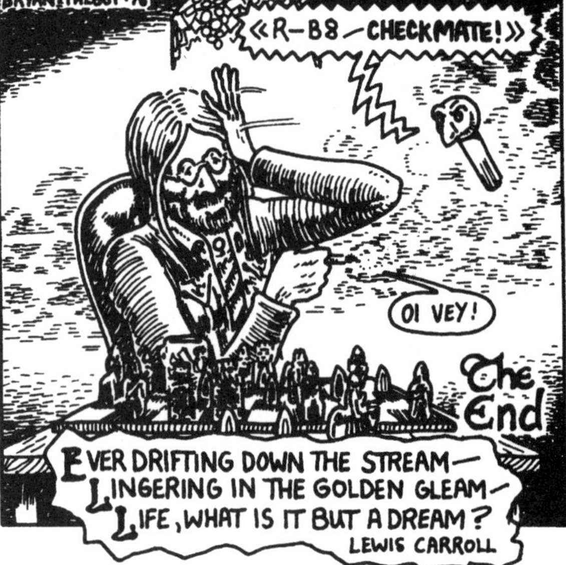
«R-B8 — CHECKMATE!»
OI VEY!
The End
EVER DRIFTING DOWN THE STREAM —
LINGERING IN THE GOLDEN GLEAM —
LIFE, WHAT IS IT BUT A DREAM?
LEWIS CARROLL

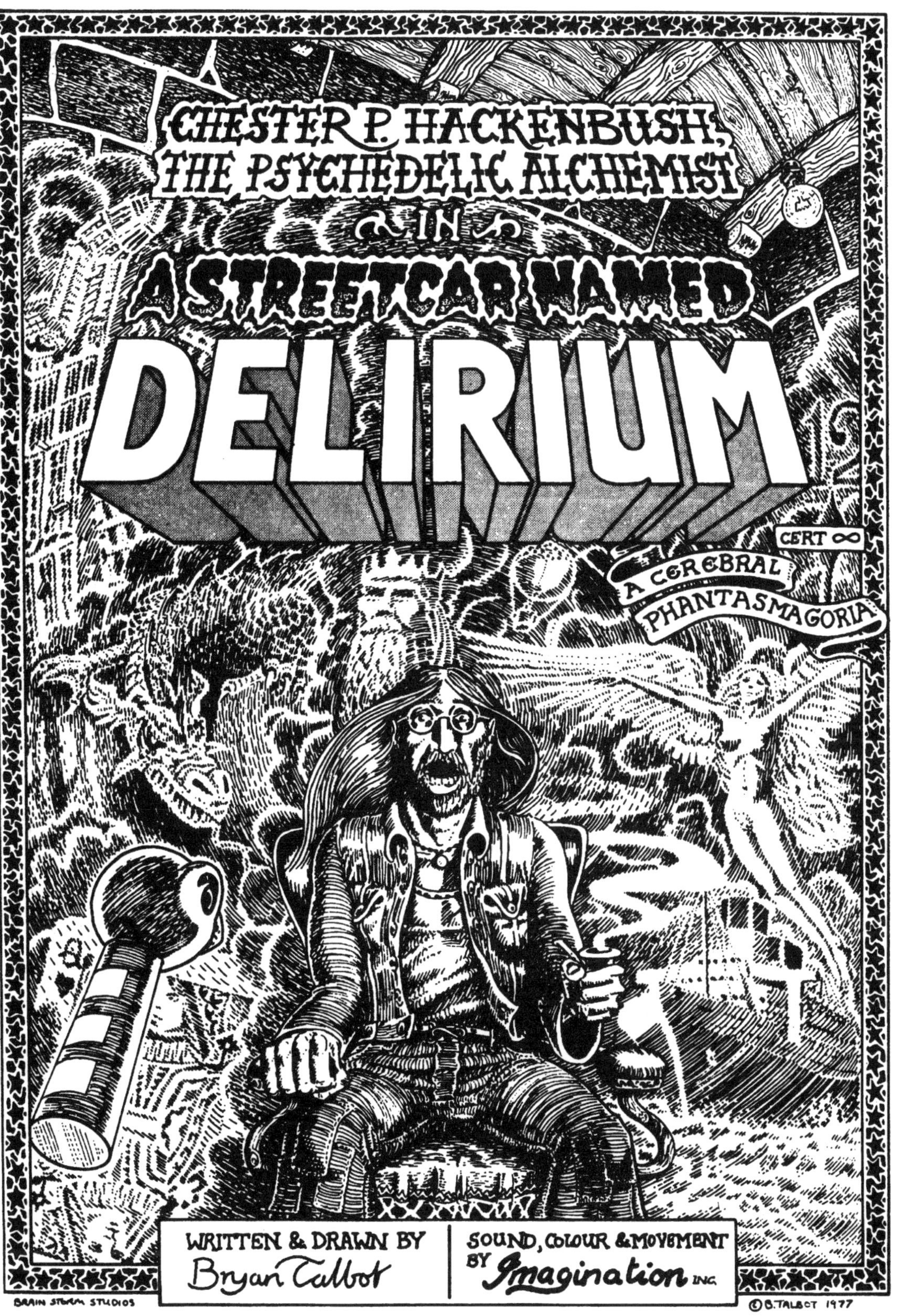
CHESTER P. HACKENBUSH,
THE PSYCHEDELIC ALCHEMIST
IN
A STREETCAR NAMED
DELIRIUM
CERT ∞
A CEREBRAL PHANTASMAGORIA
WRITTEN & DRAWN BY
Bryan Talbot
SOUND, COLOUR & MOVEMENT BY Imagination INC.
BRAIN STORM STUDIOS
© B. TALBOT 1977

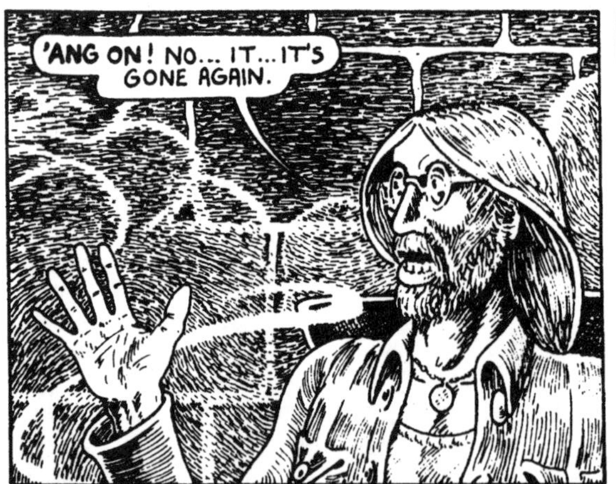
'ANG ON! NO... IT... IT'S GONE AGAIN.

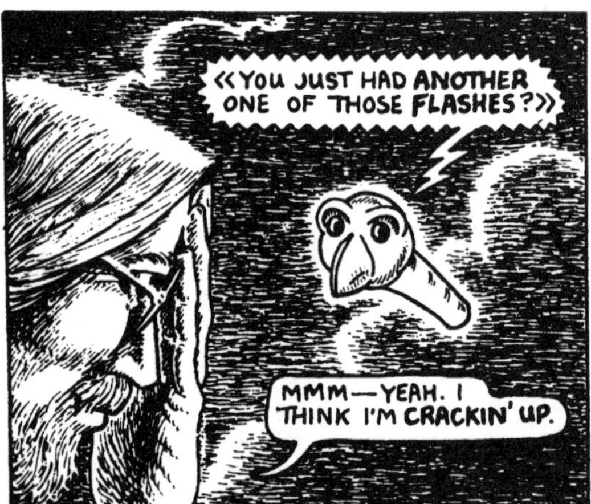
«YOU JUST HAD ANOTHER ONE OF THOSE FLASHES?»
MMM—YEAH. I THINK I'M CRACKIN' UP.

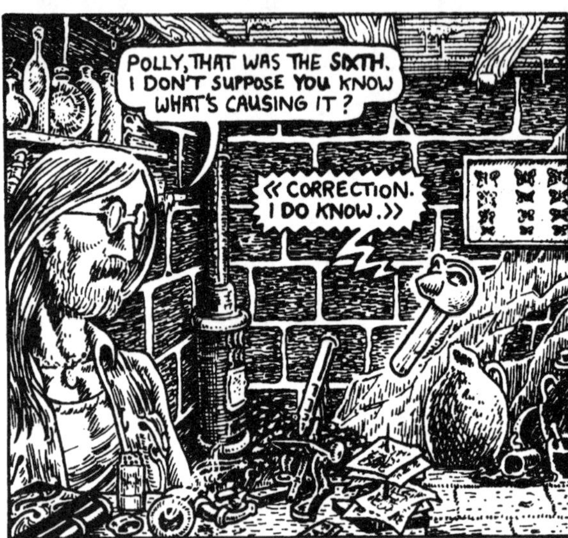
POLLY, THAT WAS THE SIXTH. I DON'T SUPPOSE YOU KNOW WHAT'S CAUSING IT?
«CORRECTION. I DO KNOW.»

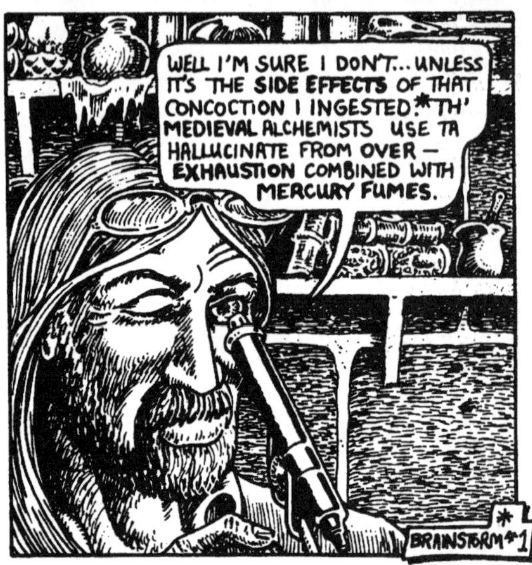
WELL I'M SURE I DON'T... UNLESS IT'S THE SIDE EFFECTS OF THAT CONCOCTION I INGESTED.* TH' MEDIEVAL ALCHEMISTS USE TA HALLUCINATE FROM OVER-EXHAUSTION COMBINED WITH MERCURY FUMES.
* BRAINSTORM #1

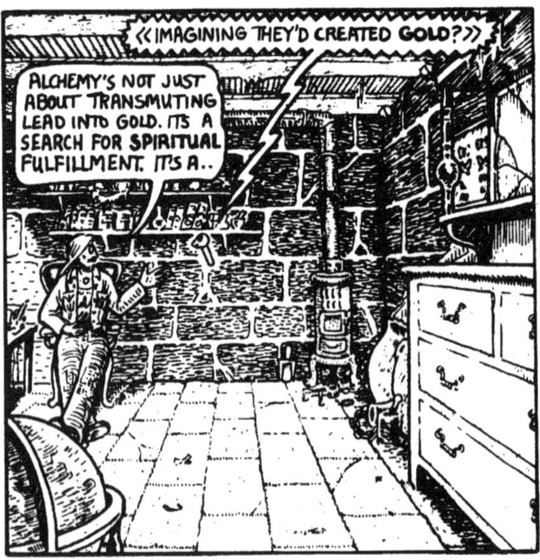
«IMAGINING THEY'D CREATED GOLD?»
ALCHEMY'S NOT JUST ABOUT TRANSMUTING LEAD INTO GOLD. ITS A SEARCH FOR SPIRITUAL FULFILLMENT. IT'S A..

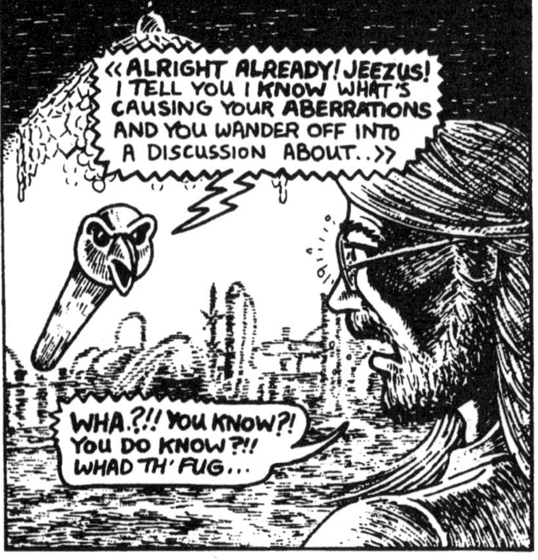
«ALRIGHT ALREADY! JEEZUS! I TELL YOU I KNOW WHAT'S CAUSING YOUR ABERRATIONS AND YOU WANDER OFF INTO A DISCUSSION ABOUT..»
WHA?!! YOU KNOW?! YOU DO KNOW?!! WHAD TH' FUG...

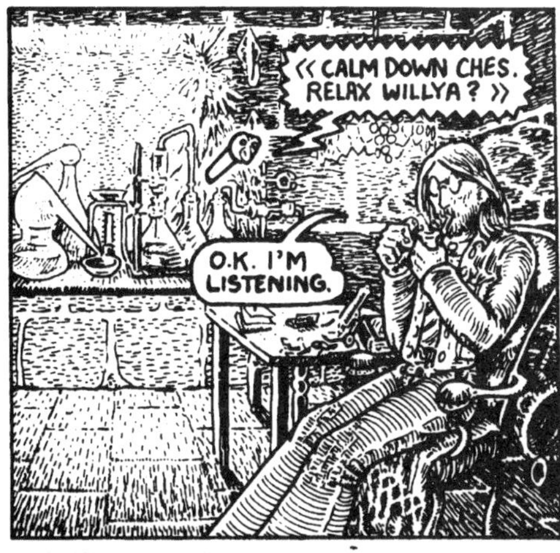
«CALM DOWN CHES. RELAX WILLYA?»
O.K. I'M LISTENING.

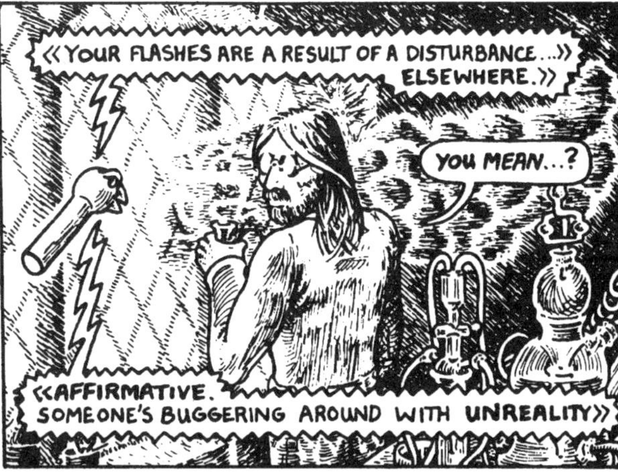
«YOUR FLASHES ARE A RESULT OF A DISTURBANCE...» ELSEWHERE.»
YOU MEAN...?
«AFFIRMATIVE. SOMEONE'S BUGGERING AROUND WITH UNREALITY»

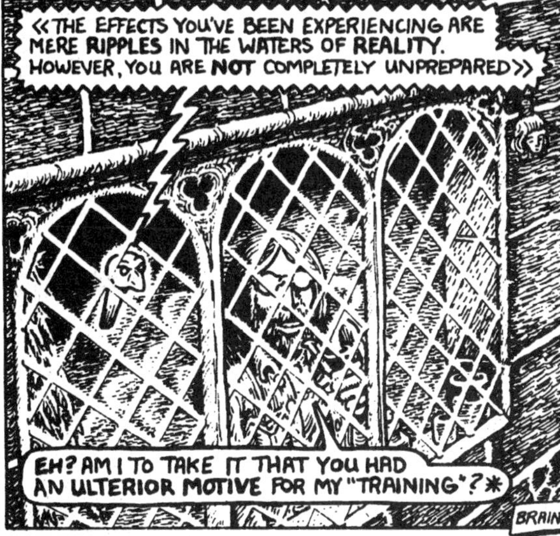
«THE EFFECTS YOU'VE BEEN EXPERIENCING ARE MERE RIPPLES IN THE WATERS OF REALITY. HOWEVER, YOU ARE NOT COMPLETELY UNPREPARED»
EH? AM I TO TAKE IT THAT YOU HAD AN ULTERIOR MOTIVE FOR MY "TRAINING"?*
* BRAINSTORM #2

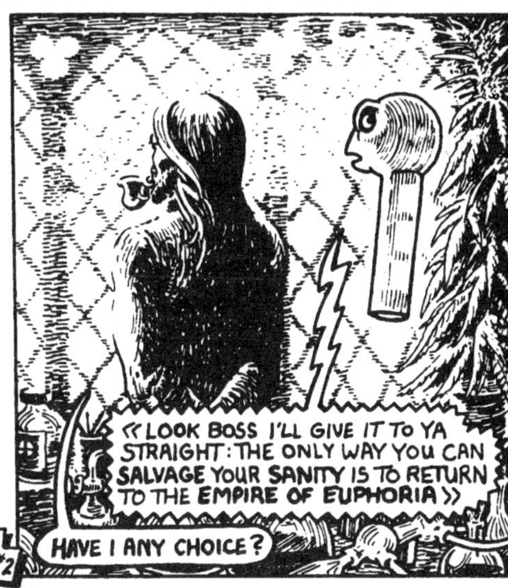
«LOOK BOSS I'LL GIVE IT TO YA STRAIGHT: THE ONLY WAY YOU CAN SALVAGE YOUR SANITY IS TO RETURN TO THE EMPIRE OF EUPHORIA»
HAVE I ANY CHOICE?

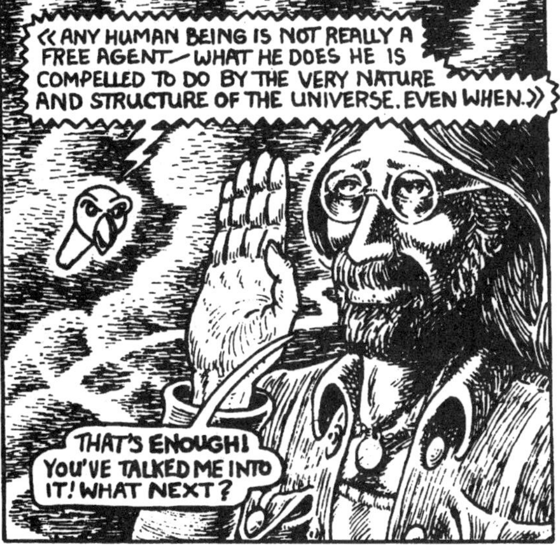
«ANY HUMAN BEING IS NOT REALLY A FREE AGENT— WHAT HE DOES HE IS COMPELLED TO DO BY THE VERY NATURE AND STRUCTURE OF THE UNIVERSE. EVEN WHEN.»
THAT'S ENOUGH! YOU'VE TALKED ME INTO IT! WHAT NEXT?

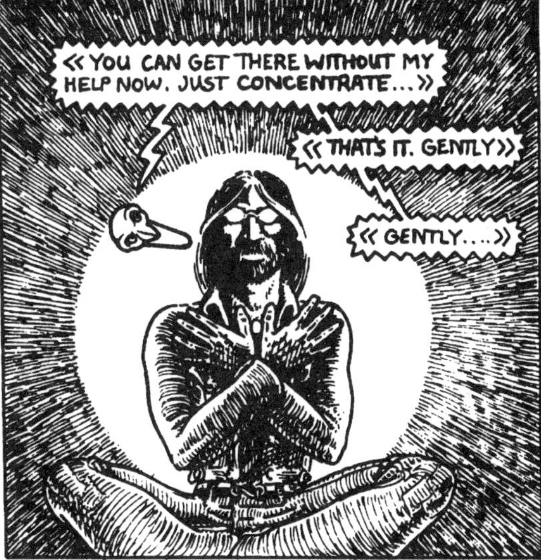
«YOU CAN GET THERE WITHOUT MY HELP NOW. JUST CONCENTRATE...»
«THAT'S IT. GENTLY»
«GENTLY....»

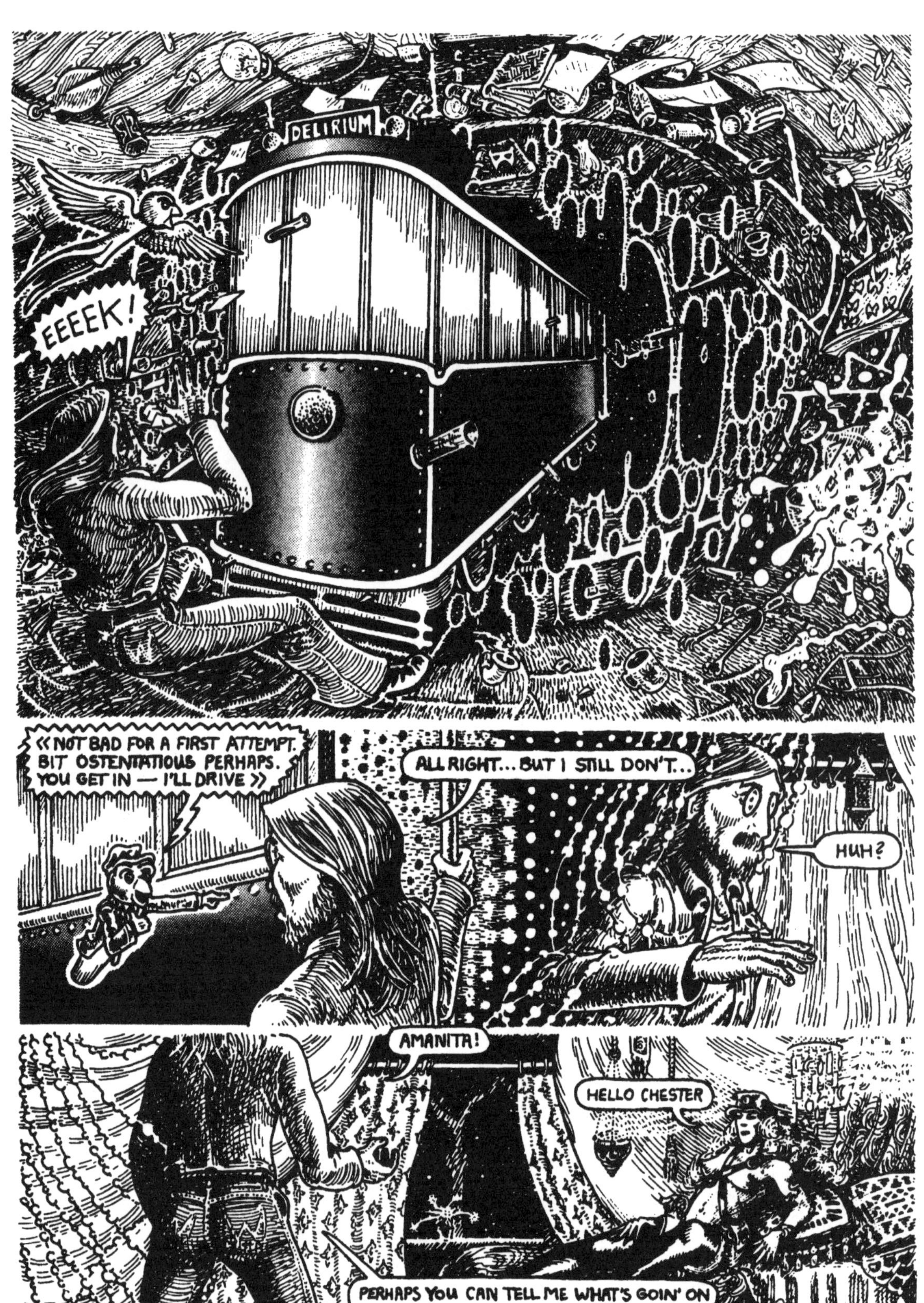
DELIRIUM
EEEEK!
«NOT BAD FOR A FIRST ATTEMPT. BIT OSTENTATIOUS PERHAPS. YOU GET IN — I'LL DRIVE»
ALL RIGHT... BUT I STILL DON'T...
HUH?
AMANITA!
HELLO CHESTER
PERHAPS YOU CAN TELL ME WHAT'S GOIN' ON

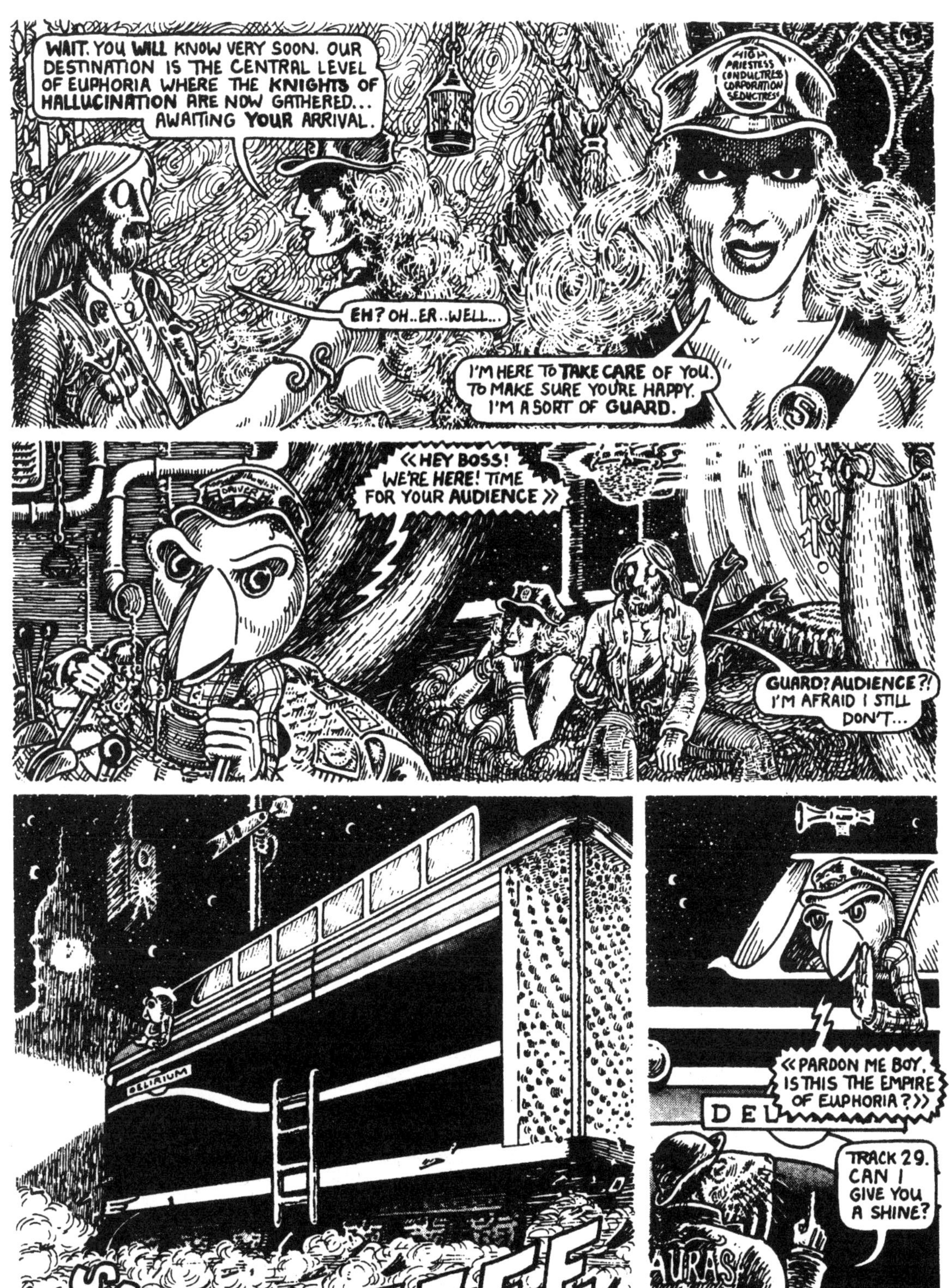
WAIT. YOU WILL KNOW VERY SOON. OUR DESTINATION IS THE CENTRAL LEVEL OF EUPHORIA WHERE THE KNIGHTS OF HALLUCINATION ARE NOW GATHERED... AWAITING YOUR ARRIVAL.
HIGH PRIESTESS CONDUCTRESS CORPORATION SEDUCTRESS
EH? OH..ER..WELL...
I'M HERE TO TAKE CARE OF YOU. TO MAKE SURE YOU'RE HAPPY. I'M A SORT OF GUARD.
DRIVER
«HEY BOSS! WE'RE HERE! TIME FOR YOUR AUDIENCE»
GUARD? AUDIENCE?! I'M AFRAID I STILL DON'T...
DELIRIUM
SKREEEEEEE
«PARDON ME BOY, IS THIS THE EMPIRE OF EUPHORIA?»
DEL
TRACK 29. CAN I GIVE YOU A SHINE?
AURAS POLISHED

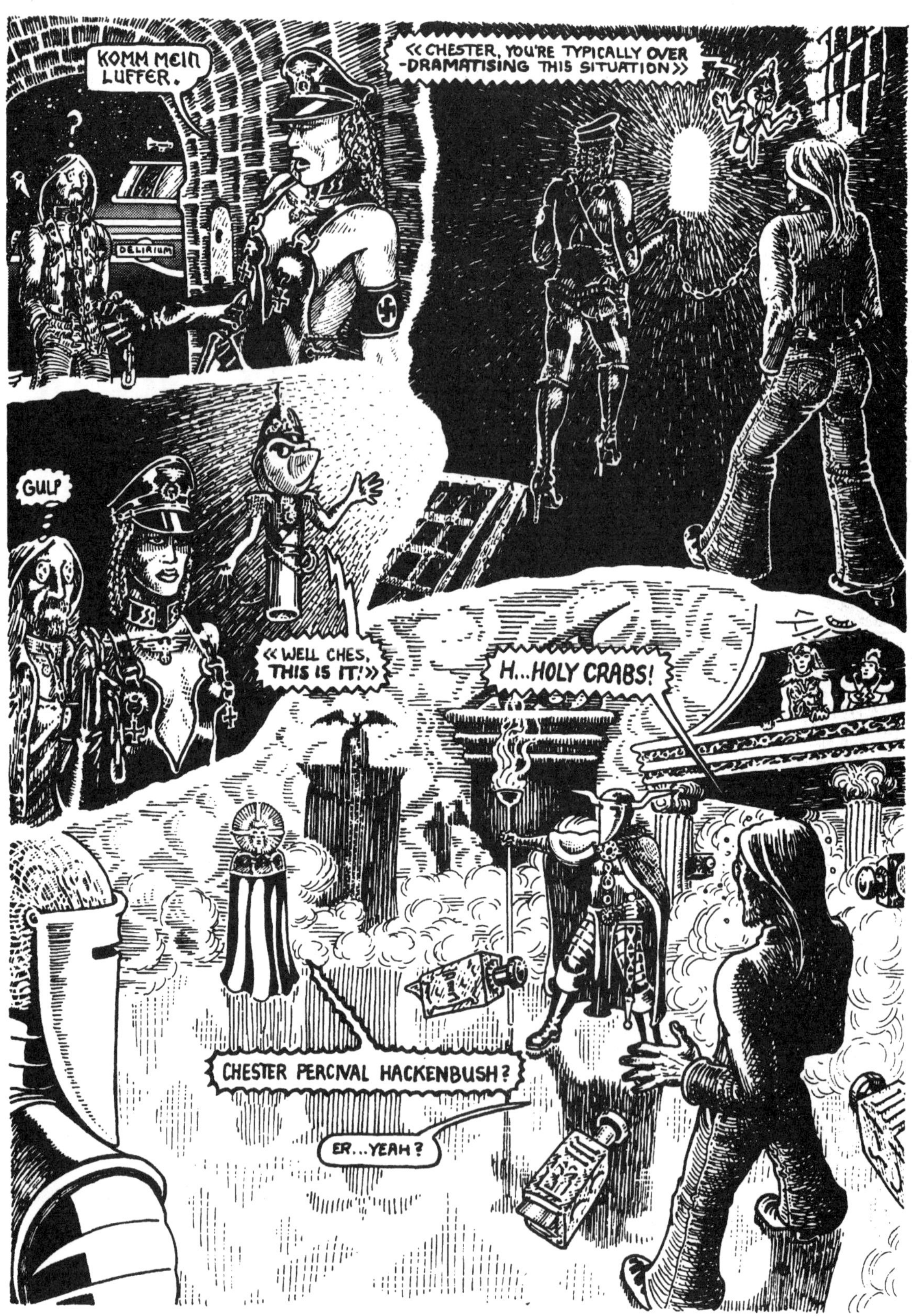
KOMM MEIN LUFFER.
?
DELIRIUM
«CHESTER, YOU'RE TYPICALLY OVER-DRAMATISING THIS SITUATION»
GULP
«WELL CHES, THIS IS IT!»
H...HOLY CRABS!
CHESTER PERCIVAL HACKENBUSH?
ER...YEAH?

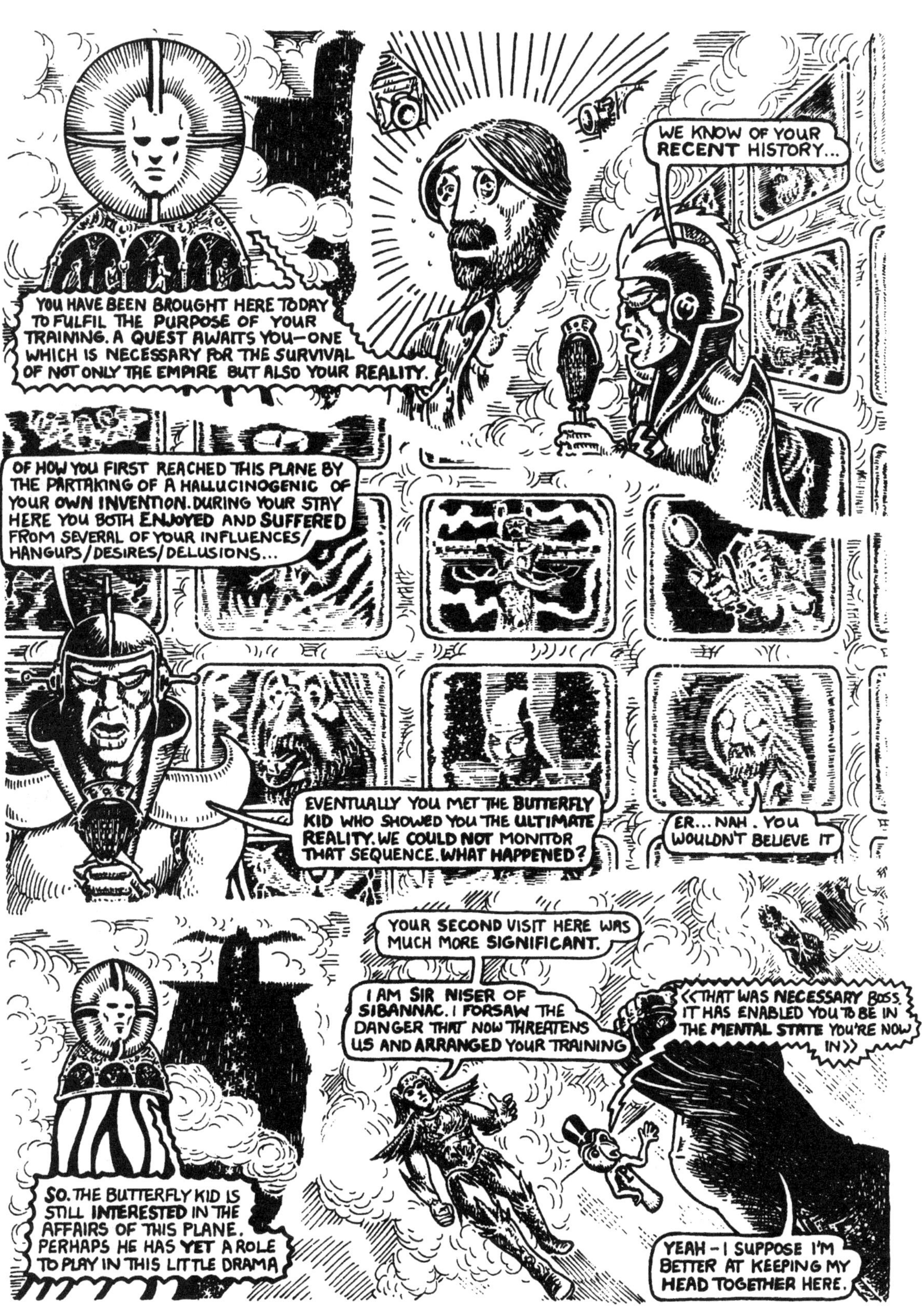
YOU HAVE BEEN BROUGHT HERE TODAY TO FULFIL THE PURPOSE OF YOUR TRAINING. A QUEST AWAITS YOU—ONE WHICH IS NECESSARY FOR THE SURVIVAL OF NOT ONLY THE EMPIRE BUT ALSO YOUR REALITY.
WE KNOW OF YOUR RECENT HISTORY...
OF HOW YOU FIRST REACHED THIS PLANE BY THE PARTAKING OF A HALLUCINOGENIC OF YOUR OWN INVENTION. DURING YOUR STAY HERE YOU BOTH ENJOYED AND SUFFERED FROM SEVERAL OF YOUR INFLUENCES/ HANGUPS/ DESIRES/ DELUSIONS...
EVENTUALLY YOU MET THE BUTTERFLY KID WHO SHOWED YOU THE ULTIMATE REALITY. WE COULD NOT MONITOR THAT SEQUENCE. WHAT HAPPENED?
ER... NAH. YOU WOULDN'T BELIEVE IT
SO. THE BUTTERFLY KID IS STILL INTERESTED IN THE AFFAIRS OF THIS PLANE. PERHAPS HE HAS YET A ROLE TO PLAY IN THIS LITTLE DRAMA
YOUR SECOND VISIT HERE WAS MUCH MORE SIGNIFICANT.
I AM SIR NISER OF SIBANNAC. I FORSAW THE DANGER THAT NOW THREATENS US AND ARRANGED YOUR TRAINING
<<THAT WAS NECESSARY BOSS. IT HAS ENABLED YOU TO BE IN THE MENTAL STATE YOU'RE NOW IN>>
YEAH - I SUPPOSE I'M BETTER AT KEEPING MY HEAD TOGETHER HERE.

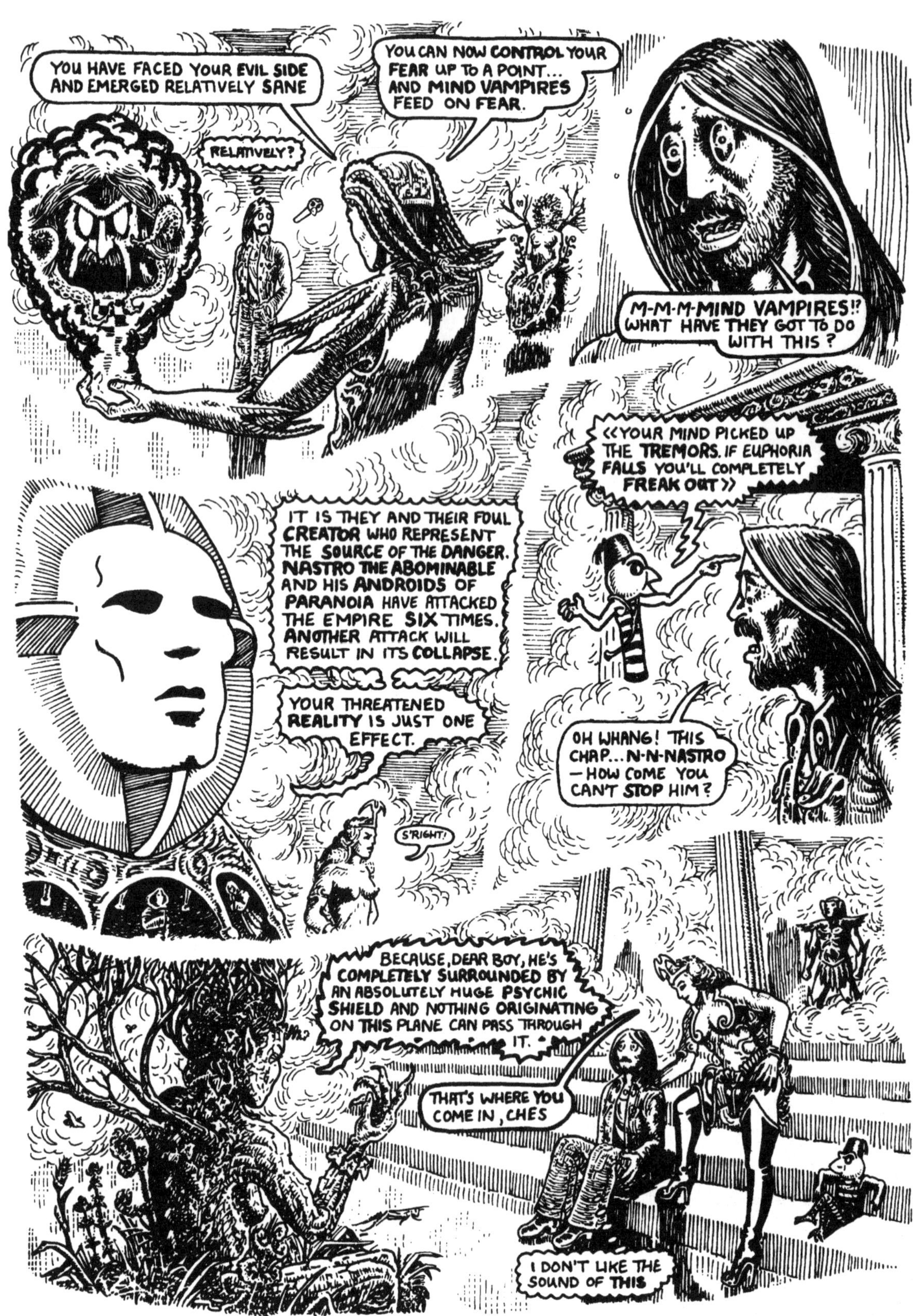
YOU HAVE FACED YOUR EVIL SIDE AND EMERGED RELATIVELY SANE
RELATIVELY?
YOU CAN NOW CONTROL YOUR FEAR UP TO A POINT... AND MIND VAMPIRES FEED ON FEAR.
M-M-M-MIND VAMPIRES!? WHAT HAVE THEY GOT TO DO WITH THIS?
IT IS THEY AND THEIR FOUL CREATOR WHO REPRESENT THE SOURCE OF THE DANGER. NASTRO THE ABOMINABLE AND HIS ANDROIDS OF PARANOIA HAVE ATTACKED THE EMPIRE SIX TIMES. ANOTHER ATTACK WILL RESULT IN ITS COLLAPSE.
YOUR THREATENED REALITY IS JUST ONE EFFECT.
S'RIGHT!
«YOUR MIND PICKED UP THE TREMORS. IF EUPHORIA FALLS YOU'LL COMPLETELY FREAK OUT»
OH WHANG! THIS CHAP... N-N-NASTRO —HOW COME YOU CAN'T STOP HIM?
BECAUSE, DEAR BOY, HE'S COMPLETELY SURROUNDED BY AN ABSOLUTELY HUGE PSYCHIC SHIELD AND NOTHING ORIGINATING ON THIS PLANE CAN PASS THROUGH IT.
THAT'S WHERE YOU COME IN, CHES
I DON'T LIKE THE SOUND OF THIS

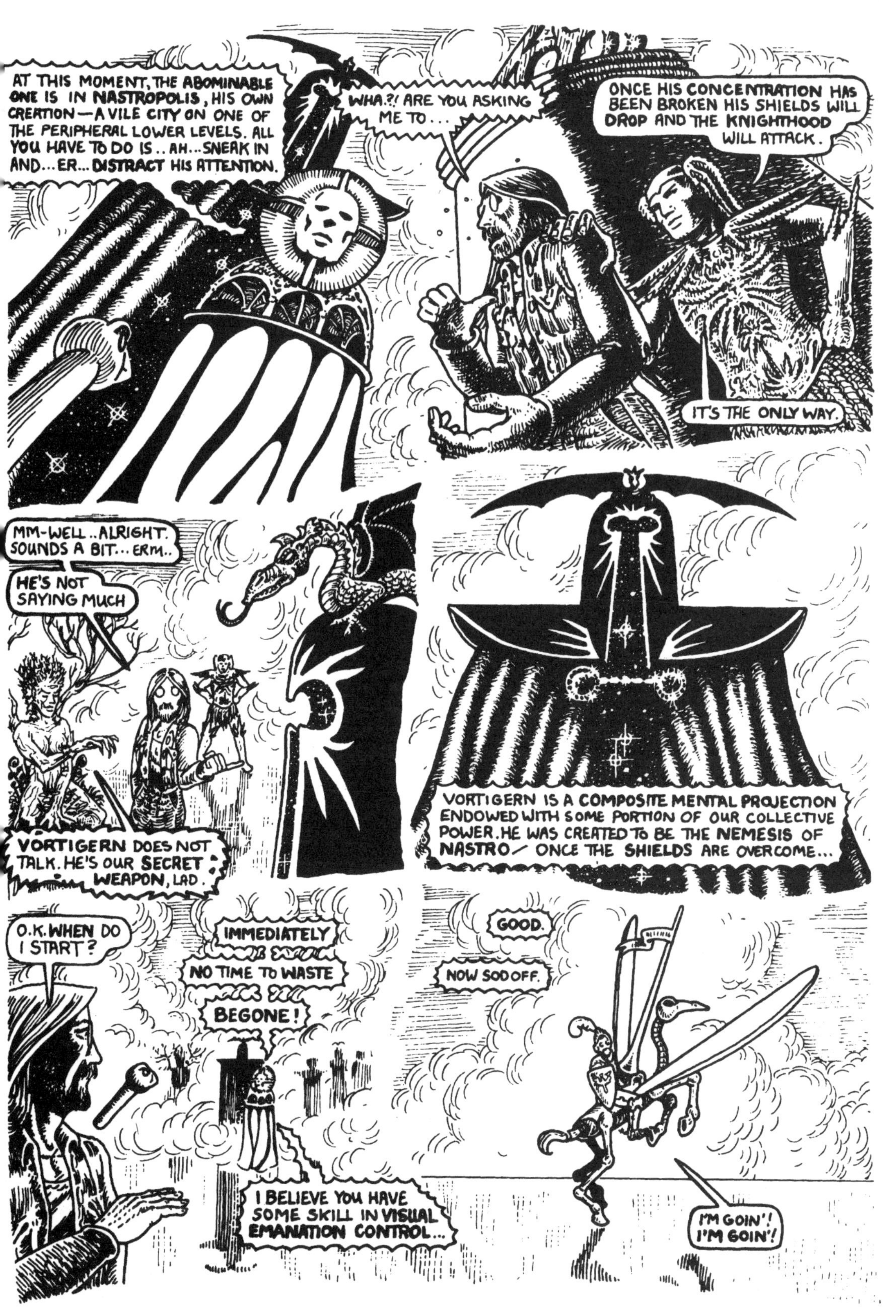
AT THIS MOMENT, THE ABOMINABLE ONE IS IN NASTROPOLIS, HIS OWN CREATION — A VILE CITY ON ONE OF THE PERIPHERAL LOWER LEVELS. ALL YOU HAVE TO DO IS.. AH... SNEAK IN AND... ER... DISTRACT HIS ATTENTION.
WHA?! ARE YOU ASKING ME TO...
ONCE HIS CONCENTRATION HAS BEEN BROKEN HIS SHIELDS WILL DROP AND THE KNIGHTHOOD WILL ATTACK.
IT'S THE ONLY WAY.
MM-WELL.. ALRIGHT. SOUNDS A BIT... ERM..
HE'S NOT SAYING MUCH
VORTIGERN DOES NOT TALK. HE'S OUR SECRET WEAPON, LAD.
VORTIGERN IS A COMPOSITE MENTAL PROJECTION ENDOWED WITH SOME PORTION OF OUR COLLECTIVE POWER. HE WAS CREATED TO BE THE NEMESIS OF NASTRO / ONCE THE SHIELDS ARE OVERCOME...
O.K. WHEN DO I START?
IMMEDIATELY
NO TIME TO WASTE
BEGONE!
I BELIEVE YOU HAVE SOME SKILL IN VISUAL EMANATION CONTROL...
GOOD.
NOW SOD OFF.
I'M GOIN'! I'M GOIN'!

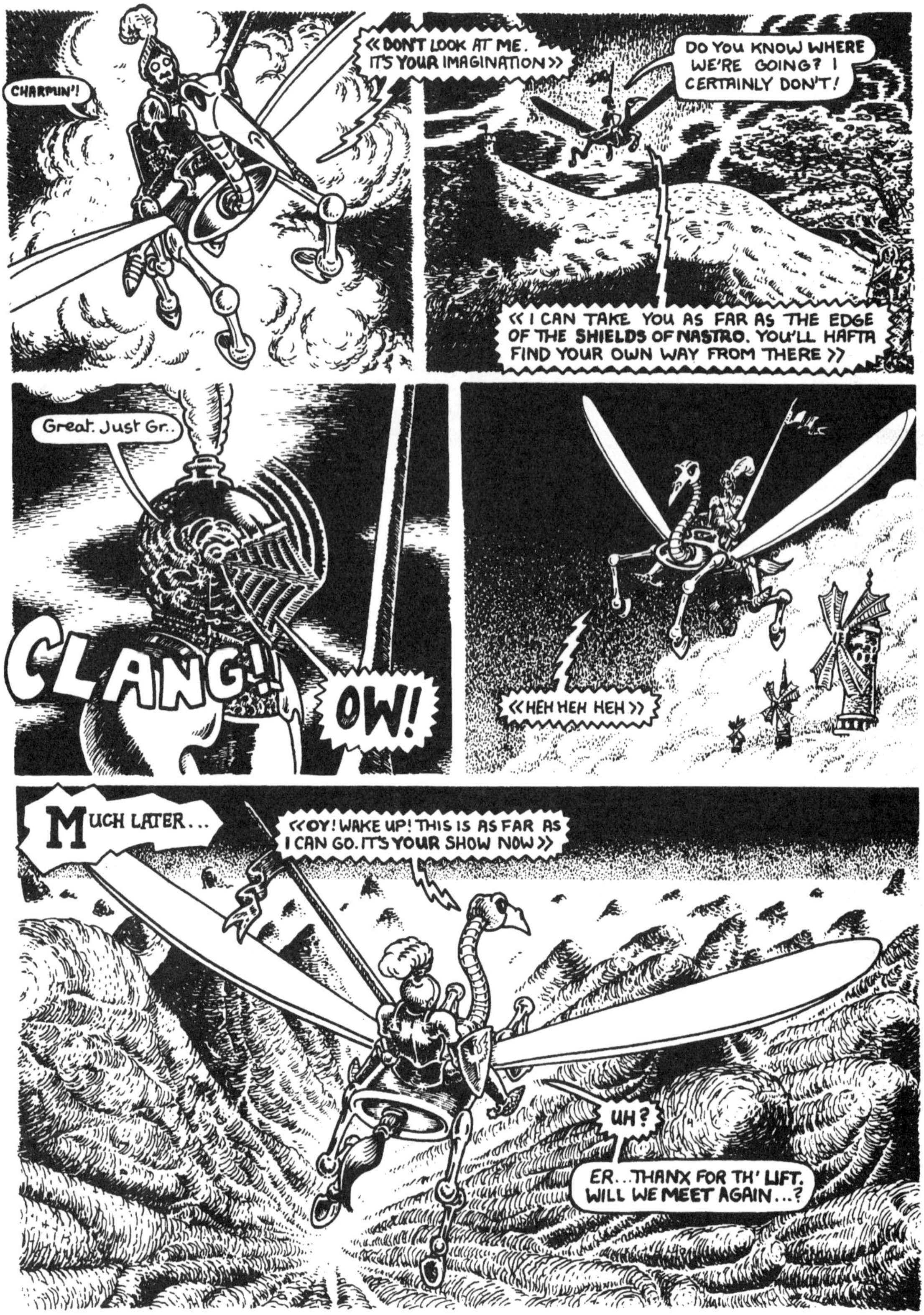

CHARMIN'!

«DON'T LOOK AT ME. IT'S **YOUR** IMAGINATION»

DO YOU KNOW **WHERE** WE'RE GOING? I CERTAINLY DON'T!

«I CAN TAKE YOU AS FAR AS THE EDGE OF THE **SHIELDS OF NASTRO**. YOU'LL HAFTA FIND YOUR OWN WAY FROM THERE»

Great. Just Gr..

CLANG!!

OW!

«HEH HEH HEH»

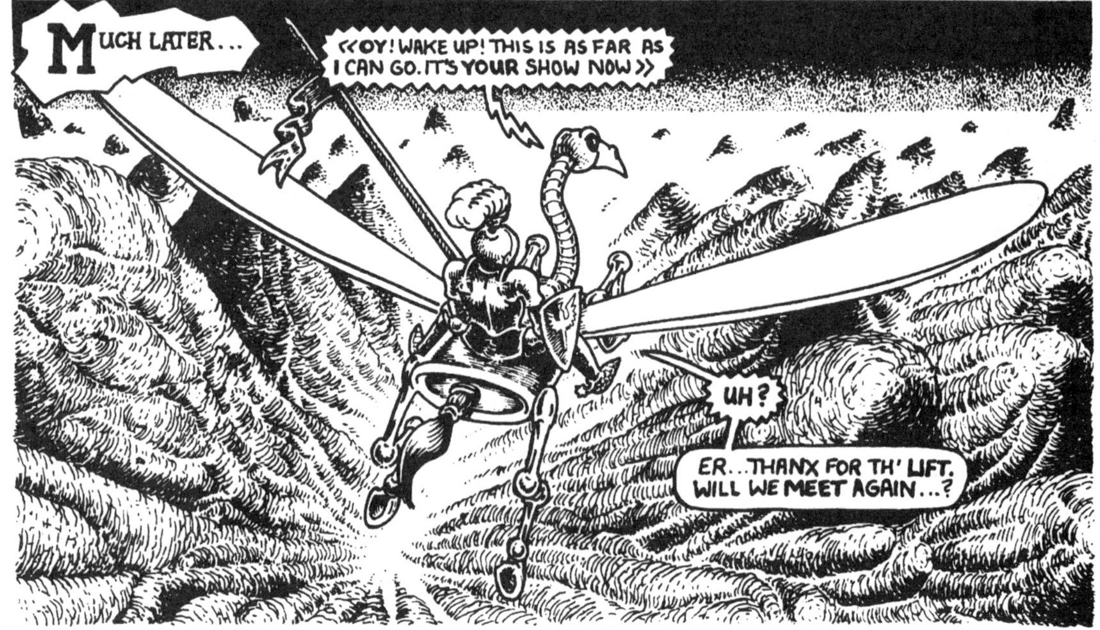

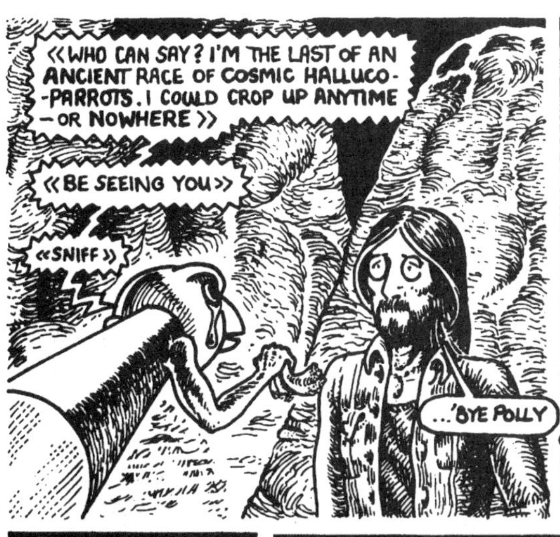
«WHO CAN SAY? I'M THE LAST OF AN ANCIENT RACE OF COSMIC HALLUCO-PARROTS. I COULD CROP UP ANYTIME — OR NOWHERE»
«BE SEEING YOU»
«SNIFF»
...'BYE POLLY

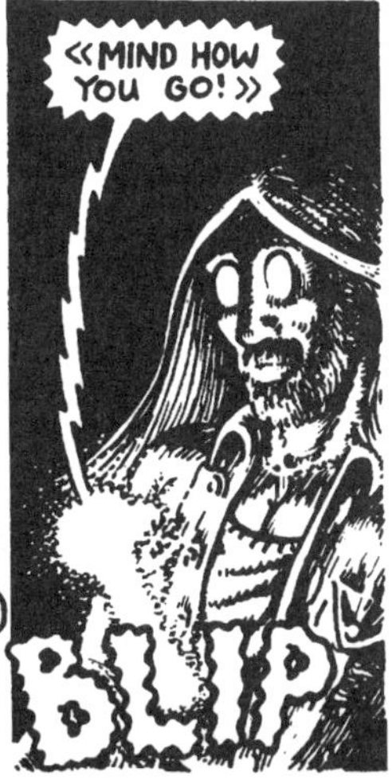
«MIND HOW YOU GO!»
BLIP

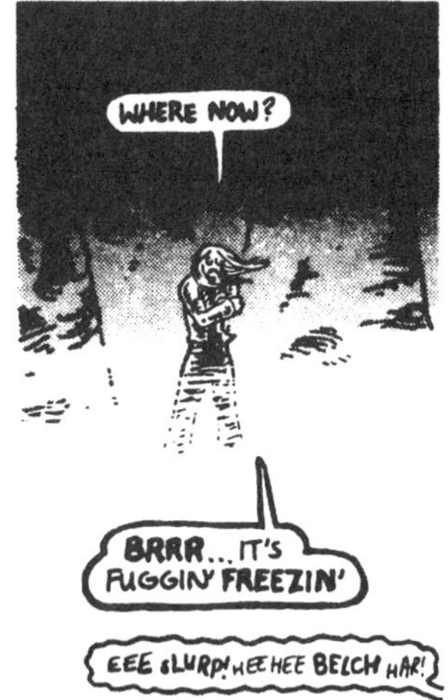
WHERE NOW?
BRRR... IT'S FUGGIN' FREEZIN'
EEE SLURP! HEE HEE BELCH HAR!

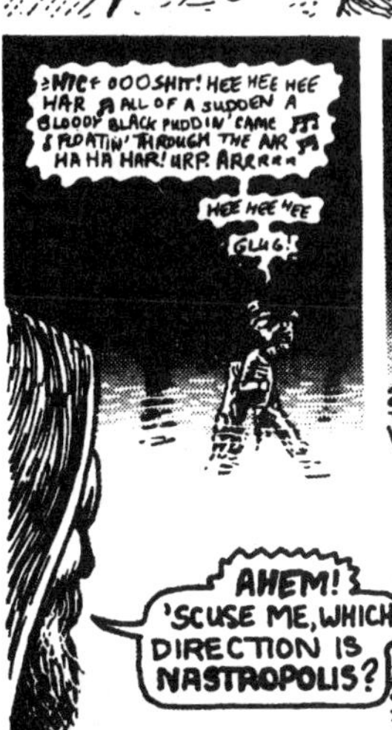
HIC OOOSHIT! HEE HEE HEE HAR ALL OF A SUDDEN A BLOODY BLACK PUDDIN' CAME FLOATIN' THROUGH THE AIR HA HA HAR! URP. ARRRRR
HEE HEE HEE
GLUG!
AHEM! 'SCUSE ME, WHICH DIRECTION IS NASTROPOLIS?

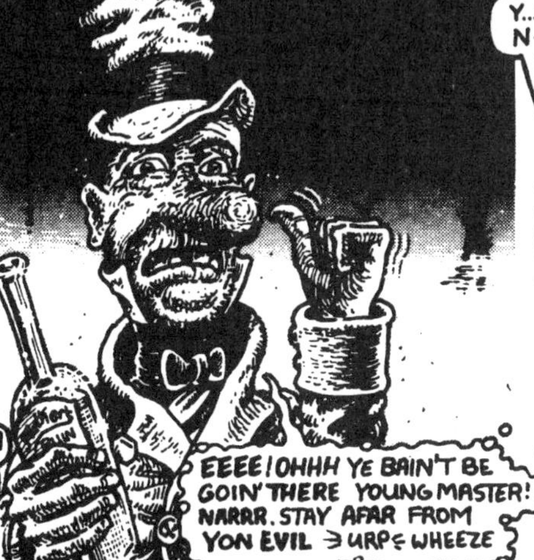
EEEE! OHHH YE BAIN'T BE GOIN' THERE YOUNG MASTER! NARRR. STAY AFAR FROM YON EVIL URP WHEEZE

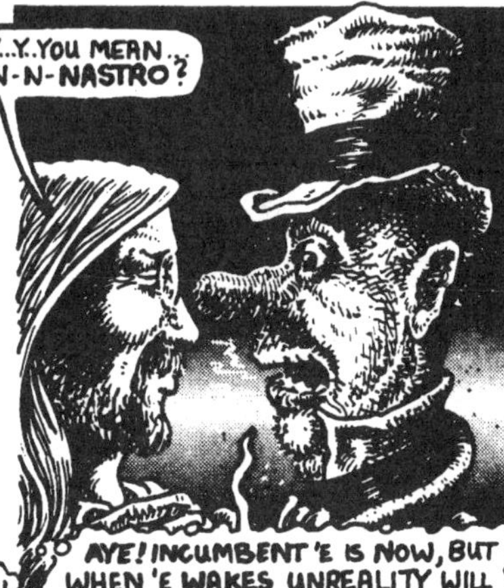
Y..Y..YOU MEAN... N-N-NASTRO?
AYE! INCUMBENT 'E IS NOW, BUT WHEN 'E WAKES UNREALITY WILL TREMBLE! EEE! T'WILL BE THE LAST ATTACK — THE FINAL BATTLE! AIEE! AIEEE! BEWARE! BEWARE...

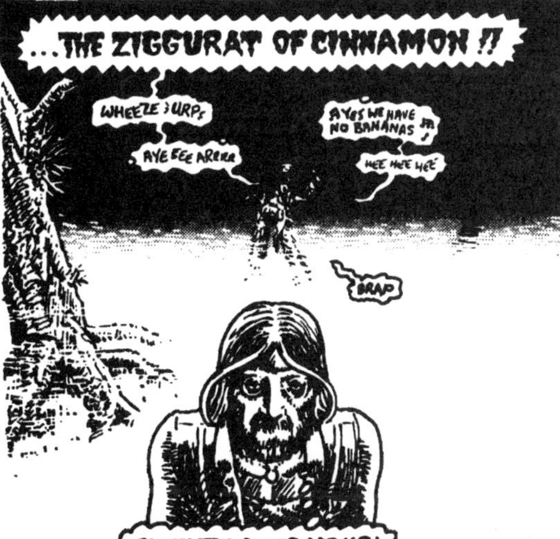
...THE ZIGGURAT OF CINNAMON !!
WHEEZE URP
AYE EEE ARRRR
YES WE HAVE NO BANANAS
HEE HEE HEE
BRAP
FANTASTIC. CHEER ME UP!

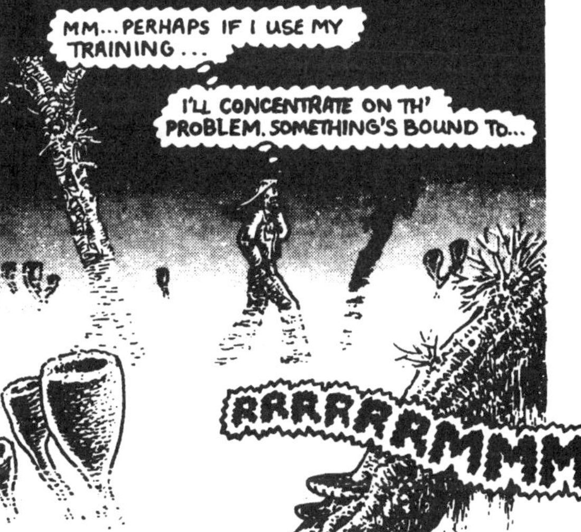
MM... PERHAPS IF I USE MY TRAINING...
I'LL CONCENTRATE ON TH' PROBLEM. SOMETHING'S BOUND TO...
RRRRRRMMMM

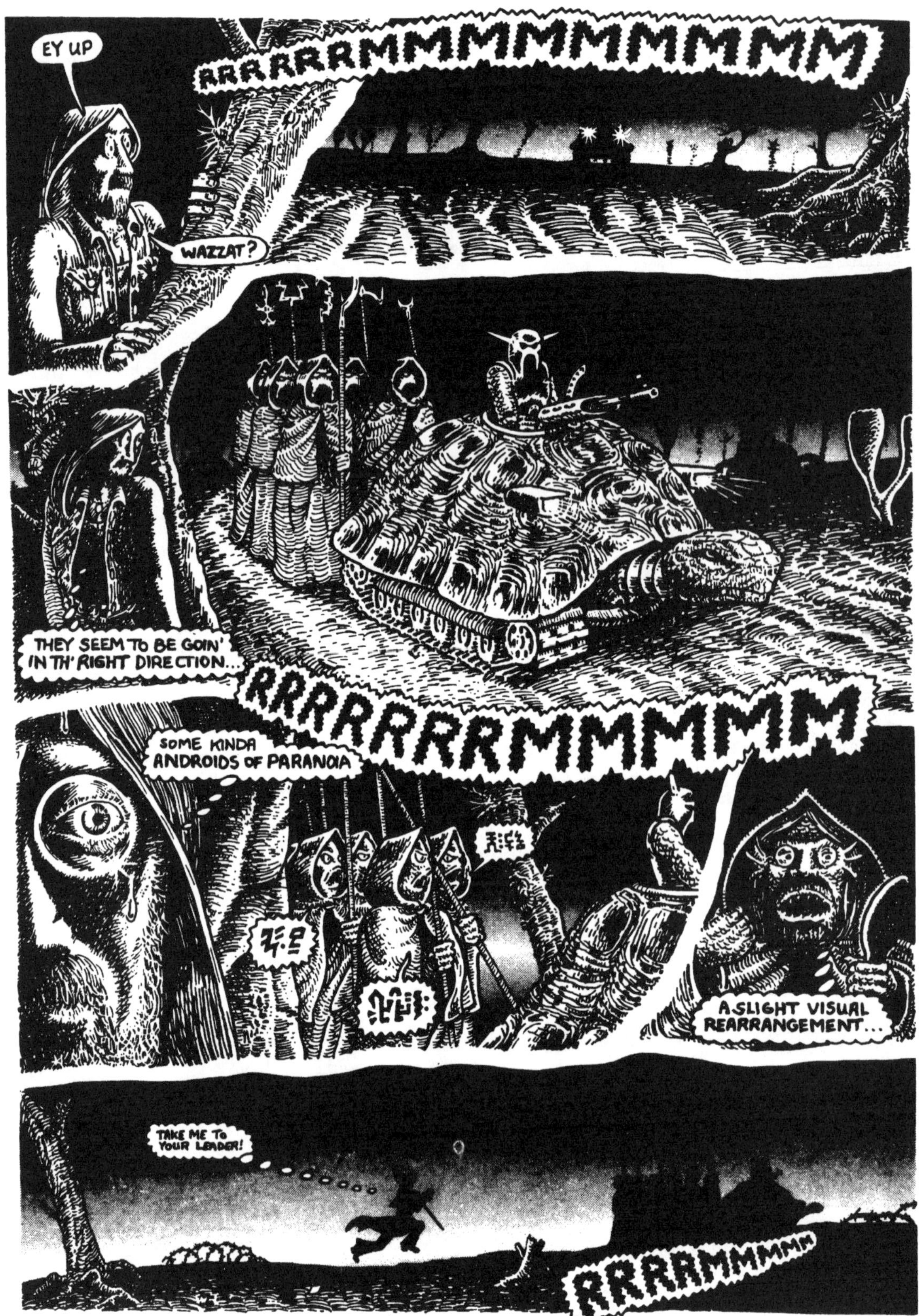
EY UP
RRRRRRMMMMMMMMMMMMM
WAZZAT?
THEY SEEM TO BE GOIN' IN TH' RIGHT DIRECTION...
RRRRRRRRMMMMMM
SOME KINDA ANDROIDS OF PARANOIA
A SLIGHT VISUAL REARRANGEMENT...
TAKE ME TO YOUR LEADER!
RRRRMMMMM

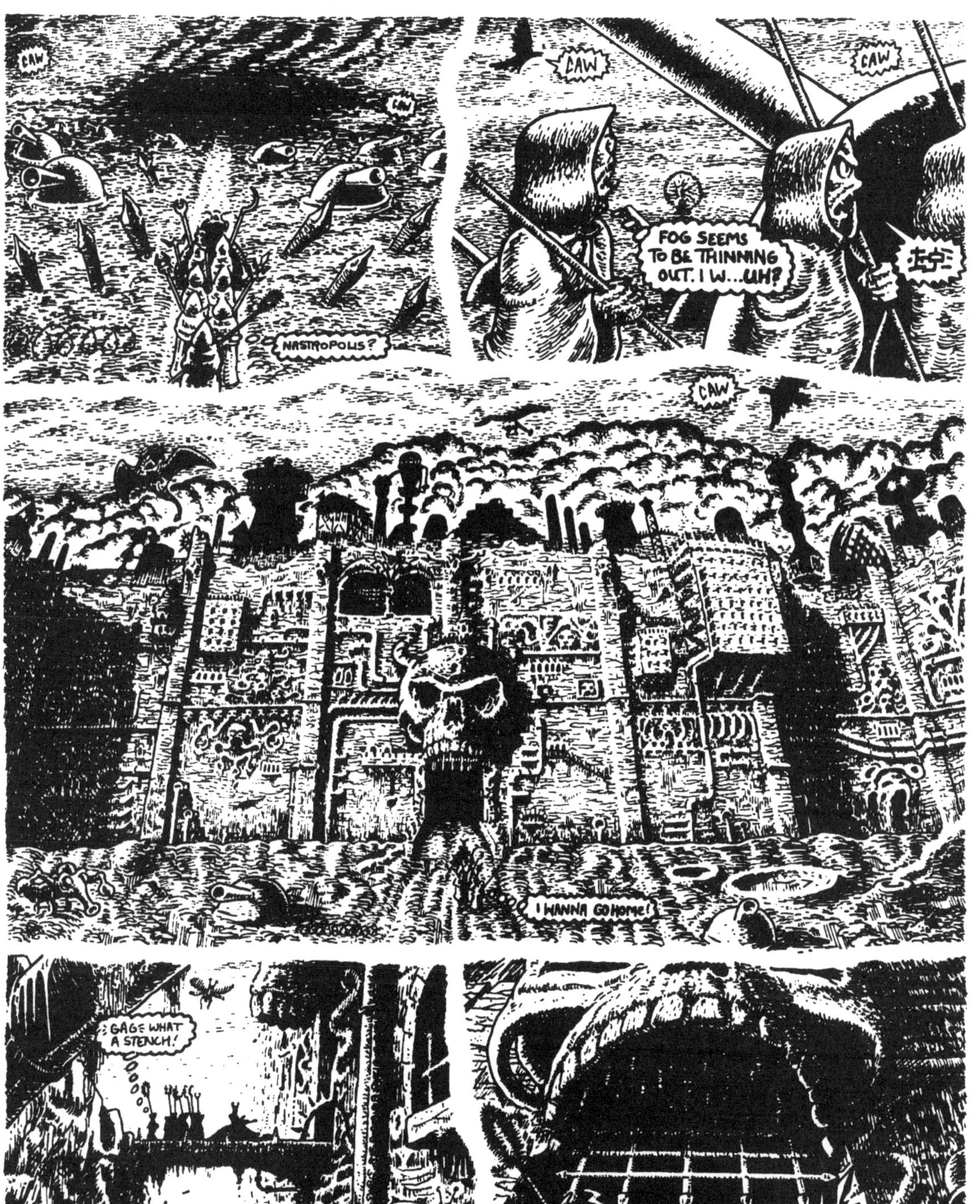
CAW
CAW
NASTROPOLIS?
CAW
CAW
FOG SEEMS TO BE THINNING OUT. I W...UH?
CAW
I WANNA GO HOME!
GAG! WHAT A STENCH!
GULP! TOO LATE TO BACK OUT NOW!

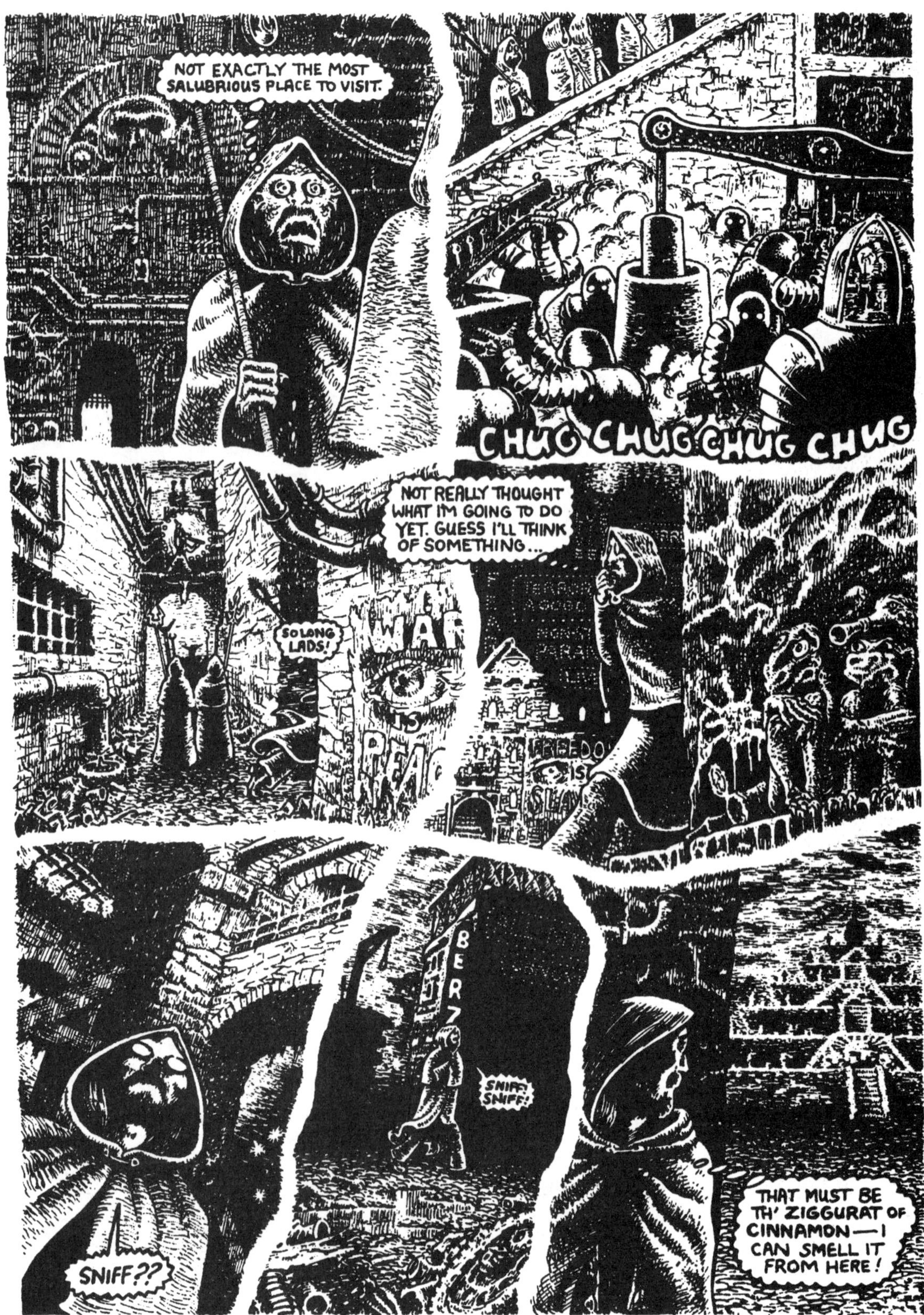
NOT EXACTLY THE MOST SALUBRIOUS PLACE TO VISIT.
CHUG CHUG CHUG CHUG
NOT REALLY THOUGHT WHAT I'M GOING TO DO YET. GUESS I'LL THINK OF SOMETHING...
SO LONG LADS!
SNIFF??
SNIFF! SNIFF!
THAT MUST BE TH' ZIGGURAT OF CINNAMON — I CAN SMELL IT FROM HERE!

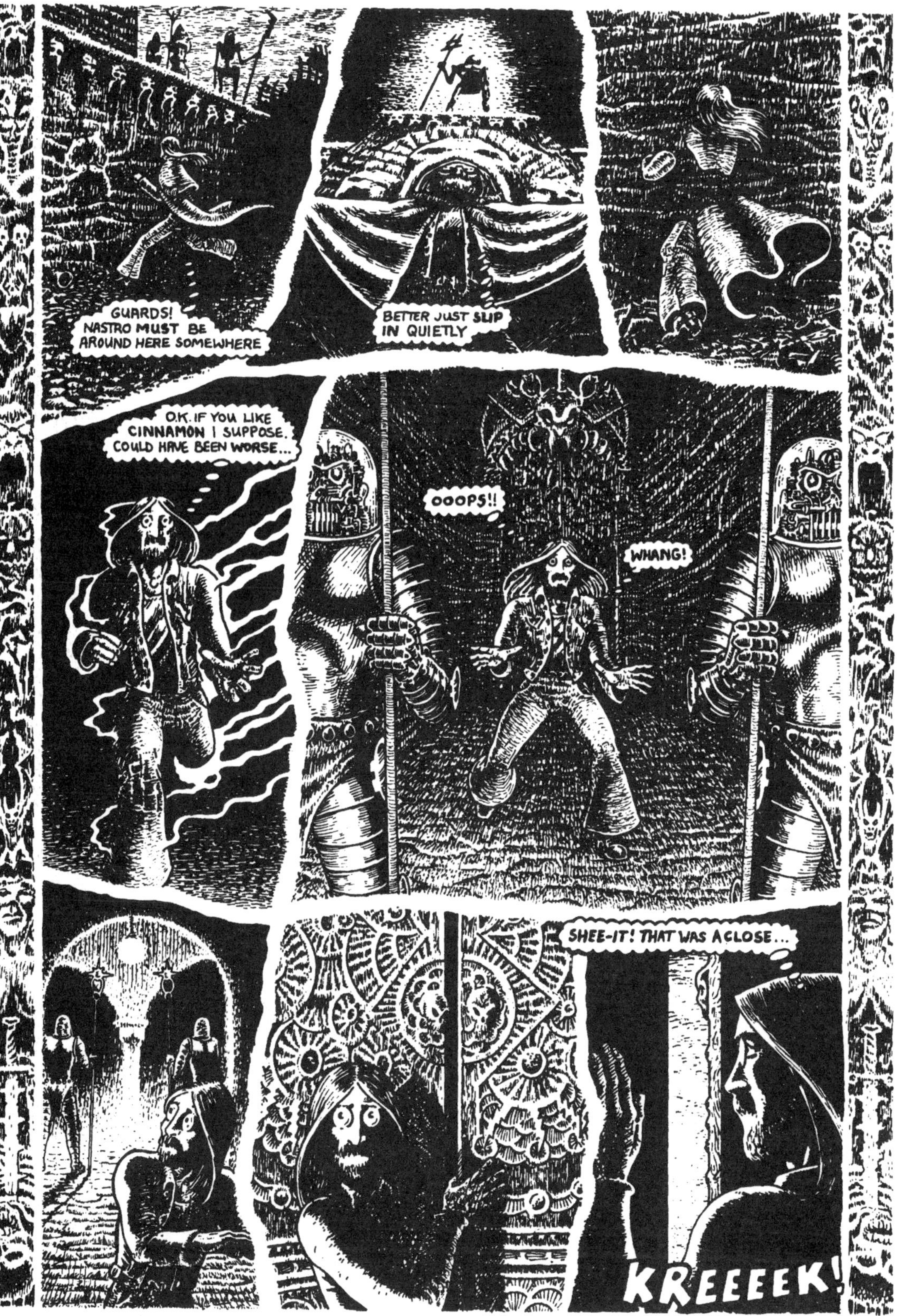
GUARDS!
NASTRO MUST BE
AROUND HERE SOMEWHERE
BETTER JUST SLIP
IN QUIETLY
O.K. IF YOU LIKE
CINNAMON I SUPPOSE.
COULD HAVE BEEN WORSE...
OOOPS!!
WHANG!
SHEE-IT! THAT WAS A CLOSE...
KREEEEK!

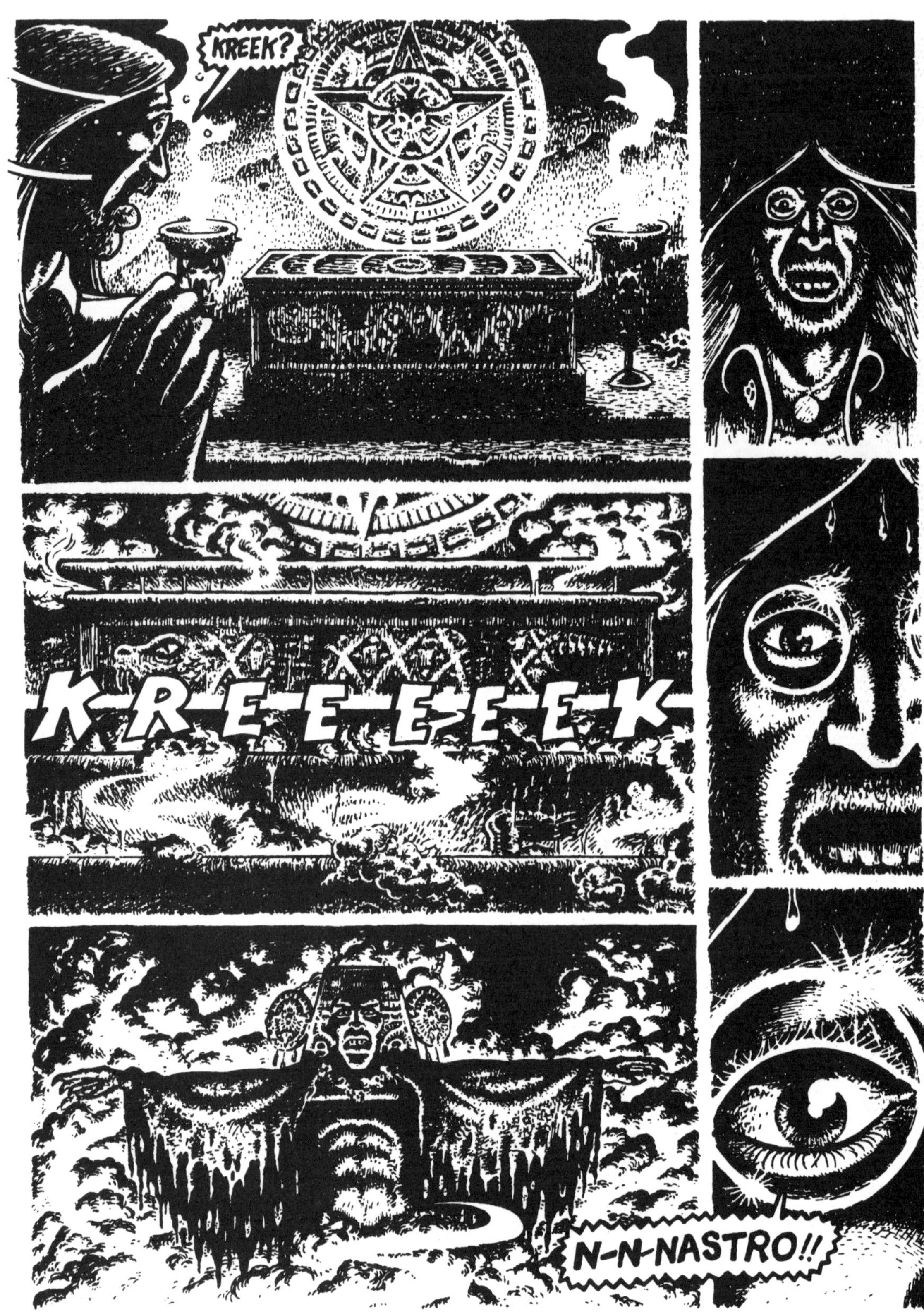
KREEK?
K-R-E-E-E-E-E-K
N-N-NASTRO!!

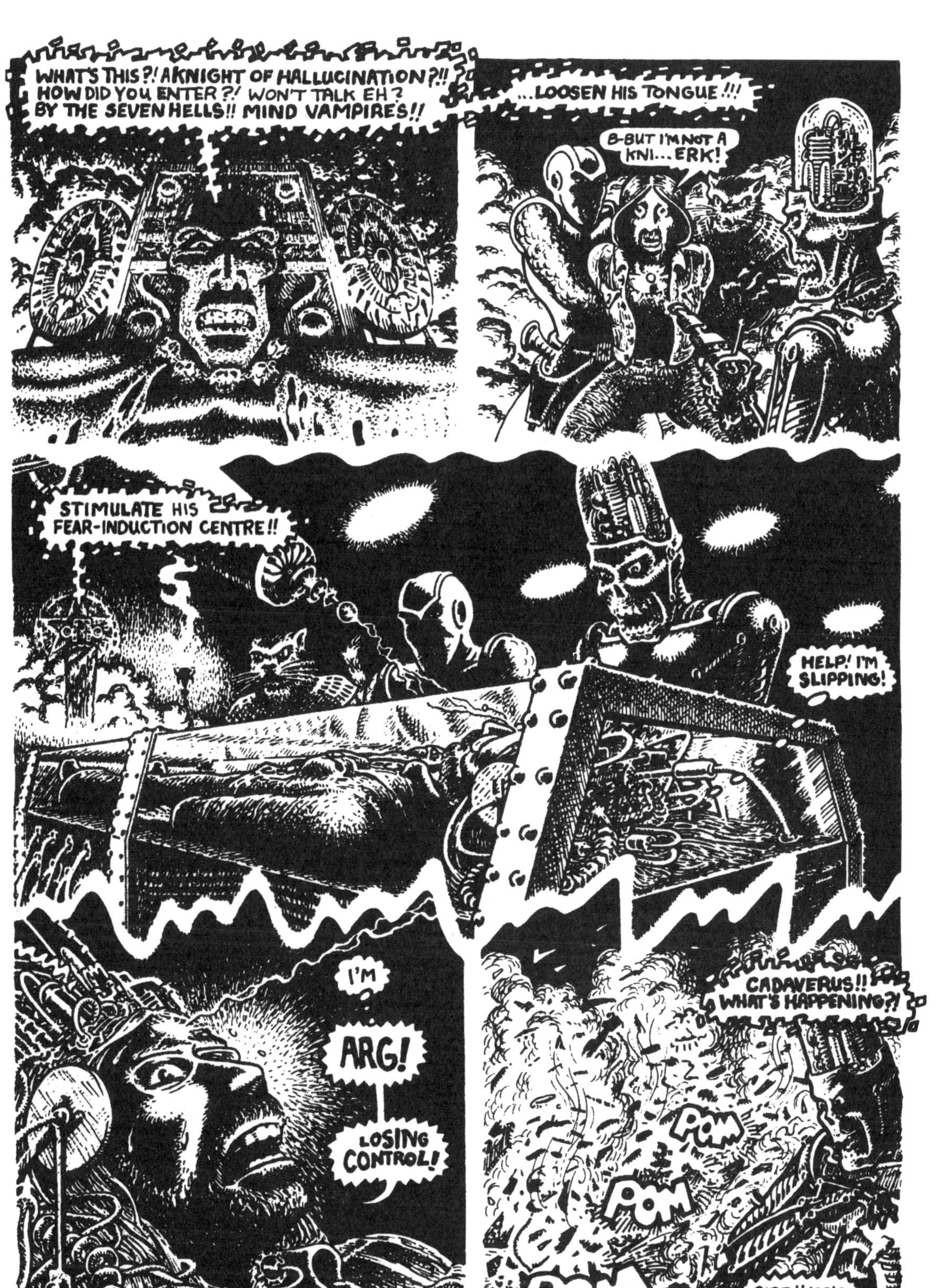
WHAT'S THIS?! A KNIGHT OF HALLUCINATION?!! HOW DID YOU ENTER?! WON'T TALK EH? BY THE SEVEN HELLS!! MIND VAMPIRES!!
...LOOSEN HIS TONGUE!!!
B-BUT I'M NOT A KNI... ERK!
STIMULATE HIS FEAR-INDUCTION CENTRE!!
HELP! I'M SLIPPING!
I'M
ARG!
LOSING CONTROL!
CADAVERUS!! WHAT'S HAPPENING?!
POM
POM
POM
SIRE!! HE'S BLOWING THE FUSES!!

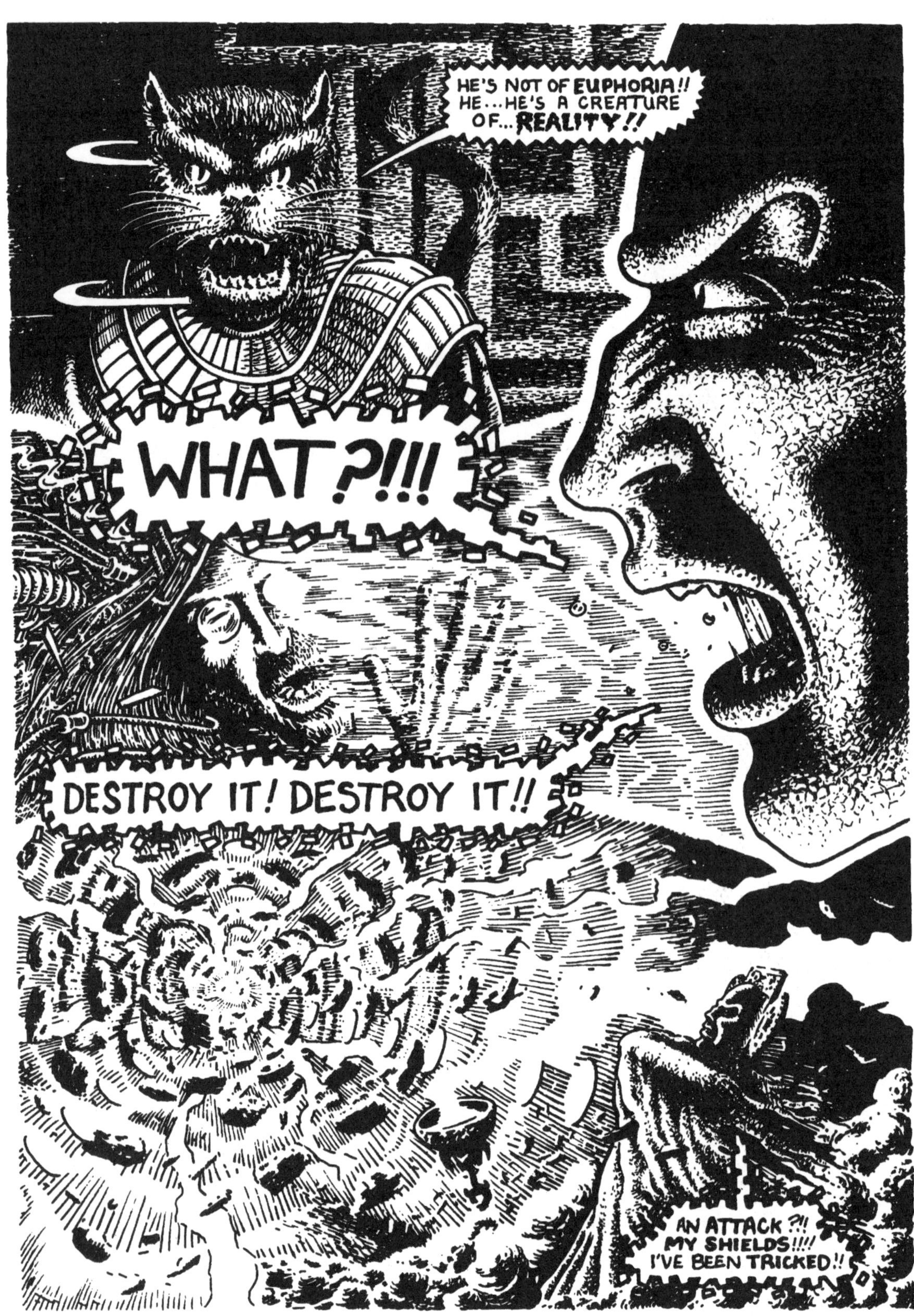
HE'S NOT OF EUPHORIA!! HE...HE'S A CREATURE OF...REALITY!!
WHAT?!!!
DESTROY IT! DESTROY IT!!
AN ATTACK?!! MY SHIELDS!!!! I'VE BEEN TRICKED!!

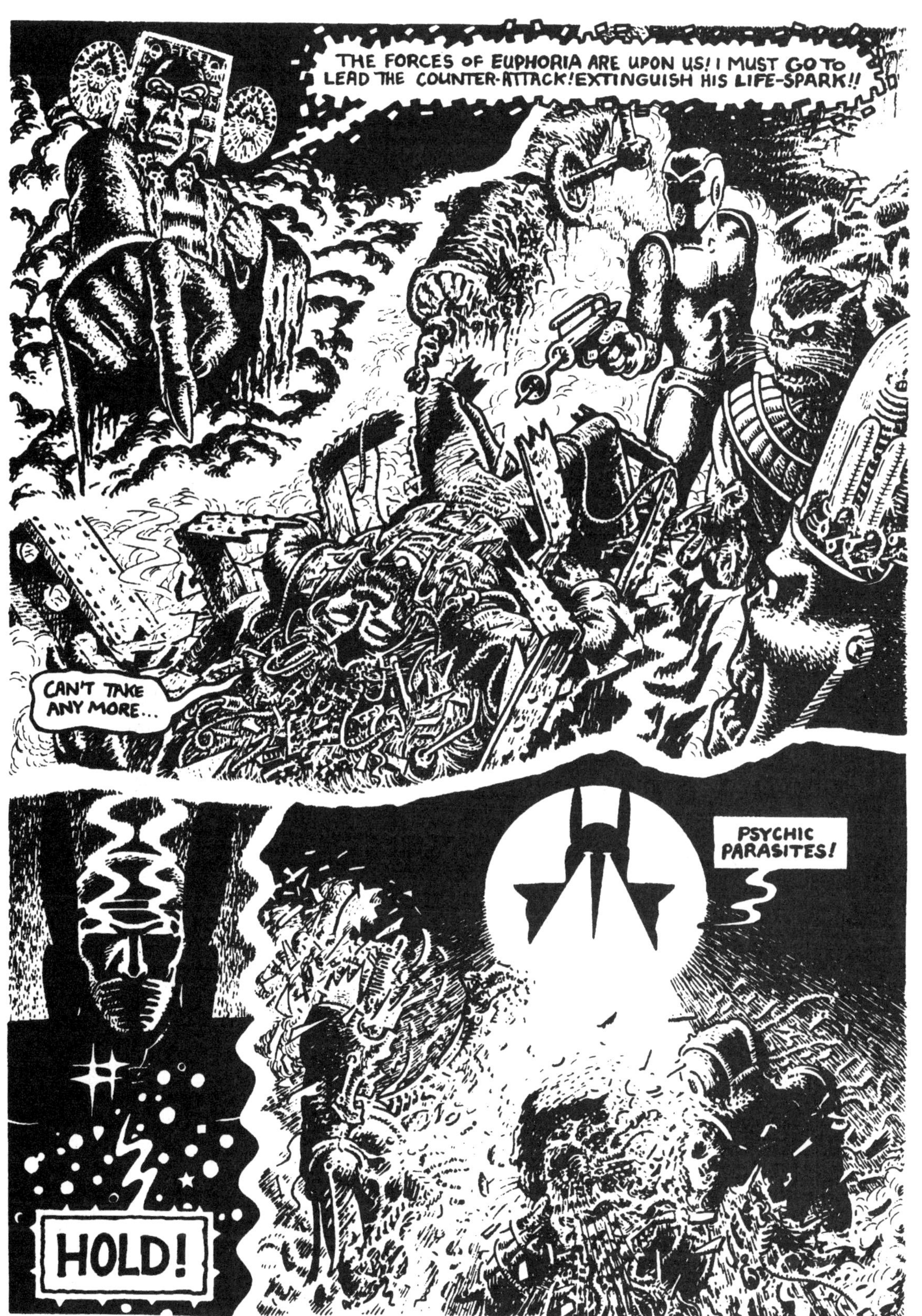
THE FORCES OF EUPHORIA ARE UPON US! I MUST GO TO LEAD THE COUNTER-ATTACK! EXTINGUISH HIS LIFE-SPARK!!
CAN'T TAKE ANY MORE...
HOLD!
PSYCHIC PARASITES!

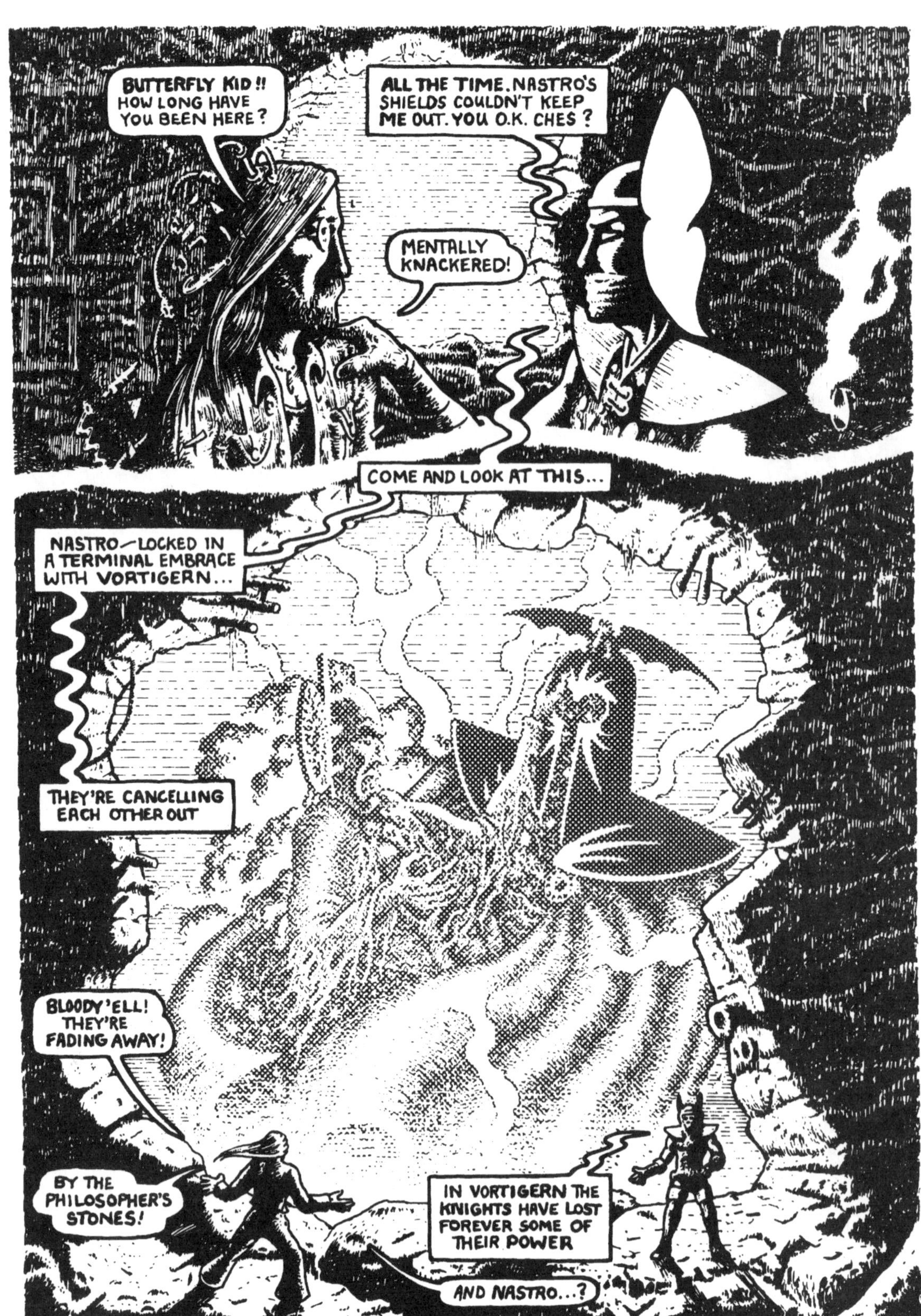
BUTTERFLY KID!! HOW LONG HAVE YOU BEEN HERE?
ALL THE TIME. NASTRO'S SHIELDS COULDN'T KEEP ME OUT. YOU O.K. CHES?
MENTALLY KNACKERED!
COME AND LOOK AT THIS...
NASTRO—LOCKED IN A TERMINAL EMBRACE WITH VORTIGERN...
THEY'RE CANCELLING EACH OTHER OUT
BLOODY 'ELL! THEY'RE FADING AWAY!
BY THE PHILOSOPHER'S STONES!
IN VORTIGERN THE KNIGHTS HAVE LOST FOREVER SOME OF THEIR POWER
AND NASTRO...?

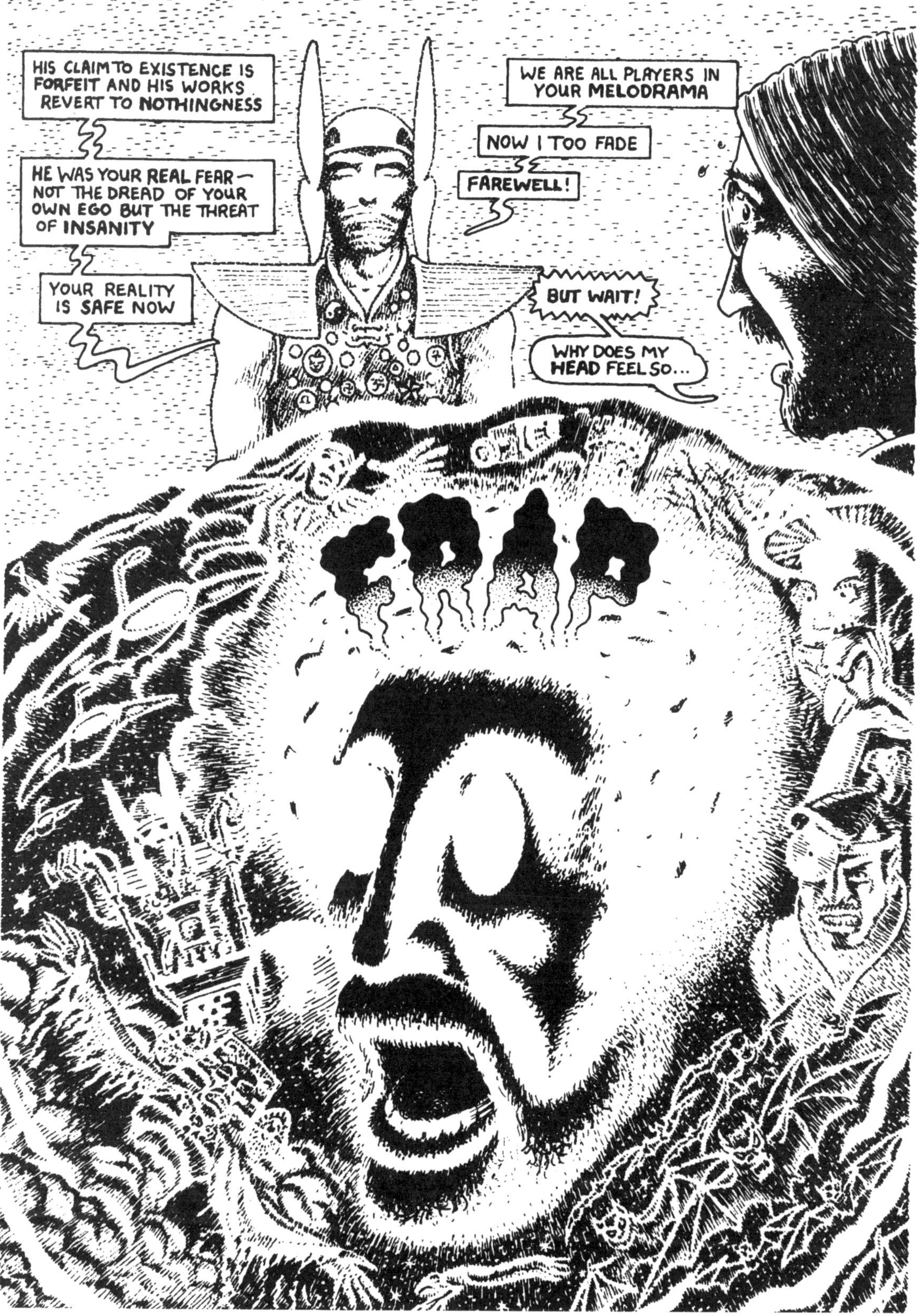
HIS CLAIM TO EXISTENCE IS FORFEIT AND HIS WORKS REVERT TO NOTHINGNESS
HE WAS YOUR REAL FEAR — NOT THE DREAD OF YOUR OWN EGO BUT THE THREAT OF INSANITY
YOUR REALITY IS SAFE NOW
WE ARE ALL PLAYERS IN YOUR MELODRAMA
NOW I TOO FADE
FAREWELL!
BUT WAIT!
WHY DOES MY HEAD FEEL SO...
CRAP

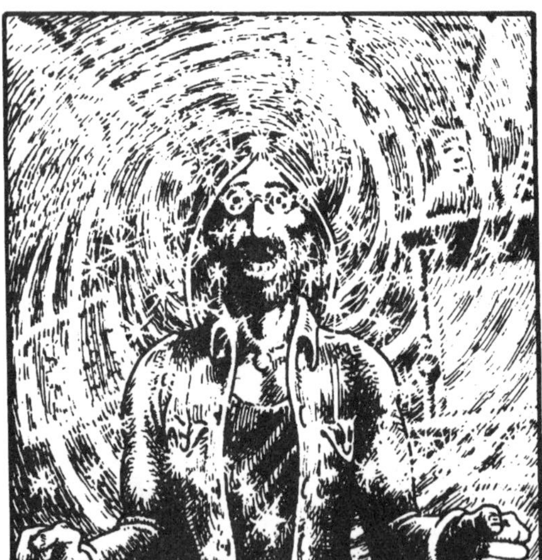
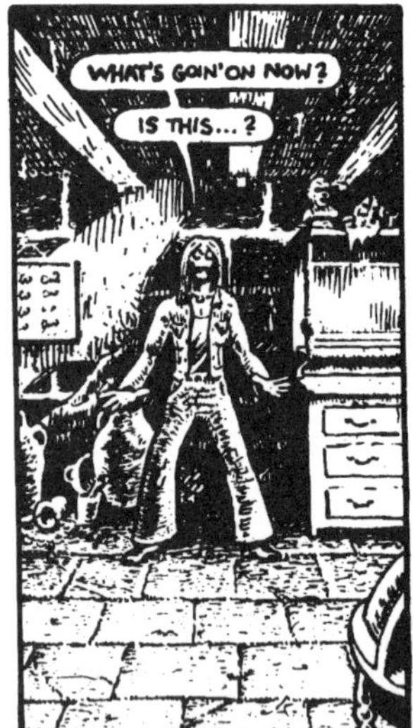
WHAT'S GOIN'ON NOW?
IS THIS...?
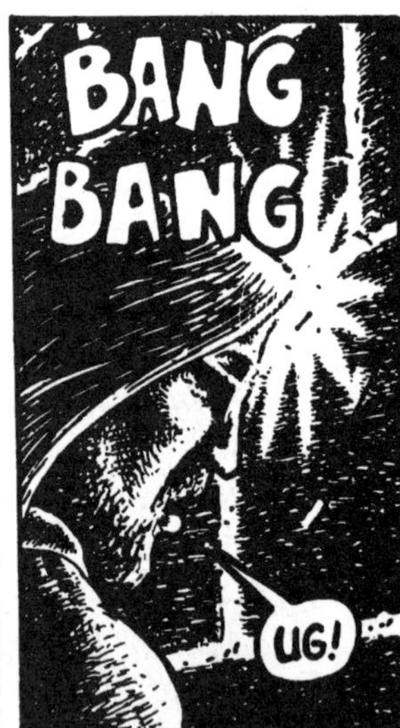
BANG
BANG
UG!
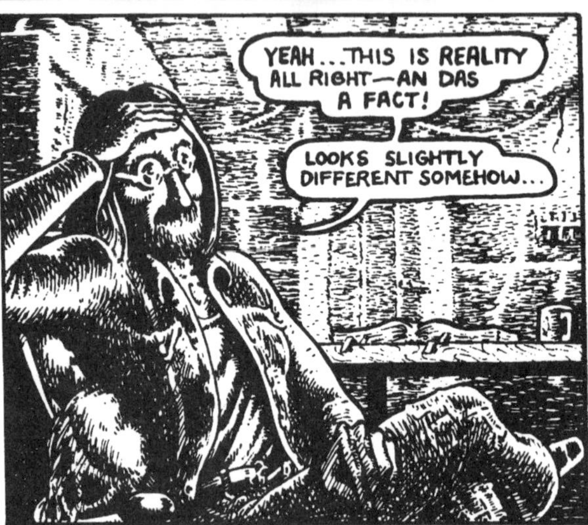
YEAH...THIS IS REALITY ALL RIGHT—AN DAS A FACT!
LOOKS SLIGHTLY DIFFERENT SOMEHOW...
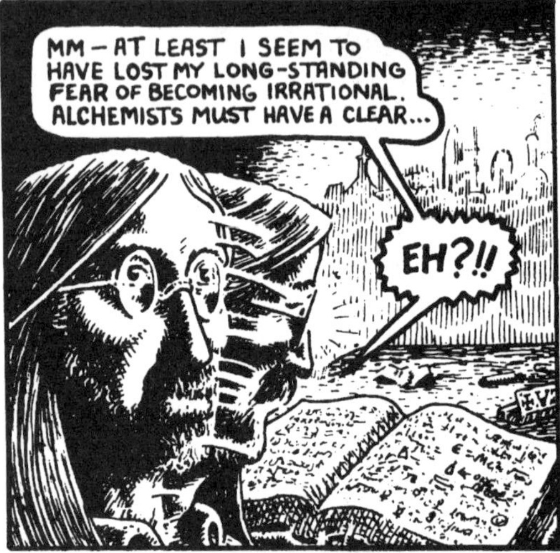
MM—AT LEAST I SEEM TO HAVE LOST MY LONG-STANDING FEAR OF BECOMING IRRATIONAL. ALCHEMISTS MUST HAVE A CLEAR...
EH?!!
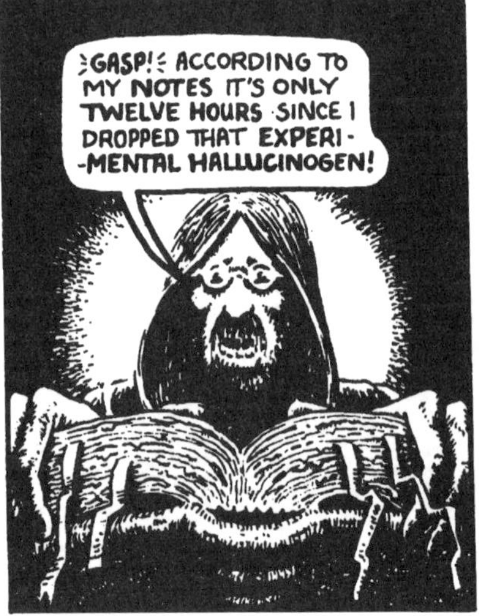
GASP! ACCORDING TO MY NOTES IT'S ONLY TWELVE HOURS SINCE I DROPPED THAT EXPERI-MENTAL HALLUCINOGEN!
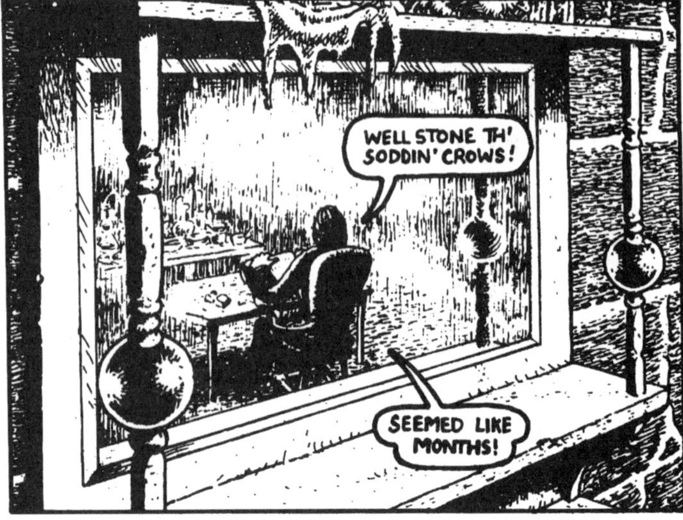
WELL STONE TH' SODDIN' CROWS!
SEEMED LIKE MONTHS!

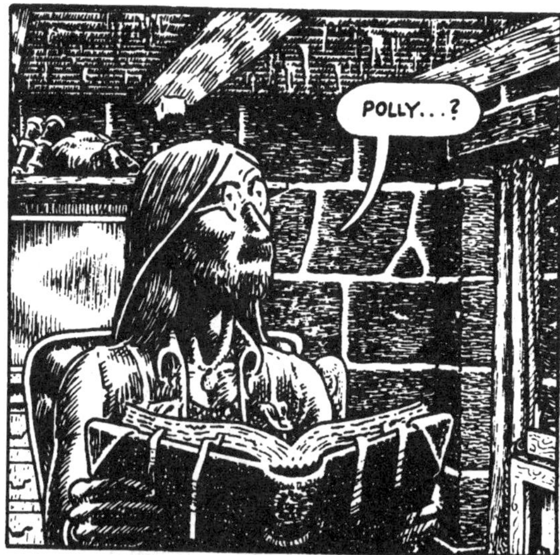

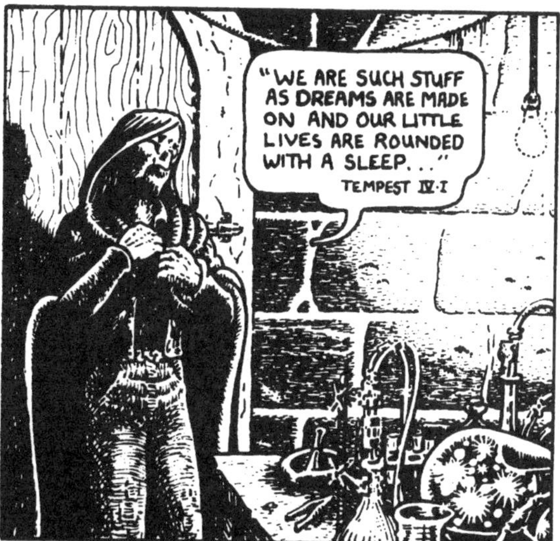

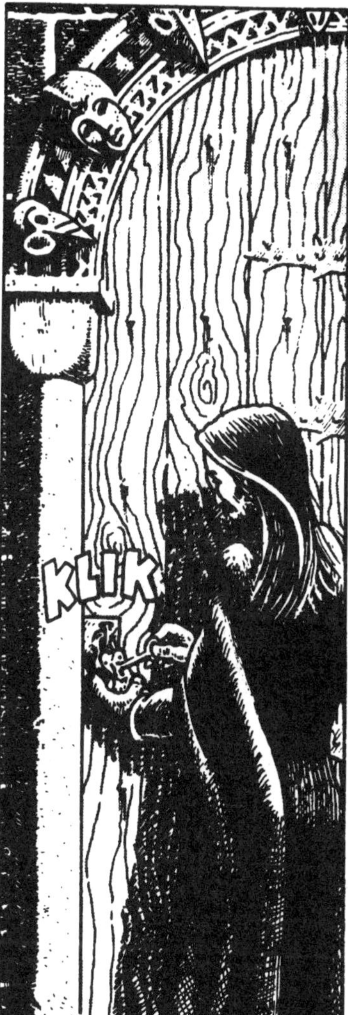

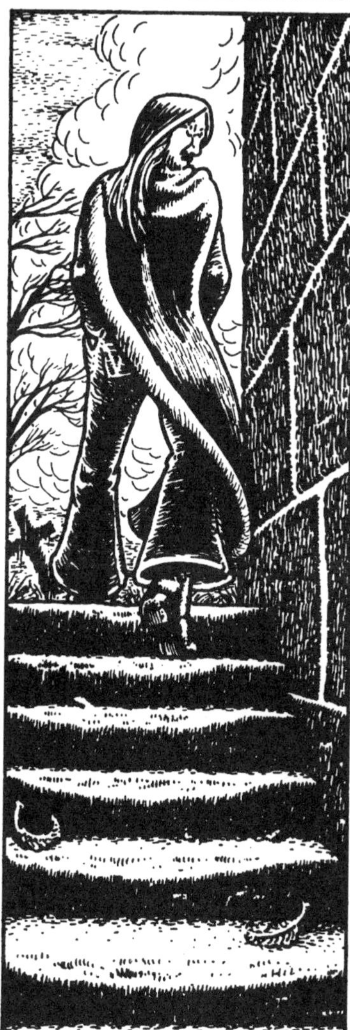

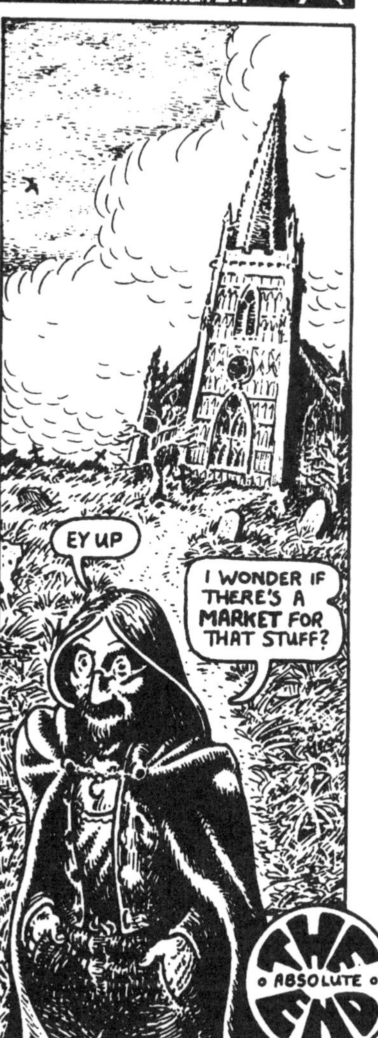

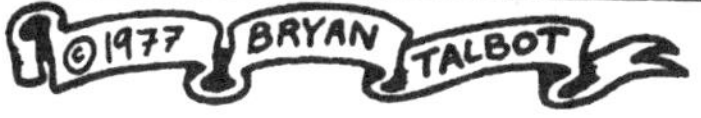

· BRAINSTORM STUDIOS ·

IT'S ALL IN THE MIND, YOU KNOW

How embarrassing.

Illustrators can always see the worst in their own work produced only a few months ago, never mind twenty five years. Is it really that long? Tempus fugit. Time flies like an arrow. Fruit flies like bananas. Jeez. I'm rambling already and I've only just started. I look back through a purple haze...

I think of this first published work as my apprenticeship in the comics medium and freely admit that I made all my mistakes in print. See, I'm self-taught. That is to say, I was taught by a very ignorant person indeed. Of course I had the same acquired knowledge of comics grammar as anybody who'd spent their life reading them but, as for the actual drawing, I'm a slow learner. Some artists seem to arrive fully-formed. I'm still learning.

At college, I did a graphic design course; the wrong choice. If I'd known I'd end up drawing comics for a living I'd have done illustration. As it was, I was taught typography and layout (which, to be fair, has fed into my storytelling) but I *should* have been exposed to life drawing, perspective, chiaroscuro et al, all of which I had to learn from practise and library books after I finished the course.

Also, the more I understood about it, the more I grew to dread the world for which I was being trained to work. I just couldn't envisage for myself a life that revolved around advertising junk that I couldn't care less about. I retreated into comics.

This was the golden age of underground comics, the comics of the counterculture, when all the staid barriers confining the medium were being ripped apart. The innocuous comic book was being redefined as a powerful instrument for communication. These new comics could not be pigeon-holed; they were experimental and as diverse as the people who wrote and drew them. They were both iconoclastic and retro. They could be as whimsical and surreal as Moscoso and Rick Griffin, or as socially aware and gut-wrenchingly gritty as Tom Veitch and Greg Irons, whose Vietnam strips were literally years ahead of their equivalents in other, supposedly more respectable media. They could be as sexist as Crumb or S. Clay Wilson or as feminist as Trina Robbins, as knowingly shocking as Robert Williams or as poignant as Justin Green, as grim as *Slow Death* or as funny as Gilbert Shelton.

The illustration styles and storytelling techniques were equally diverse and groundbreaking as the medium was pushed to its limit. Panels overlapped in new and ingenious ways and multiple images and audacious metapanels were used for specific effect. Drawing styles from other artforms, such as book illustration or poster design were introduced. Influences from avant-garde literature and art movies were incorporated, resulting in non-linear plots and astonishing pictorial compositions. In time, this was all assimilated into mainstream comics and

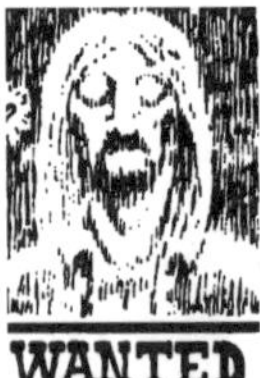

had a profound effect on the medium as a whole.

There was the usual percentage of bad stuff you get in any medium - naive, poorly executed or irredeemably self-indulgent (which makes it sound like most modern Fine Art) - but this definitely was an exciting time in comics.

In 1973, whilst still at college, I ran a headshop along with my wife Mary and her brother Steve. It was called *White Rabbit*, though the title *Church Mice* would have been more appropriate. Still, the shop kept us alive for a year and, through it, we met many long term friends, one of which was Lee Harris. I'd met Lee in his shop (Alchemy in Portobello Road. It's still there - go and see) and he became of our main suppliers of paraphenalia, joss sticks and ginseng, all on credit, all on trust.

Lee is a wonderful man, passionate about his beliefs and interests and with an amazing history. From being one of the first white members of the ANC in South Africa, through his years as a playwright and actor, to his publishing of *Home Grown* magazine and his battles with the law he is, in his own words, "a footsoldier of the counterculture". I keep pestering him to write his autobiography. It'll be fascinating.

"If you ever do a comic, I'll publish it". This was the rash offer he made to me whilst I was in London in 1974 to submit a strip to Cozmic Comics. The strip was accepted, but they never used it, never paid me and I never saw the artwork again. Publisher Felix Dennis, one of the "Oz three", went on to produce poster mags and become a millionaire with a vast publishing empire. A thinly veiled skit of him is in the strip Komix Comics.

Two years after Lee's offer of publication I'd reached a complete dead end. I'd finished college and been unemployed for a year. Mary, our young sons Robin and Alwyn and I were living on the breadline. Instead of doing something sensible, such as getting a job as a dustman (don't laugh; I did apply for it) I decided to do the comic for Lee.

I'd aready done about four pages of *Out Of The Crucible* whilst at college, two of which I redrew. The other sixteen pages took me five months. I hitched down to London from Preston, Lancashire and presented it to Lee. True to his word, he published them and told me to get on with the next one. It was the start of my career in comics.

A chance meeting of Lee and Mal Burns resulted in Lee bringing him on board as editor. He had an unbounded enthusiasm for and an encyclopeadic knowledge of underground comics and was a perfect choice. Later Mal was instrumental in getting *Luther Arkwright* to a wider audience in Serge Boissevain's *Pssst!*. One of the great pleasures of working on this collection has been the renewal of my friendship with Mal and Lee.

I plucked the title *Brainstorm* from the section on insanity in *Roget's Thesaurus*. It just sounded right. There was a track of the same name by Hawkwind (who advertised in the first issue) and it also put me in mind of the *Professor Branestawm* illustrations by Heath Robinson.

By 1975, the psychedelic adventure story was already an established underground genre. Creators such as Sheridan and Schreiber had laid the groundwork, charting the exploits of their madcap psychonauts in the infinite possibilities of inner space, and were a big influence on *Crucible*. The tradition goes back further, though, to *Alice In Wonderland* and *Pilgrim's Progress* and probably beyond, depending upon how you interpret myth and folklore.

Swiping names from my good mate Chester West and Groucho Marx's Dr. Hackenbush from *A Day At The Races*, I had my first protagonist. I never stopped to consider characterisation; his reactions were basically my own. One of the hardest things to do when first drawing a comic is to ensure characters are easily identifiable from different angles and from a distance, hence the beard, straight nose and glasses.

My favourite Chester story is *From Here To Infinity*. The first story was little more than a picture book for trippers, but the second was a lot more considered. I'd been studying classic book illustrators, such as Arthur Rackham, and was trying to produce a synthesis of their styles and American underground styles. The theme is duality and the story inspired by *Alice*. Like *Through The Looking Glass*, it can be played through as a chess game, moves and pieces indicated by visual clues. It's also a self-referential adventure story; the various characters and plot devices pointed out to the readers as they happen. Yes, I was trying to be a smart-ass.

Chester has never really gone away. Apart from his apperances in *The Omega Report* and the later *Smokey Bears* and his parallel self, Parsifal, in *The Adventures Of Luther Arkwright* and the recent *Heart Of Empire*, he seems to have assumed an independent existence. *Brainstorm* was read by many of today's "Brit Pack" writers, such as Alan Moore, Grant Morrison and Neil Gaiman. There are influences from *Brainstorm* in *Animal Man* and *Shade The Changing Man*. Chester was "americanised" into Chester Williams in *Swamp Thing* and he and other Brainstorm characters have cameos in Bob Walker's Hawklords graphic novel *Ledge Of Darkness* (as seen here), *The Bush Telegraph* and Ben Hunt's *Vogarth*. And here he is again in this new reprint.

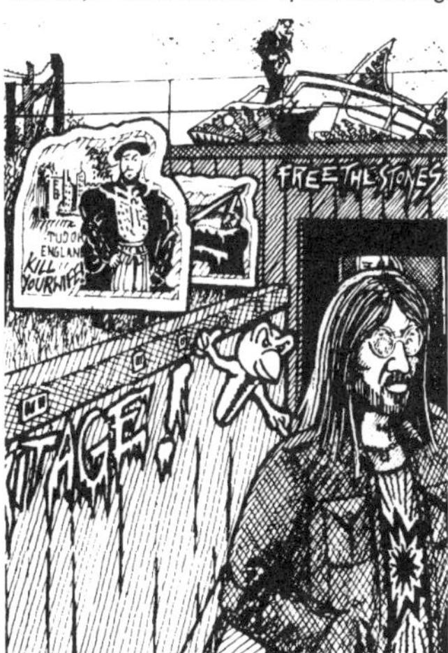

He's also in *The Tribe*, a strip produced for one of the 1970's incarnations of the alternative newspaper *International Times* that never got off the ground because the would-be publishers were so stupifyingly stoned that they never managed to get it together (and lost the artwork to boot). It was meant to be the first episode of an ongoing underground soap opera of which I'd plotted the first year's storyline. I later used the group of characters as the basis for the *Smokey Bears* shorts, intended to be a sort of British *Furry Freak Brothers*, for Lee's *Home Grown* magazine.

My first professional piece of comic work, *Hassan-I-Sabbah*, was comissioned by Craig Sams for *Seed* - The Journal of Organic Living, in 1976. I'd discovered halftone, and the following story was the result...

The Papist Affair was an excuse to do a "ground-level" strip in line and watercolour wash and was directly inspired by the *Jerry Cornelius* stories of Michael Moorcock. After this, Arkwright took on his own personality and I developed his own milieu , but this was his very first appearance. Now, just having finished the new Arkwright graphic novel, *Heart Of Empire*, I realise that he, like Chester, will never be far from my side.

I'm still very pleased with the concept and plot of*The Omega Report*, which was produced years before several comparable comic strips and films. The artwork though, is another thing. Interesting would perhaps be a kind word for it. All the Chester stories were drawn using Rotring technical pens. For this story, I tried to simulate the feel of fifties black and white private dick movies by inking heavily with a brush and using lots of mechanical tints in attempt to create a film noir atmosphere. I'd never inked with a brush before and it took me three months to realise that it was supposed to go to a fine pinpoint at the end. In case this was published "before your time", I have to point out that the whole story is littered with references to 70's rock music.

A few years ago I was at a large media event at Olympia, part of which was an attempt to interest the general public in the comic medium. I was spreading the word to one of the punters, a large, respectable-looking business gent, when he suddenly discovered that I was the the guy who used to do *Brainstorm*. He whooped loudly and snatched me up in a huge bear hug, exclaiming "I loved those comics! Thank you! Thank you!" And this wasn't an isolated incident. There are people who still treasure the comic (usually through some fond acid memory) and think it's the best thing I've ever done. Perhaps they're right. It's all subjective, isn't it?

Perhaps no reason then, to be embarrassed.

`Scuse me while I kiss the sky.

Bryan Talbot
Brainstorm Studios

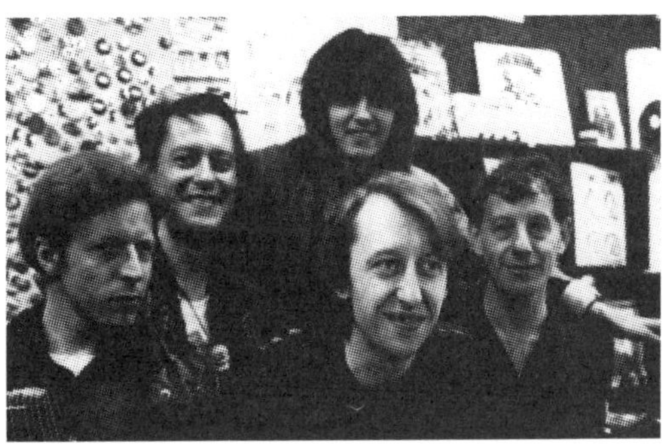

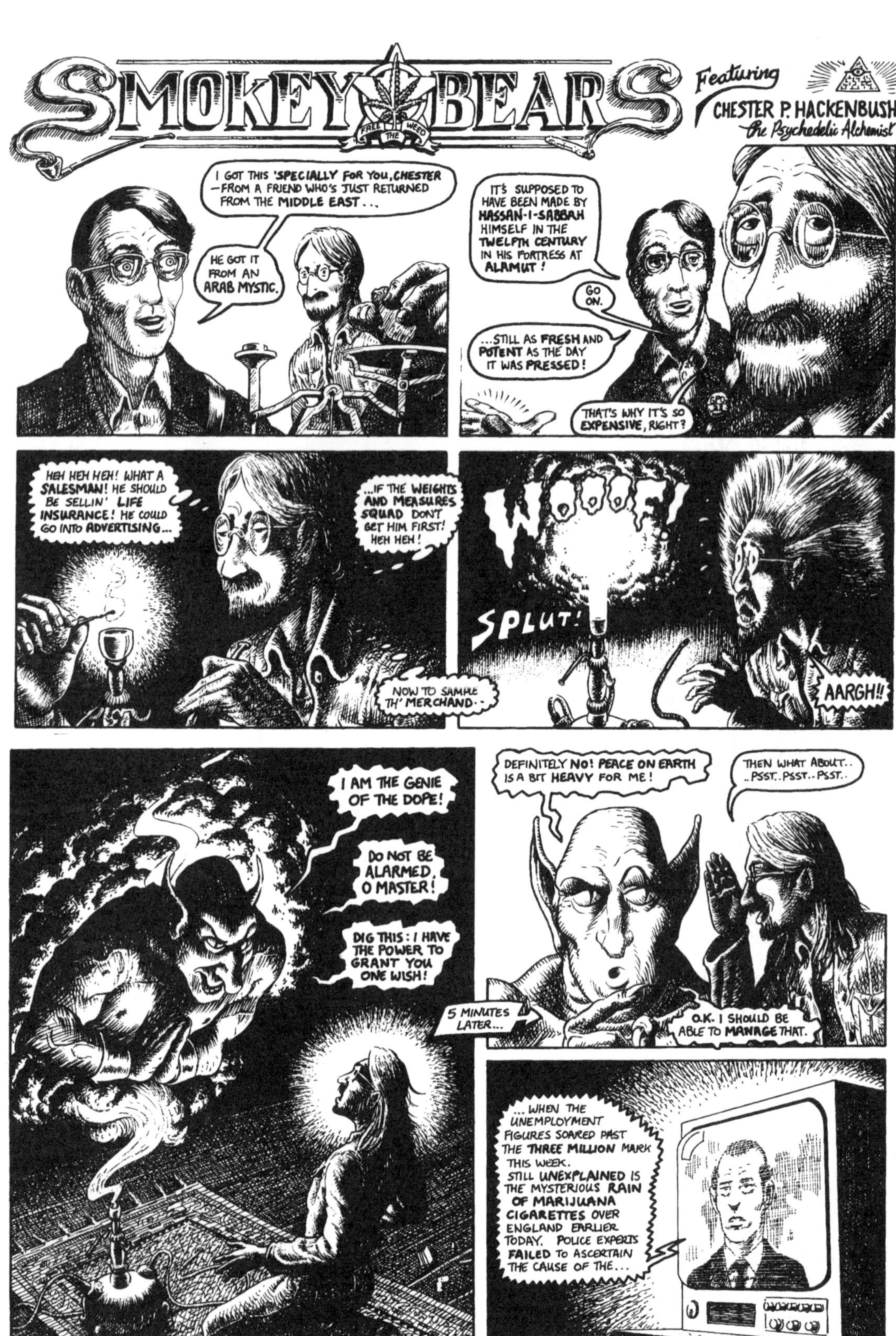
SMOKEY BEARS
FREE THE WEED
Featuring
CHESTER P. HACKENBUSH
The Psychedelic Alchemist
I GOT THIS 'SPECIALLY FOR YOU, CHESTER —FROM A FRIEND WHO'S JUST RETURNED FROM THE MIDDLE EAST...
HE GOT IT FROM AN ARAB MYSTIC.
IT'S SUPPOSED TO HAVE BEEN MADE BY HASSAN-I-SABBAH HIMSELF IN THE TWELFTH CENTURY IN HIS FORTRESS AT ALAMUT!
GO ON.
...STILL AS FRESH AND POTENT AS THE DAY IT WAS PRESSED!
THAT'S WHY IT'S SO EXPENSIVE, RIGHT?
HEH HEH HEH! WHAT A SALESMAN! HE SHOULD BE SELLIN' LIFE INSURANCE! HE COULD GO INTO ADVERTISING...
...IF THE WEIGHTS AND MEASURES SQUAD DON'T GET HIM FIRST! HEH HEH!
NOW TO SAMPLE TH' MERCHAND-
WOOOF!
SPLUT!
AARGH!!
I AM THE GENIE OF THE DOPE!
DO NOT BE ALARMED, O MASTER!
DIG THIS: I HAVE THE POWER TO GRANT YOU ONE WISH!
5 MINUTES LATER...
DEFINITELY NO! PEACE ON EARTH IS A BIT HEAVY FOR ME!
THEN WHAT ABOUT.. ..PSST..PSST..PSST..
O.K. I SHOULD BE ABLE TO MANAGE THAT.
... WHEN THE UNEMPLOYMENT FIGURES SOARED PAST THE THREE MILLION MARK THIS WEEK. STILL UNEXPLAINED IS THE MYSTERIOUS RAIN OF MARIJUANA CIGARETTES OVER ENGLAND EARLIER TODAY. POLICE EXPERTS FAILED TO ASCERTAIN THE CAUSE OF THE...
FINIS
BRAINSTORM STUDIOS
©B.TALBOT 1980

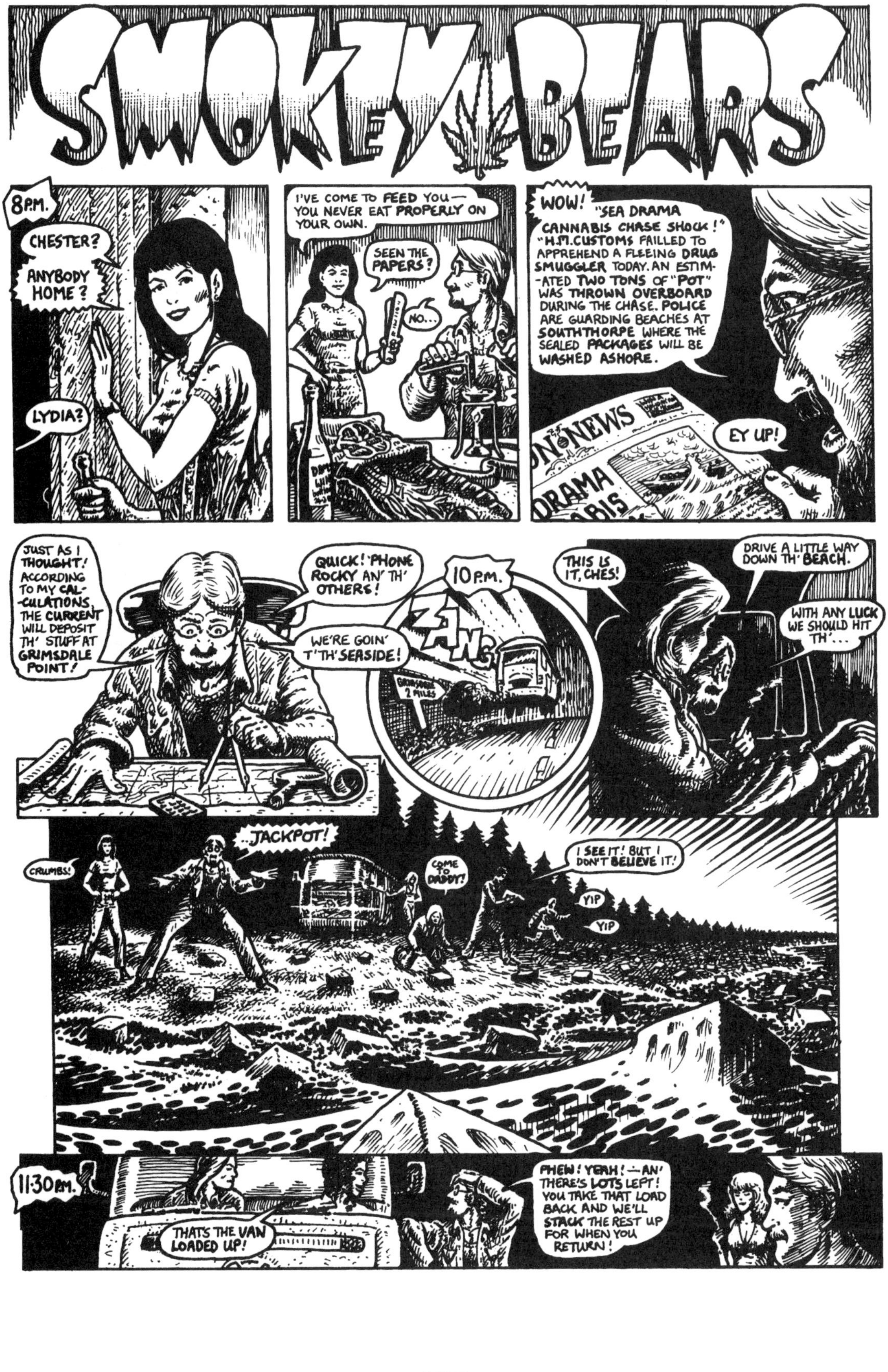

SMOKEY BEARS

8P.M.
CHESTER?
ANYBODY HOME?
LYDIA?

I'VE COME TO FEED YOU— YOU NEVER EAT PROPERLY ON YOUR OWN.
SEEN THE PAPERS?
NO...

WOW! "SEA DRAMA CANNABIS CHASE SHOCK!" "H.M.CUSTOMS FAILLED TO APPREHEND A FLEEING DRUG SMUGGLER TODAY. AN ESTIM-ATED TWO TONS OF "POT" WAS THROWN OVERBOARD DURING THE CHASE. POLICE ARE GUARDING BEACHES AT SOUTHTHORPE WHERE THE SEALED PACKAGES WILL BE WASHED ASHORE.
NEWS
DRAMA
EY UP!

JUST AS I THOUGHT! ACCORDING TO MY CAL-CULATIONS THE CURRENT WILL DEPOSIT TH' STUFF AT GRIMSDALE POINT!
QUICK! 'PHONE ROCKY AN' TH' OTHERS!
WE'RE GOIN' T'TH'SEASIDE!

10P.M.
ZAN
GRIMSDALE 2 MILES

THIS IS IT, CHES!
DRIVE A LITTLE WAY DOWN TH' BEACH.
WITH ANY LUCK WE SHOULD HIT TH'...

CRUMBS!
..JACKPOT!
COME TO DADDY!
I SEE IT! BUT I DON'T BELIEVE IT!
YIP
YIP

11:30P.M.
THAT'S THE VAN LOADED UP!
PHEW! YEAH! —AN' THERE'S LOTS LEFT! YOU TAKE THAT LOAD BACK AND WE'LL STACK THE REST UP FOR WHEN YOU RETURN!

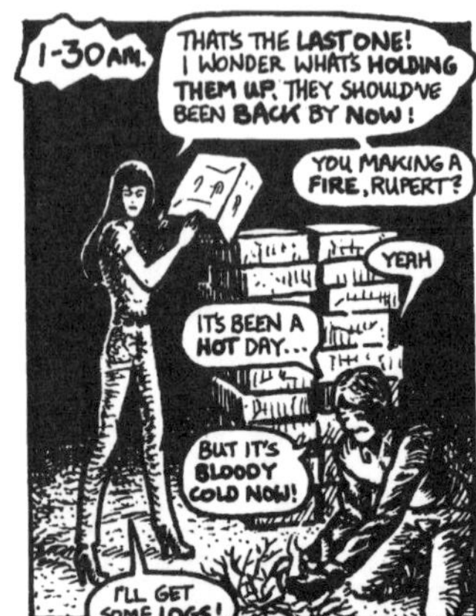

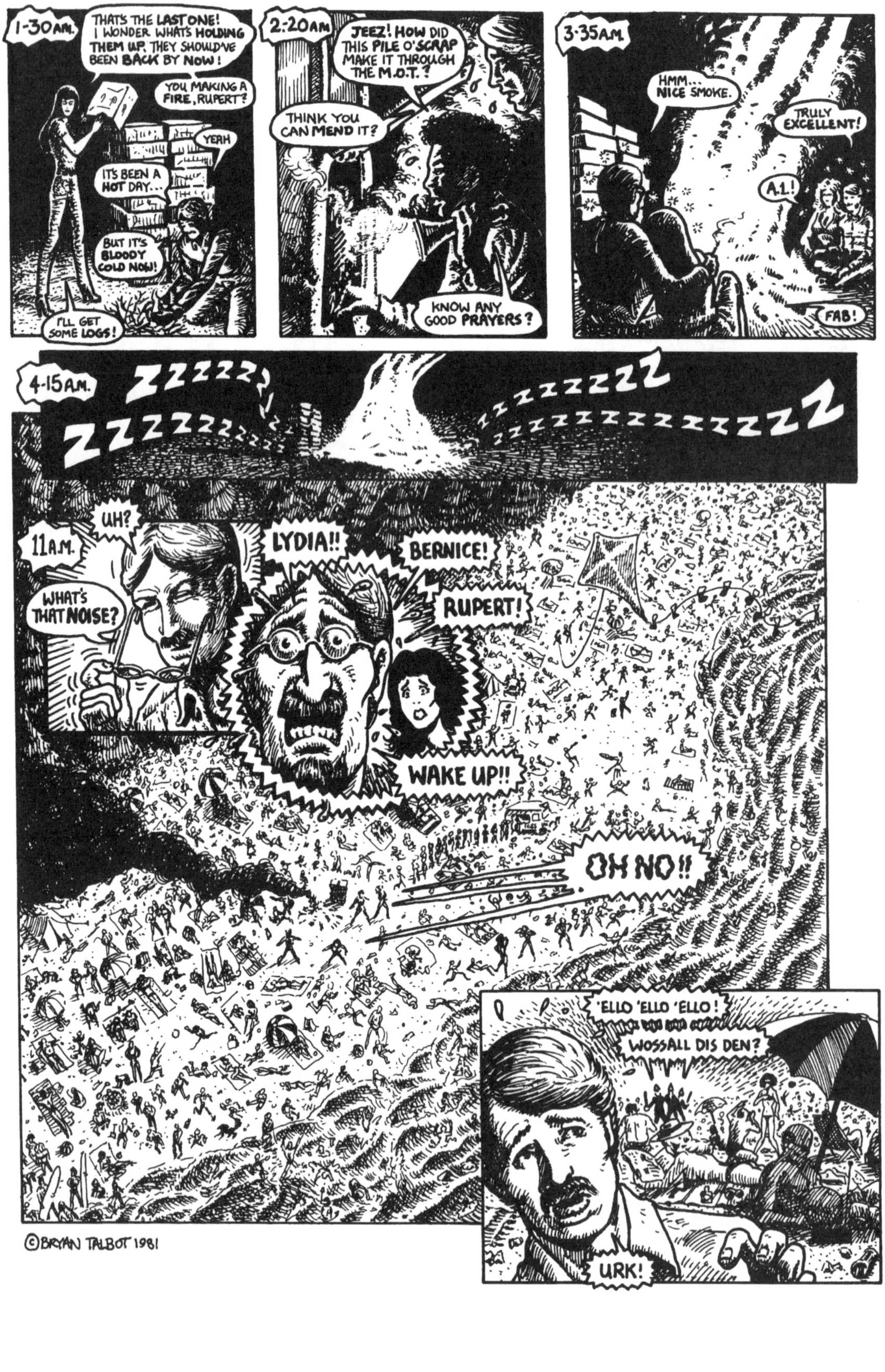

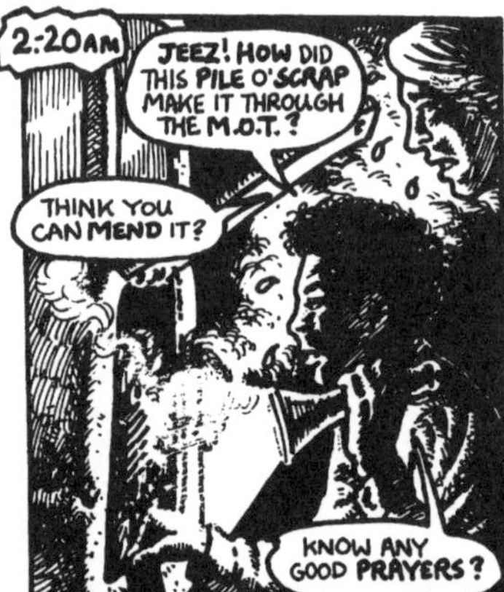

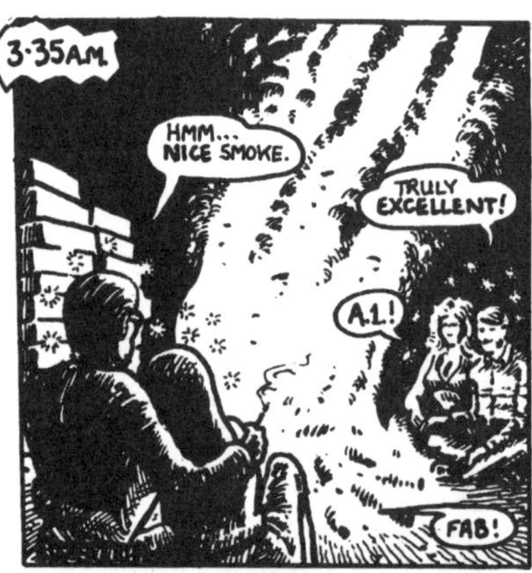

4-15 A.M.
ZZZZZZ
ZZZZZZZZZZ
ZZZZZZZZZ
ZZZZZZZZZZZZZZZZ

11 A.M.
UH?
WHAT'S THAT NOISE?
LYDIA!!
BERNICE!
RUPERT!
WAKE UP!!
OH NO!!
'ELLO 'ELLO 'ELLO!
WOSSALL DIS DEN?
URK!

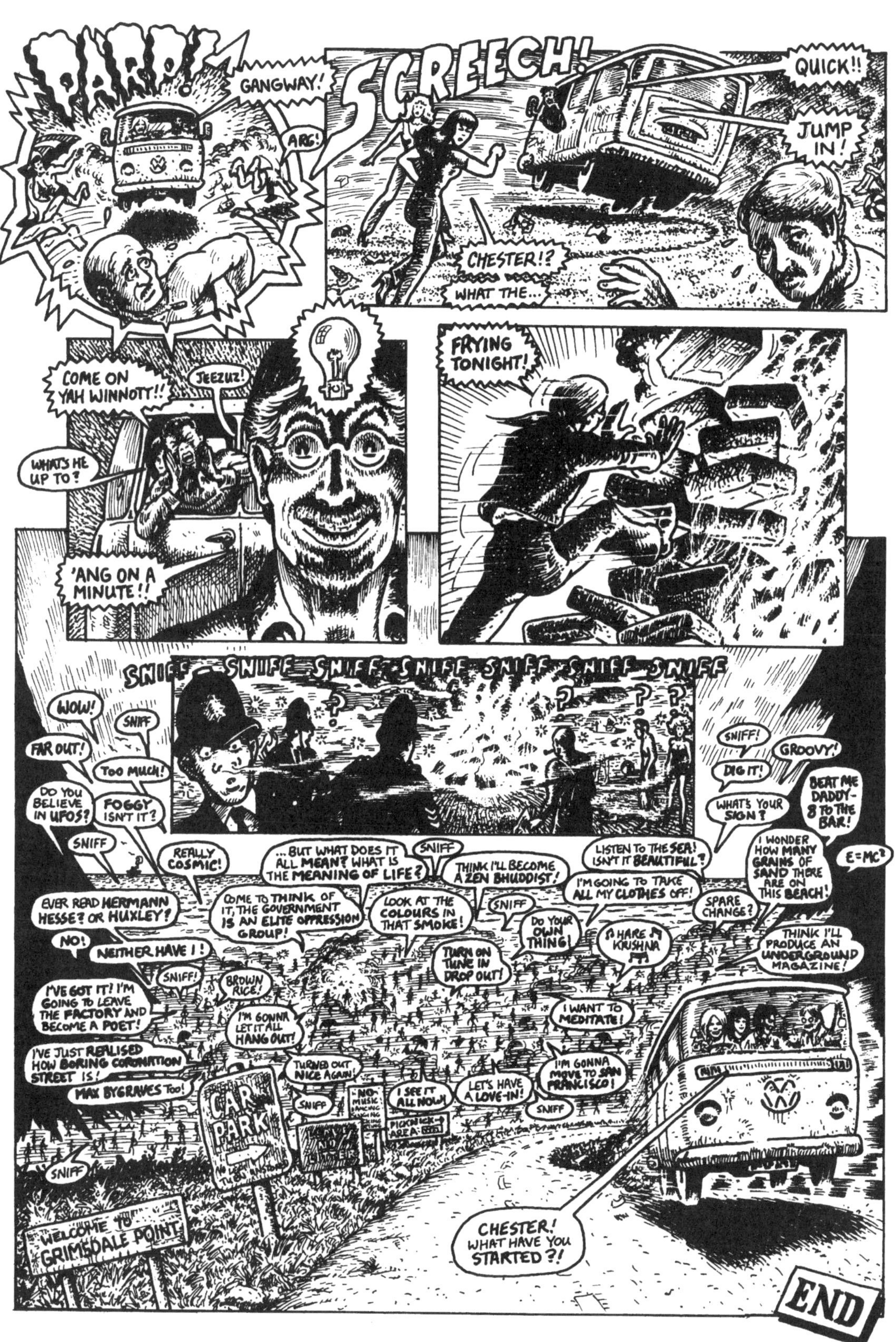
PARP!!
GANGWAY!
ARG!
SCREECH!
QUICK!!
JUMP IN!
CHESTER!?
WHAT THE...
COME ON YAH WINNOTT!!
JEEZUZ!
WHAT'S HE UP TO?
'ANG ON A MINUTE!!
FRYING TONIGHT!
SNIFF SNIFF SNIFF SNIFF SNIFF SNIFF SNIFF
WOW!
SNIFF
FAR OUT!
TOO MUCH!
DO YOU BELIEVE IN UFOS?
FOGGY ISN'T IT?
SNIFF!
DIG IT!
GROOVY!
WHAT'S YOUR SIGN?
BEAT ME DADDY-8 TO THE BAR!
SNIFF
REALLY COSMIC!
...BUT WHAT DOES IT ALL MEAN? WHAT IS THE MEANING OF LIFE?
SNIFF
THINK I'LL BECOME A ZEN BHUDDIST!
LISTEN TO THE SEA! ISN'T IT BEAUTIFUL!
I WONDER HOW MANY GRAINS OF SAND THERE ARE ON THIS BEACH!
E=MC²
EVER READ HERMANN HESSE? OR HUXLEY?
COME TO THINK OF IT, THE GOVERNMENT IS AN ELITE OPPRESSION GROUP!
LOOK AT THE COLOURS IN THAT SMOKE!
SNIFF
I'M GOING TO TAKE ALL MY CLOTHES OFF!
SPARE CHANGE?
DO YOUR OWN THING!
HARE KRISHNA
THINK I'LL PRODUCE AN UNDERGROUND MAGAZINE!
NO!
NEITHER HAVE I!
TURN ON TUNE IN DROP OUT!
SNIFF!
BROWN RICE!
I'VE GOT IT! I'M GOING TO LEAVE THE FACTORY AND BECOME A POET!
I'M GONNA LET IT ALL HANG OUT!
I WANT TO MEDITATE!
I'VE JUST REALISED HOW BORING CORONATION STREET IS!
MAX BYGRAVES TOO!
TURNED OUT NICE AGAIN!
I SEE IT ALL NOW!
LET'S HAVE A LOVE-IN!
I'M GONNA MOVE TO SAN FRANCISCO!
SNIFF
SNIFF
CAR PARK
NO MUSIC
PICKNICK AREA
SNIFF
WELCOME TO GRIMSDALE POINT
CHESTER! WHAT HAVE YOU STARTED?!
END

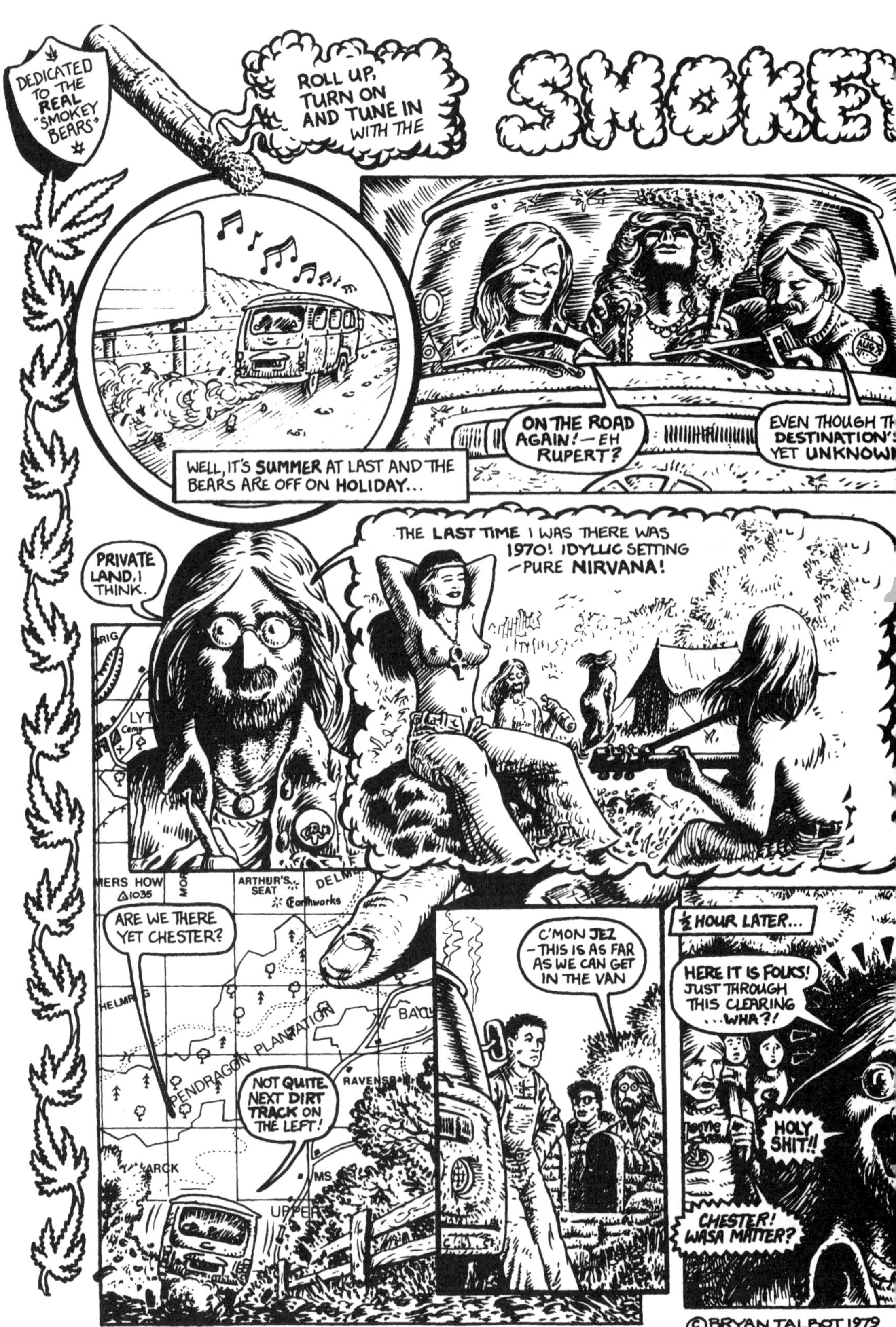
DEDICATED TO THE REAL "SMOKEY BEARS"
ROLL UP, TURN ON AND TUNE IN WITH THE
SMOKE
WELL, IT'S SUMMER AT LAST AND THE BEARS ARE OFF ON HOLIDAY...
ON THE ROAD AGAIN! — EH RUPERT?
EVEN THOUGH TH DESTINATION'S YET UNKNOW
PRIVATE LAND, I THINK.
THE LAST TIME I WAS THERE WAS 1970! IDYLLIC SETTING — PURE NIRVANA!
ARE WE THERE YET CHESTER?
NOT QUITE. NEXT DIRT TRACK ON THE LEFT!
ARTHUR'S SEAT
Earthworks
PENDRAGON PLANTATION
C'MON JEZ — THIS IS AS FAR AS WE CAN GET IN THE VAN
½ HOUR LATER...
HERE IT IS FOLKS! JUST THROUGH THIS CLEARING ...WHA?!
HOLY SHIT!!
CHESTER! WASA MATTER?
BRAINSTORM STUDIOS
©BRYAN TALBOT 1979

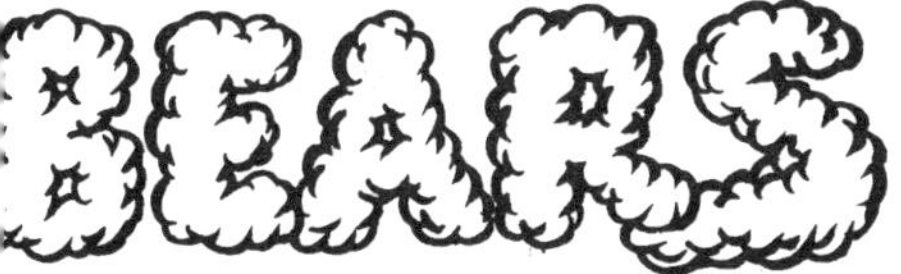
BEARS

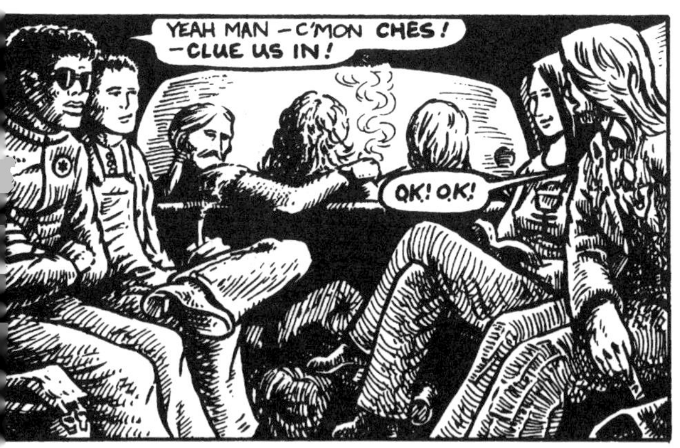
YEAH MAN – C'MON CHES! – CLUE US IN!
OK! OK!

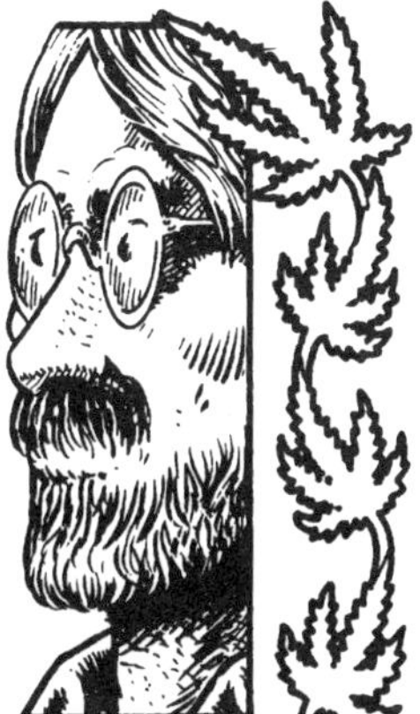
IT'S JUST A REALLY NICE BEAUTY SPOT! – A SUN TRAP!
CRAWLING WITH BLOODY TOURISTS!
HELL NO! IT'S A SMALL VALLEY – COMPLETELY SECLUDED. NO ONE GOES THERE

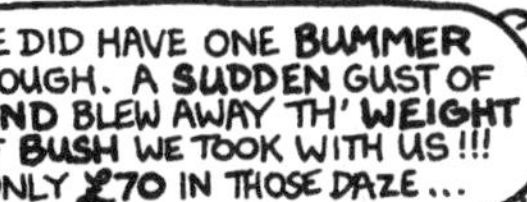
E DID HAVE ONE BUMMER
HOUGH. A SUDDEN GUST OF
IND BLEW AWAY TH' WEIGHT
F BUSH WE TOOK WITH US!!!
ONLY £70 IN THOSE DAZE...

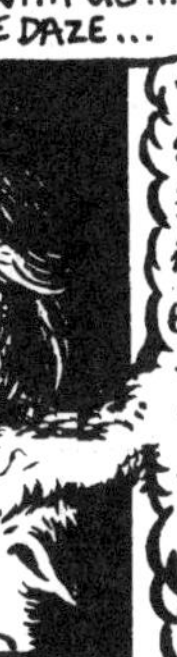

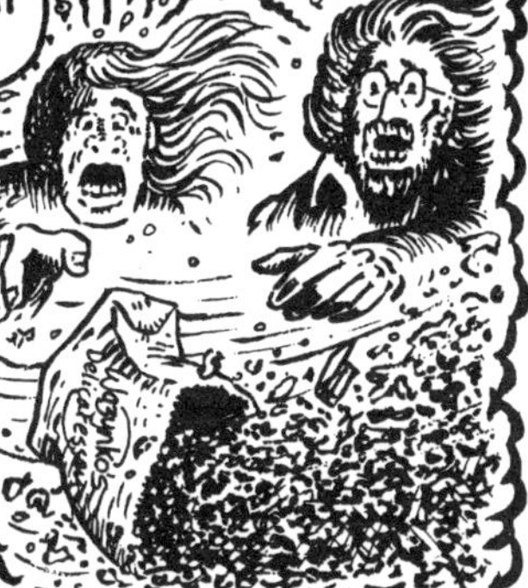

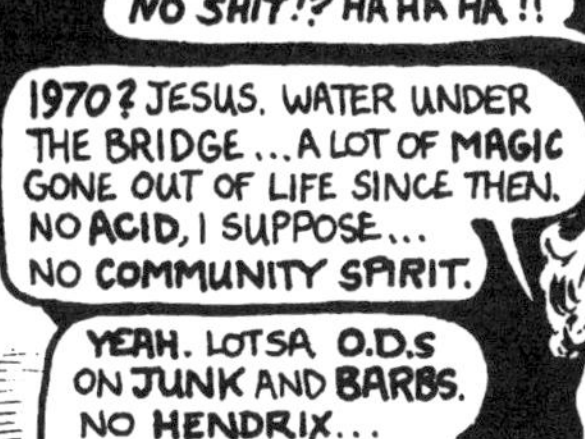
NO SHIT!? HA HA HA!!
1970? JESUS. WATER UNDER THE BRIDGE... A LOT OF MAGIC GONE OUT OF LIFE SINCE THEN. NO ACID, I SUPPOSE... NO COMMUNITY SPIRIT.

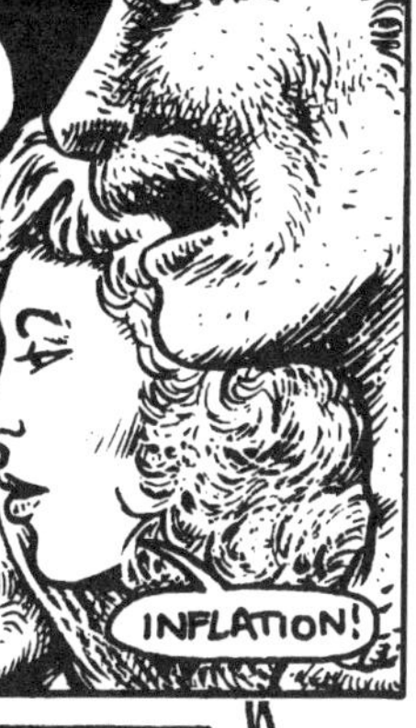
YEAH. LOTSA O.D.S ON JUNK AND BARBS. NO HENDRIX... WATERGATE... ROCK & ROLL HYPE... PEOPLE SELLING OUT LIKE CRAZY... COLDER WEATHER!
INFLATION!

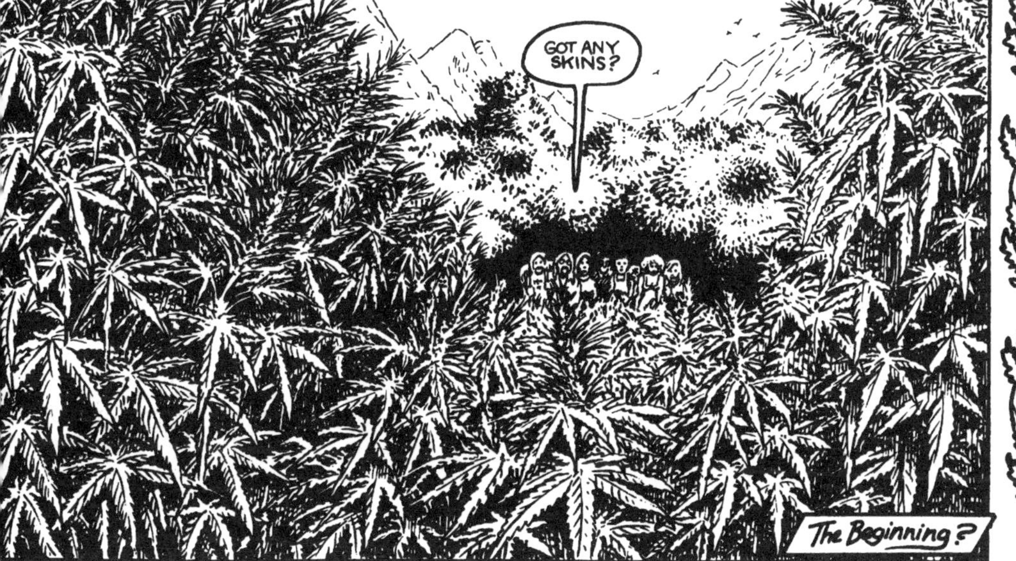
GOT ANY SKINS?
The Beginning?

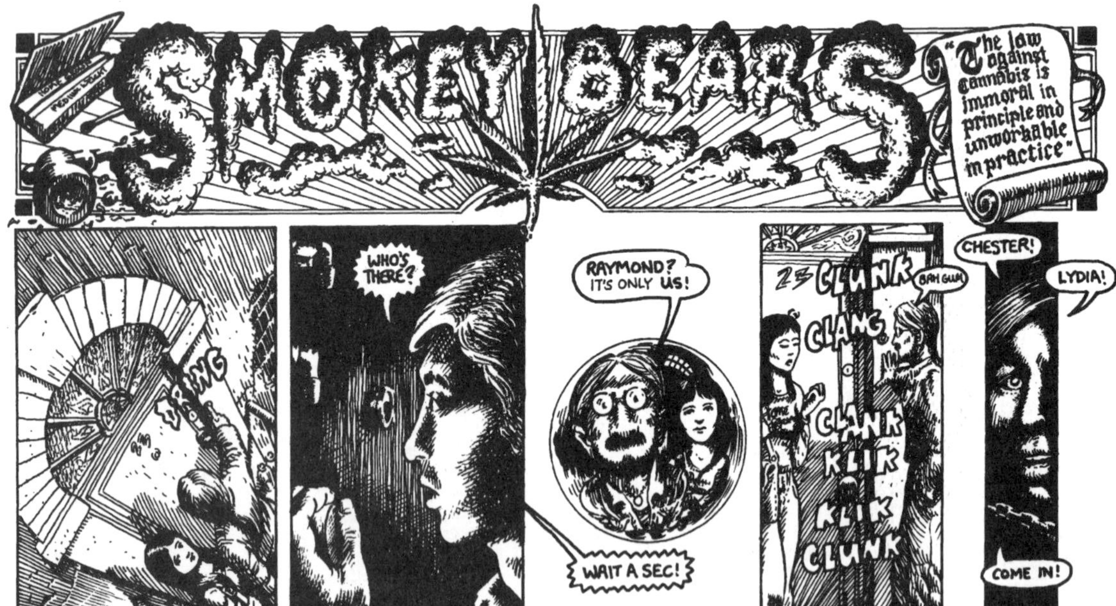

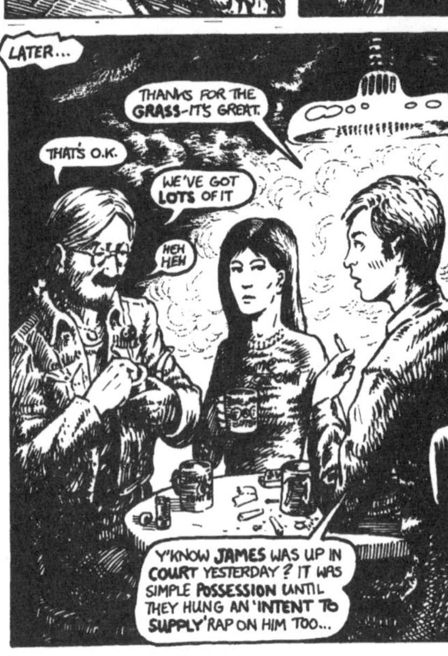

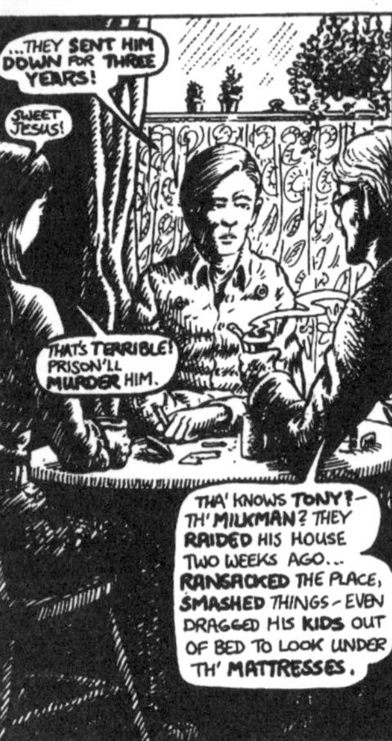

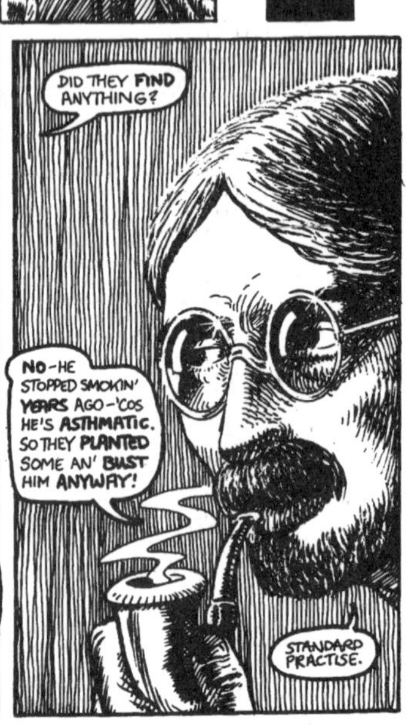

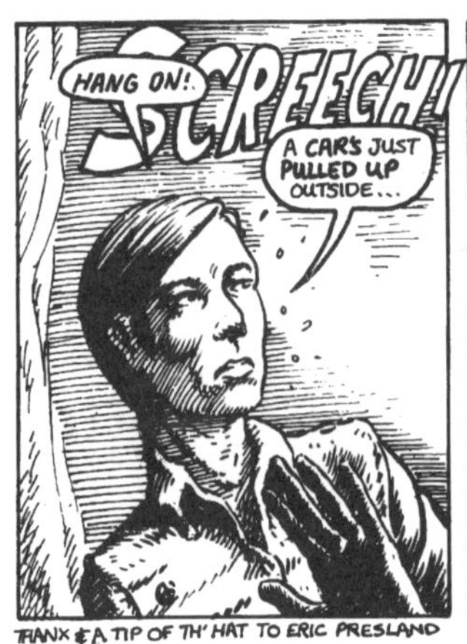

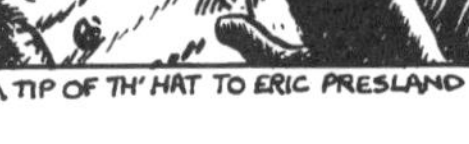

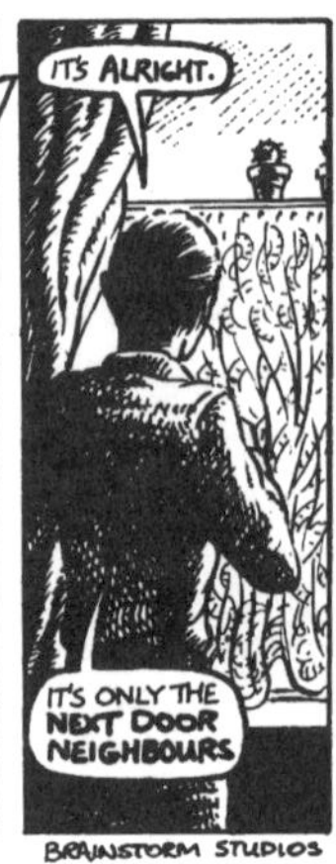

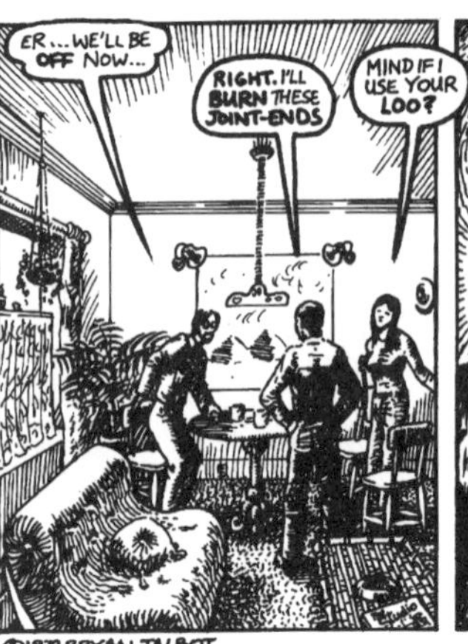

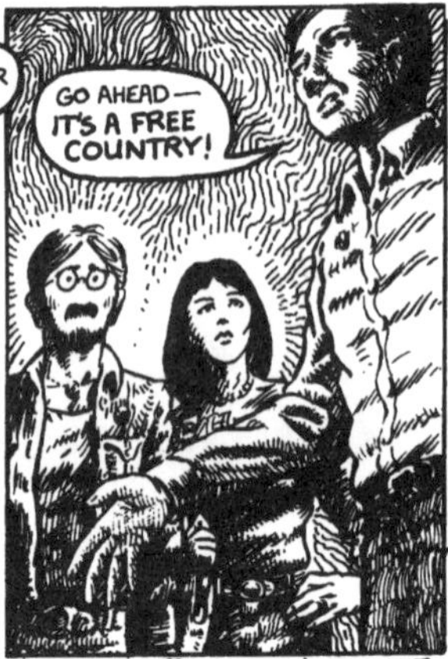

BRAINSTORM STUDIOS ©1979 BRYAN TALBOT

FREEZE SHOT & FADE OUT...

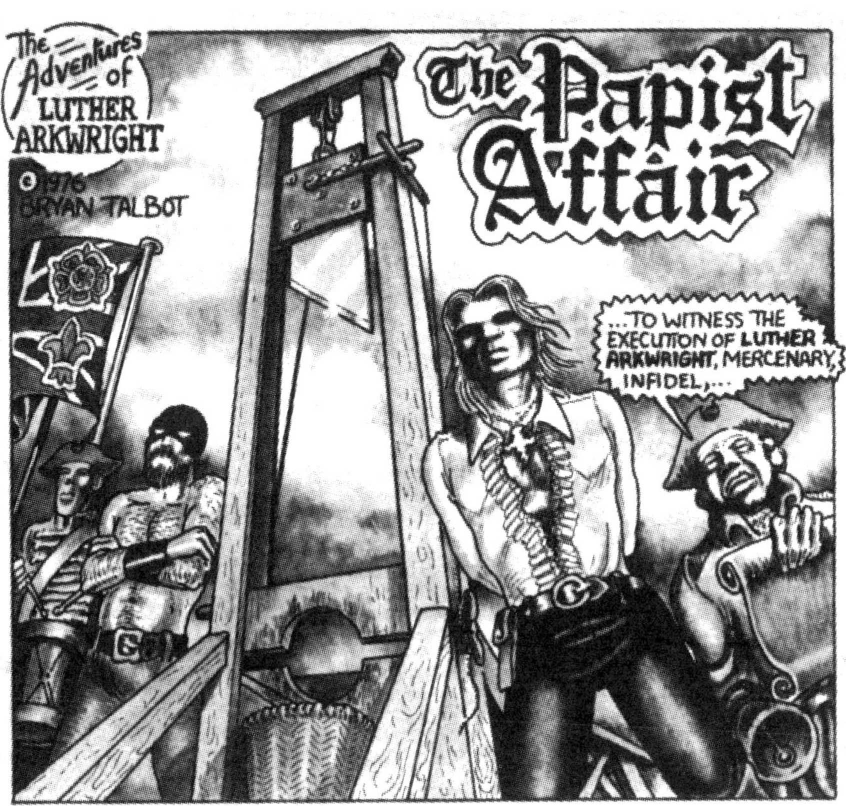

LOCATION:
PARALLEL ENGLAND Nº185
VARIATION:
IN 1524, CATHERINE OF ARAGON BORE A SON TO HENRY VIII. HENRY DID NOT MARRY AGAIN. CONSEQUENTLY ENGLAND NEVER BROKE RELATIONS WITH ROME + ELIZABETH I WAS NEVER BORN. HENRY IX WAS A TYRANT, A RELIGIOUS FANATIC WHO CRUSHED ALL THOSE WHO DID NOT SUBSCRIBE TO CATHOLICISM...
THE TUDORS HELD ONTO THE CROWN. COUNTRIES FELL BEFORE ENGLAND'S MIGHT.
WORLD WARS I + II NEVER TOOK PLACE.
DECADENCE SET IN.
1977: THE TOTTERING HOLY BRITISH EMPIRE STILL HOLDS SWAY OVER EUROPE + THE AMERICAS.

BUT HENRY IX's MADNESS HAS LIVED ON THROUGH THE CENTURIES + INTERNAL DISSENTION IS STILL RIFE....

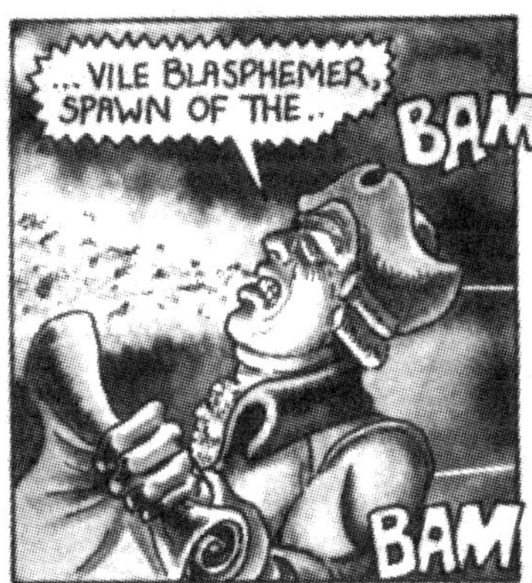

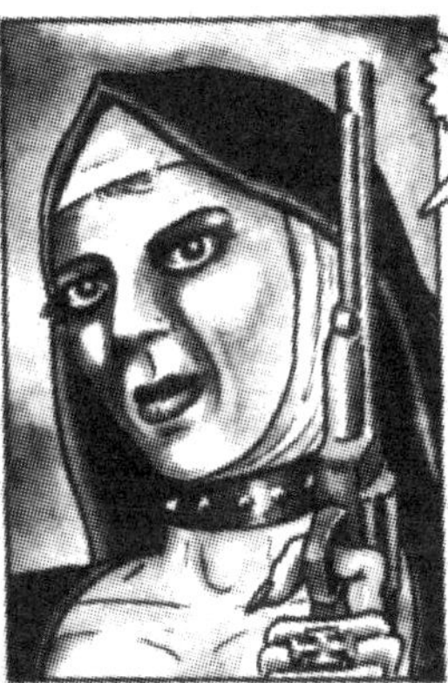

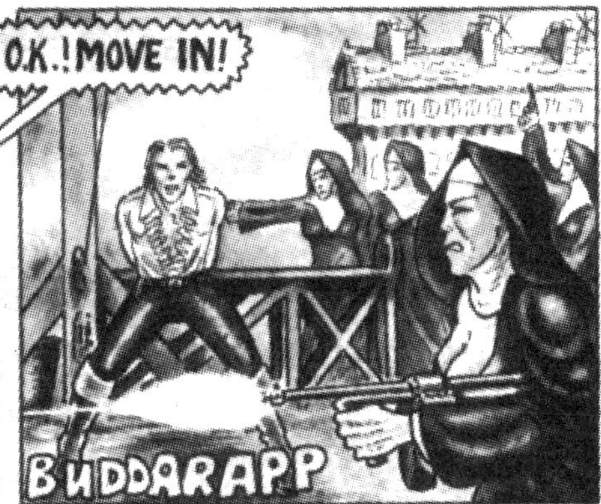

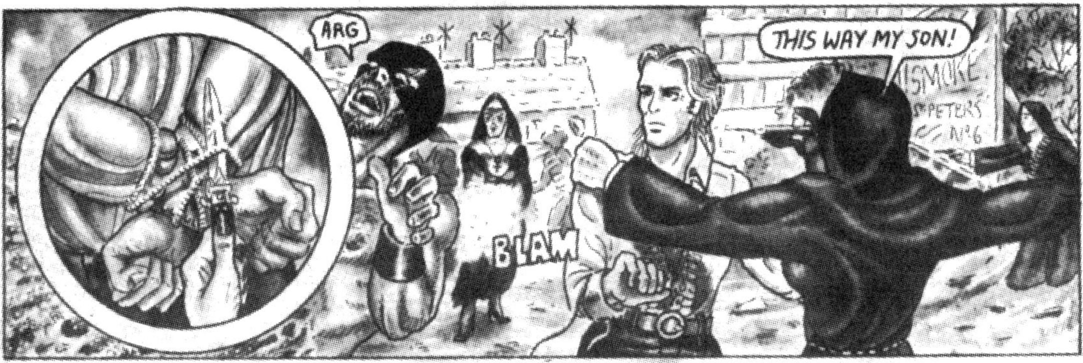

TIME LAPSE:
TEN MINUTES.
SITUATION:
HEADING WEST-WARDS ALONG THE HENRY V HIGHWAY.
DESTINATION:
SALISBURY PLAIN
METEOROLOGICAL REPORT:
THE STORMCLOUDS **DARKEN**...

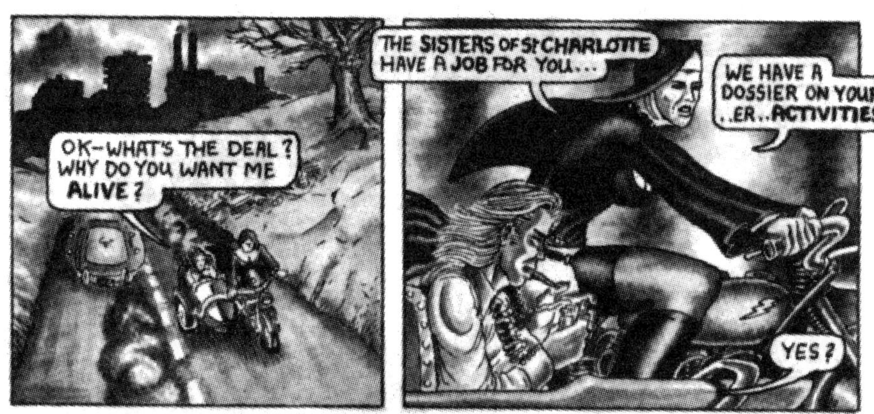

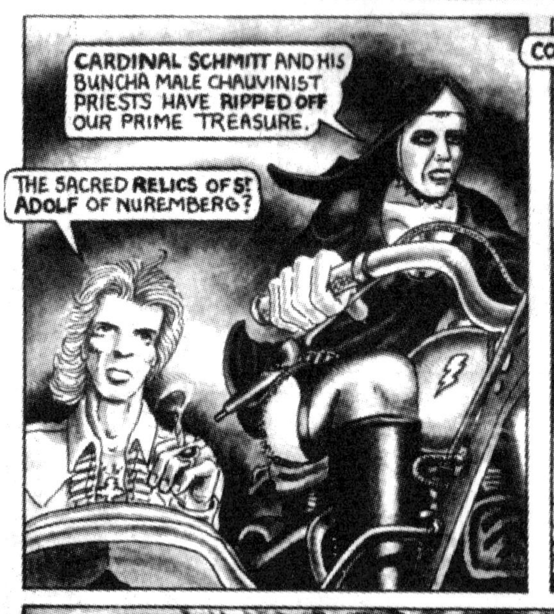

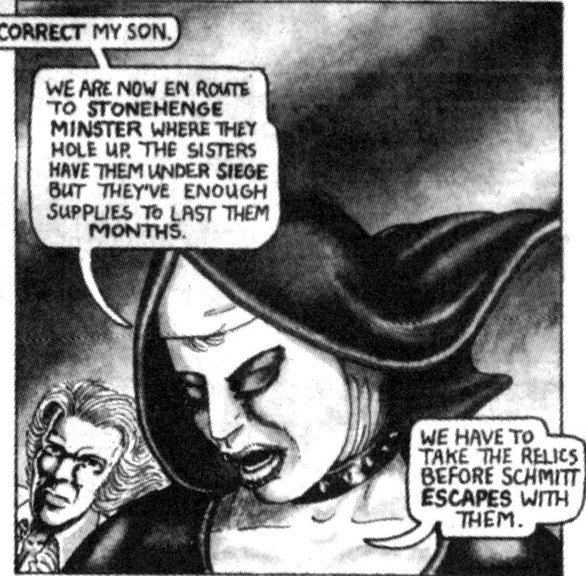

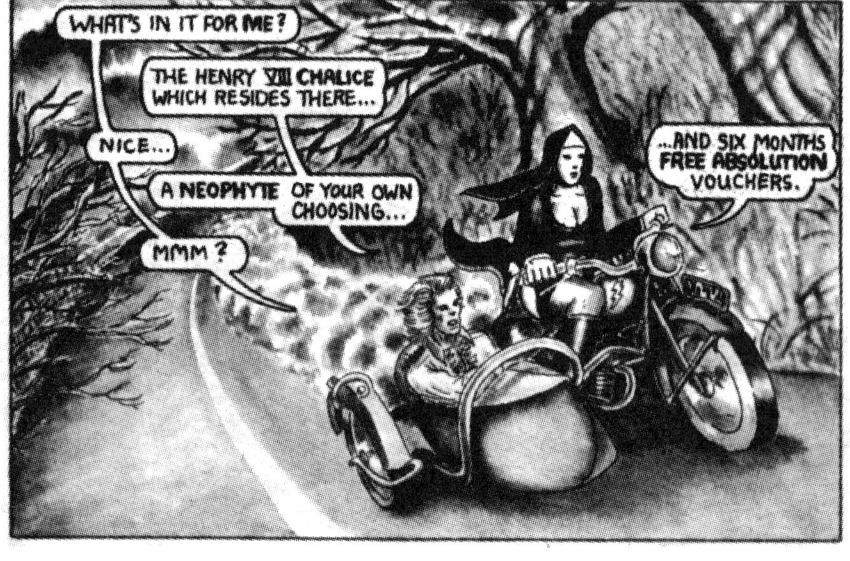

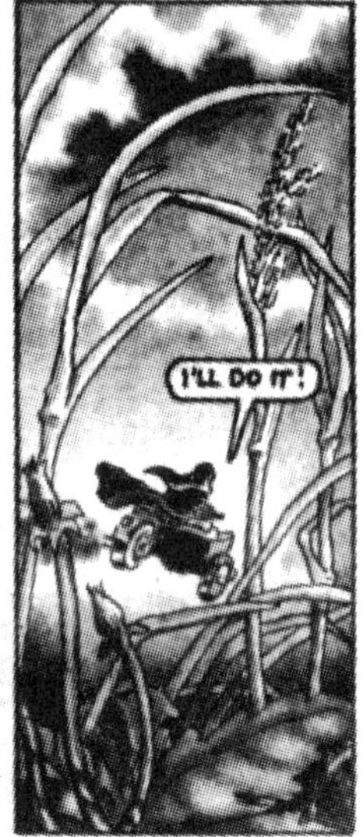

TIME LAPSE: 2 HOURS 17 MIN.

LOCATION: STONEHENGE MINSTER, A GOTHIC CATHEDRAL BUILT ON THE SITE OF AN ANCIENT **STONE CIRCLE**.

INCONSISTENCY: CATHEDRAL POWER SOURCE READINGS PARADOXICALLY **HIGH**.

ARKWRIGHT STARES AT THE BLACK VELVET HABITS OF THE SISTERS OF St CHARLOTTE AND MENTALLY **PREPARES** HIMSELF. **NO** SLIP UPS THIS TIME. THE **FUTURE** HISTORY OF THE 185TH PARALLEL IS IN THE **BALANCE**.

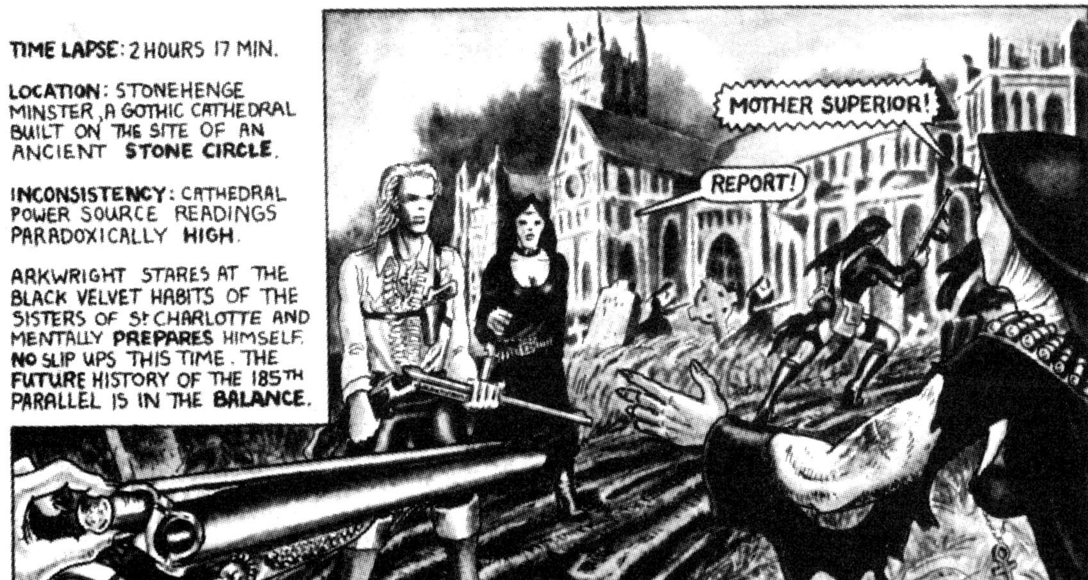

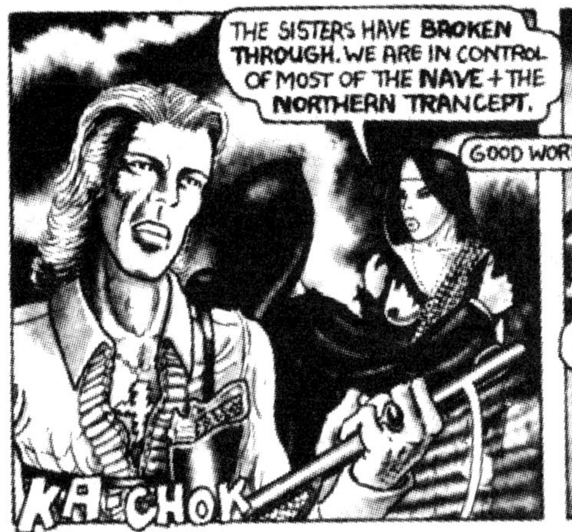

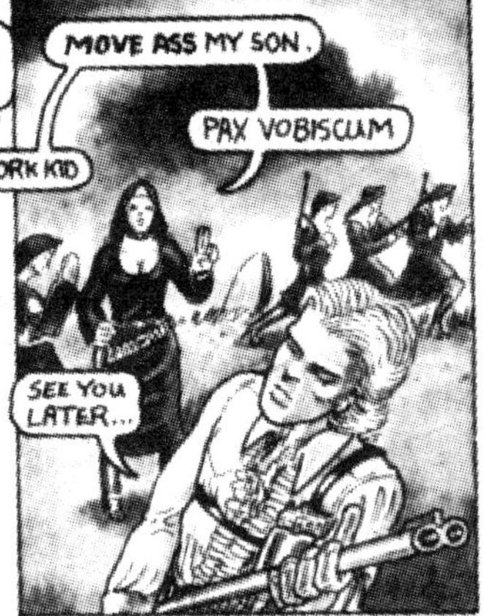

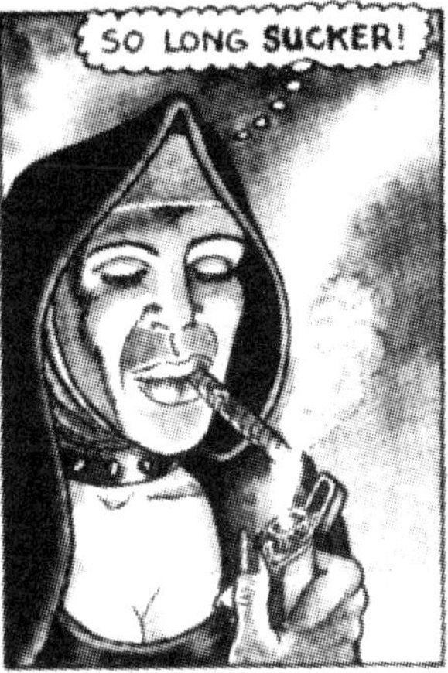

IMPRESSION: IN THE GREAT MEDIEVAL NAVE CLOYING **FRANKINCENSE** MINGLES WITH ACRID **GUNSMOKE**. GIBBERING MACHINEGUNS, ROARING SHOTGUNS, BARKING REVOLVERS, SHOUTS AND SCREAMS CREATE A **DEAFENING** WALL OF SOUND.

ARKWRIGHT, AS **ALWAYS**, IS AWARE OF HIS MISSION —MAINTAINING THE **EQUILIBRIUM** OF THE PARALLELS. **NOW** HIS FIRST PRIORITY IS TO **LIQUIDATE** CARDINAL SCHMITT, WHOSE **DISRUPTIVE** INFLUENCE HAS PRECIPITATED THIS CRISIS OF **IMBALANCE**.

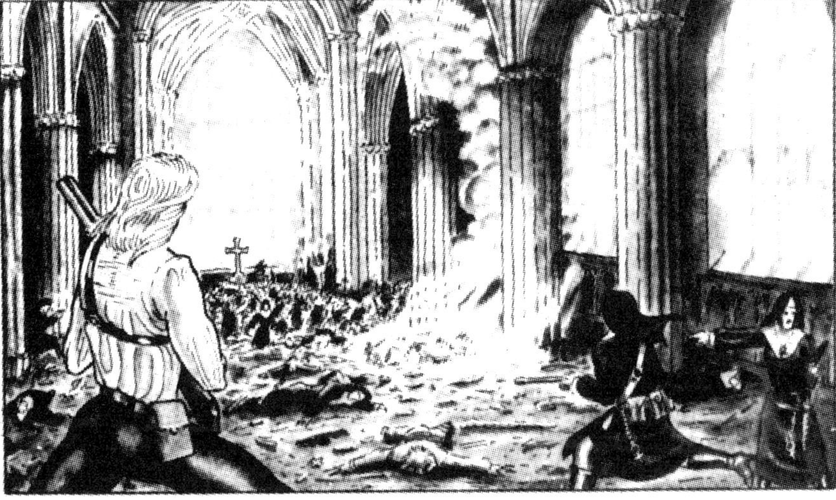

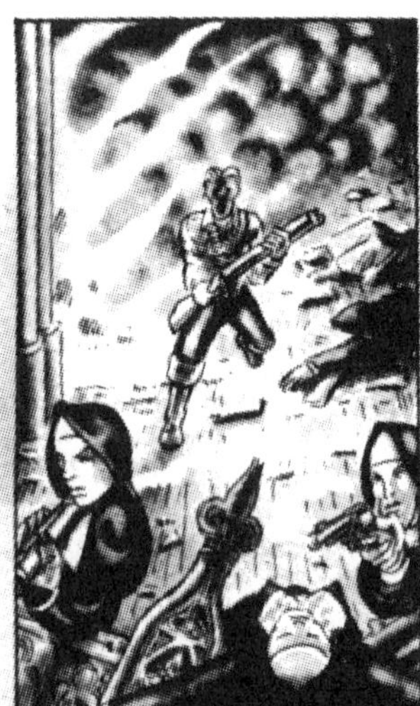

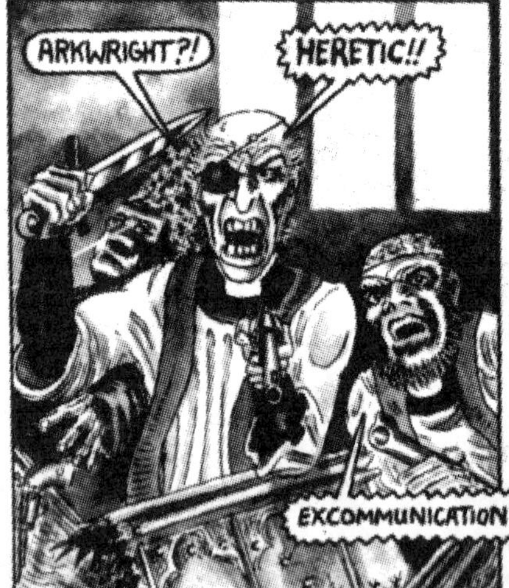
ARKWRIGHT?!
HERETIC!!
EXCOMMUNICATION!

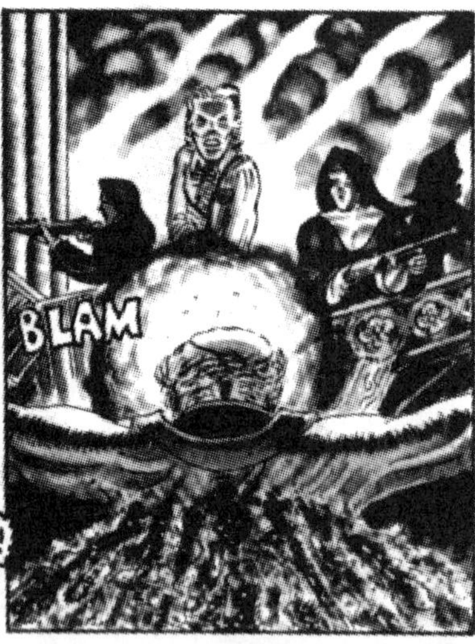
BLAM

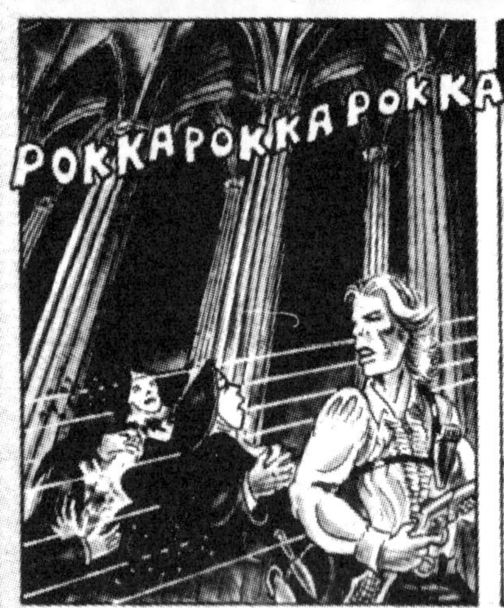
POKKAPOKKAPOKKA

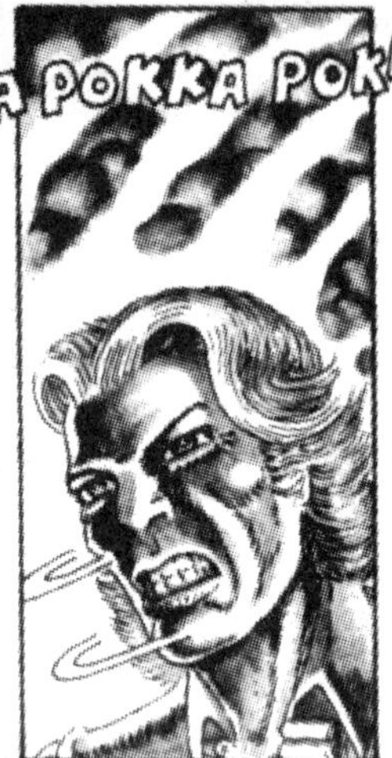
POKKA POKKA

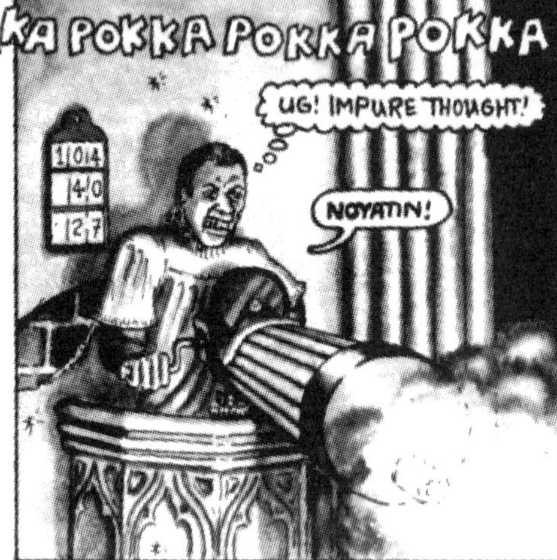
POKKA POKKA POKKA
UG! IMPURE THOUGHT!
NOYATIN!

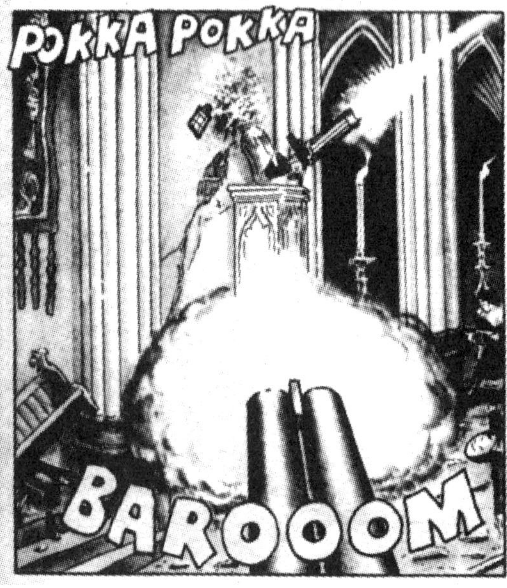
POKKA POKKA
BAROOOM

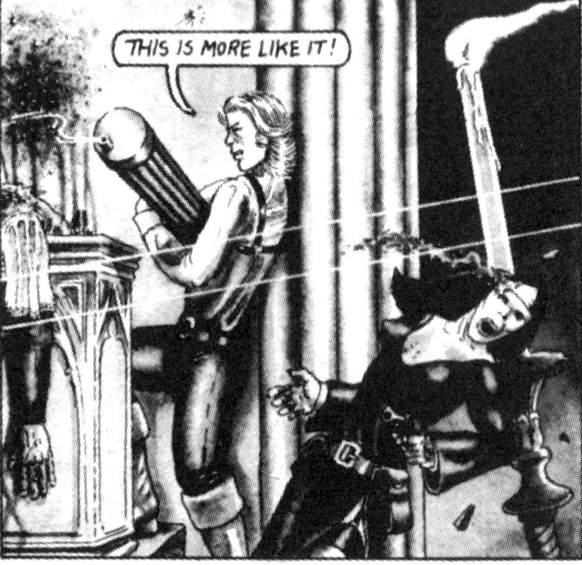
THIS IS MORE LIKE IT!

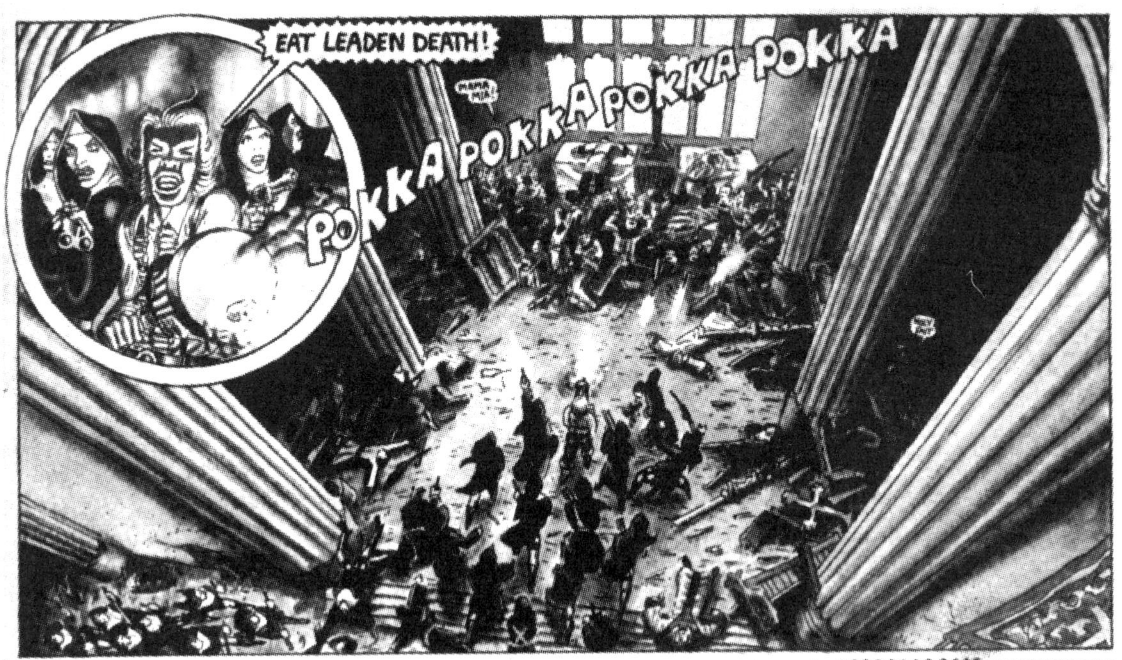

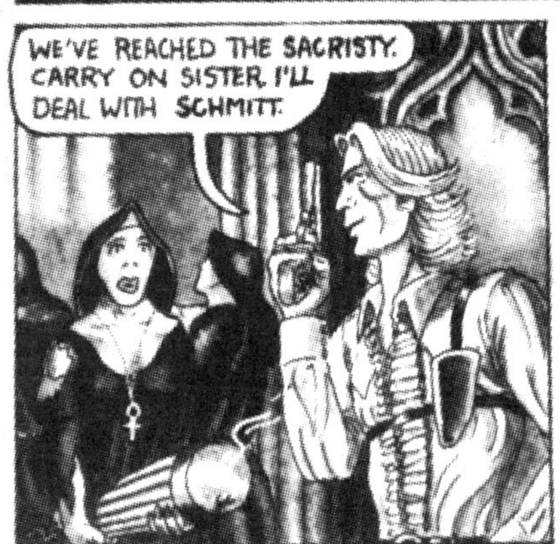

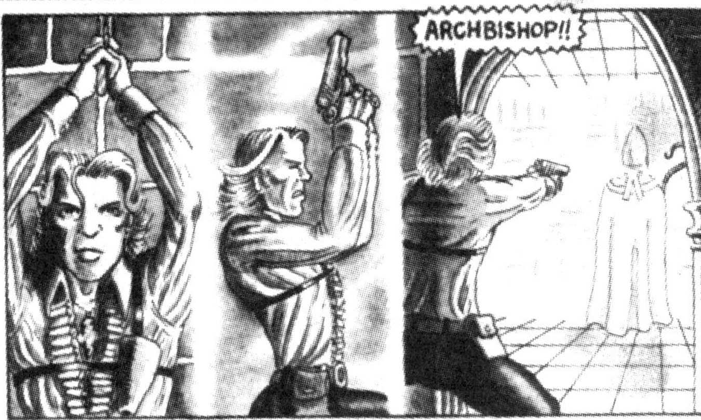

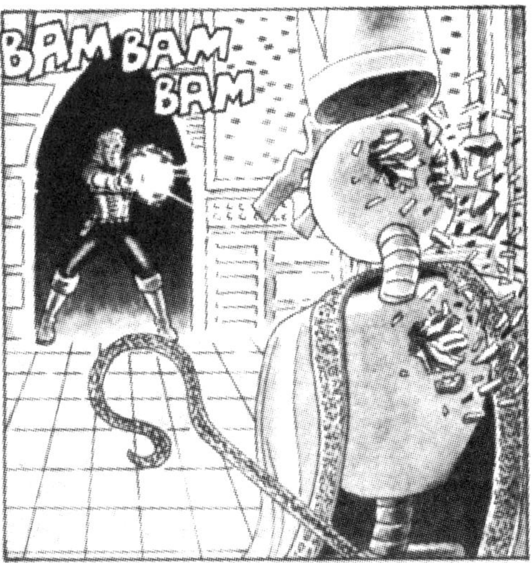

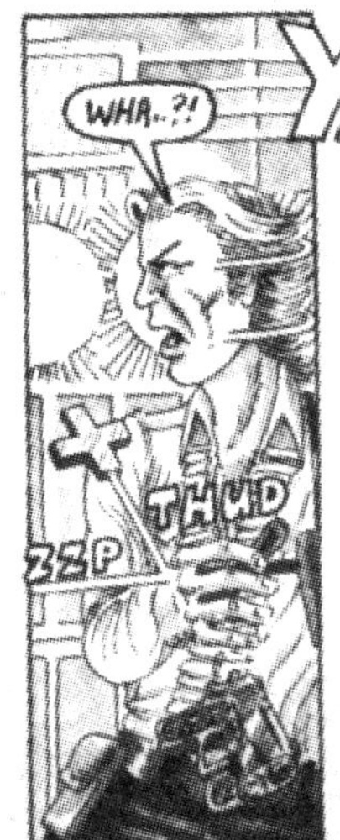

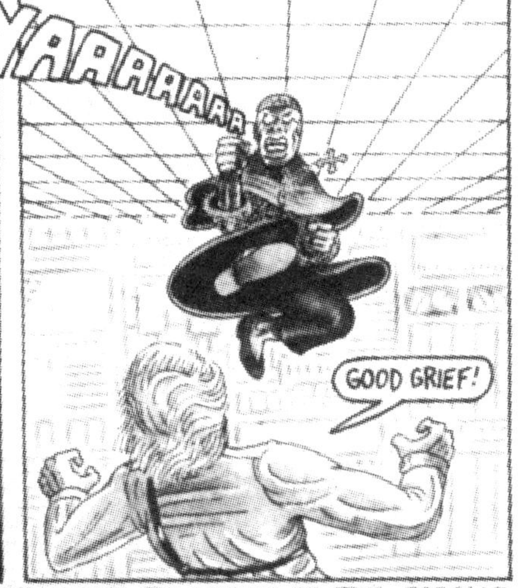

INCONSISTENCY: THIS SET UP IS FAR IN ADVANCE OF ANY TECHNOLOGY BELONGING TO THIS PARALLEL

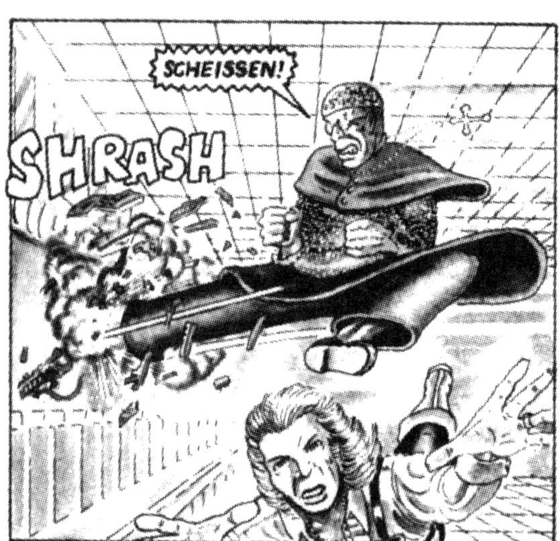
SCHEISSEN!
SHRASH

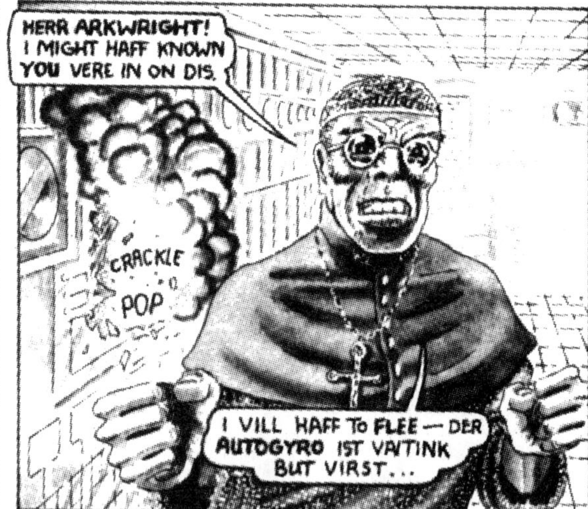
HERR ARKWRIGHT! I MIGHT HAFF KNOWN YOU VERE IN ON DIS.
CRACKLE
POP
I VILL HAFF TO FLEE — DER AUTOGYRO IST VAITINK BUT VIRST...

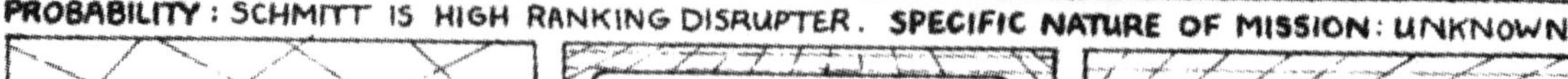
PROBABILITY: SCHMITT IS HIGH RANKING DISRUPTER. SPECIFIC NATURE OF MISSION: UNKNOWN.

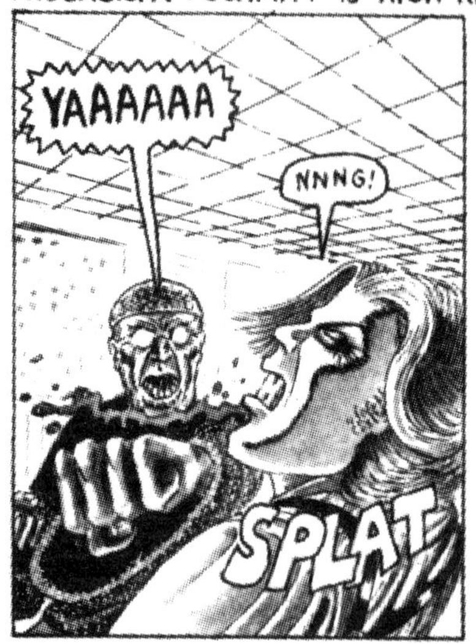
YAAAAAA
NNNG!
SPLAT

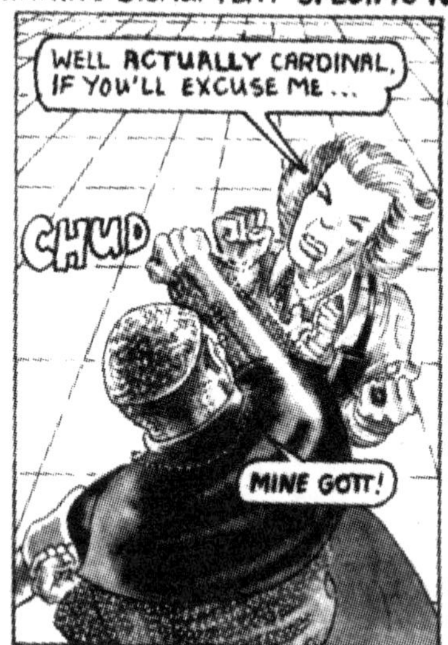
WELL ACTUALLY CARDINAL, IF YOU'LL EXCUSE ME...
CHUD
MINE GOTT!

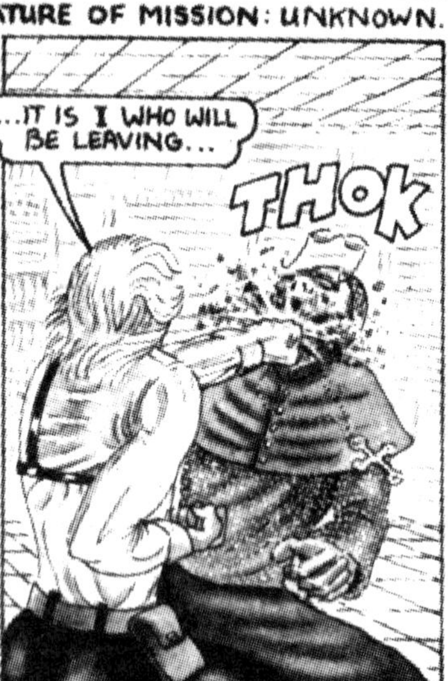
...IT IS I WHO WILL BE LEAVING...
THOK

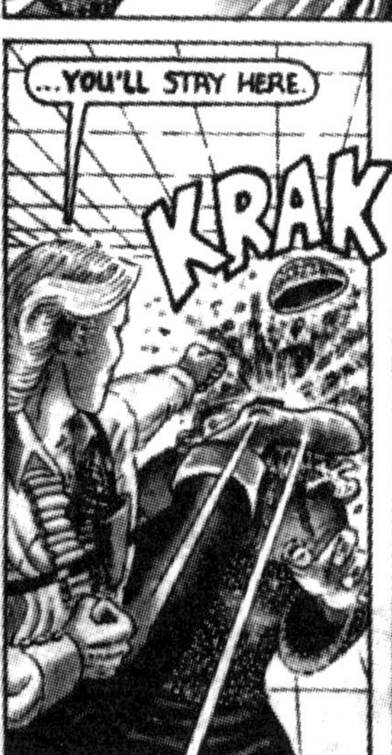
...YOU'LL STAY HERE.
KRAK

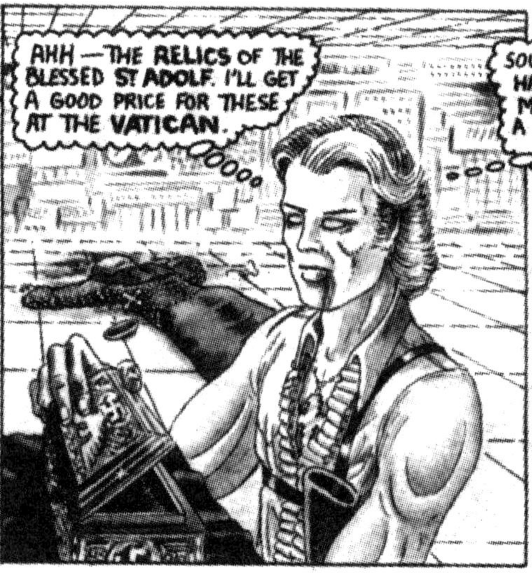
AHH — THE RELICS OF THE BLESSED ST ADOLF. I'LL GET A GOOD PRICE FOR THESE AT THE VATICAN.

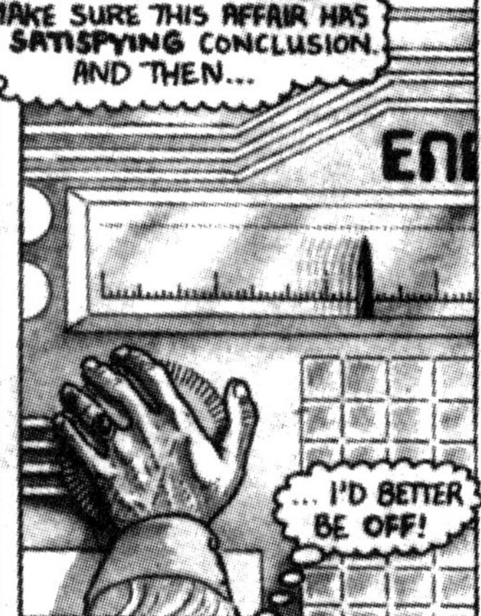
SOUNDS LIKE THE HOSTILITIES HAVE CEASED. I'LL JUST MAKE SURE THIS AFFAIR HAS A SATISFYING CONCLUSION. AND THEN...
...I'D BETTER BE OFF!

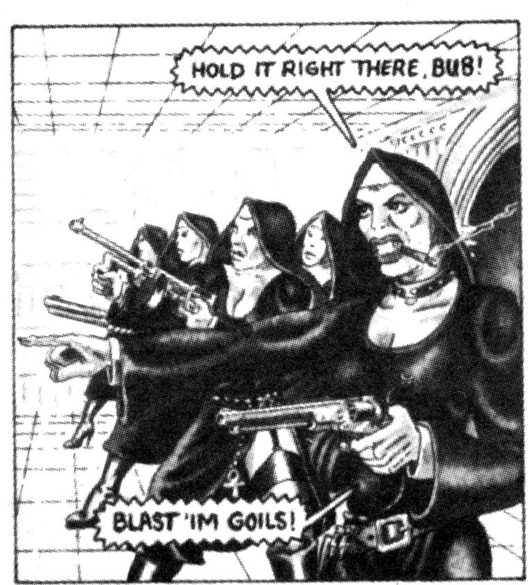
HOLD IT RIGHT THERE, BUB!
BLAST 'IM GOILS!

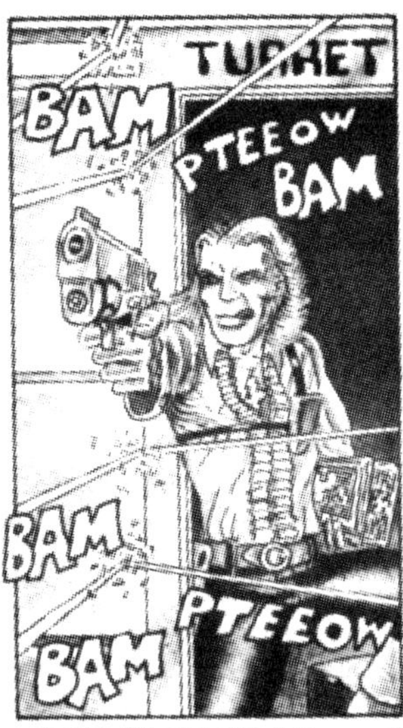
TURRET
BAM
PTEEOW
BAM
BAM
PTEEOW
BAM

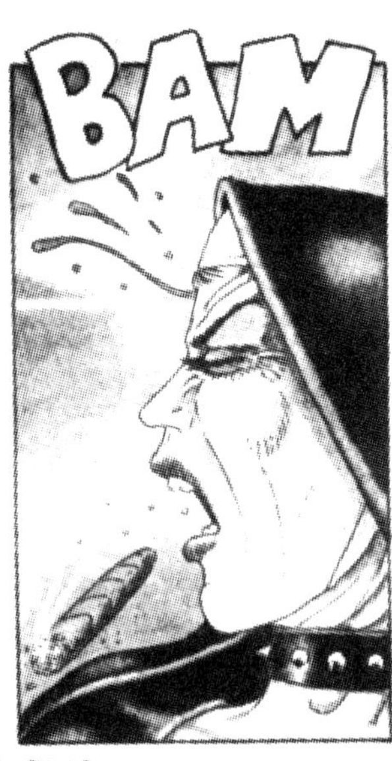
BAM

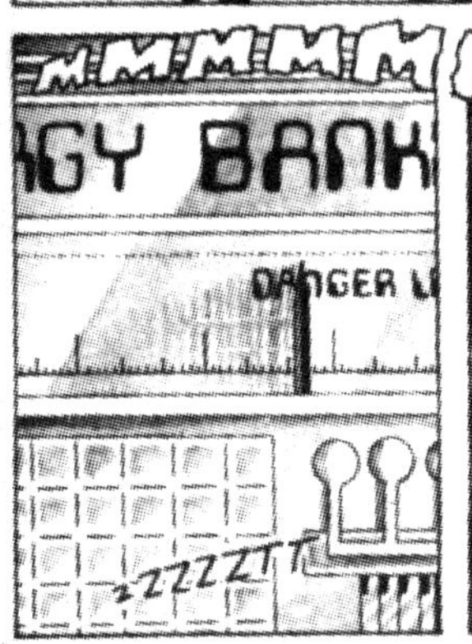
MMMMMMMMMMMMMMMMMMMMMM
GY BANK
DANGER L
ZZZZZTT

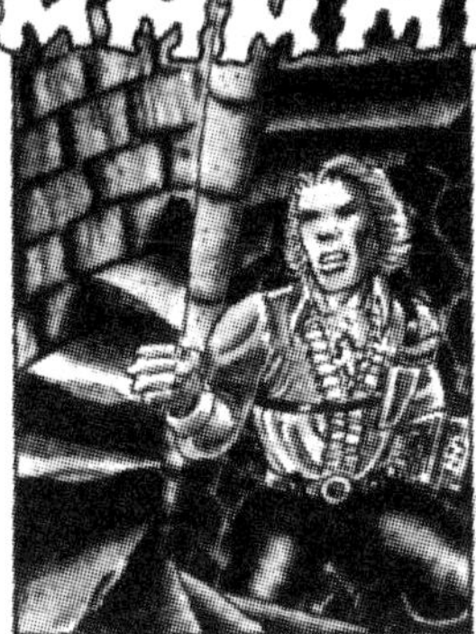

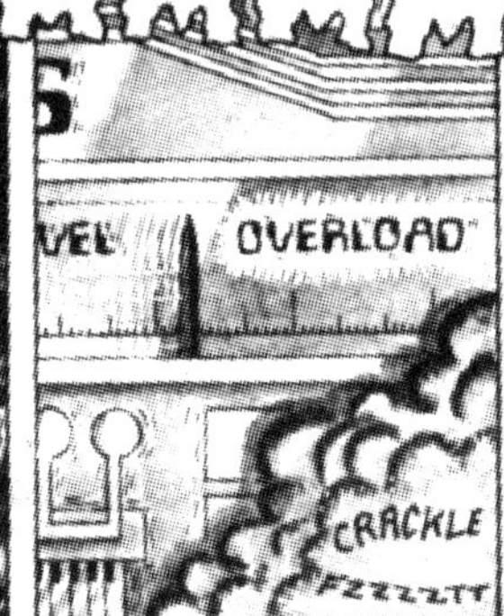
S
VEL
"OVERLOAD"
CRACKLE
FZZZZTT

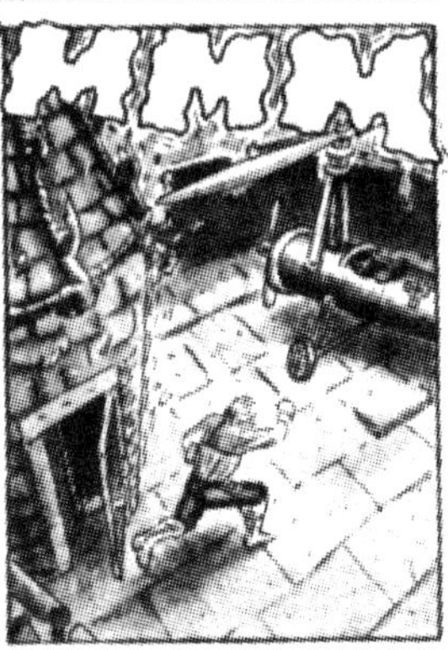

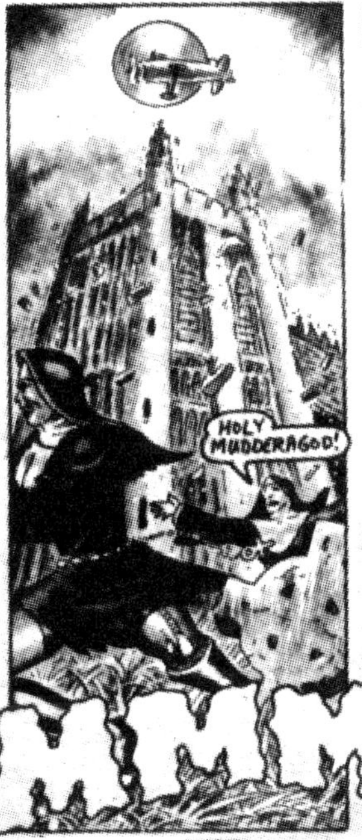
HOLY MUDDERAGOD!

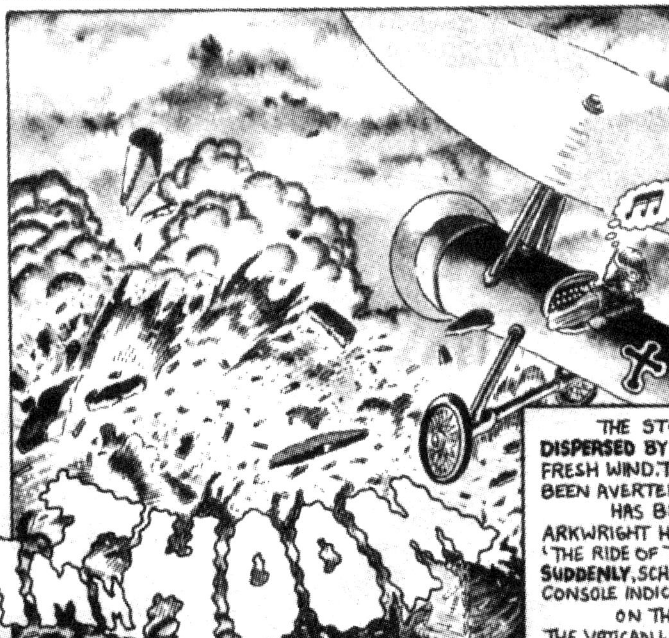
MMMMHOOM
THE STORMCLOUDS ARE DISPERSED BY A STRONG, FRESH WIND. THE STORM HAS BEEN AVERTED - THE BALANCE HAS BEEN RESTORED. ARKWRIGHT HUMS WAGNER'S 'THE RIDE OF THE VALKYRIES'. SUDDENLY, SCHMITT'S AUTOGYRO CONSOLE INDICATES DISRUPTION ON THE 95TH PARALLEL. THE VATICAN WILL HAVE TO WAIT...
End

GLAD YOU'RE BACK

On April Fool's Day 1972, Alchemy began trading as a headshop in an indoor market in London's Portobello Road. It was a colourful time when nearly everyone you met had either just been to India or was about to embark on the journey. On the tide of great gurus you encountered beautific smiles and enlightened spirits. If you saw some long-haired 'freak' in his sheepskin coat and flares walking down the Portobello on a Saturday, you'd greet him thus: 'Hi man, far out!'

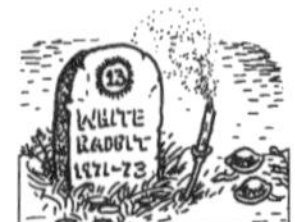

I met Bryan Talbot during that first year. While at art college he was running a basement shop in his home town of Preston, Lancashire, called White Rabbit and I supplied him with incense, perfumed oils, herbs and balms from the East.

In September 1975 Bryan arranged to come down to London to show me the comic story he had just finished. It was almost two years since I'd last seen him. He reminded me that I'd once said that if he got his comic together, I'd be interested in publishing it. He had spent three months working on it and it was finally complete. I had hardly read a comic in years, let alone published one.

On the day he came to my flat, I had just been ripped-off by some 'bob-a-job' kids who I had let in to clean the place up. They had taken some small change and other items and I had gone out to look for them but couldn't find them. I felt dejected and sad that I had been robbed while I trusted them.

When I returned to the flat, Bryan was already waiting for me. My girlfriend Brigitte had made him some tea. I sat down and Bryan put the pages of artwork in my lap. As I turned the pages over I felt deeply moved. Something had been taken from me and here was something being given. I felt as if it had been drawn especially for me. Chester P Hackenbush had restored my faith in humanity.

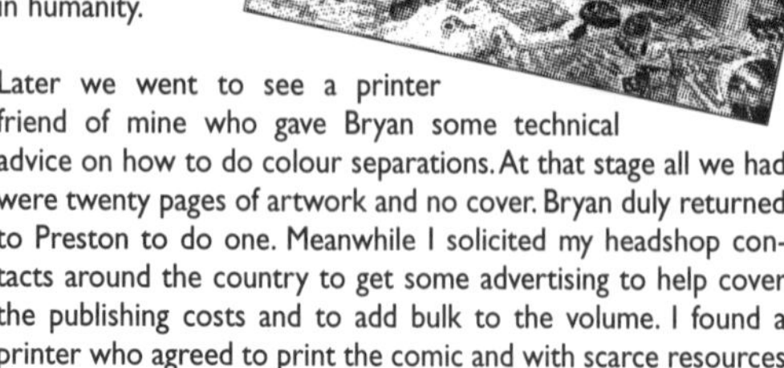

Later we went to see a printer friend of mine who gave Bryan some technical advice on how to do colour separations. At that stage all we had were twenty pages of artwork and no cover. Bryan duly returned to Preston to do one. Meanwhile I solicited my headshop contacts around the country to get some advertising to help cover the publishing costs and to add bulk to the volume. I found a printer who agreed to print the comic and with scarce resources went ahead.

Two magical events took place on the same day - the 26th of November 1975.

On that day Brigitte and I were married in a Buddhist temple. The ceremony was attended by a few close friends of whom Bryan was one and he took the photograph shown here. Afterwards, Brigitte and I cooked and served a meal for the five Thai monks who had blessed us and then we returned to the flat for a party.

Many friends had gathered and were sitting cross-legged on the

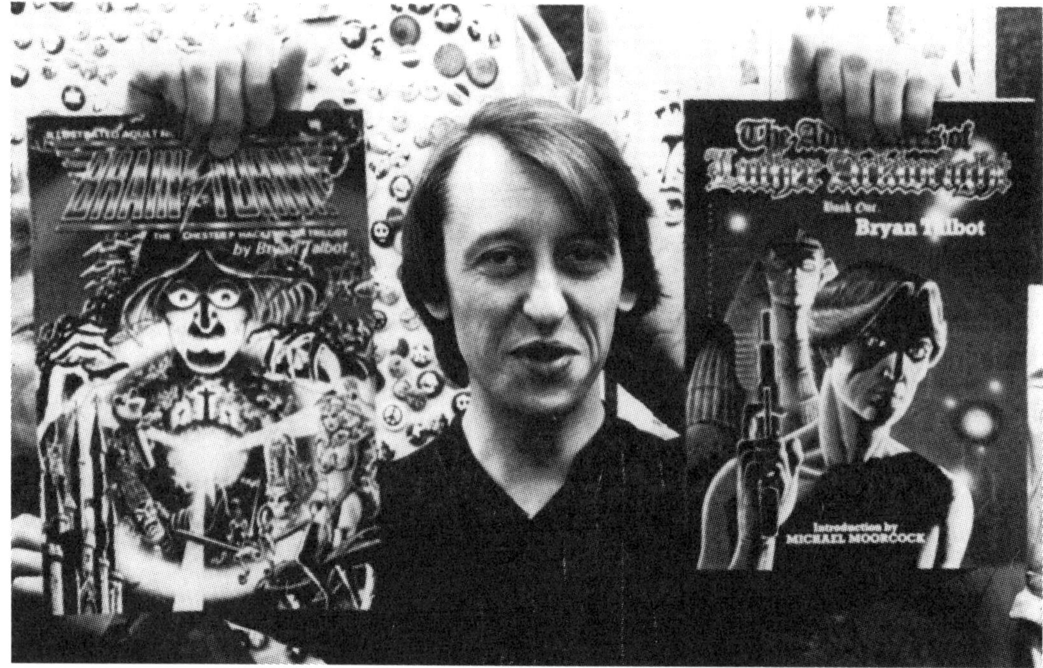

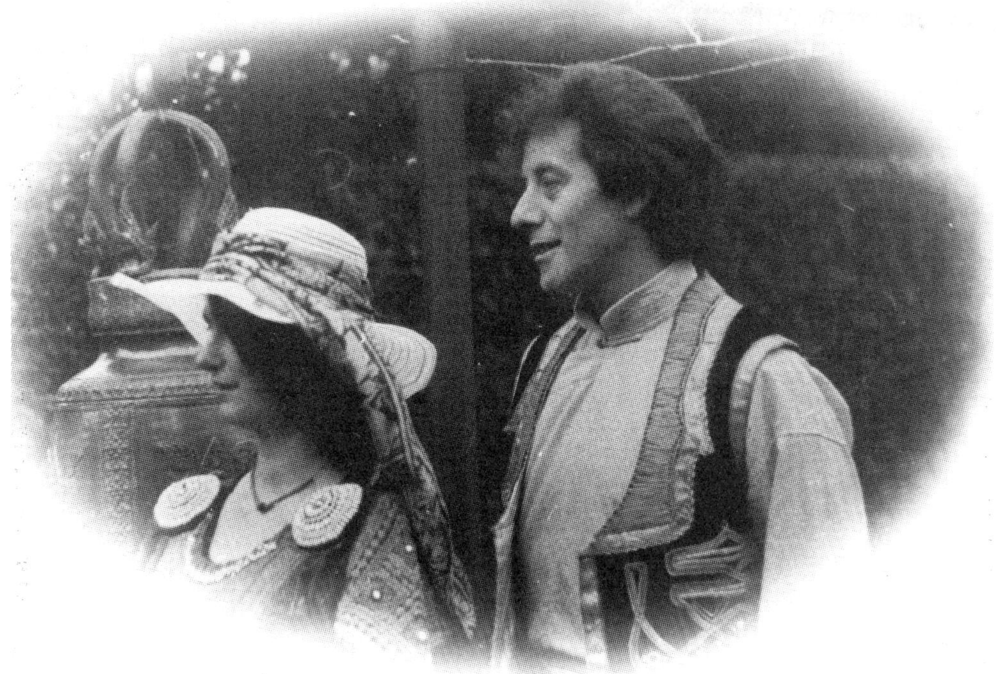

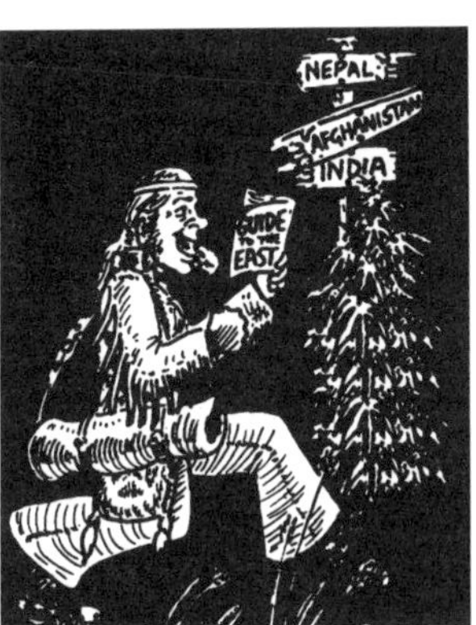

carpets or lounging on cushions. Then I got a call from the printer informing me that the first batch of comics would be arriving at nearby Paddington railway station. Bryan and I rushed off to pick them up.

When we got back to the party we opened up the parcel and there they were - Brainstorm Comix number one with their bright red covers. Bryan took one out and just looked at it in awe and wonderment. I passed a few copies around and a little while later everyone was reading them.

I republished the Chester trilogy in one volume, seven y6ears later on the 26th November 1982. Bryan came down to Alchemy, which had by then moved to larger premises a few doors up the road, to do a signing for both it and the first Luther Arkwright book which came out at the same time. The accompanying photo was taken then.

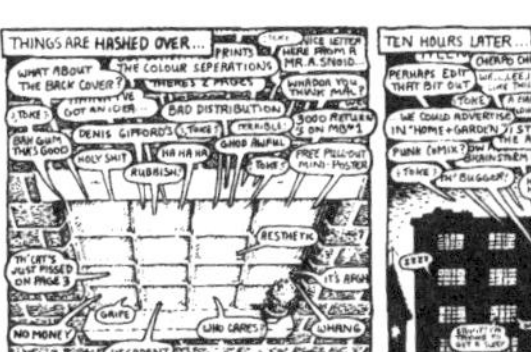

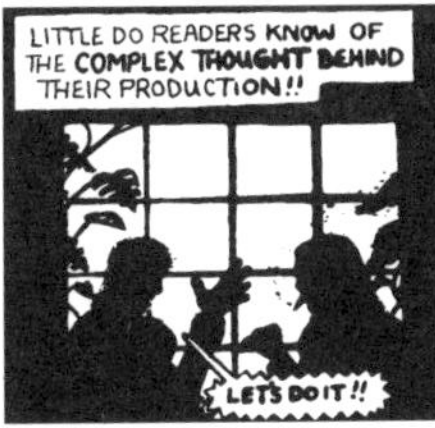

The three epic adventures of Chester P Hackenbush were a seminal work, an experiment in visual story-telling styles that encompasses many popular cultural influences. Chester's cerebral journeys into inner and outer space takes us along a mystical quest for spiritual unity. Like an alchemical text, it is riddled with subtle hidden references and allegorical situations that delight the adept and enlighten the apprentice.

I am pleased and proud to have made friends with Bryan and Chester all those years ago.

Lee Harris
Publisher

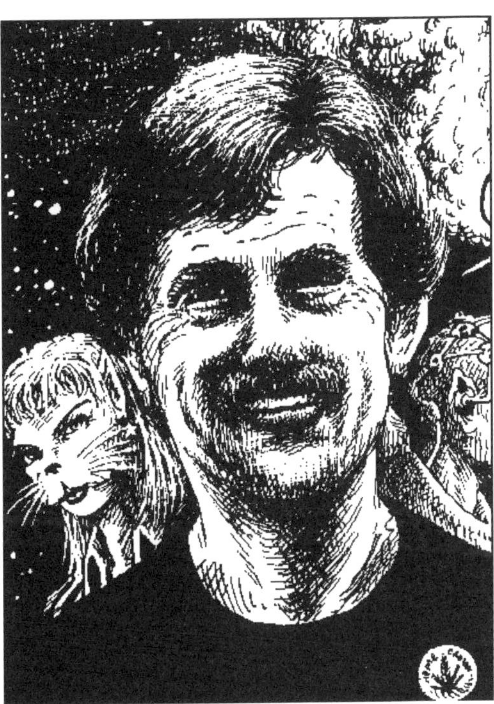

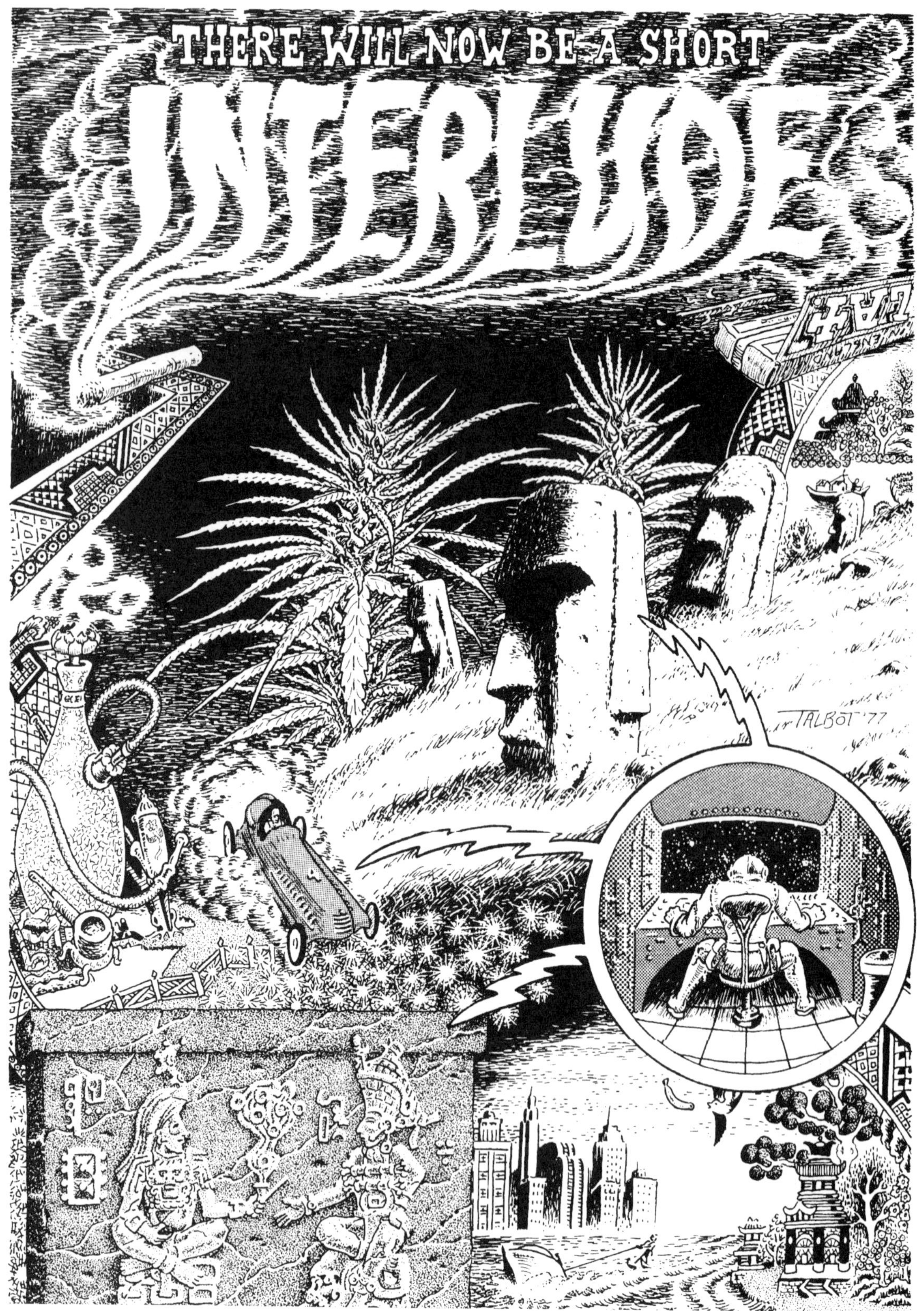
THERE WILL NOW BE A SHORT
INTERLUDE
TALBOT '77

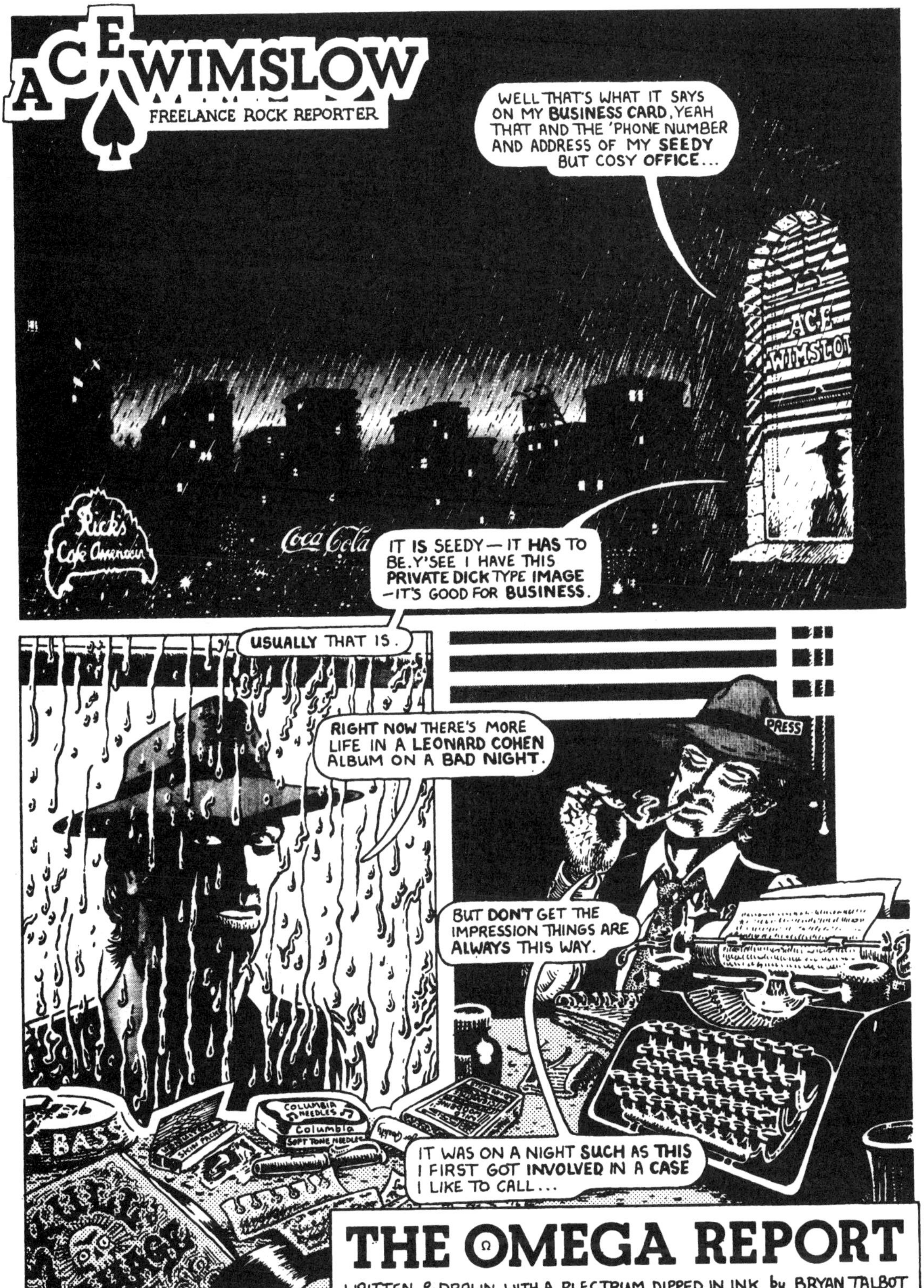

ACE WIMSLOW

FREELANCE ROCK REPORTER

WELL THAT'S WHAT IT SAYS ON MY BUSINESS CARD, YEAH THAT AND THE 'PHONE NUMBER AND ADDRESS OF MY SEEDY BUT COSY OFFICE...

ACE WIMSLOW

Rick's Café Americain

Coca-Cola

IT IS SEEDY — IT HAS TO BE. Y'SEE I HAVE THIS PRIVATE DICK TYPE IMAGE — IT'S GOOD FOR BUSINESS.

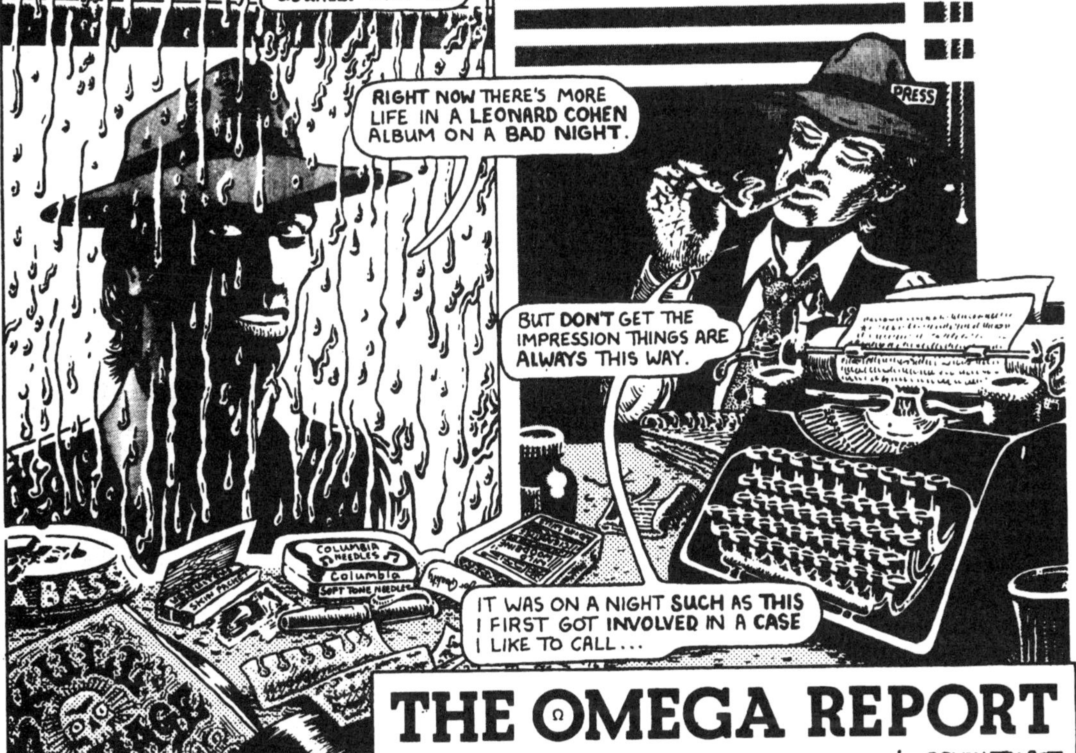

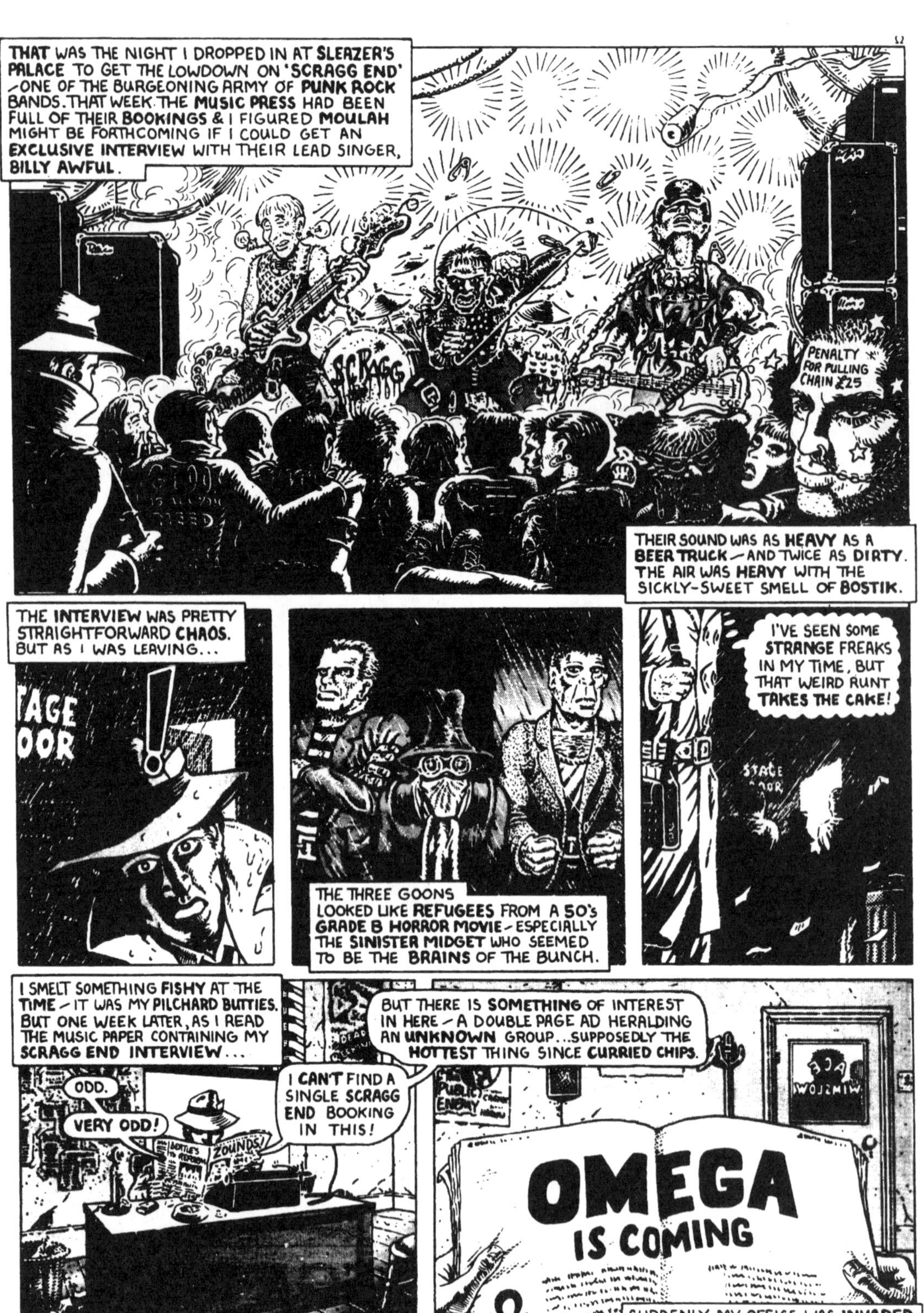
THAT WAS THE NIGHT I DROPPED IN AT SLEAZER'S PALACE TO GET THE LOWDOWN ON 'SCRAGG END' – ONE OF THE BURGEONING ARMY OF PUNK ROCK BANDS. THAT WEEK THE MUSIC PRESS HAD BEEN FULL OF THEIR BOOKINGS & I FIGURED MOULAH MIGHT BE FORTHCOMING IF I COULD GET AN EXCLUSIVE INTERVIEW WITH THEIR LEAD SINGER, BILLY AWFUL.
SCRAGG
PENALTY FOR PULLING CHAIN £25
THEIR SOUND WAS AS HEAVY AS A BEER TRUCK – AND TWICE AS DIRTY. THE AIR WAS HEAVY WITH THE SICKLY-SWEET SMELL OF BOSTIK.
THE INTERVIEW WAS PRETTY STRAIGHTFORWARD CHAOS. BUT AS I WAS LEAVING...
TAGE OOR
!
THE THREE GOONS LOOKED LIKE REFUGEES FROM A 50's GRADE B HORROR MOVIE – ESPECIALLY THE SINISTER MIDGET WHO SEEMED TO BE THE BRAINS OF THE BUNCH.
I'VE SEEN SOME STRANGE FREAKS IN MY TIME, BUT THAT WEIRD RUNT TAKES THE CAKE!
I SMELT SOMETHING FISHY AT THE TIME – IT WAS MY PILCHARD BUTTIES. BUT ONE WEEK LATER, AS I READ THE MUSIC PAPER CONTAINING MY SCRAGG END INTERVIEW...
ODD.
VERY ODD!
ZOUNDS!
I CAN'T FIND A SINGLE SCRAGG END BOOKING IN THIS!
BUT THERE IS SOMETHING OF INTEREST IN HERE – A DOUBLE PAGE AD HERALDING AN UNKNOWN GROUP... SUPPOSEDLY THE HOTTEST THING SINCE CURRIED CHIPS.
PUBLIC ENEMY
OMEGA IS COMING
Ω
SUDDENLY MY OFFICE WAS INVADED.

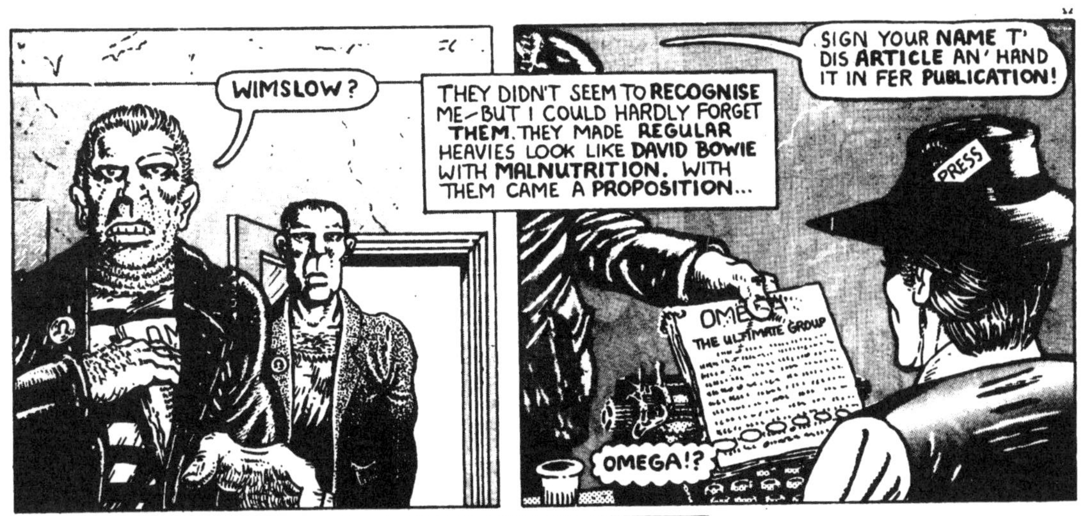
WIMSLOW?
THEY DIDN'T SEEM TO RECOGNISE ME—BUT I COULD HARDLY FORGET THEM. THEY MADE REGULAR HEAVIES LOOK LIKE DAVID BOWIE WITH MALNUTRITION. WITH THEM CAME A PROPOSITION...
SIGN YOUR NAME T' DIS ARTICLE AN' HAND IT IN FER PUBLICATION!
PRESS
OMEGA
THE ULTIMATE GROUP
OMEGA!?

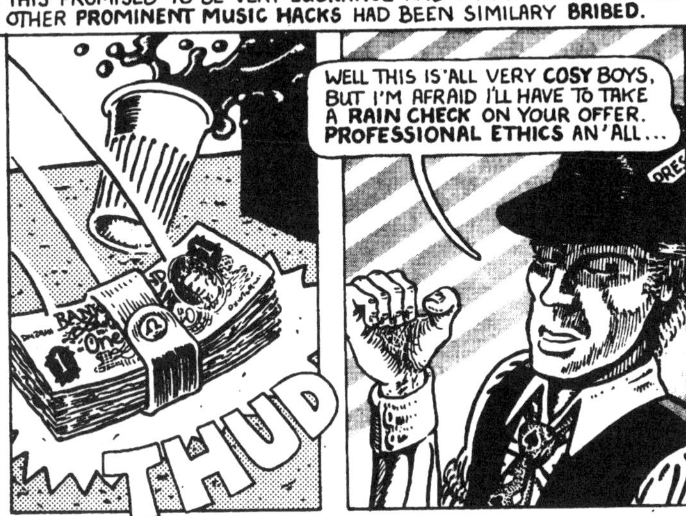
THIS PROMISED TO BE VERY LUCRATIVE AND I WAS INFORMED THAT OTHER PROMINENT MUSIC HACKS HAD BEEN SIMILARY BRIBED.
THUD
WELL THIS IS ALL VERY COSY BOYS, BUT I'M AFRAID I'LL HAVE TO TAKE A RAIN CHECK ON YOUR OFFER. PROFESSIONAL ETHICS AN' ALL...

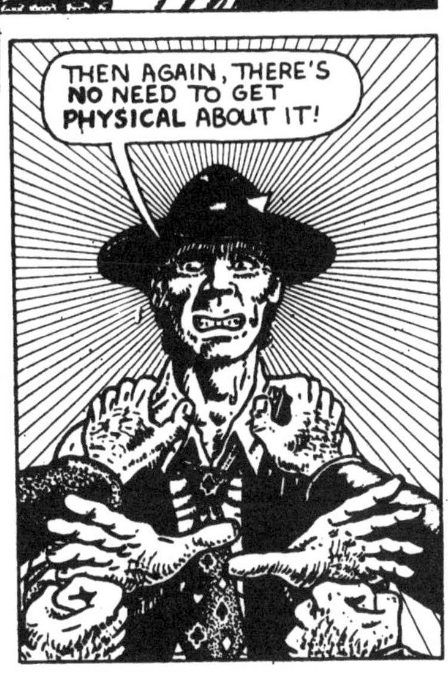
THEN AGAIN, THERE'S NO NEED TO GET PHYSICAL ABOUT IT!

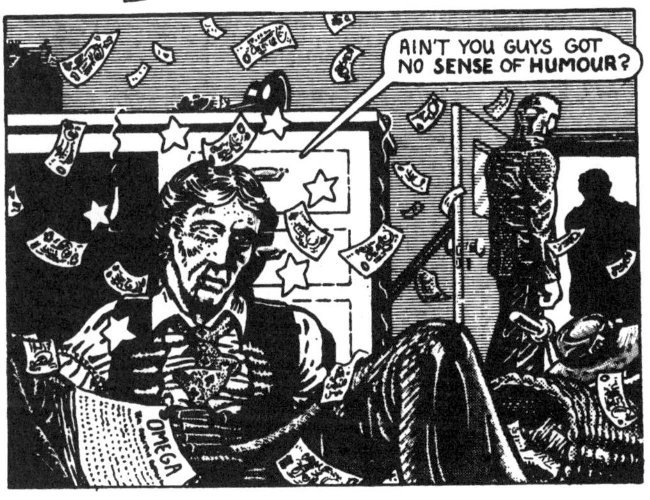
AIN'T YOU GUYS GOT NO SENSE OF HUMOUR?
OMEGA

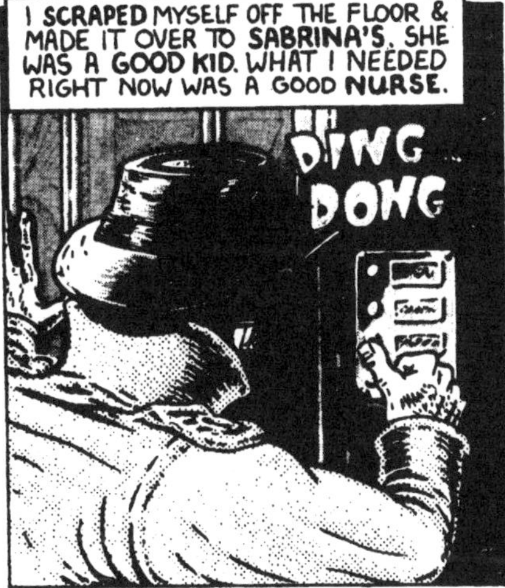
I SCRAPED MYSELF OFF THE FLOOR & MADE IT OVER TO SABRINA'S. SHE WAS A GOOD KID. WHAT I NEEDED RIGHT NOW WAS A GOOD NURSE.
DING DONG

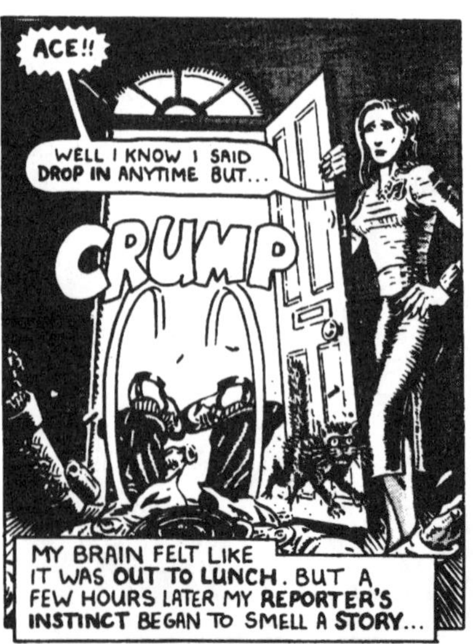
ACE!!
WELL I KNOW I SAID DROP IN ANYTIME BUT...
CRUMP
MY BRAIN FELT LIKE IT WAS OUT TO LUNCH. BUT A FEW HOURS LATER MY REPORTER'S INSTINCT BEGAN TO SMELL A STORY...

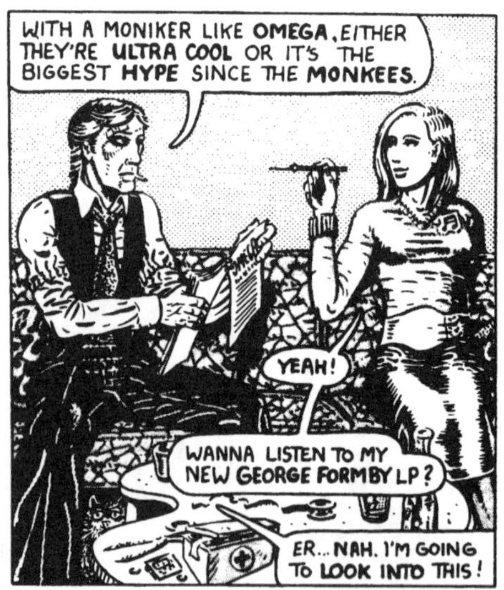
WITH A MONIKER LIKE OMEGA, EITHER THEY'RE ULTRA COOL OR IT'S THE BIGGEST HYPE SINCE THE MONKEES.
YEAH!
WANNA LISTEN TO MY NEW GEORGE FORMBY LP?
ER... NAH. I'M GOING TO LOOK INTO THIS!

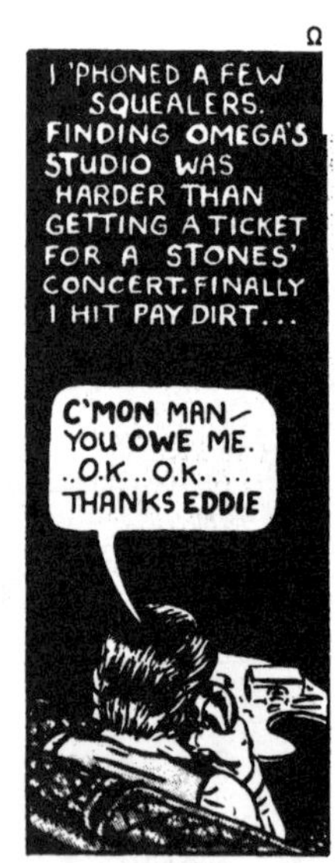
I 'PHONED A FEW SQUEALERS. FINDING OMEGA'S STUDIO WAS HARDER THAN GETTING A TICKET FOR A STONES' CONCERT. FINALLY I HIT PAY DIRT...
C'MON MAN- YOU OWE ME. ..O.K...O.K..... THANKS EDDIE

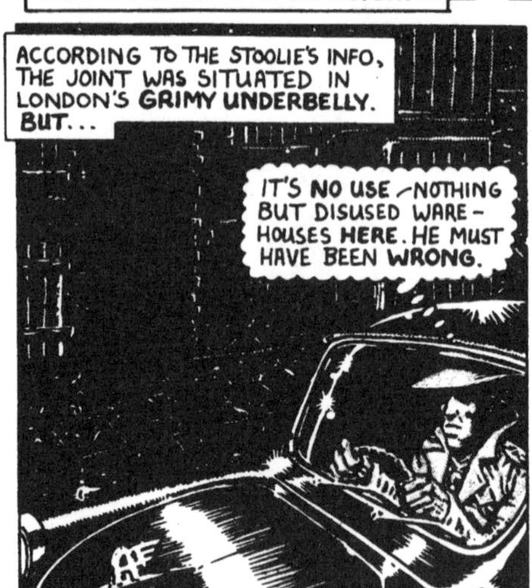
ACCORDING TO THE STOOLIE'S INFO, THE JOINT WAS SITUATED IN LONDON'S GRIMY UNDERBELLY. BUT...
IT'S NO USE - NOTHING BUT DISUSED WARE-HOUSES HERE. HE MUST HAVE BEEN WRONG.

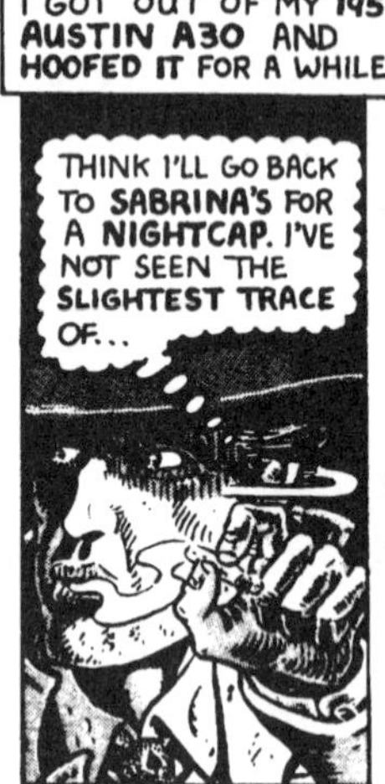
I GOT OUT OF MY 1952 AUSTIN A30 AND HOOFED IT FOR A WHILE.
THINK I'LL GO BACK TO SABRINA'S FOR A NIGHTCAP. I'VE NOT SEEN THE SLIGHTEST TRACE OF...

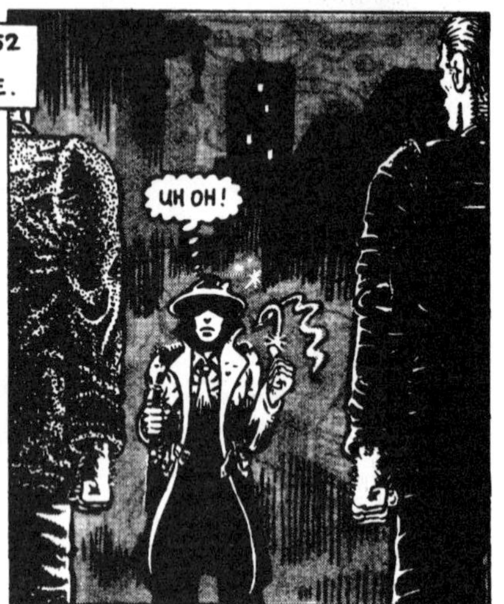
UH OH!

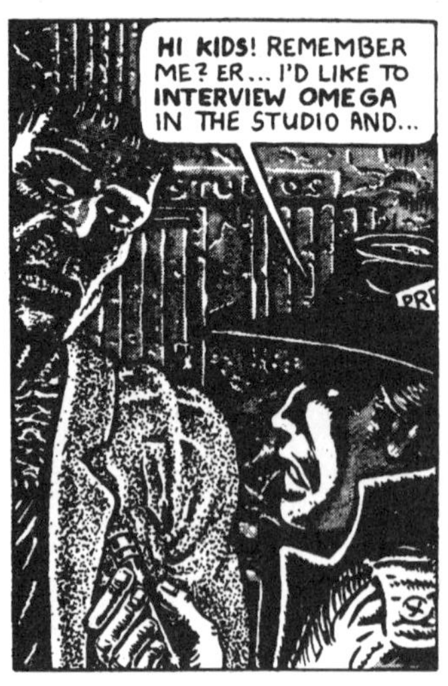
HI KIDS! REMEMBER ME? ER... I'D LIKE TO INTERVIEW OMEGA IN THE STUDIO AND...

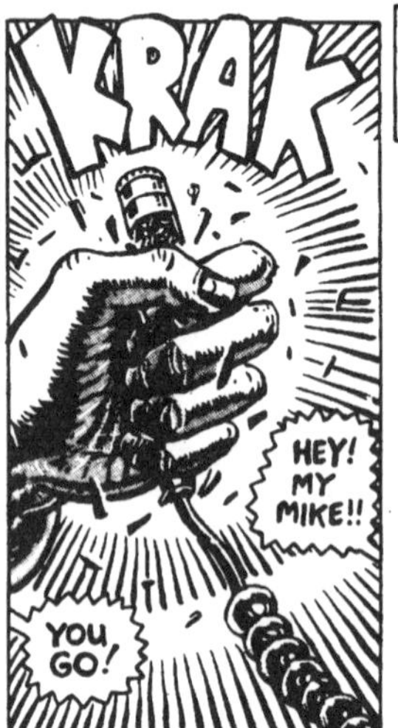
KRAK
HEY! MY MIKE!!
YOU GO!

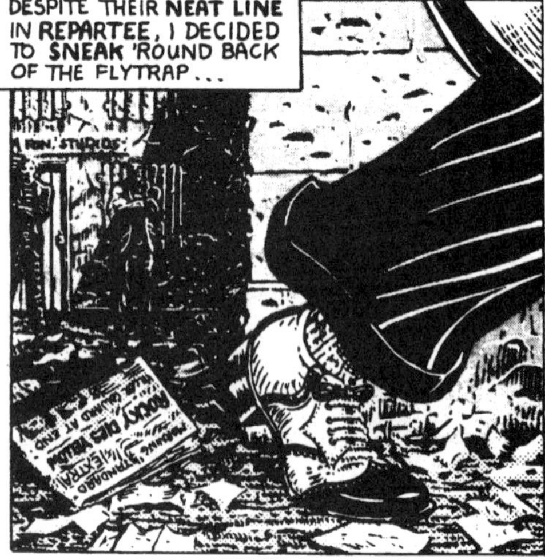
DESPITE THEIR NEAT LINE IN REPARTEE, I DECIDED TO SNEAK 'ROUND BACK OF THE FLYTRAP...

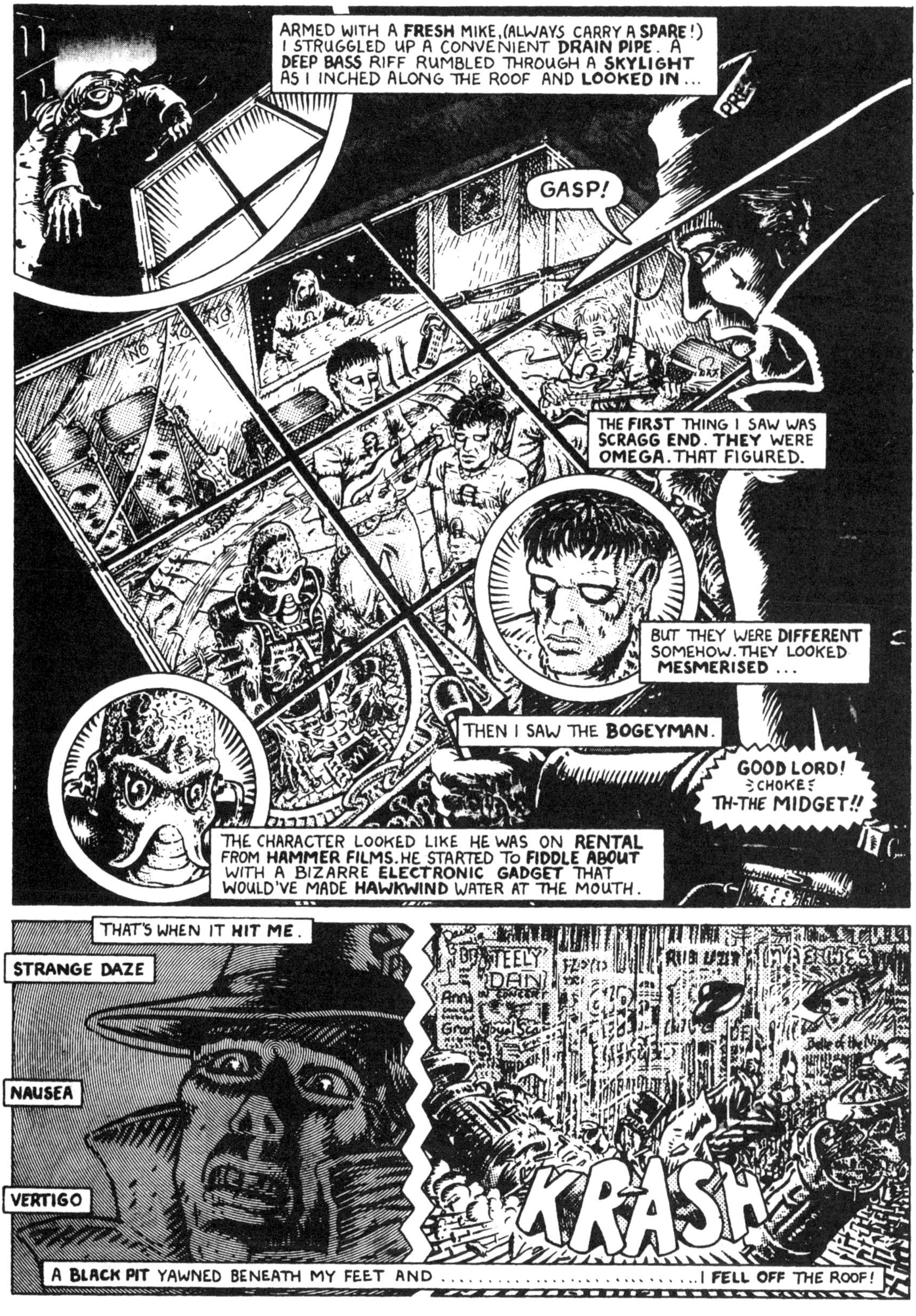

ARMED WITH A **FRESH** MIKE, (ALWAYS CARRY A **SPARE**!) I STRUGGLED UP A CONVENIENT **DRAIN PIPE**. A **DEEP BASS** RIFF RUMBLED THROUGH A **SKYLIGHT** AS I INCHED ALONG THE ROOF AND **LOOKED IN**...

GASP!

THE **FIRST** THING I SAW WAS **SCRAGG END**. **THEY** WERE **OMEGA**. THAT FIGURED.

BUT THEY WERE **DIFFERENT** SOMEHOW. THEY LOOKED **MESMERISED**...

THEN I SAW THE **BOGEYMAN**.

GOOD LORD! CHOKE TH-THE MIDGET!!

THE CHARACTER LOOKED LIKE HE WAS ON **RENTAL** FROM **HAMMER FILMS**. HE STARTED TO **FIDDLE ABOUT** WITH A BIZARRE **ELECTRONIC GADGET** THAT WOULD'VE MADE **HAWKWIND** WATER AT THE MOUTH.

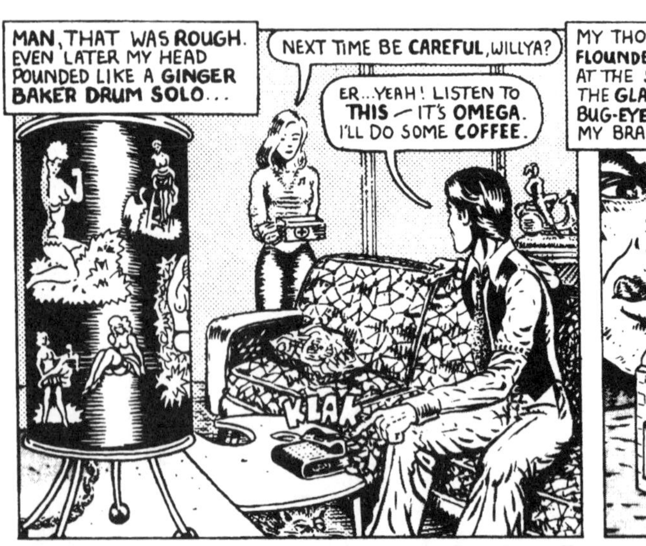
MAN, THAT WAS ROUGH. EVEN LATER MY HEAD POUNDED LIKE A GINGER BAKER DRUM SOLO...
NEXT TIME BE CAREFUL, WILLYA?
ER...YEAH! LISTEN TO THIS — IT'S OMEGA. I'LL DO SOME COFFEE.
KLAK

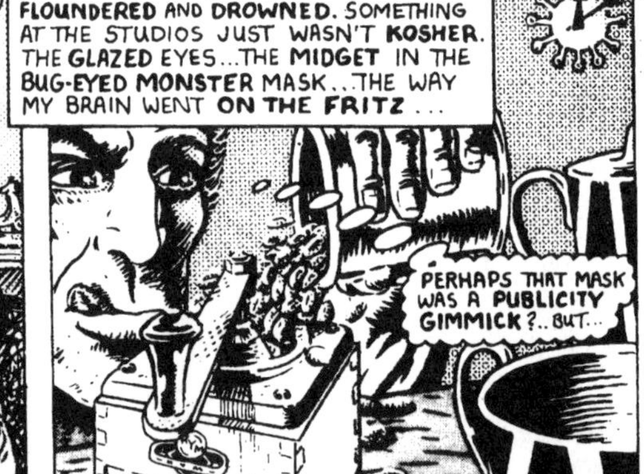
MY THOUGHTS WERE SWIMMING. THEY FLOUNDERED AND DROWNED. SOMETHING AT THE STUDIOS JUST WASN'T KOSHER. THE GLAZED EYES...THE MIDGET IN THE BUG-EYED MONSTER MASK...THE WAY MY BRAIN WENT ON THE FRITZ...
PERHAPS THAT MASK WAS A PUBLICITY GIMMICK?..BUT...
I SWITCHED OFF MY MIND AND SET ABOUT CONCOCTING MY PERSONAL BLEND OF COSTA RICAN AND JAVA.

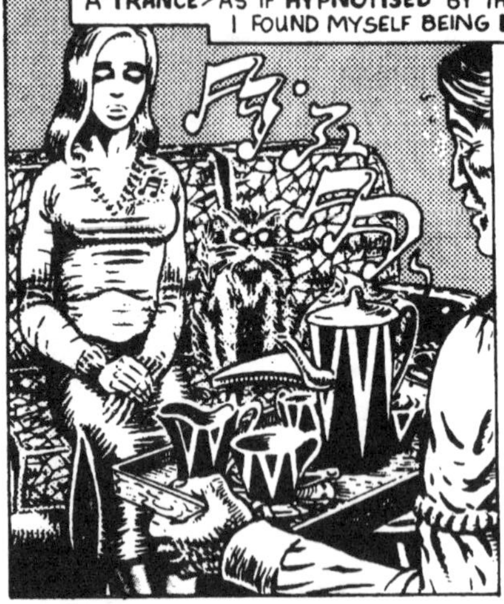
I RE-ENTERED SABRINA'S RECONSTRUCTION 1950's LIVINGROOM TO FIND HER AND IGGY THE CAT IN A TRANCE — AS IF HYPNOTISED BY THE MUSIC. I FOUND MYSELF BEING DRAWN IN...

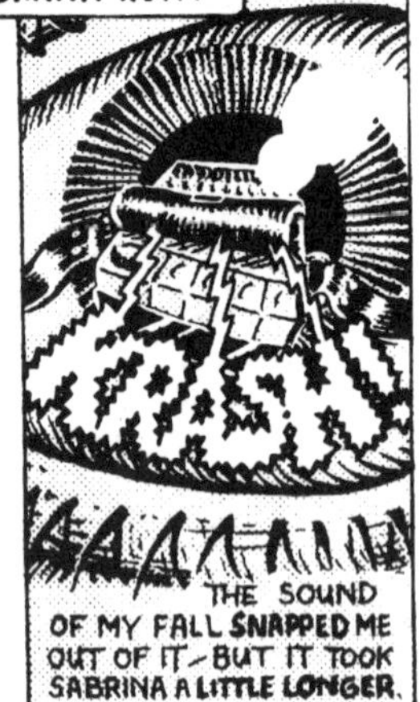
CRASH
AAAAAA
THE SOUND OF MY FALL SNAPPED ME OUT OF IT — BUT IT TOOK SABRINA A LITTLE LONGER.

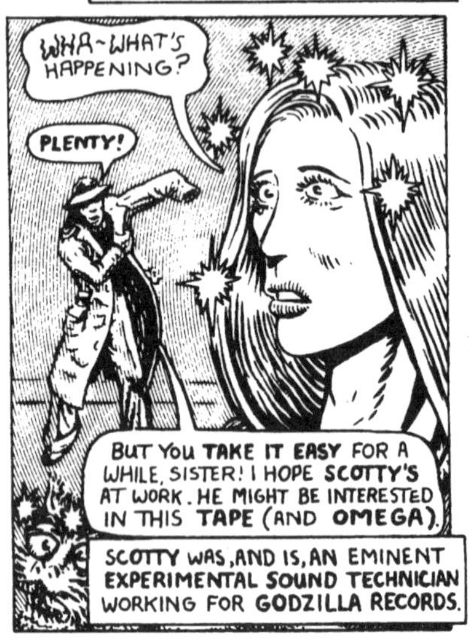
WHA-WHAT'S HAPPENING?
PLENTY!
BUT YOU TAKE IT EASY FOR A WHILE, SISTER! I HOPE SCOTTY'S AT WORK. HE MIGHT BE INTERESTED IN THIS TAPE (AND OMEGA).
SCOTTY WAS, AND IS, AN EMINENT EXPERIMENTAL SOUND TECHNICIAN WORKING FOR GODZILLA RECORDS.

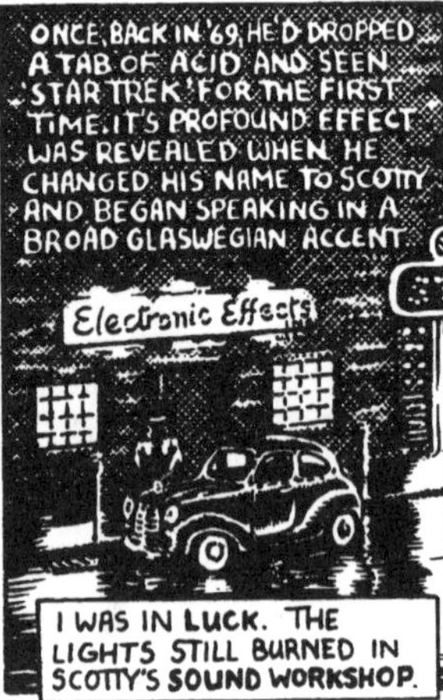
ONCE, BACK IN '69, HE'D DROPPED A TAB OF ACID AND SEEN 'STAR TREK' FOR THE FIRST TIME. IT'S PROFOUND EFFECT WAS REVEALED WHEN HE CHANGED HIS NAME TO SCOTTY AND BEGAN SPEAKING IN A BROAD GLASWEGIAN ACCENT.
Electronic Effects
I WAS IN LUCK. THE LIGHTS STILL BURNED IN SCOTTY'S SOUND WORKSHOP.

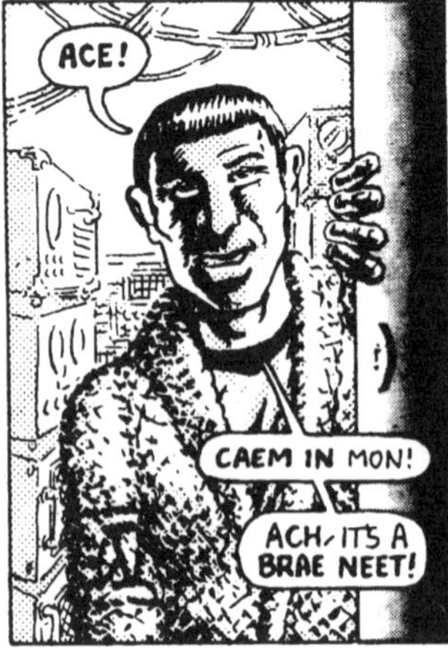
ACE!
CAEM IN MON!
ACH, IT'S A BRAE NEET!

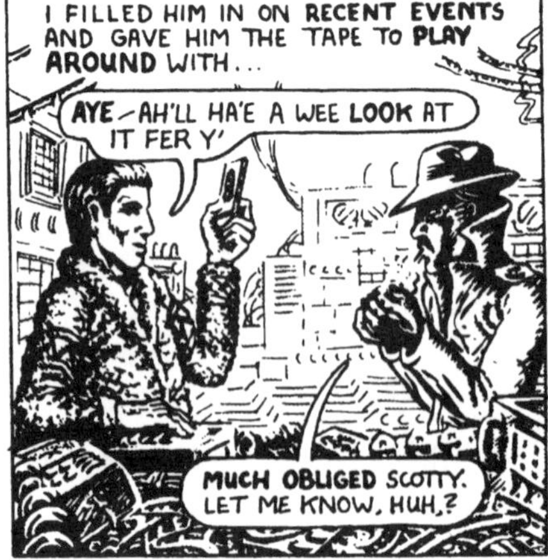
I FILLED HIM IN ON RECENT EVENTS AND GAVE HIM THE TAPE TO PLAY AROUND WITH...
AYE — AH'LL HA'E A WEE LOOK AT IT FER Y'
MUCH OBLIGED SCOTTY. LET ME KNOW, HUH,?

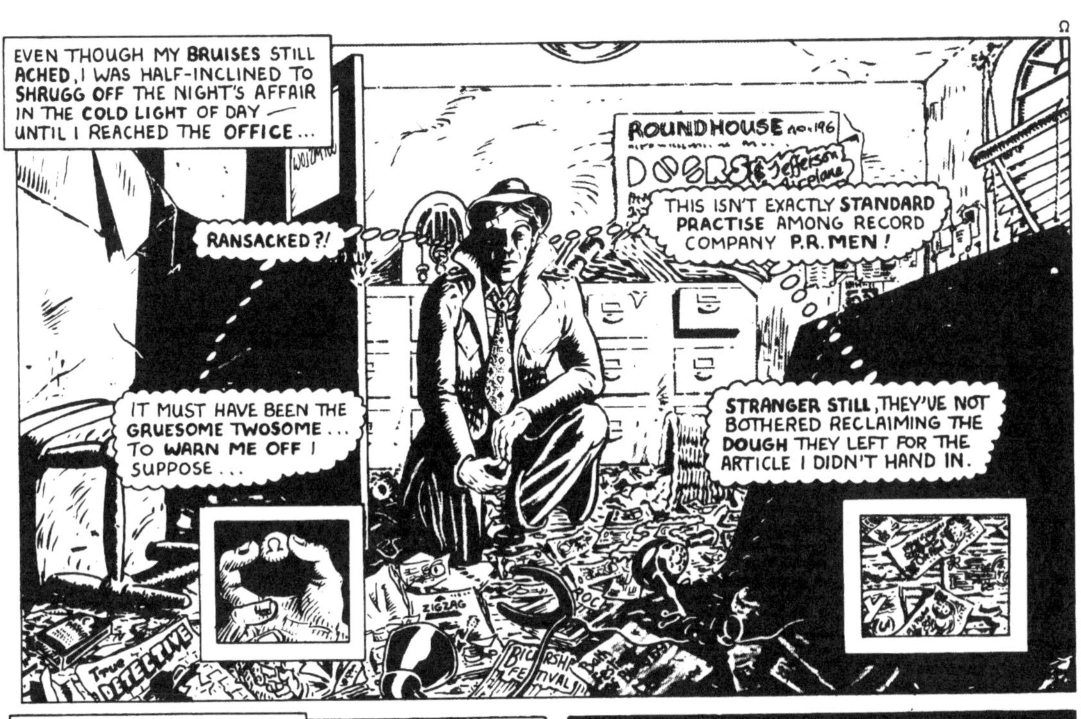
EVEN THOUGH MY BRUISES STILL ACHED, I WAS HALF-INCLINED TO SHRUGG OFF THE NIGHT'S AFFAIR IN THE COLD LIGHT OF DAY — UNTIL I REACHED THE OFFICE...
ROUNDHOUSE no. 196
DOORS & Jefferson Airplane
RANSACKED?!
THIS ISN'T EXACTLY STANDARD PRACTISE AMONG RECORD COMPANY P.R. MEN!
IT MUST HAVE BEEN THE GRUESOME TWOSOME... TO WARN ME OFF I SUPPOSE...
STRANGER STILL, THEY'VE NOT BOTHERED RECLAIMING THE DOUGH THEY LEFT FOR THE ARTICLE I DIDN'T HAND IN.
ZIGZAG
True DETECTIVE
BICKERSHAW FESTIVAL

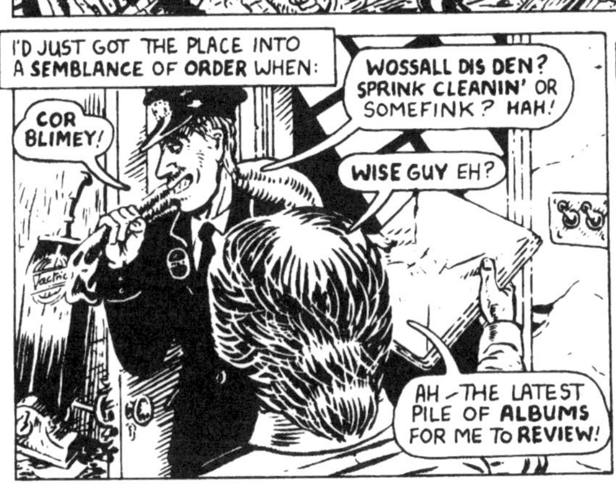
I'D JUST GOT THE PLACE INTO A SEMBLANCE OF ORDER WHEN:
COR BLIMEY!
WOSSALL DIS DEN? SPRINK CLEANIN' OR SOMEFINK? HAH!
WISE GUY EH?
AH - THE LATEST PILE OF ALBUMS FOR ME TO REVIEW!

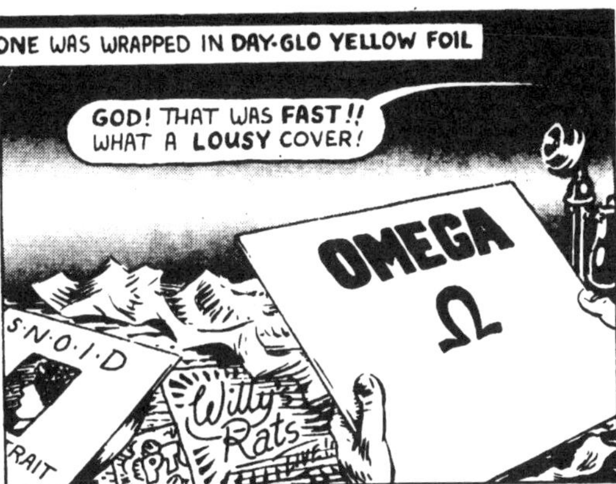
ONE WAS WRAPPED IN DAY-GLO YELLOW FOIL
GOD! THAT WAS FAST!! WHAT A LOUSY COVER!
OMEGA
Ω
S·N·O·I·D
Willy Rats

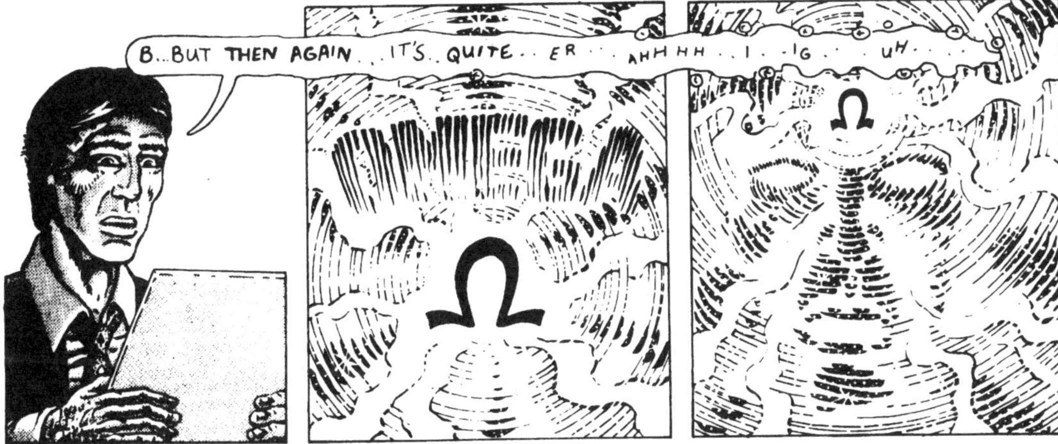
B... BUT THEN AGAIN... IT'S... QUITE... ER... AHHHH... I... G... UH...

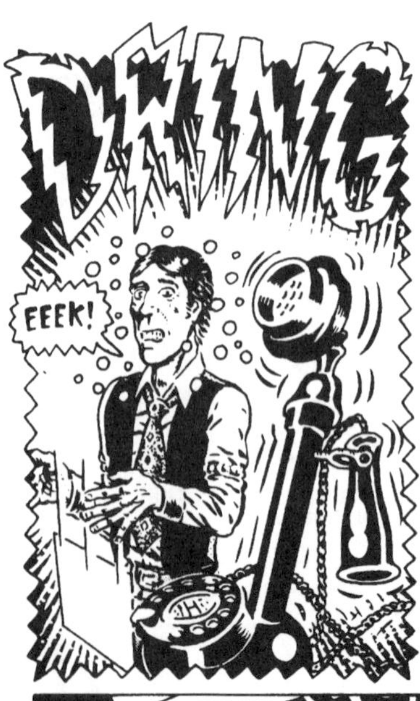
DRING
EEEK!

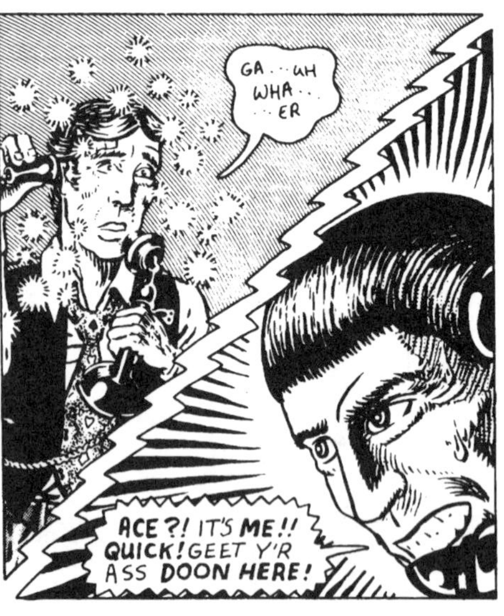
GA... UH WHA... ...ER
ACE?! IT'S ME!! QUICK! GEET Y'R ASS DOON HERE!

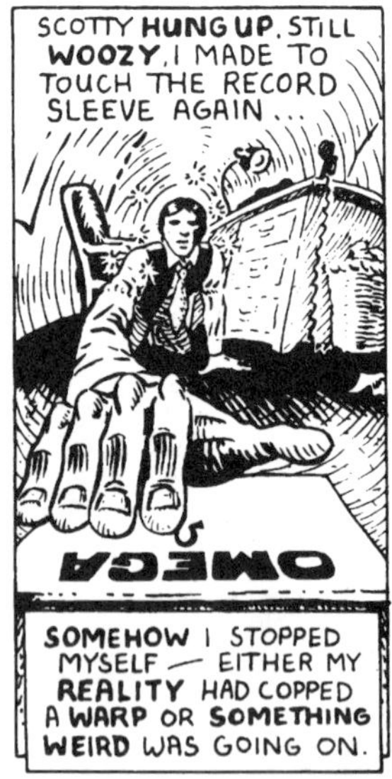
SCOTTY HUNG UP, STILL WOOZY, I MADE TO TOUCH THE RECORD SLEEVE AGAIN...
SOMEHOW I STOPPED MYSELF — EITHER MY REALITY HAD COPPED A WARP OR SOMETHING WEIRD WAS GOING ON.

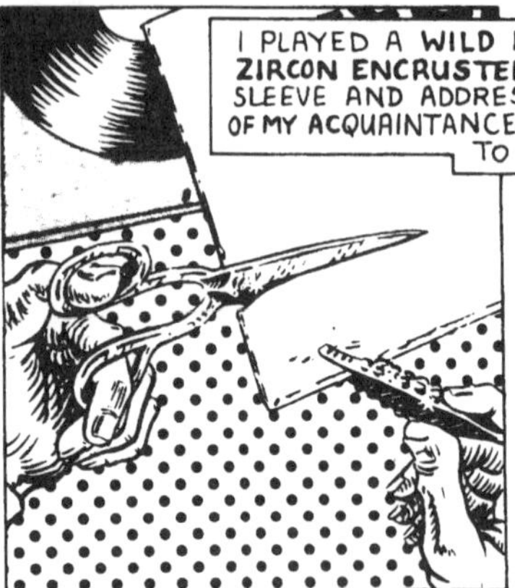
I PLAYED A WILD HUNCH. WITH THE AID OF MY SCISSORS AND ZIRCON ENCRUSTED TWEEZERS, I PACKAGED A SECTION OF THE SLEEVE AND ADDRESSED IT TO A CERTAIN PSYCHEDELIC ALCHEMIST OF MY ACQUAINTANCE. ON THE WAY OVER TO SCOTTY'S I FED IT TO A DOUBLE BARRELLED VICTORIAN PILLARBOX.

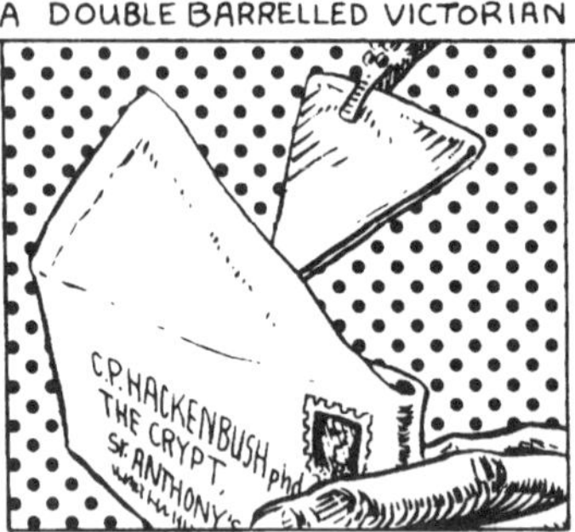
C.P. HACKENBUSH phd
THE CRYPT
ST ANTHONY'S

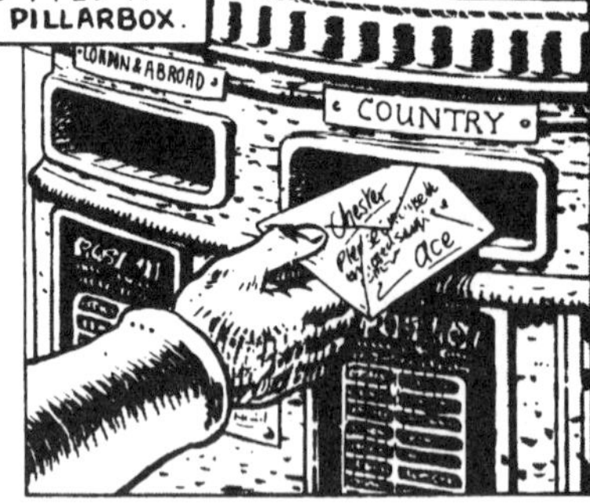
LONDON & ABROAD
COUNTRY

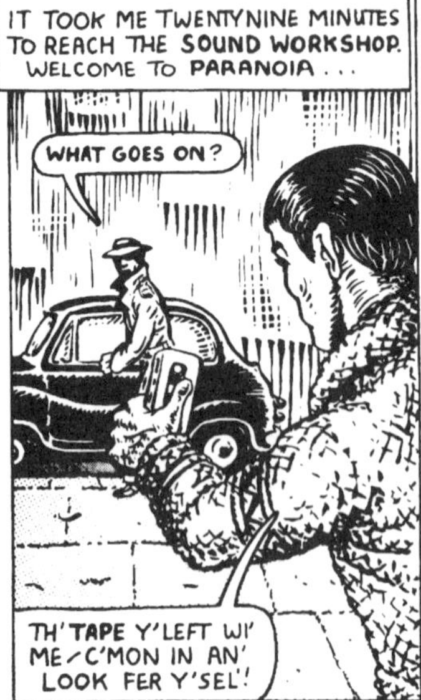
IT TOOK ME TWENTYNINE MINUTES TO REACH THE SOUND WORKSHOP. WELCOME TO PARANOIA...
WHAT GOES ON?
TH' TAPE Y'LEFT WI' ME — C'MON IN AN' LOOK FER Y'SEL'!

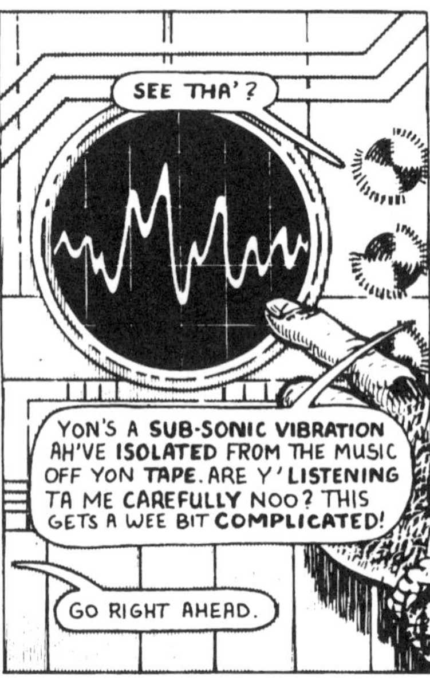
SEE THA'?
YON'S A SUB-SONIC VIBRATION AH'VE ISOLATED FROM THE MUSIC OFF YON TAPE. ARE Y' LISTENING TA ME CAREFULLY NOO? THIS GETS A WEE BIT COMPLICATED!
GO RIGHT AHEAD.

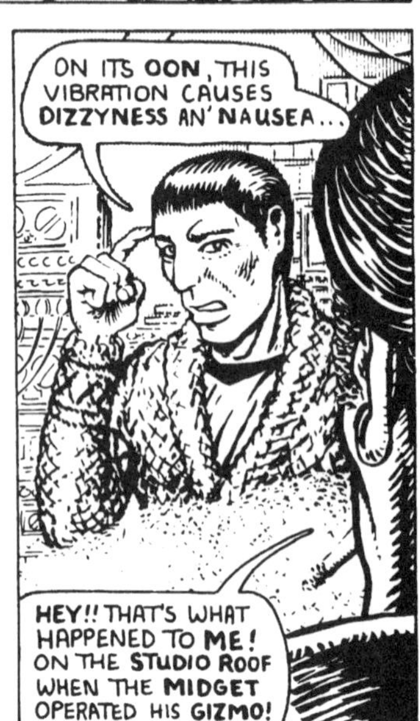
ON ITS OON, THIS VIBRATION CAUSES DIZZYNESS AN' NAUSEA...
HEY!! THAT'S WHAT HAPPENED TO ME! ON THE STUDIO ROOF WHEN THE MIDGET OPERATED HIS GIZMO!

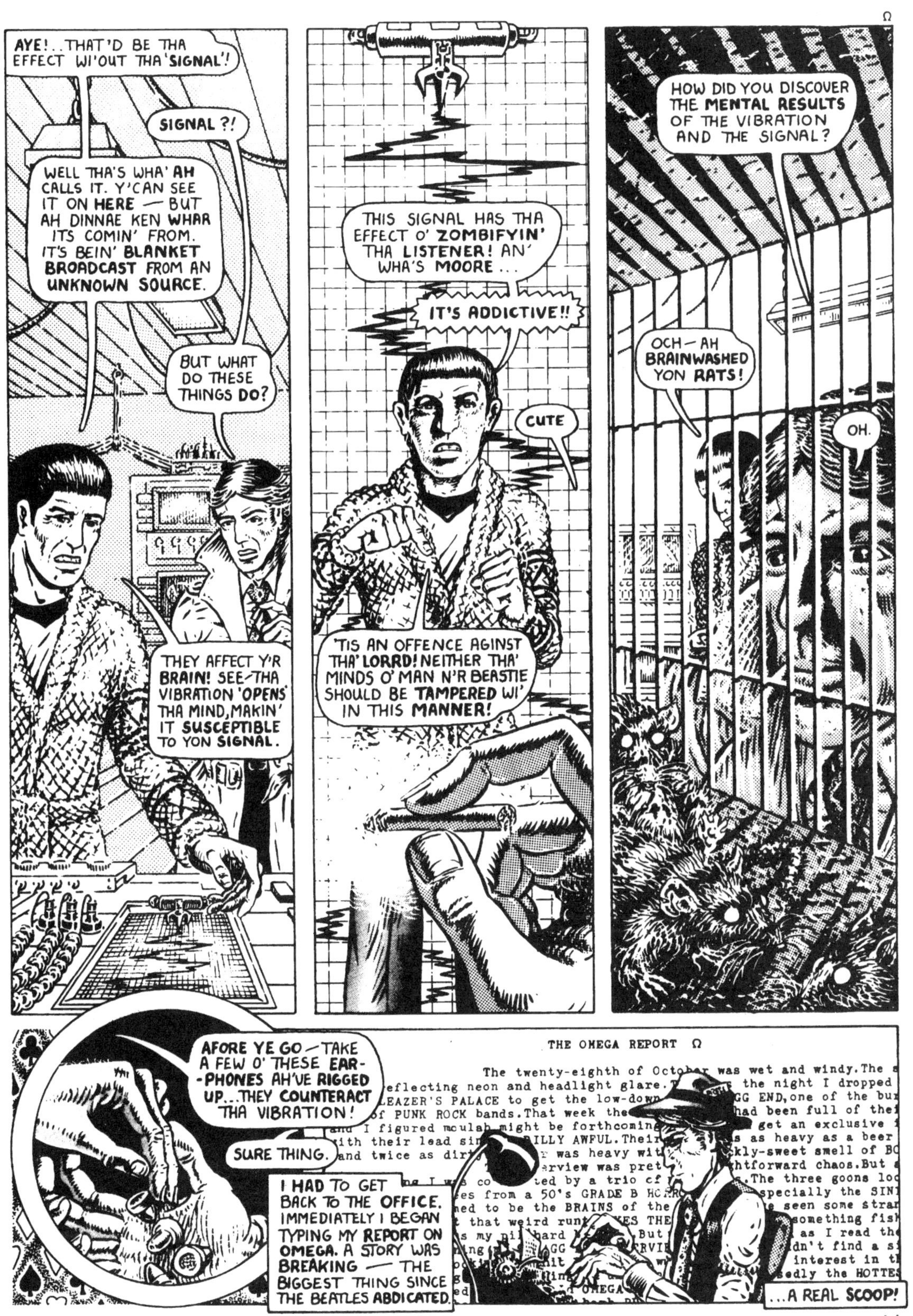
Ω
AYE!..THAT'D BE THA EFFECT WI'OUT THA 'SIGNAL'!
SIGNAL ?!
WELL THA'S WHA' AH CALLS IT. Y'CAN SEE IT ON HERE — BUT AH DINNAE KEN WHAR ITS COMIN' FROM. IT'S BEIN' BLANKET BROADCAST FROM AN UNKNOWN SOURCE.
BUT WHAT DO THESE THINGS DO?
THEY AFFECT Y'R BRAIN! SEE-THA VIBRATION 'OPENS' THA MIND, MAKIN' IT SUSCEPTIBLE TO YON SIGNAL.
THIS SIGNAL HAS THA EFFECT O' ZOMBIFYIN' THA LISTENER! AN' WHA'S MOORE...
IT'S ADDICTIVE!!
CUTE
'TIS AN OFFENCE AGINST THA' LORRD! NEITHER THA' MINDS O' MAN N'R BEASTIE SHOULD BE TAMPERED WI' IN THIS MANNER!
HOW DID YOU DISCOVER THE MENTAL RESULTS OF THE VIBRATION AND THE SIGNAL?
OCH-AH BRAINWASHED YON RATS!
OH.
AFORE YE GO-TAKE A FEW O' THESE EAR-PHONES AH'VE RIGGED UP...THEY COUNTERACT THA VIBRATION!
SURE THING.
I HAD TO GET BACK TO THE OFFICE. IMMEDIATELY I BEGAN TYPING MY REPORT ON OMEGA. A STORY WAS BREAKING — THE BIGGEST THING SINCE THE BEATLES ABDICATED.
THE OMEGA REPORT Ω
The twenty-eighth of October was wet and windy.
...A REAL SCOOP!

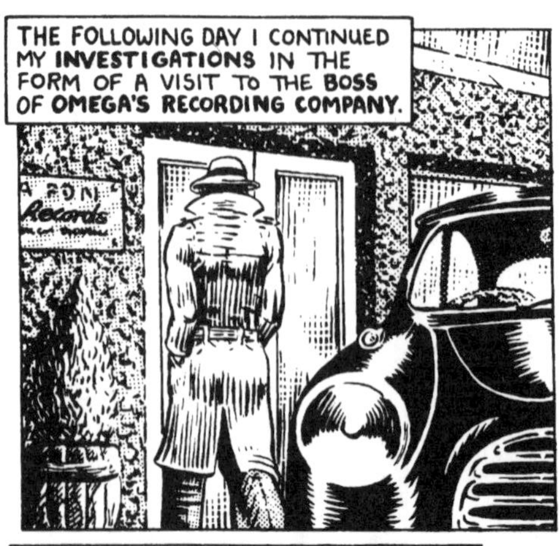
THE FOLLOWING DAY I CONTINUED MY INVESTIGATIONS IN THE FORM OF A VISIT TO THE BOSS OF OMEGA'S RECORDING COMPANY.

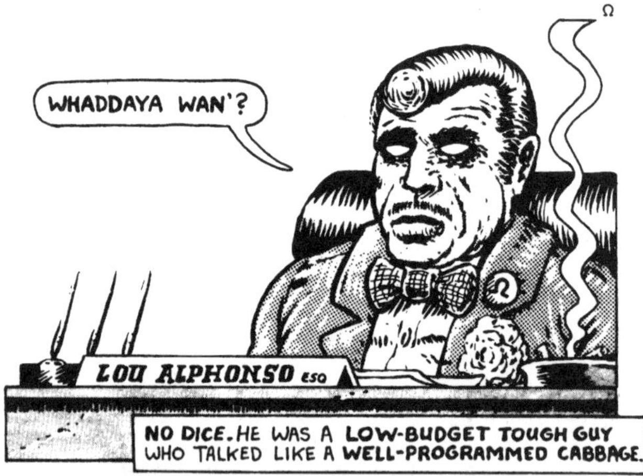
WHADDAYA WAN'?
LOU ALPHONSO ESQ
NO DICE. HE WAS A LOW-BUDGET TOUGH GUY WHO TALKED LIKE A WELL-PROGRAMMED CABBAGE.

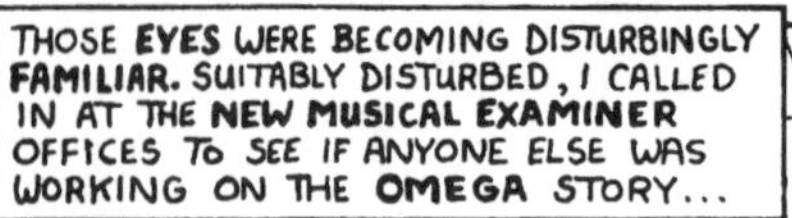
THOSE EYES WERE BECOMING DISTURBINGLY FAMILIAR. SUITABLY DISTURBED, I CALLED IN AT THE NEW MUSICAL EXAMINER OFFICES TO SEE IF ANYONE ELSE WAS WORKING ON THE OMEGA STORY...

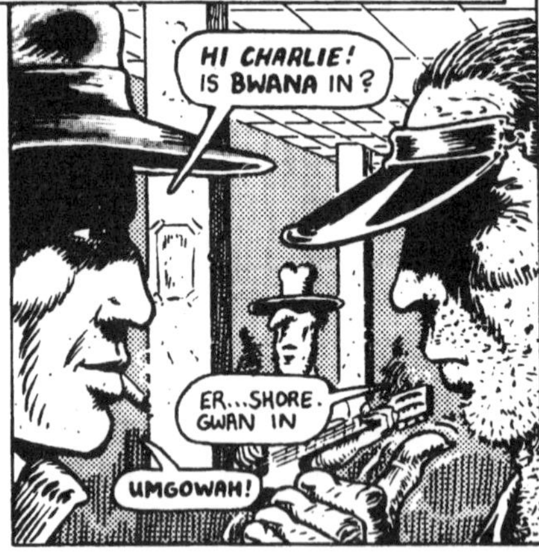
HI CHARLIE! IS BWANA IN?
ER...SHORE. GWAN IN
UMGOWAH!

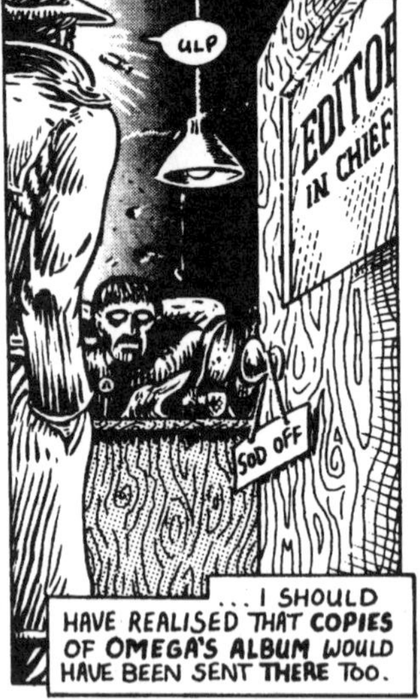
ULP
EDITOR IN CHIEF
SOD OFF
...I SHOULD HAVE REALISED THAT COPIES OF OMEGA'S ALBUM WOULD HAVE BEEN SENT THERE TOO.

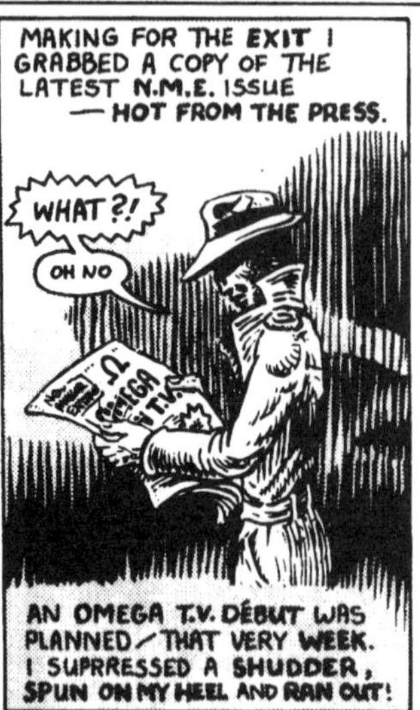
MAKING FOR THE EXIT I GRABBED A COPY OF THE LATEST N.M.E. ISSUE — HOT FROM THE PRESS.
WHAT?!
OH NO
AN OMEGA T.V. DÉBUT WAS PLANNED — THAT VERY WEEK. I SUPRRESSED A SHUDDER, SPUN ON MY HEEL AND RAN OUT!

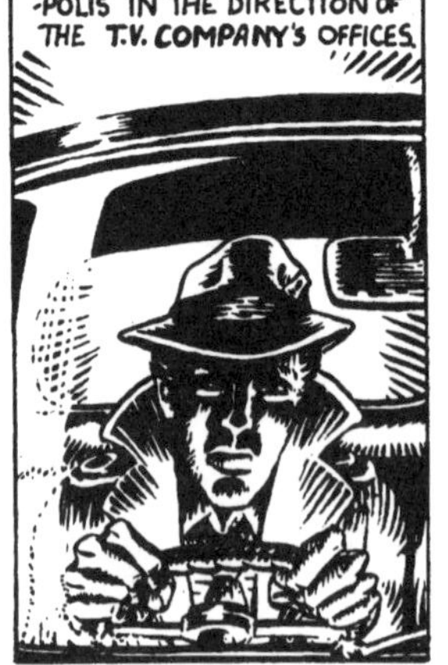
HENDRIX'S 'HOUSE BURNING DOWN' RANG OUT OF THE CAR STEREO AS MY AUSTIN A30 — 'THE FLYING FART' — SPED THROUGH THE METRO-POLIS IN THE DIRECTION OF THE T.V. COMPANY'S OFFICES.

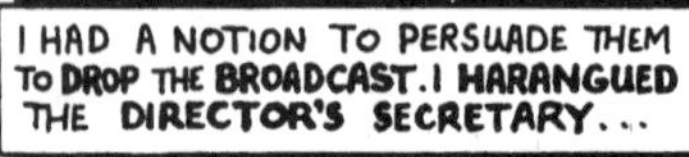
I HAD A NOTION TO PERSUADE THEM TO DROP THE BROADCAST. I HARANGUED THE DIRECTOR'S SECRETARY...

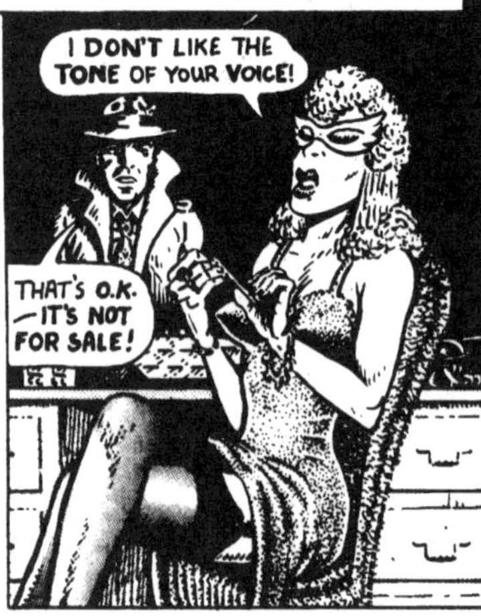
I DON'T LIKE THE TONE OF YOUR VOICE!
THAT'S O.K. — IT'S NOT FOR SALE!

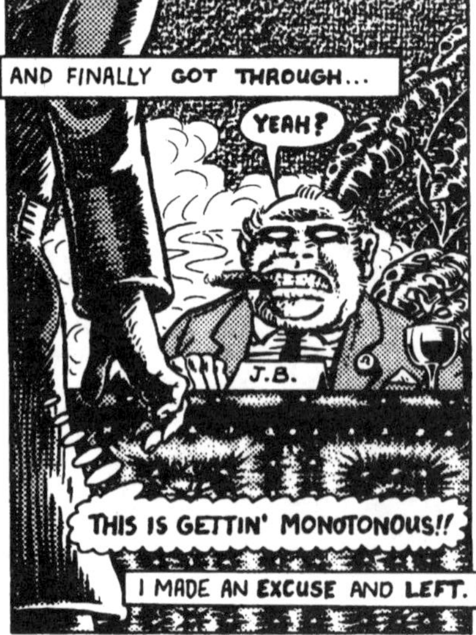
AND FINALLY GOT THROUGH...
YEAH?
J.B.
THIS IS GETTIN' MONOTONOUS!!
I MADE AN EXCUSE AND LEFT.

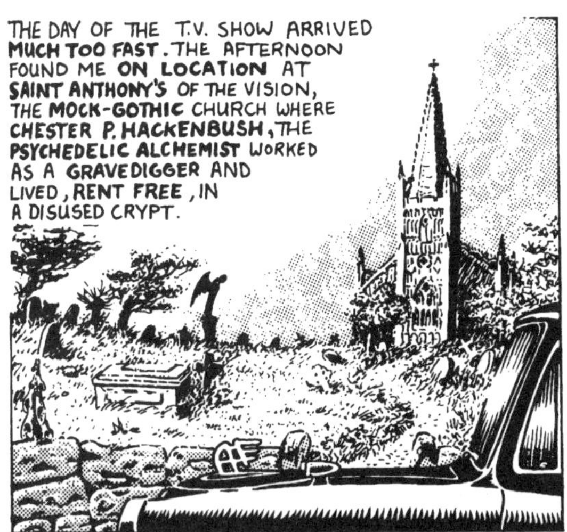
THE DAY OF THE T.V. SHOW ARRIVED MUCH TOO FAST. THE AFTERNOON FOUND ME ON LOCATION AT SAINT ANTHONY'S OF THE VISION, THE MOCK-GOTHIC CHURCH WHERE CHESTER P. HACKENBUSH, THE PSYCHEDELIC ALCHEMIST WORKED AS A GRAVEDIGGER AND LIVED, RENT FREE, IN A DISUSED CRYPT.

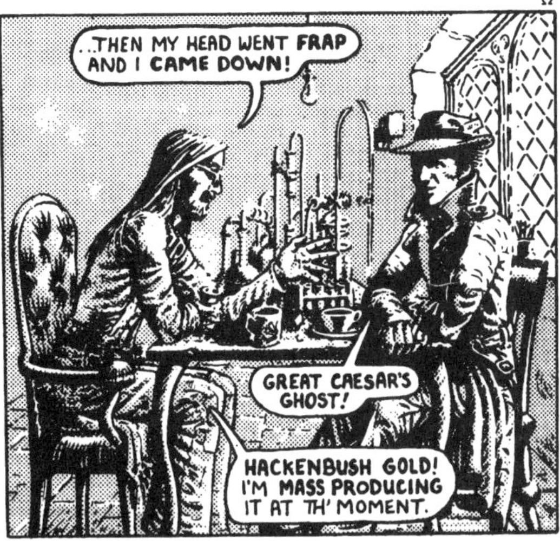
..THEN MY HEAD WENT FRAP AND I CAME DOWN!
GREAT CAESAR'S GHOST!
HACKENBUSH GOLD! I'M MASS PRODUCING IT AT TH' MOMENT.

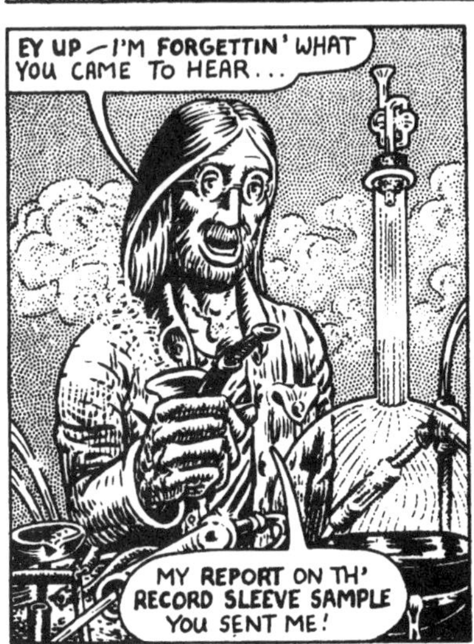
EY UP — I'M FORGETTIN' WHAT YOU CAME TO HEAR...
MY REPORT ON TH' RECORD SLEEVE SAMPLE YOU SENT ME!

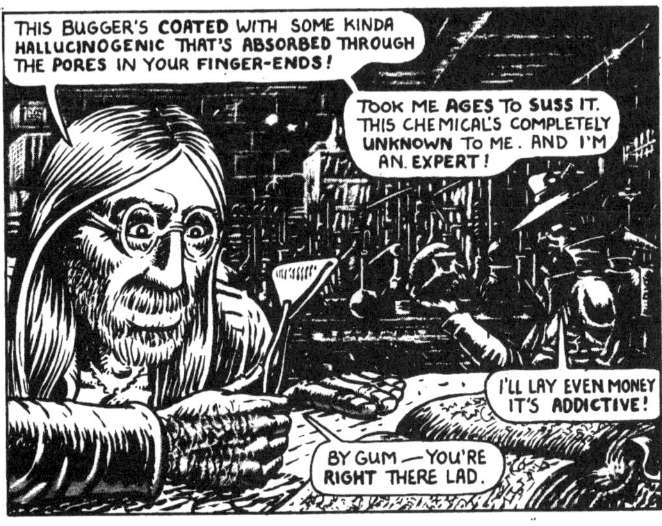
THIS BUGGER'S COATED WITH SOME KINDA HALLUCINOGENIC THAT'S ABSORBED THROUGH THE PORES IN YOUR FINGER-ENDS!
TOOK ME AGES TO SUSS IT. THIS CHEMICAL'S COMPLETELY UNKNOWN TO ME. AND I'M AN EXPERT!
I'LL LAY EVEN MONEY IT'S ADDICTIVE!
BY GUM — YOU'RE RIGHT THERE LAD.

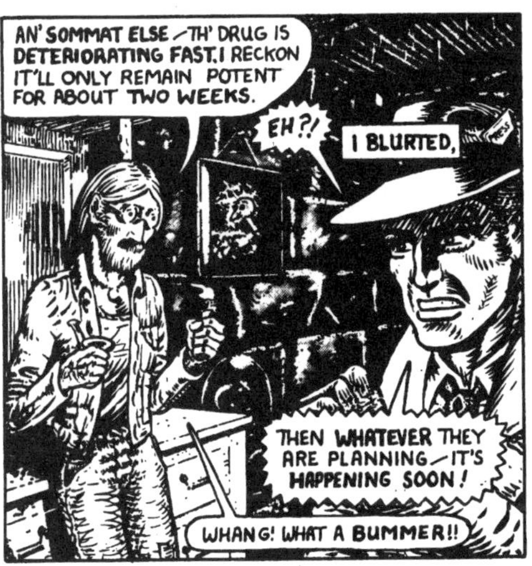
AN' SOMMAT ELSE — TH' DRUG IS DETERIORATING FAST. I RECKON IT'LL ONLY REMAIN POTENT FOR ABOUT TWO WEEKS.
EH?!
I BLURTED,
THEN WHATEVER THEY ARE PLANNING — IT'S HAPPENING SOON!
WHANG! WHAT A BUMMER!!

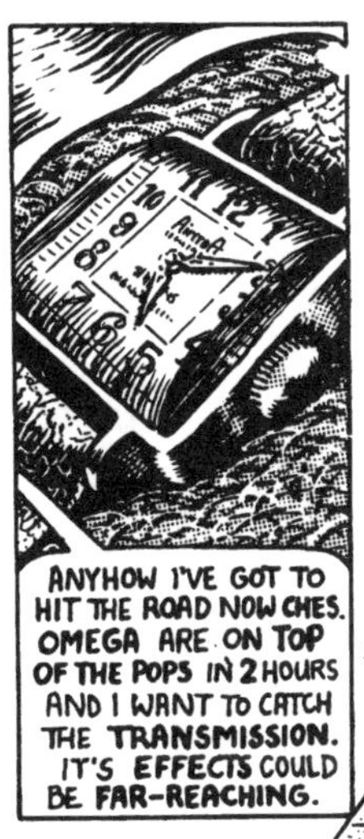
ANYHOW I'VE GOT TO HIT THE ROAD NOW CHES. OMEGA ARE ON TOP OF THE POPS IN 2 HOURS AND I WANT TO CATCH THE TRANSMISSION. IT'S EFFECTS COULD BE FAR-REACHING.

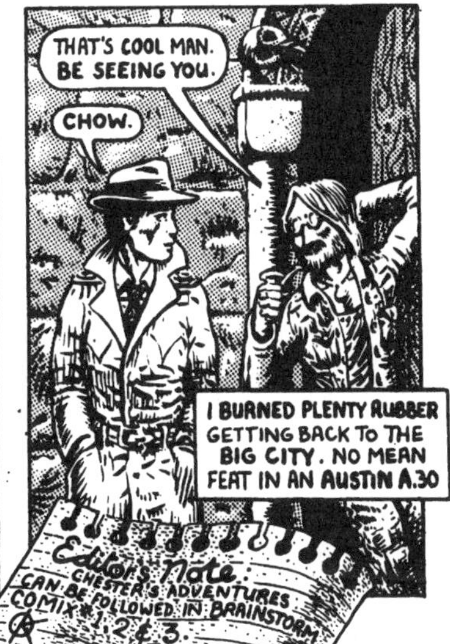
THAT'S COOL MAN. BE SEEING YOU.
CHOW.
I BURNED PLENTY RUBBER GETTING BACK TO THE BIG CITY. NO MEAN FEAT IN AN AUSTIN A.30
Editor's Note: CHESTER'S ADVENTURES CAN BE FOLLOWED IN BRAINSTORM COMIX #1, 2 & 3.

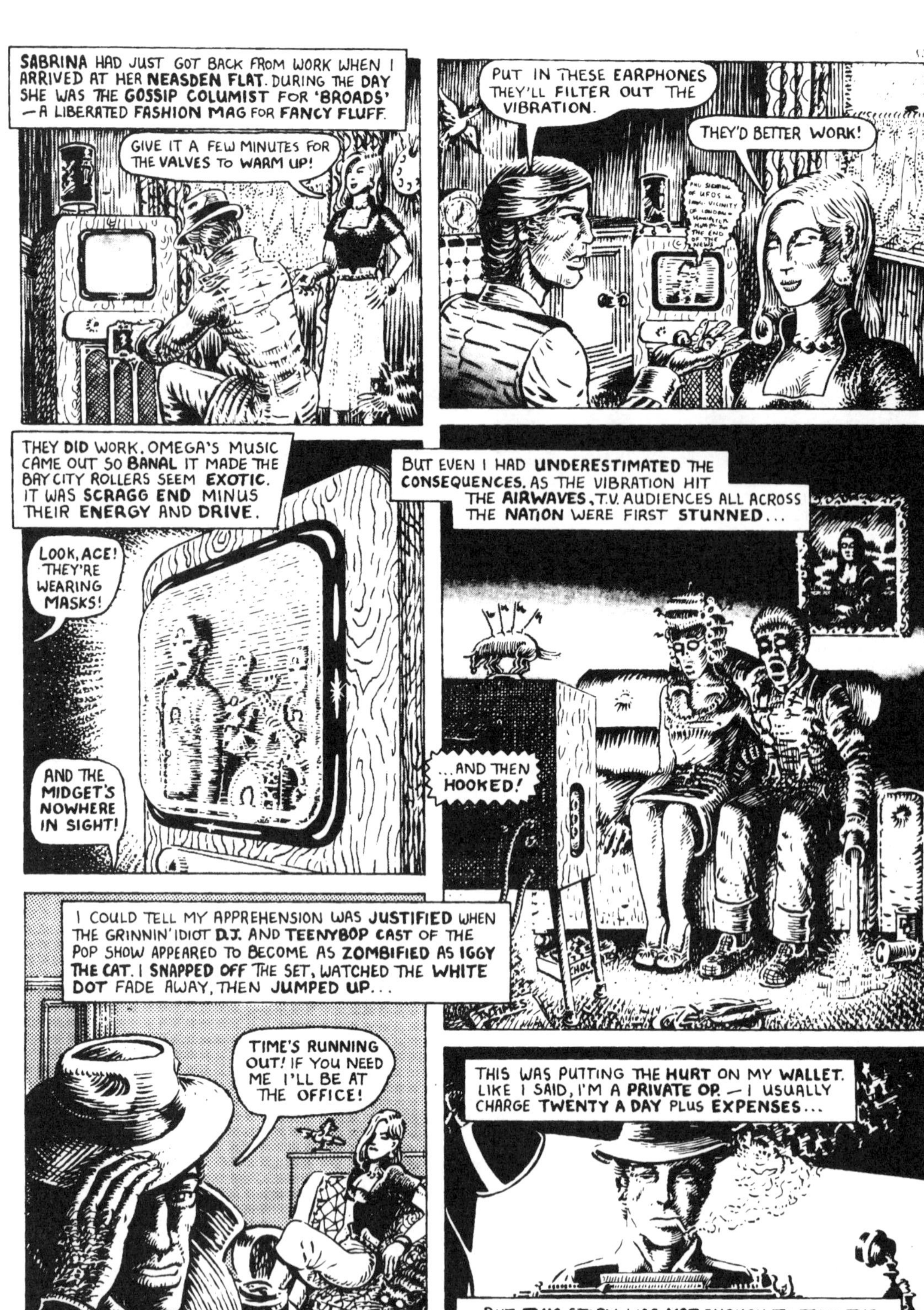
SABRINA HAD JUST GOT BACK FROM WORK WHEN I ARRIVED AT HER NEASDEN FLAT. DURING THE DAY SHE WAS THE GOSSIP COLUMIST FOR 'BROADS' —A LIBERATED FASHION MAG FOR FANCY FLUFF.
GIVE IT A FEW MINUTES FOR THE VALVES TO WARM UP!
PUT IN THESE EARPHONES THEY'LL FILTER OUT THE VIBRATION.
THEY'D BETTER WORK!
THEY DID WORK. OMEGA'S MUSIC CAME OUT SO BANAL IT MADE THE BAY CITY ROLLERS SEEM EXOTIC. IT WAS SCRAGG END MINUS THEIR ENERGY AND DRIVE.
LOOK, ACE! THEY'RE WEARING MASKS!
AND THE MIDGET'S NOWHERE IN SIGHT!
BUT EVEN I HAD UNDERESTIMATED THE CONSEQUENCES. AS THE VIBRATION HIT THE AIRWAVES, T.V. AUDIENCES ALL ACROSS THE NATION WERE FIRST STUNNED...
...AND THEN HOOKED!
I COULD TELL MY APPREHENSION WAS JUSTIFIED WHEN THE GRINNIN' IDIOT D.J. AND TEENYBOP CAST OF THE POP SHOW APPEARED TO BECOME AS ZOMBIFIED AS IGGY THE CAT. I SNAPPED OFF THE SET, WATCHED THE WHITE DOT FADE AWAY, THEN JUMPED UP...
TIME'S RUNNING OUT! IF YOU NEED ME I'LL BE AT THE OFFICE!
THIS WAS PUTTING THE HURT ON MY WALLET. LIKE I SAID, I'M A PRIVATE OP. — I USUALLY CHARGE TWENTY A DAY PLUS EXPENSES...
...BUT THIS STORY WAS HOT ENOUGH TO TAKE THE PAINT OFF A FENDER STRATOCASTER AT TWO HUNDRED YARDS. I WORKED THROUGH THE NIGHT...

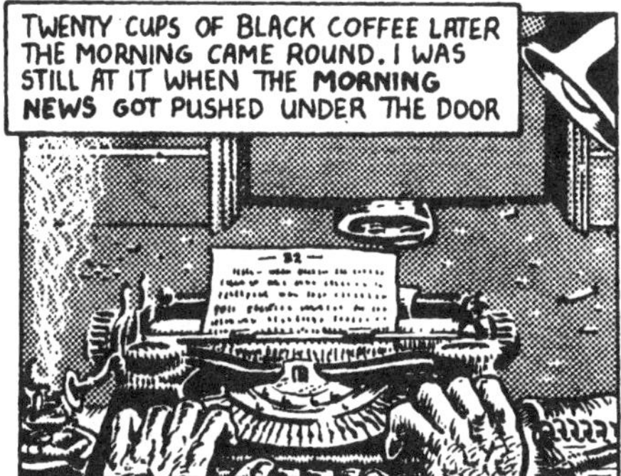
TWENTY CUPS OF BLACK COFFEE LATER THE MORNING CAME ROUND. I WAS STILL AT IT WHEN THE MORNING NEWS GOT PUSHED UNDER THE DOOR

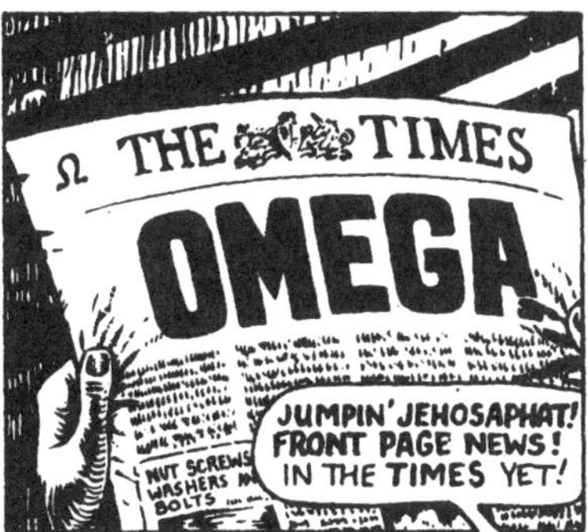
THE TIMES
OMEGA
NUT SCREWS WASHERS N BOLTS
JUMPIN' JEHOSAPHAT! FRONT PAGE NEWS! IN THE TIMES YET!

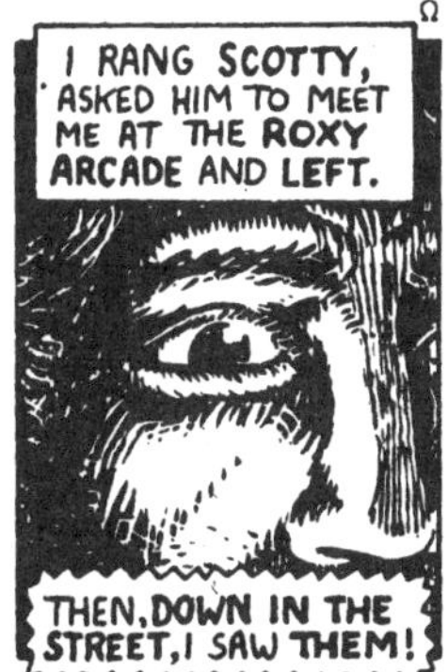
I RANG SCOTTY, ASKED HIM TO MEET ME AT THE ROXY ARCADE AND LEFT.
THEN, DOWN IN THE STREET, I SAW THEM!

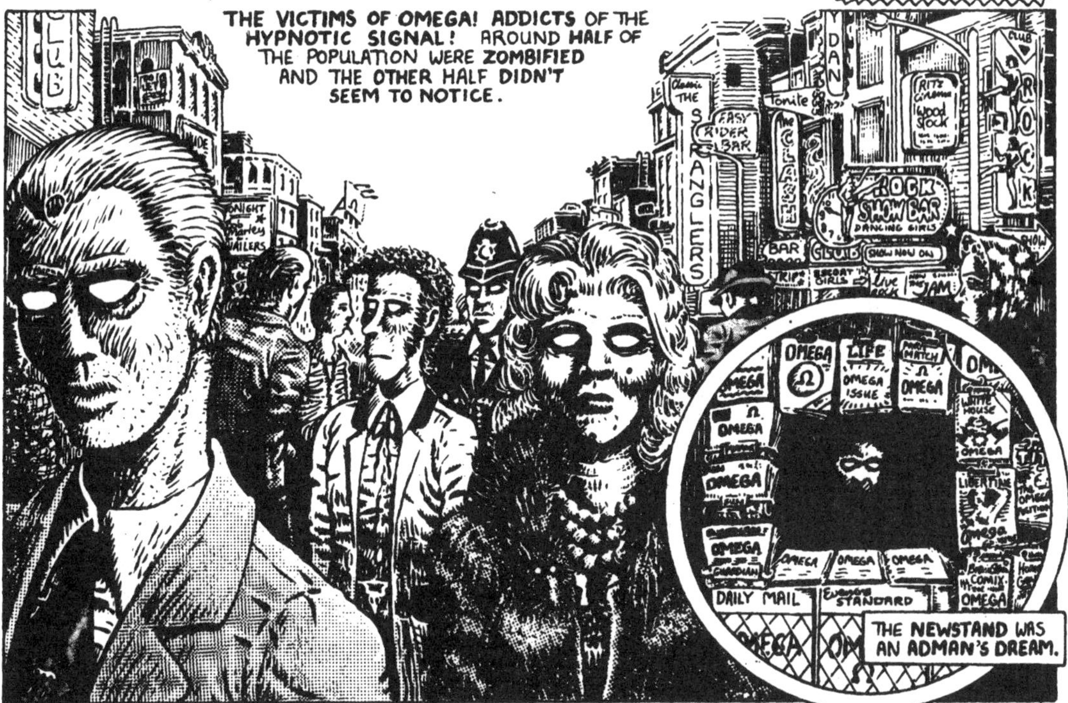
THE VICTIMS OF OMEGA! ADDICTS OF THE HYPNOTIC SIGNAL! AROUND HALF OF THE POPULATION WERE ZOMBIFIED AND THE OTHER HALF DIDN'T SEEM TO NOTICE.
STRANGLERS
EASY RIDER BAR
ROCK SHOW BAR
DANCING GIRLS
OMEGA
LIFE
OMEGA ISSUE
DAILY MAIL
STANDARD
THE NEWSTAND WAS AN ADMAN'S DREAM.

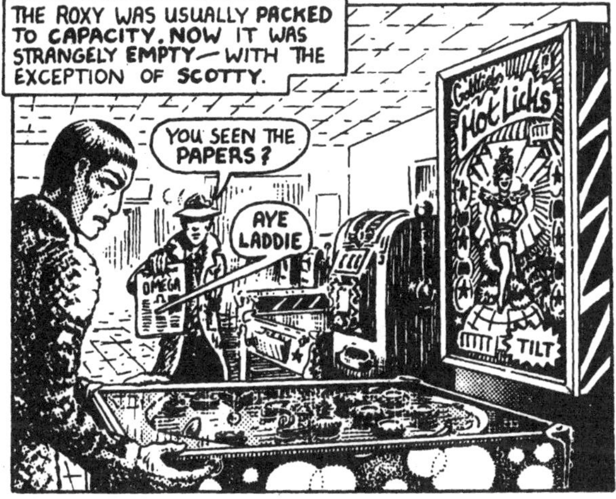
THE ROXY WAS USUALLY PACKED TO CAPACITY. NOW IT WAS STRANGELY EMPTY— WITH THE EXCEPTION OF SCOTTY.
YOU SEEN THE PAPERS?
AYE LADDIE
OMEGA
Hot Licks
TILT

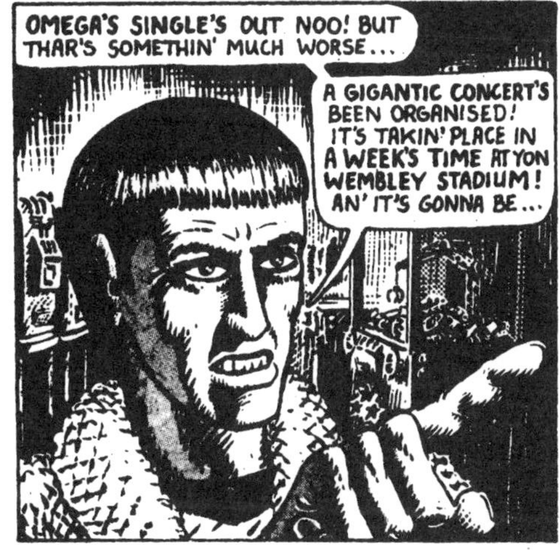
OMEGA'S SINGLE'S OUT NOO! BUT THAR'S SOMETHIN' MUCH WORSE...
A GIGANTIC CONCERT'S BEEN ORGANISED! IT'S TAKIN' PLACE IN A WEEK'S TIME AT YON WEMBLEY STADIUM! AN' IT'S GONNA BE...

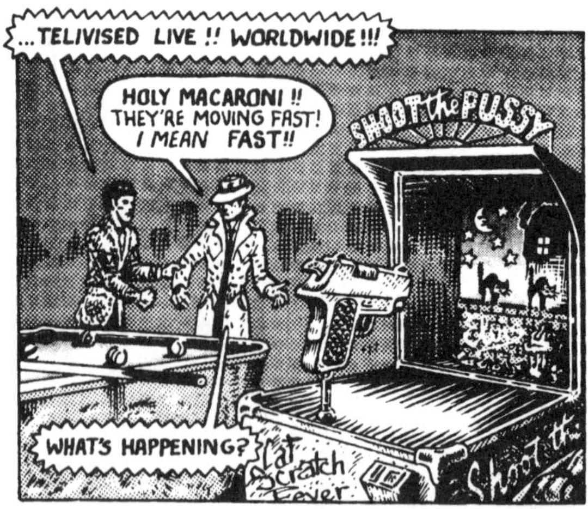
...TELIVISED LIVE !! WORLDWIDE!!!
HOLY MACARONI !! THEY'RE MOVING FAST! I MEAN FAST!!
SHOOT the PUSSY
WHAT'S HAPPENING?

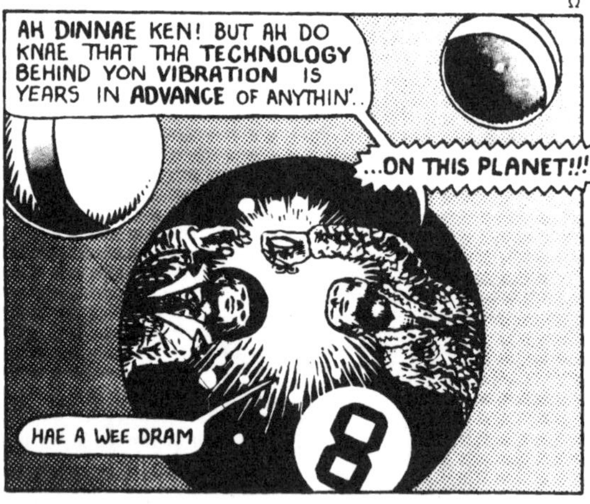
AH DINNAE KEN! BUT AH DO KNAE THAT THA TECHNOLOGY BEHIND YON VIBRATION IS YEARS IN ADVANCE OF ANYTHIN'..
...ON THIS PLANET!!!
HAE A WEE DRAM
8

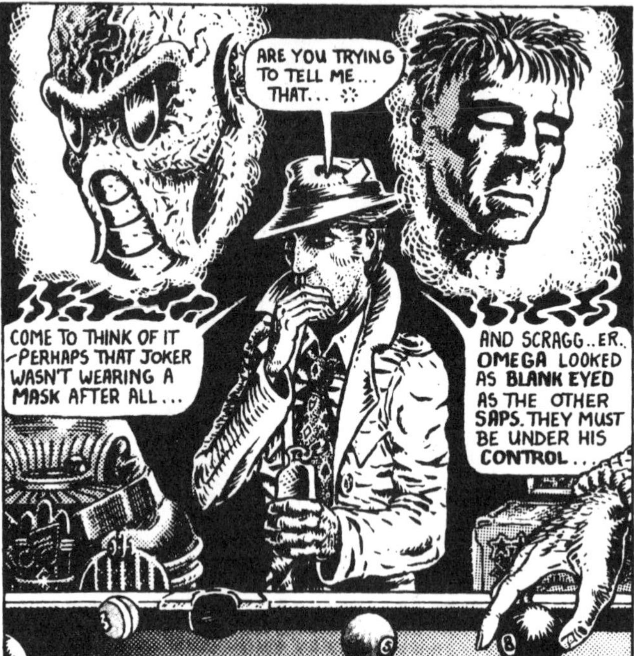
ARE YOU TRYING TO TELL ME... THAT...
COME TO THINK OF IT -PERHAPS THAT JOKER WASN'T WEARING A MASK AFTER ALL...
AND SCRAGG..ER. OMEGA LOOKED AS BLANK EYED AS THE OTHER SAPS. THEY MUST BE UNDER HIS CONTROL..

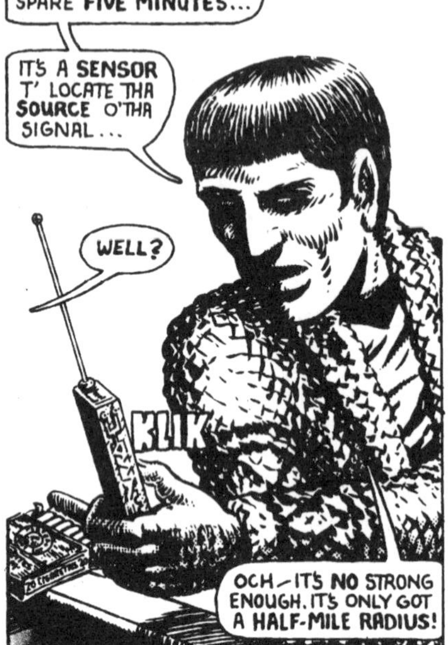
SEE HERE - AH KNOCKED THIS THING UP IN A SPARE FIVE MINUTES...
IT'S A SENSOR T' LOCATE THA SOURCE O'THA SIGNAL...
WELL?
KLIK
OCH - IT'S NO STRONG ENOUGH. IT'S ONLY GOT A HALF-MILE RADIUS!

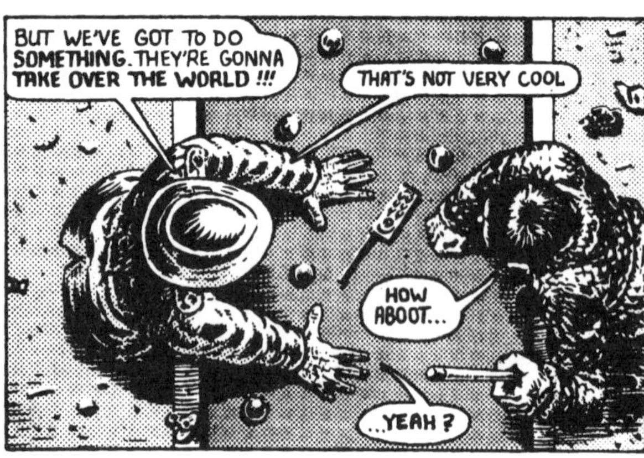
BUT WE'VE GOT TO DO SOMETHING. THEY'RE GONNA TAKE OVER THE WORLD !!!
THAT'S NOT VERY COOL
HOW ABOOT...
...YEAH ?

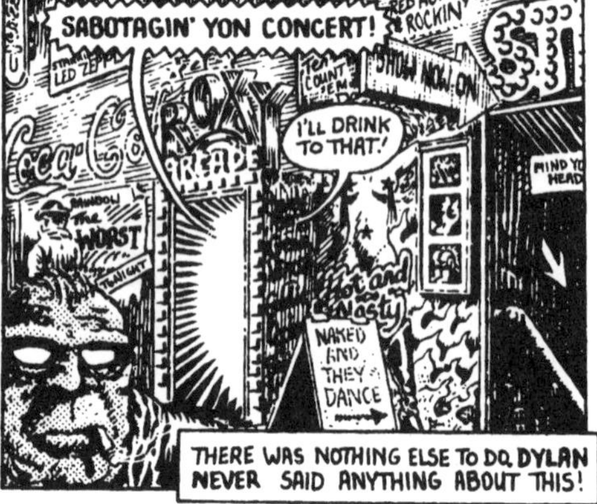
SABOTAGIN' YON CONCERT!
ROXY
I'LL DRINK TO THAT!
NAKED AND THEY DANCE
MIND YO HEAD
THERE WAS NOTHING ELSE TO DO. DYLAN NEVER SAID ANYTHING ABOUT THIS!

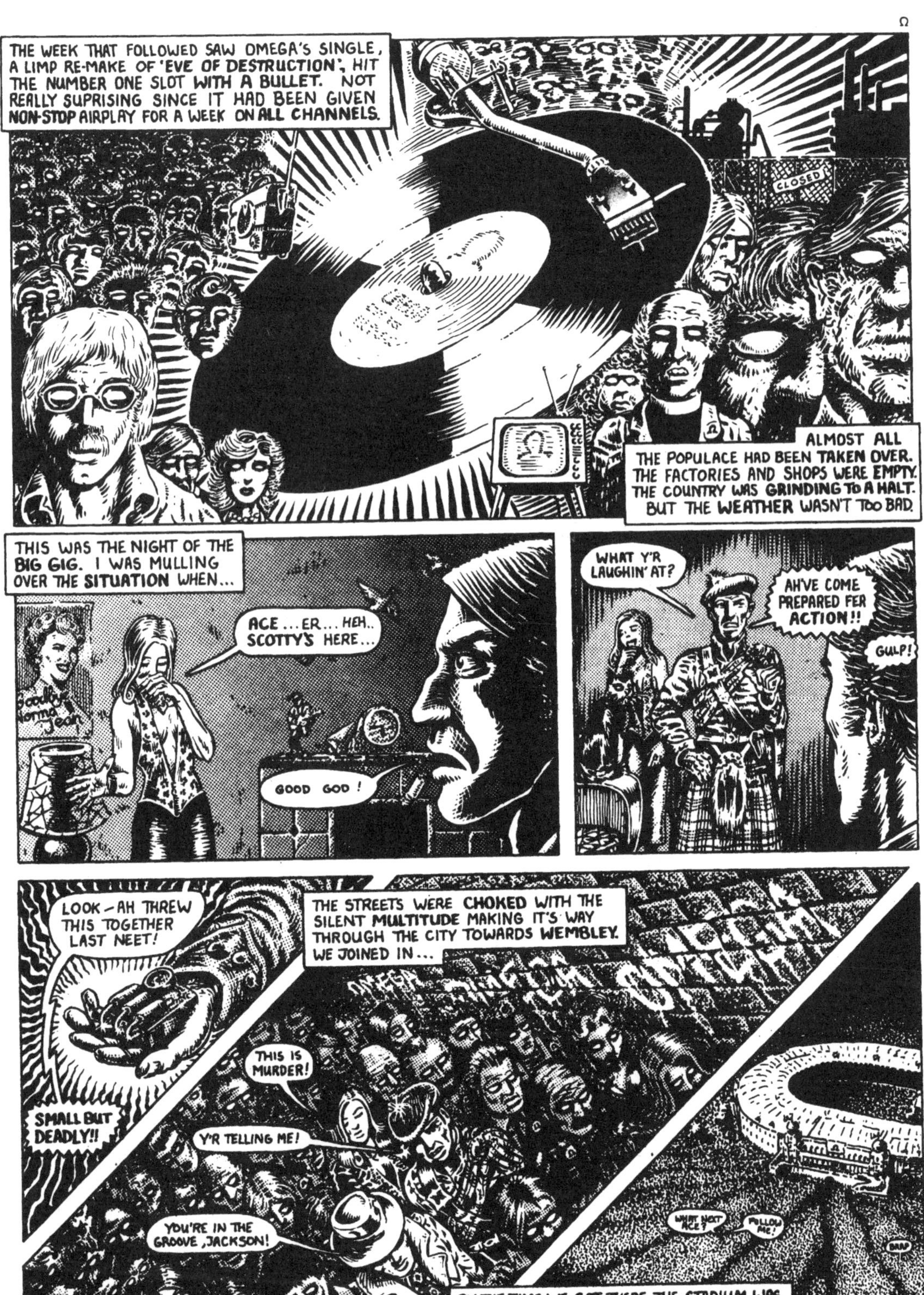
THE WEEK THAT FOLLOWED SAW OMEGA'S SINGLE, A LIMP RE-MAKE OF 'EVE OF DESTRUCTION', HIT THE NUMBER ONE SLOT WITH A BULLET. NOT REALLY SUPRISING SINCE IT HAD BEEN GIVEN NON-STOP AIRPLAY FOR A WEEK ON ALL CHANNELS.
CLOSED
ALMOST ALL THE POPULACE HAD BEEN TAKEN OVER. THE FACTORIES AND SHOPS WERE EMPTY. THE COUNTRY WAS GRINDING TO A HALT. BUT THE WEATHER WASN'T TOO BAD.
THIS WAS THE NIGHT OF THE BIG GIG. I WAS MULLING OVER THE SITUATION WHEN...
ACE... ER... HEH.. SCOTTY'S HERE...
GOOD GOD!
WHAT Y'R LAUGHIN' AT?
AH'VE COME PREPARED FER ACTION!!
GULP!
LOOK – AH THREW THIS TOGETHER LAST NEET!
SMALL BUT DEADLY!!
THE STREETS WERE CHOKED WITH THE SILENT MULTITUDE MAKING IT'S WAY THROUGH THE CITY TOWARDS WEMBLEY. WE JOINED IN...
THIS IS MURDER!
Y'R TELLING ME!
YOU'RE IN THE GROOVE, JACKSON!
WHAT NEXT ACE?
FOLLOW ME!
BY THE TIME WE GOT THERE, THE STADIUM WAS ALREADY FULL WITH 'FANS' WHO'D BEEN QUEUING OUTSIDE FOR THE PAST SIX DAYS.

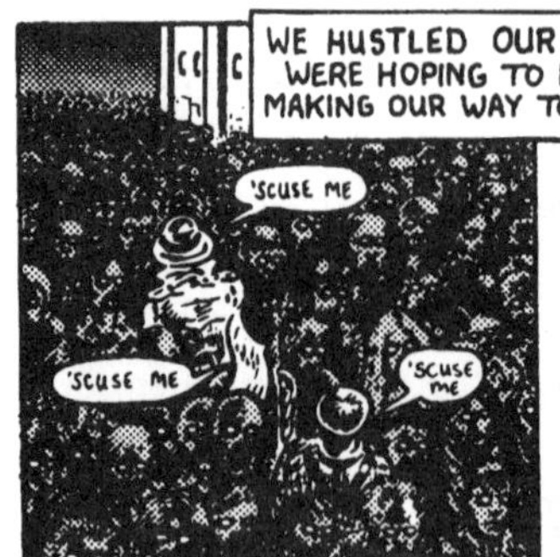
WE HUSTLED OUR WAY THROUGH THE THRONGS WHO WERE HOPING TO HEAR OMEGA FROM OUTSIDE — MAKING OUR WAY TO A LITTLE-KNOWN ENTRANCE I'VE USED MANY TIMES BEFORE...
'SCUSE ME
'SCUSE ME
'SCUSE ME

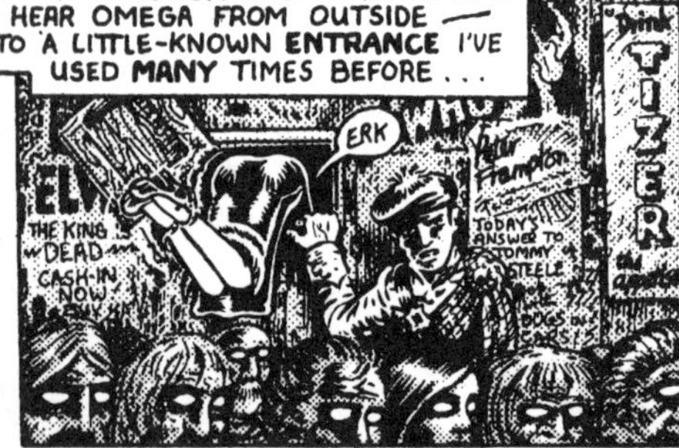
ERK
ELV
THE KING DEAD
CASH-IN NOW
TODAY'S ANSWER TO TOMMY STEELE
TIZER

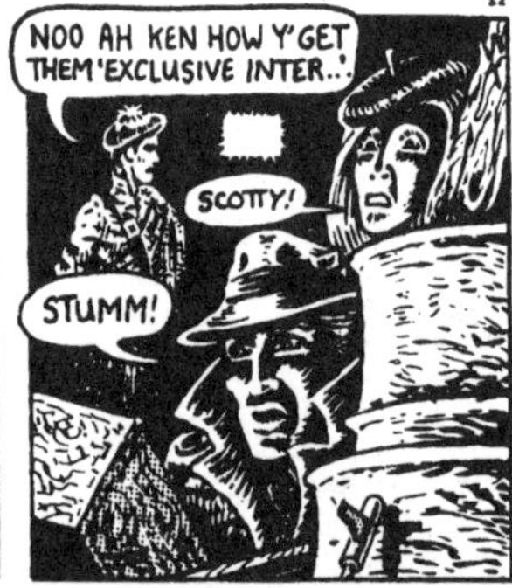
NOO AH KEN HOW Y'GET THEM 'EXCLUSIVE INTER..'
SCOTTY!
STUMM!

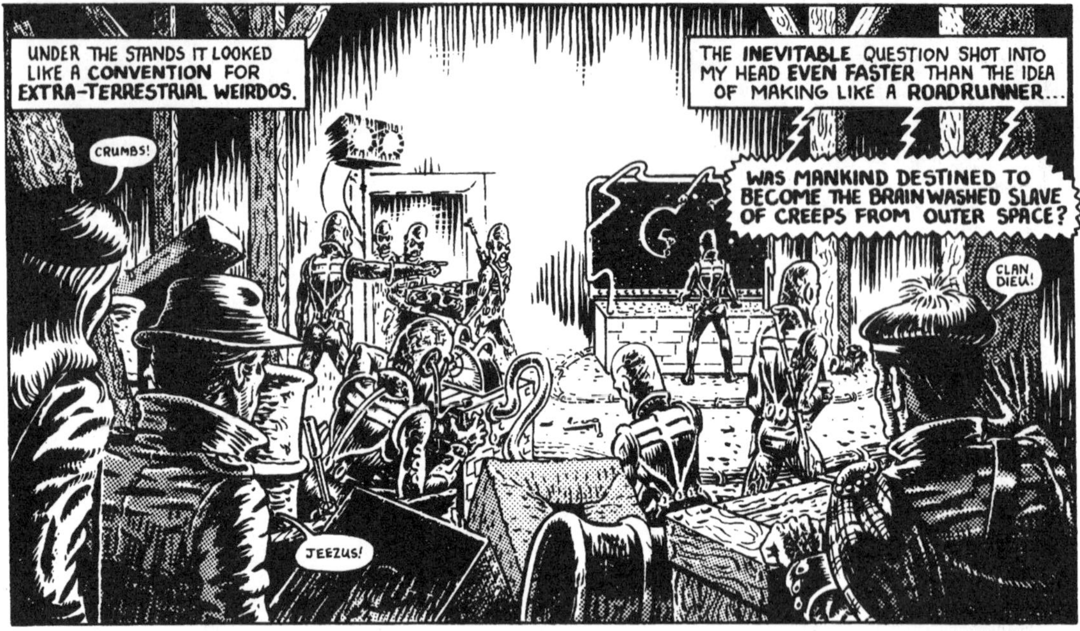
UNDER THE STANDS IT LOOKED LIKE A CONVENTION FOR EXTRA-TERRESTRIAL WEIRDOS.
THE INEVITABLE QUESTION SHOT INTO MY HEAD EVEN FASTER THAN THE IDEA OF MAKING LIKE A ROADRUNNER...
WAS MANKIND DESTINED TO BECOME THE BRAINWASHED SLAVE OF CREEPS FROM OUTER SPACE?
CRUMBS!
CLAN DIEU!
JEEZUS!

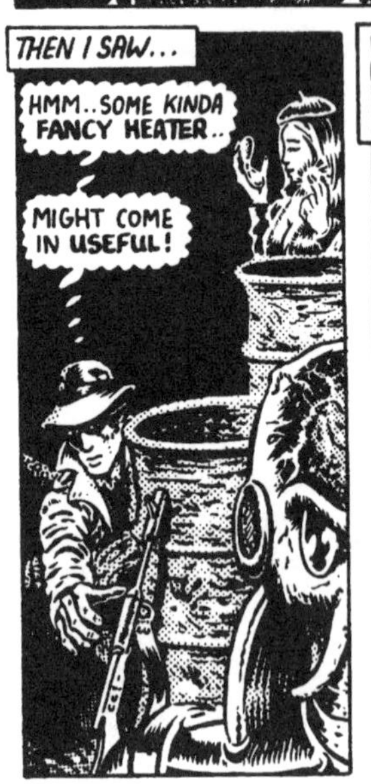
THEN I SAW...
HMM..SOME KINDA FANCY HEATER..
MIGHT COME IN USEFUL!

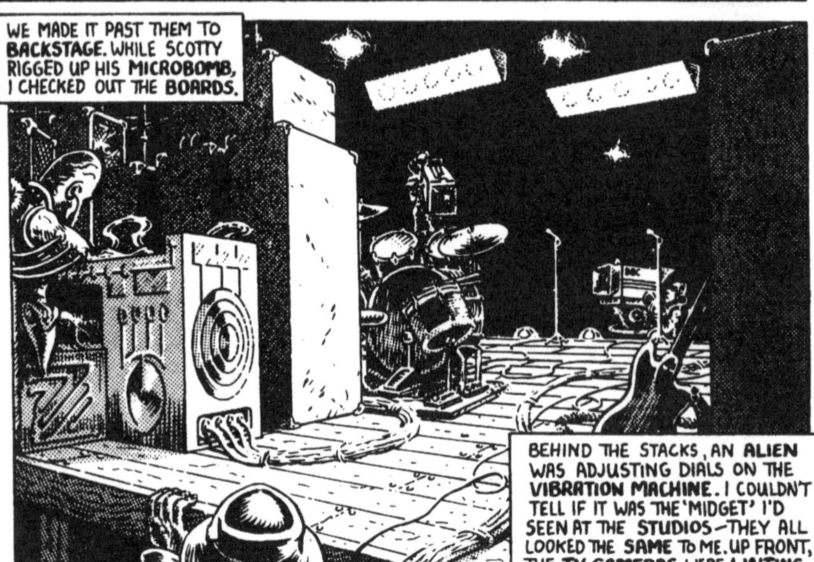
WE MADE IT PAST THEM TO BACKSTAGE. WHILE SCOTTY RIGGED UP HIS MICROBOMB, I CHECKED OUT THE BOARDS.
BEHIND THE STACKS, AN ALIEN WAS ADJUSTING DIALS ON THE VIBRATION MACHINE. I COULDN'T TELL IF IT WAS THE 'MIDGET' I'D SEEN AT THE STUDIOS—THEY ALL LOOKED THE SAME TO ME. UP FRONT, THE T.V. CAMERAS WERE WAITING...

Ω

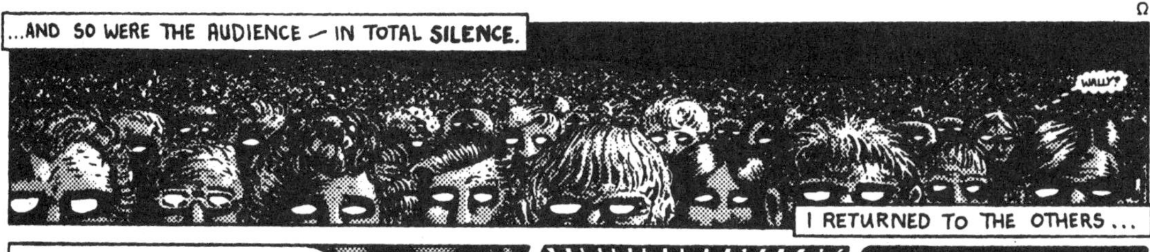
...AND SO WERE THE AUDIENCE — IN TOTAL SILENCE.
WALLY?
I RETURNED TO THE OTHERS...

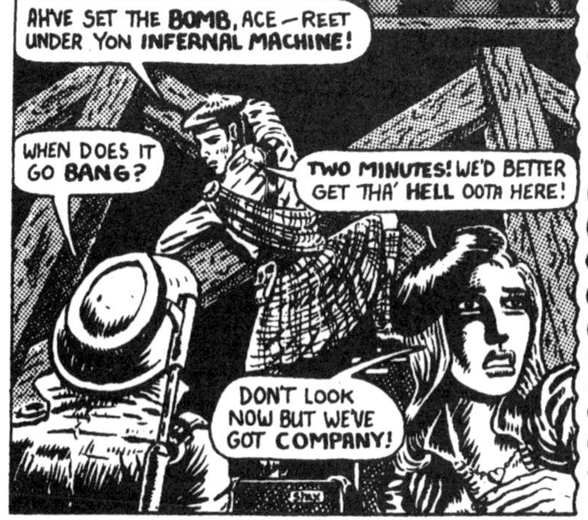
AH'VE SET THE BOMB, ACE—REET UNDER YON INFERNAL MACHINE!
WHEN DOES IT GO BANG?
TWO MINUTES! WE'D BETTER GET THA' HELL OOTA HERE!
DON'T LOOK NOW BUT WE'VE GOT COMPANY!

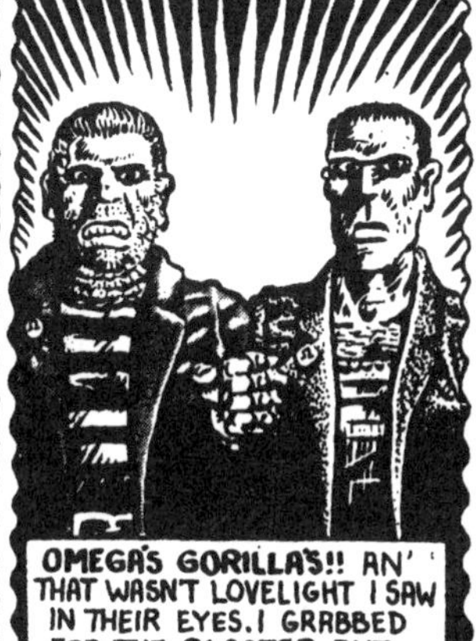
OMEGA'S GORILLA'S!! AN' THAT WASN'T LOVELIGHT I SAW IN THEIR EYES. I GRABBED FOR THE BLASTER BUT...

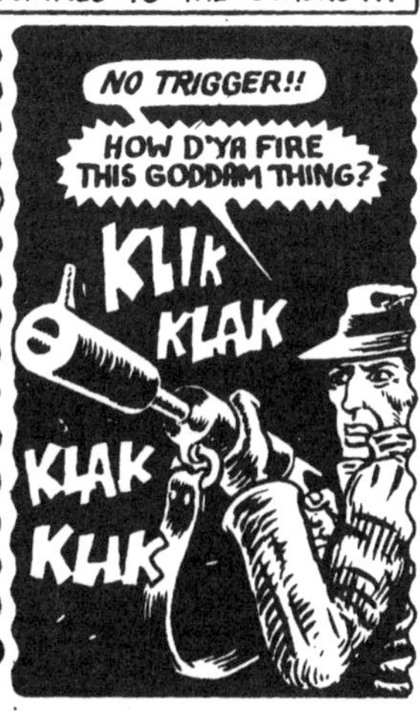
NO TRIGGER!!
HOW D'YA FIRE THIS GODDAM THING?
KLIK
KLAK
KLAK
KLIK

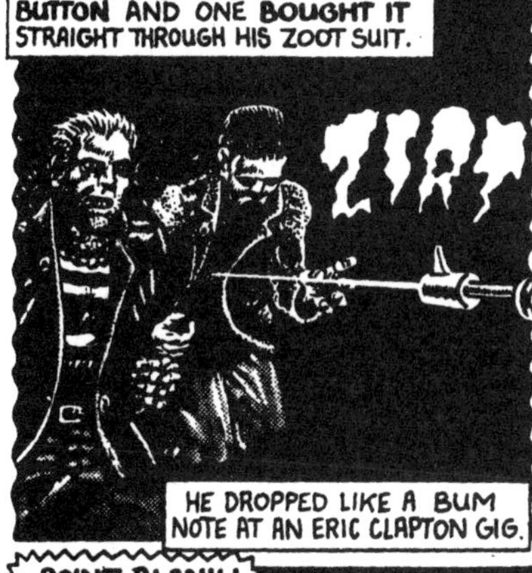
I GOT LUCKY. I PRESSED THE RIGHT BUTTON AND ONE BOUGHT IT STRAIGHT THROUGH HIS ZOOT SUIT.
ZIRT
HE DROPPED LIKE A BUM NOTE AT AN ERIC CLAPTON GIG.

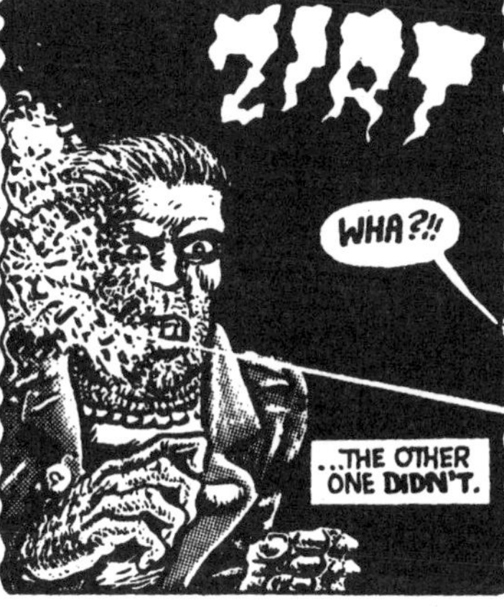
ZIRT
WHA?!!
...THE OTHER ONE DIDN'T.

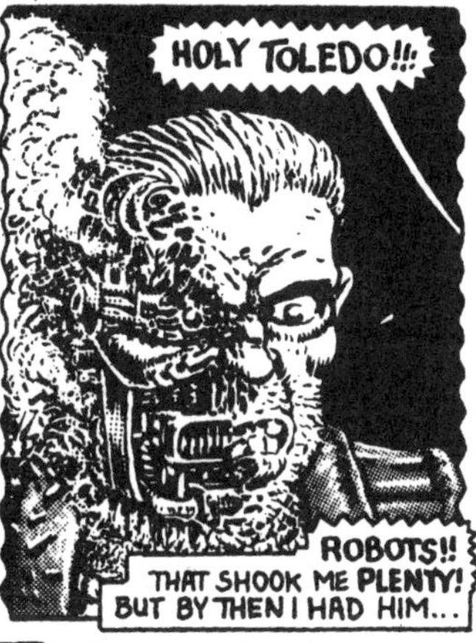
HOLY TOLEDO!!!
ROBOTS!! THAT SHOOK ME PLENTY! BUT BY THEN I HAD HIM...

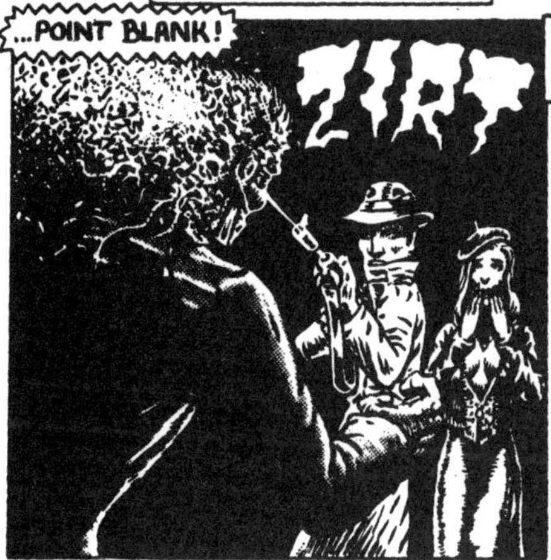
...POINT BLANK!
ZIRT

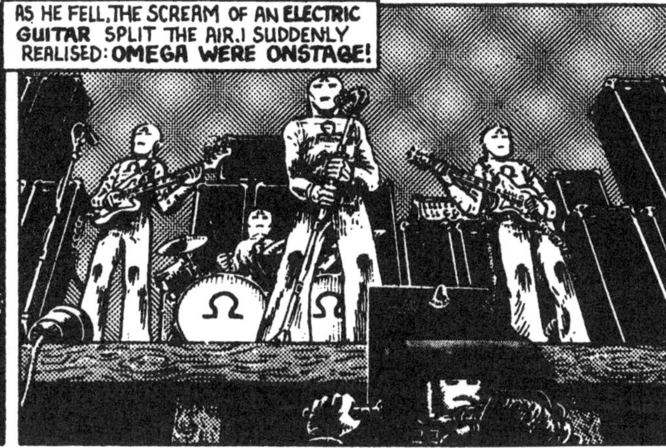
AS HE FELL, THE SCREAM OF AN ELECTRIC GUITAR SPLIT THE AIR. I SUDDENLY REALISED: OMEGA WERE ONSTAGE!

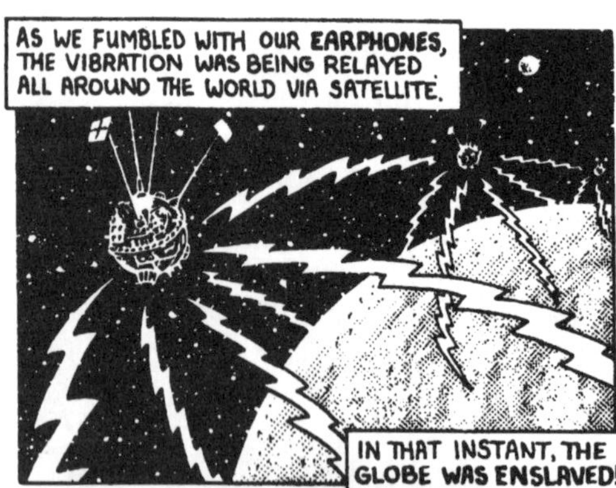
AS WE FUMBLED WITH OUR EARPHONES, THE VIBRATION WAS BEING RELAYED ALL AROUND THE WORLD VIA SATELLITE.
IN THAT INSTANT, THE GLOBE WAS ENSLAVED!

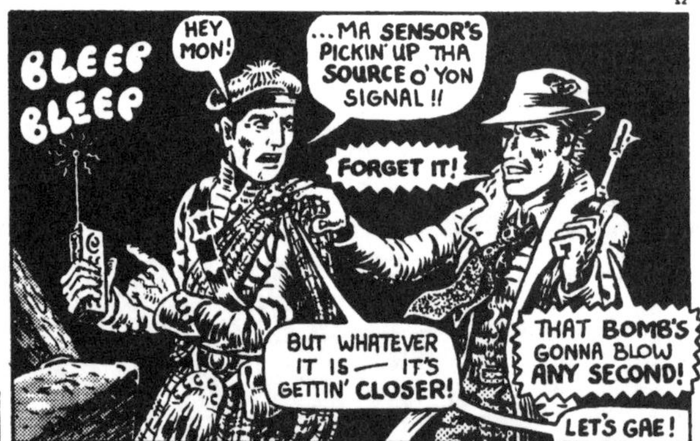
BLEEP BLEEP
HEY MON!
...MA SENSOR'S PICKIN' UP THA SOURCE O' YON SIGNAL!!
FORGET IT!
BUT WHATEVER IT IS — IT'S GETTIN' CLOSER!
THAT BOMB'S GONNA BLOW ANY SECOND!
LET'S GAE!

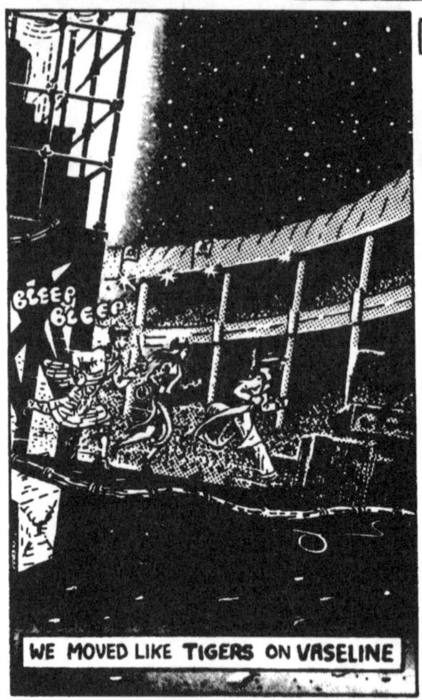
BLEEP BLEEP
WE MOVED LIKE TIGERS ON VASELINE

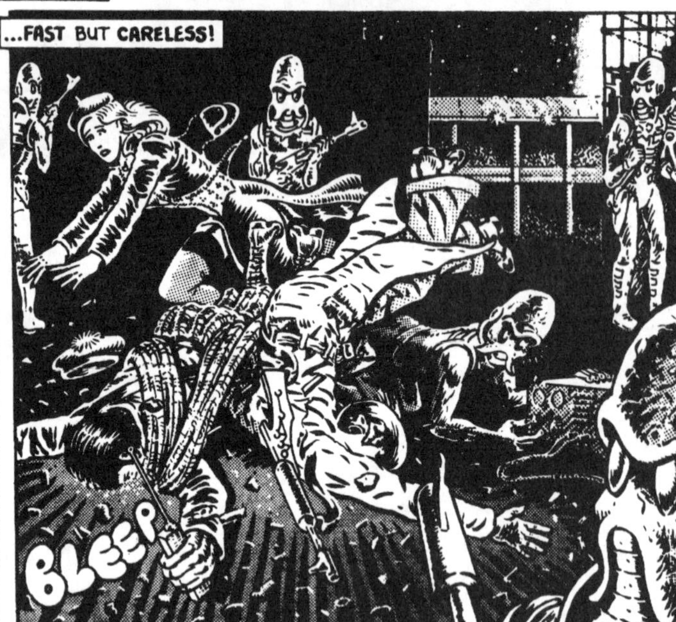
...FAST BUT CARELESS!
BLEEP

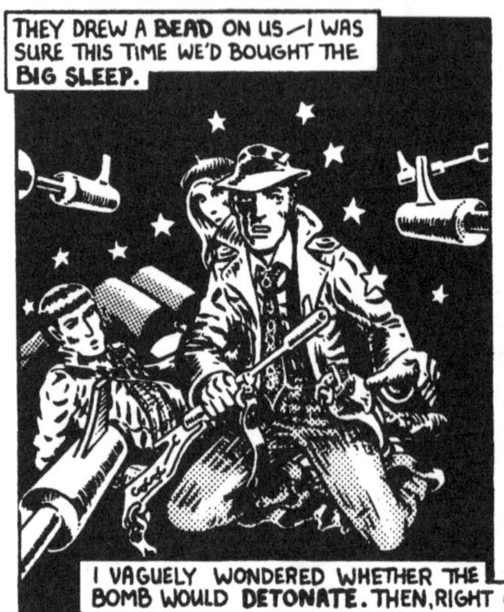
THEY DREW A BEAD ON US — I WAS SURE THIS TIME WE'D BOUGHT THE BIG SLEEP.
I VAGUELY WONDERED WHETHER THE BOMB WOULD DETONATE. THEN, RIGHT ON CUE... IT DID.

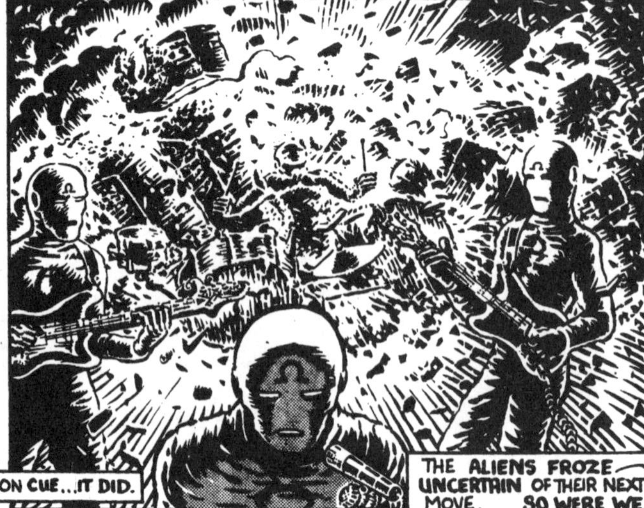
THE ALIENS FROZE — UNCERTAIN OF THEIR NEXT MOVE. SO WERE WE.

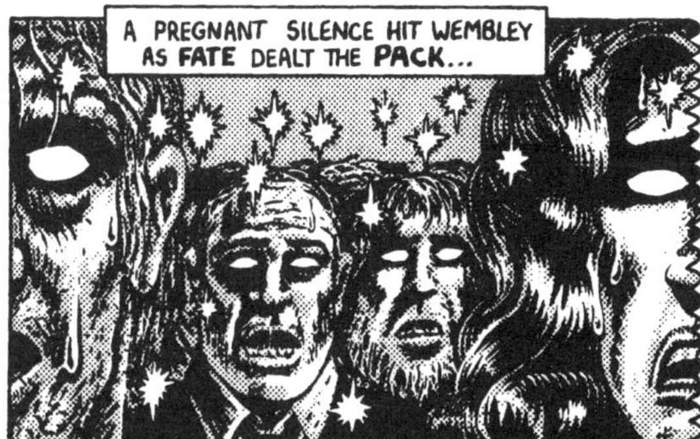
A PREGNANT SILENCE HIT WEMBLEY AS FATE DEALT THE PACK...

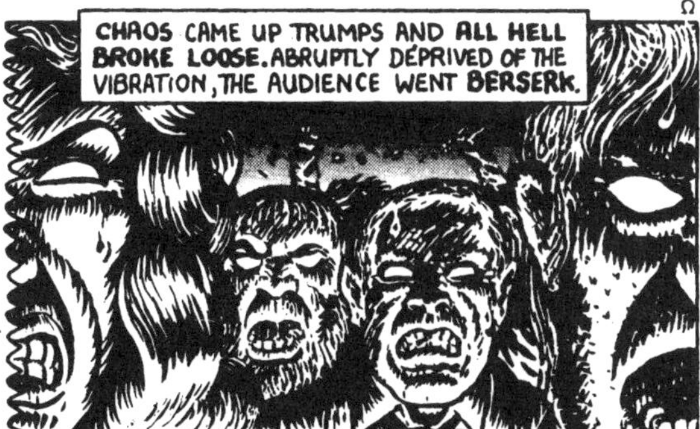
CHAOS CAME UP TRUMPS AND ALL HELL BROKE LOOSE. ABRUPTLY DEPRIVED OF THE VIBRATION, THE AUDIENCE WENT BERSERK.

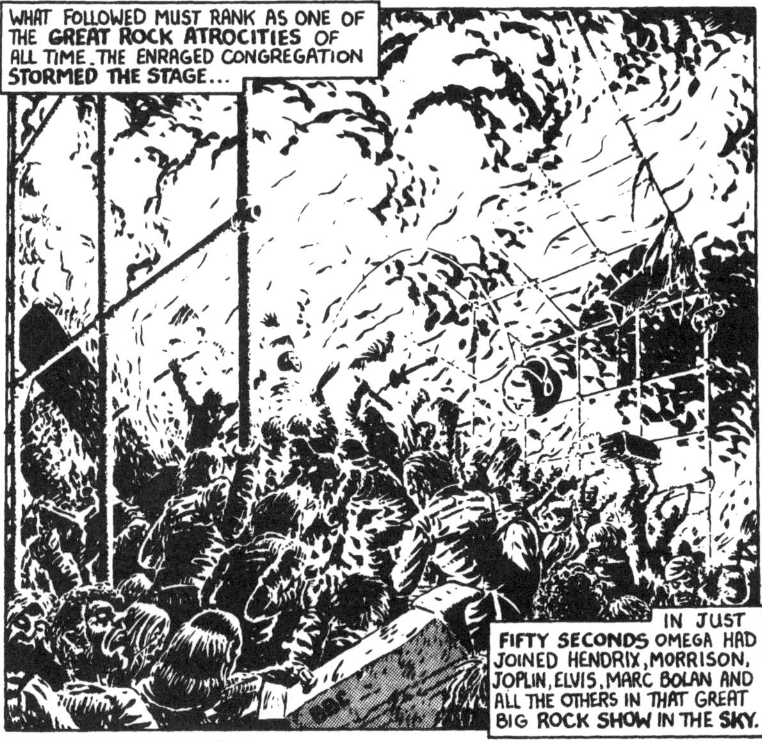
WHAT FOLLOWED MUST RANK AS ONE OF THE GREAT ROCK ATROCITIES OF ALL TIME. THE ENRAGED CONGREGATION STORMED THE STAGE...
IN JUST FIFTY SECONDS OMEGA HAD JOINED HENDRIX, MORRISON, JOPLIN, ELVIS, MARC BOLAN AND ALL THE OTHERS IN THAT GREAT BIG ROCK SHOW IN THE SKY.

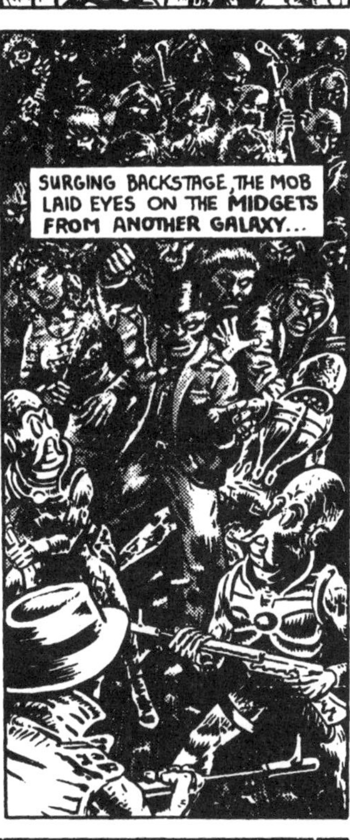
SURGING BACKSTAGE, THE MOB LAID EYES ON THE MIDGETS FROM ANOTHER GALAXY...

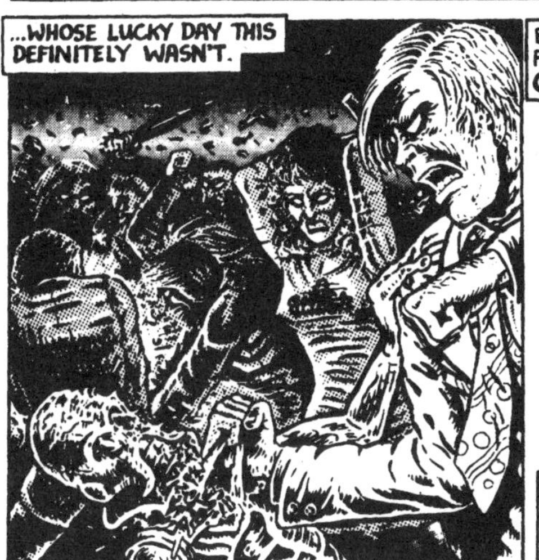
...WHOSE LUCKY DAY THIS DEFINITELY WASN'T.

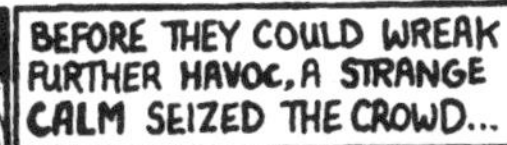
BEFORE THEY COULD WREAK FURTHER HAVOC, A STRANGE CALM SEIZED THE CROWD...

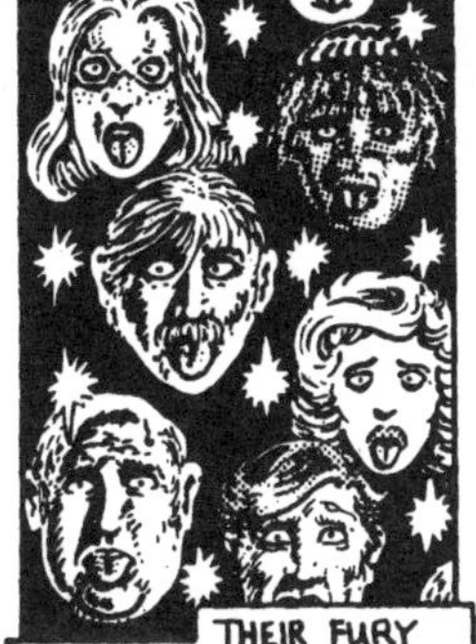
THEIR FURY SPENT, ALL ENERGY DRAINED, THEY TROOPED OUT OF THE STADIUM EN MASSE —DAZED AND CONFUSED.

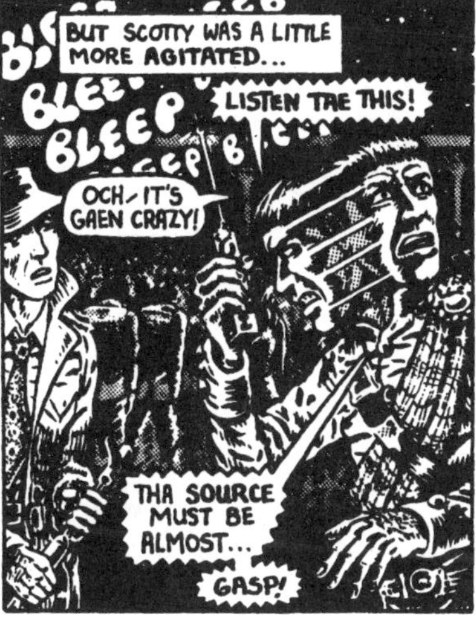
BUT SCOTTY WAS A LITTLE MORE AGITATED...
BLEEP
BLEEP
LISTEN TAE THIS!
OCH - IT'S GAEN CRAZY!
THA SOURCE MUST BE ALMOST...
GASP!

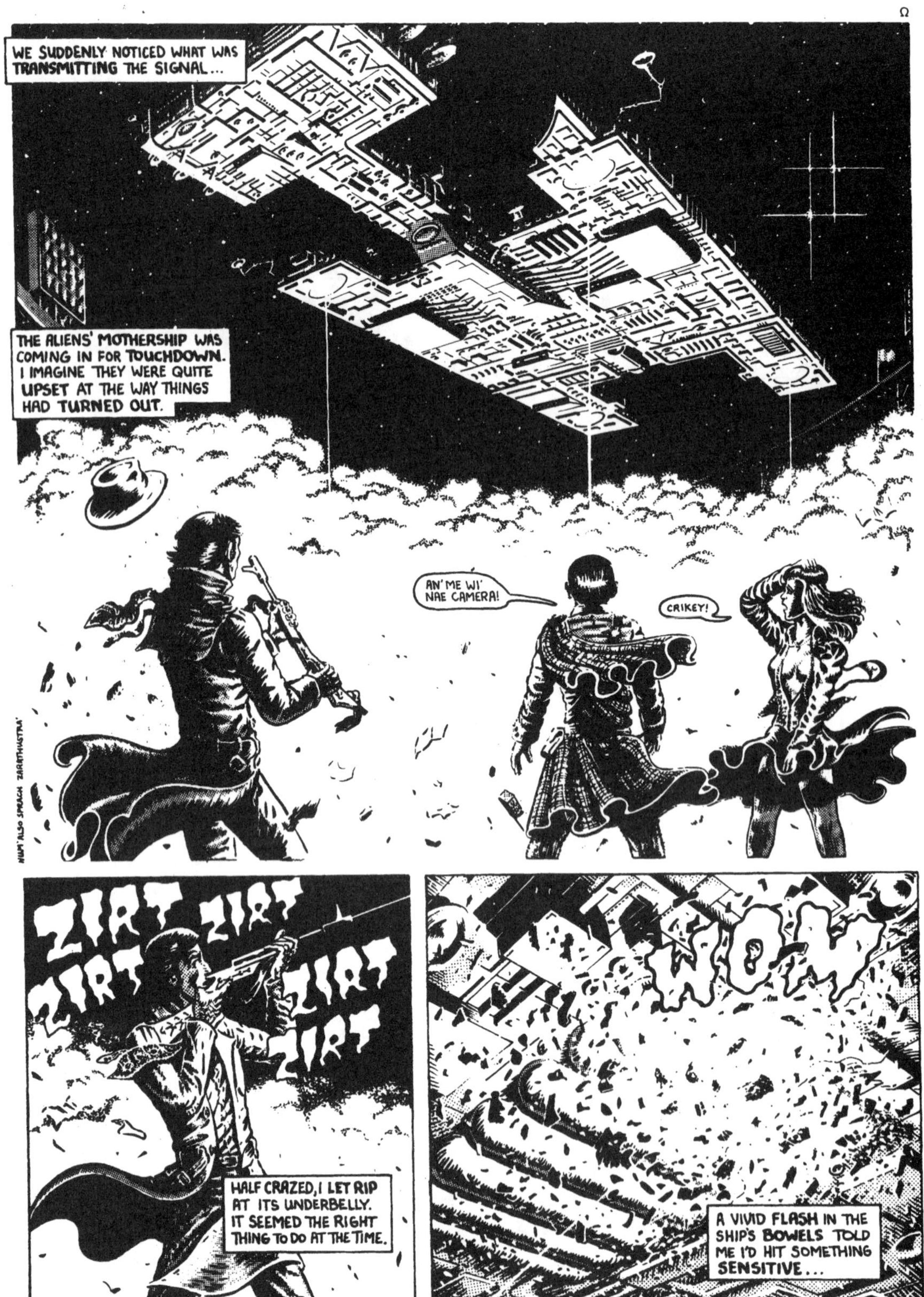

WE SUDDENLY NOTICED WHAT WAS TRANSMITTING THE SIGNAL...
THE ALIENS' MOTHERSHIP WAS COMING IN FOR TOUCHDOWN. I IMAGINE THEY WERE QUITE UPSET AT THE WAY THINGS HAD TURNED OUT.
HUM' ALSO SPRACH ZARATHUSTRA'
AN' ME WI' NAE CAMERA!
CRIKEY!
ZIRT ZIRT ZIRT ZIRT ZIRT ZIRT
HALF CRAZED, I LET RIP AT ITS UNDERBELLY. IT SEEMED THE RIGHT THING TO DO AT THE TIME.
WOM
A VIVID FLASH IN THE SHIP'S BOWELS TOLD ME I'D HIT SOMETHING SENSITIVE...

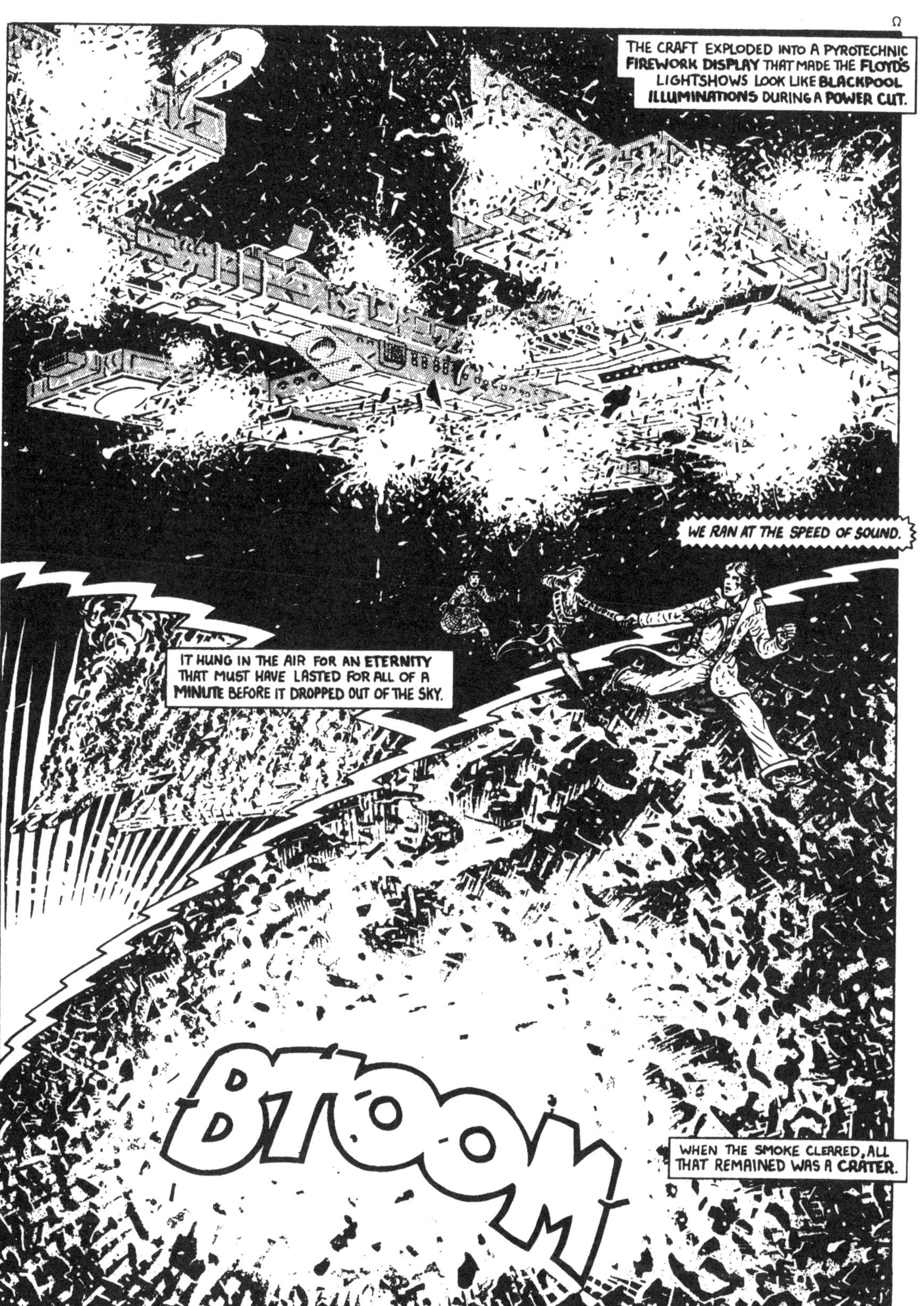
THE CRAFT EXPLODED INTO A PYROTECHNIC FIREWORK DISPLAY THAT MADE THE FLOYD'S LIGHTSHOWS LOOK LIKE BLACKPOOL ILLUMINATIONS DURING A POWER CUT.
WE RAN AT THE SPEED OF SOUND.
IT HUNG IN THE AIR FOR AN ETERNITY THAT MUST HAVE LASTED FOR ALL OF A MINUTE BEFORE IT DROPPED OUT OF THE SKY.
BTOOM
WHEN THE SMOKE CLEARED, ALL THAT REMAINED WAS A CRATER.

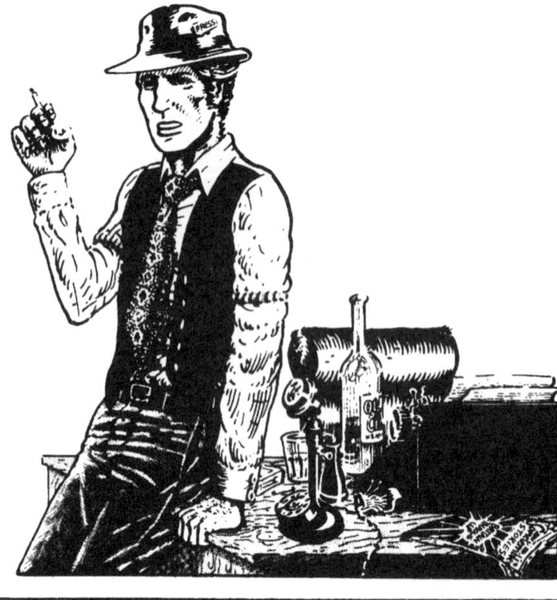

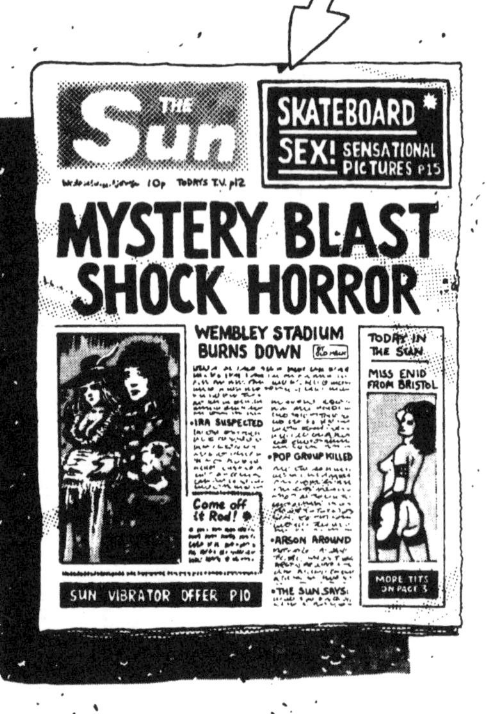

THE Sun

SKATEBOARD SEX! SENSATIONAL PICTURES P15

10p TODAYS T.V. p12

MYSTERY BLAST SHOCK HORROR

WEMBLEY STADIUM BURNS DOWN

•IRA SUSPECTED

•POP GROUP KILLED

Come off it Rod!

•ARSON AROUND

•THE SUN SAYS:

TODAY IN THE SUN

MISS ENID FROM BRISTOL

MORE TITS ON PAGE 3

SUN VIBRATOR OFFER P10

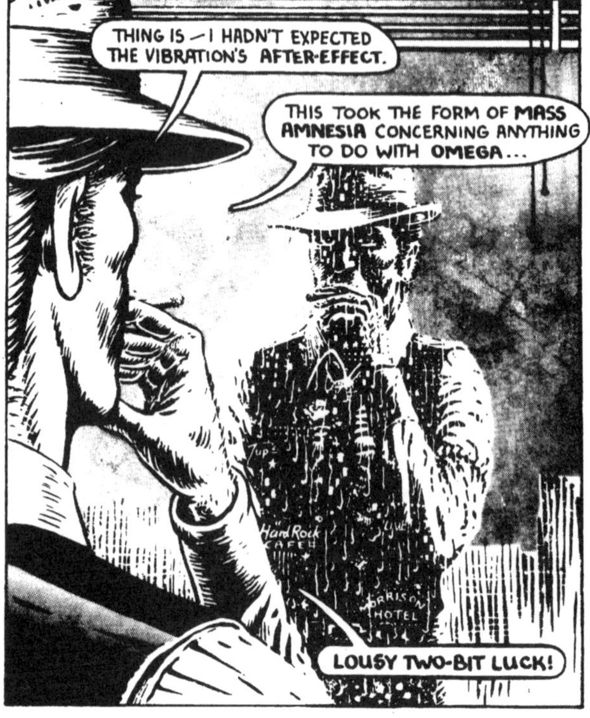

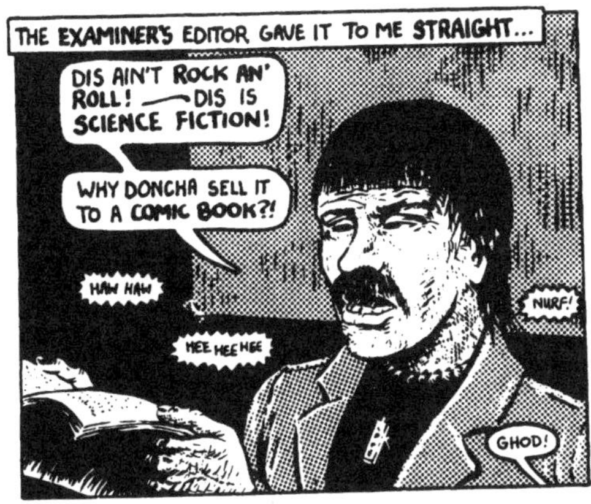

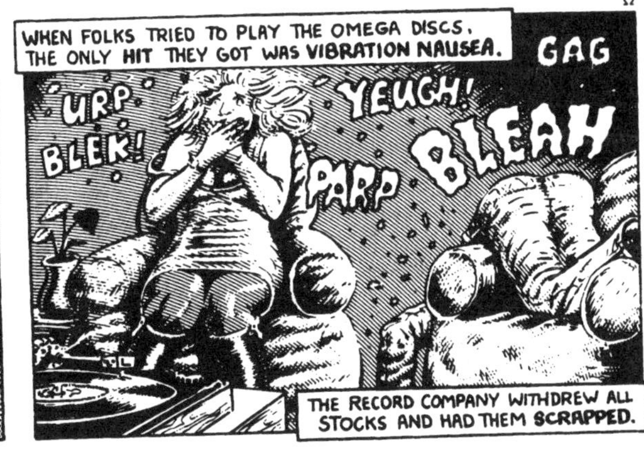

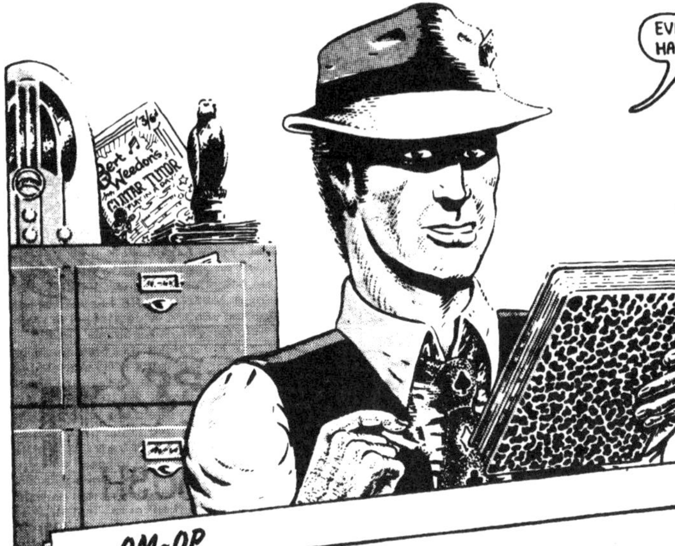

OM-OP

OMEGA

PERSONNEL: Billy Awful, *vocals*, Matt Black, *bass*, 'Astro' Quimby, *lead guitar*, 'Bongo' Ackroyd, *percussion*.

FORMED: 1967 as *PLF* (Peace, Love, Flowers).

1968: Masqueraded as *THE ELECTRIC PRUNES* at UFO. Thrown out.

Same year *Asto* O.D.'s on banana leaves at Southport Flower Show. Replaced by *Mick O'Riley* (stage name: 'Thunderclap Gascoine').

1969: Scunthorpe Magistrates' Court: *PLF* sent down for two years (Theft, Possession of Drugs, Damage to Hotel Furniture, Embezzlement, Indecent Exposure, Evasion of Income Tax, Rape).

1971: Released. Name changed to *THE 3-CHORD HEAVIES*.

1972: Beaten up by *Deep Purple* at Manchester Free Trade Hall.

1973: Released from Hospital. Name changed to *THE TERRY TINSEL BAND*.

Bongo killed by stray dart during gig at *The Miners Arms*, Bradford. Replaced by ex-*PILES* drummer, *Lynsey Dumbo*.

1974: Bankrupt by costume expenses after sequin prices rocket.

1975: Name changed to *VINCE DRAPE AND THE BROTHEL CREEPERS*.

1976: One-night-stand at *Bluto's*, Wigan. Beaten up by Female Backing Group, *TITZ*.

1977: Name changed to *SCRAGG END*. Tour many Punk Rock venues including *Nasty Ethel's* and *Sleazer's Palace*.

1978: Name changed to *OMEGA*. Big publicity build-up shortly before they all perished in one of the *London Terror Bombings* frequent around that time.

DISCOGRAPHY

SINGLES:

1968: *SAN FRANCISCAN POLICEMEN/LUV YOU ALL.*
1971: *MANDRAX MADNESS/HEAVY METAL WALTZ.*
1973: *YOUR GANG SUCKS/WIDE EYED AND GORMLESS.*
1975: *GREAT BALLS OF FIRE/GOOD GOLLY MISS MOLLY.*
1977: *GILBERT GRIMSHAW'S EYES/GOB.*
1978: *EVE OF DESTRUCTION/THE PRISONER*

L.P.s.

1978: *OMEGA.* Ω

ALL RECORDS DELETED.

SEE YA ON THE BREADLINE!

THE END

BRAINSTORM STUDIOS

WHAT THEY SAID

Brainstorm was a 'light' burning through the dark days of the 70's.

Brian Barritt, Author of The Road of Excess (PSI Publishing 1998)

In England, psychedelic comix are just coming into their own. Brainstorm comics is just out, looking like a stoned version of Dr Strange... let me just say this - Bryan Talbots From Here to Infinity is one damned fine comic story and any collector worth his salt is going to want a couple of both issues in his stash.

Clay Geerdes in Comix World

Bryan Talbot is a masterful comic artist and writer. He is one of those creators whose work other creators look forward to seeing. Chester P Hackenbush, the psychedelic alchemist is his first and, I think, most endearing character.

Tasha Lowe,
www.The Comic Store.Com

Today the alternative comic is beginning to revive with Brainstorm... Instead of simply copying the styles and formats of the major comics, they are out to create something new. A new market with new ideas and new artists. Maybe along the way we will find not another Frank Bellamy, Ron Embleton, Frank Hampson or Don Lawrence, but an alternative Bellamy, Embleton, Hampson or Lawrence. And maybe it is here in this issue of Brainstorm.

Denis Gifford in the Mixed Bunch

Trippin' comix live again! Thanks for getting together the kind of comic I've always wanted but could never find. It was a truly cosmic crusade, the plot was a real mind-blower and the artwork beautiful. I hope you have success - there will be a lot of happy heads around if you do.

The Furry Freaks, Cornwall, 1976

It was a cold Saturday morning and I was on my way to meet Bryan Talbot in Liverpool. It is a weird thing to meet your hero: what would he be like in real life? I have been reading his work for a year and it has always had a profound effect on me.

The call went round: Bryan has arrived! Then he walked in. I have never been so overwhelmed in my life. No other artist has had anywhere near as big effect on me and here he was, large as life.

He was really cool! Here's a total sad fanboy who gave him a fan-

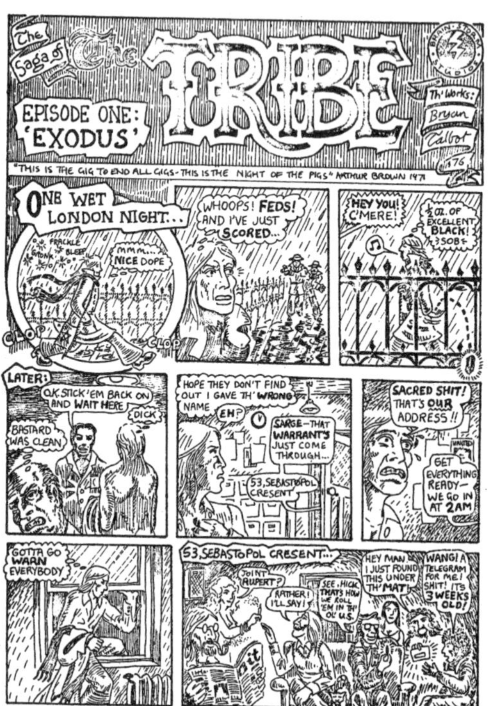

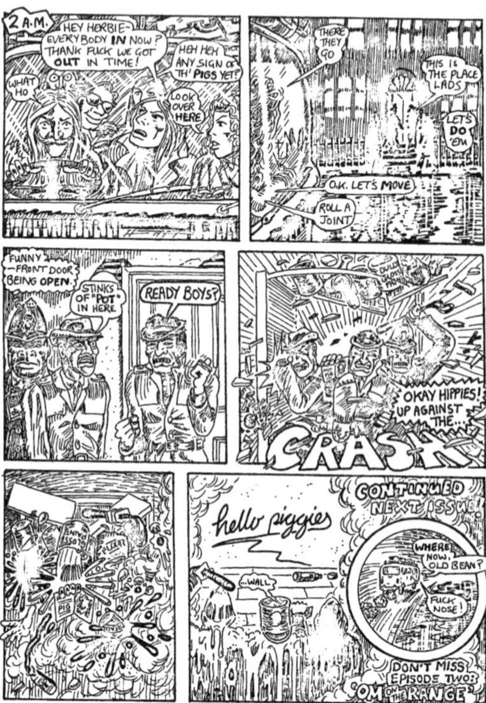

page on the web and he's talking to me like an old friend. Then there was the work that I had known about for years but never actually seen and now he's casually dishing copies out to me.

All in all it was deeply satisfying, meeting this chap who I have harboured a mental picture of over the years based on his work, and then being befriended by him. I know Bryan checks up on his webpage from time to time and although I don't want to embarass him too much: suffice to say that you've made one fanboy very happy.

James Robertson
webmaster @ www.bryan-talbot.com

Bryan Talbot's Chester P Hackenbush is clearly a character whose time has arrived. Hackenbush is not just another wacked-out wastrel, he is a mystic knight of psychedelia.

Bruce Sweeney, Comics Scen

Trust my intuition to find something both aesthetically pleasing as it is cerebrally provocative. I could swear that these life-like figures were moving across a screen. This British comic has a distinctive, delectable flavour - it captures, perpetuates that ever-important essence of what can be defined as 'fun'. I must thank all at Brainstorm for bequeathing to me this real treasure.

Glen A Ritchie
Ontario, Canada, April 1980

Bryan Talbot is a talent I don't think earlier underground comics could have visualised.

Mike Weller

I purchased issue one of the Brainstorm Trilogy in 1975 when I first met Lee Harris at 253 Portobello Road on one of my teenage pilgrimages to the big city.

As a young student of magic and alchemy, I coveted Chester P Hackenbush's fantastic crypt and soon my apartment began to resemble my hero's place of abode, with bundles of various herbs drying everywhere!

A few years later as fate would have it, I rented Lee Harris' London flat, whereupon I had the pleasure of meeting Bryan Talbot on more than one occasion.

It is now twenty four years later and I am pleased to see Talbot's Brainstorm trilogy available once again, wielding its power over our curiousity and whetting the appetite of another generation's need for the inner 'alchemical' adventure.

Let us celebrate twenty-five years of the undisputed master of British underground comix.

Jaz Coleman
Composer and Musician, 1999

Inner landscapes shift as the hero adopts one guise after another to suit the action. The overall resolution of a lot of diverse imagary makes for a pretty tasty effect.

Comix Plus

In many ways, Brainstorm Comix was the last underground comic to be produced in Britain. Underground because of the hallucinogenic adventures of its main character and the densely layered artwork of its creator, Bryan Talbot.

I was impressed: here was a proper underground comic in the American mould - colour covers, poor quality interior paper and a really strange story. Unfortunately the adventures of Chester P Hackenbush were too short-lived, but the talent of Bryan Talbot went on to feature on characters as diverse as Luther Arkwright, Nemesis the Warlock and the Batman.

Dr David Huxley
Author, forthcoming Nasty Tales: The Strange History of British Underground Comics (Headpress) 1999

The Silver Surfer has his surfboard, Howard the Duck has his cigar, Krazy Cat got a brick, but - Chester P Hackenbush has got a Pollymorphous Talking Walking Stick of Headland Rock! Brainstorm is beautiful and its concepts truly remarkable.

The Golux, Aberdeen, 1977

Brainstorm is the best thing to happen to British comics since the Eagle folded. The Bryan Talbot effort was a superb piece of workmanship and I find it impossible to re-read it and not find something I'd previously missed. Classic is definitely the word for any story that manages to combine 2001, Flash Gordon, Frankenstein and Rupert the Bear into an intelligible plotline, and Polly must be the most incredible character since Howard the Duck.

William Gillespie in Mixed Bunch, Reading

Dear Bryan. Many thanks for Brainstorm Comix. I got a kick out of it and turned it over to the bullpen so they could bask in the radiance of its magnificence - just as I did. Nice of you to think of us and many thanks for the kind words and thought. I wish you lots of luck in your endeavours but don't get so good you put us out of business.

Stan Lee, Marvel Comics, 1977

One of the best. I feel I detect a sense of cosmic adventure and awareness in the mirror of your minds expanded on paper. The flavour of acidic journeys and Moorcockesque atmosphere combine to render your offering essential reading. Words are inherently dull and slow in comparison with the sharp clear essence of entity described so inadequately by the vision in my mind.

Graham, Plymouth, 1977

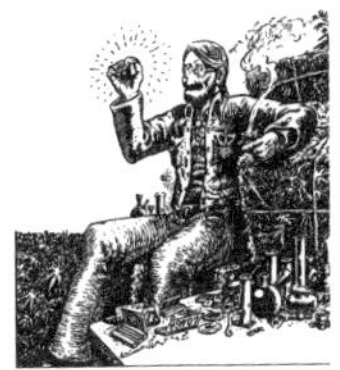

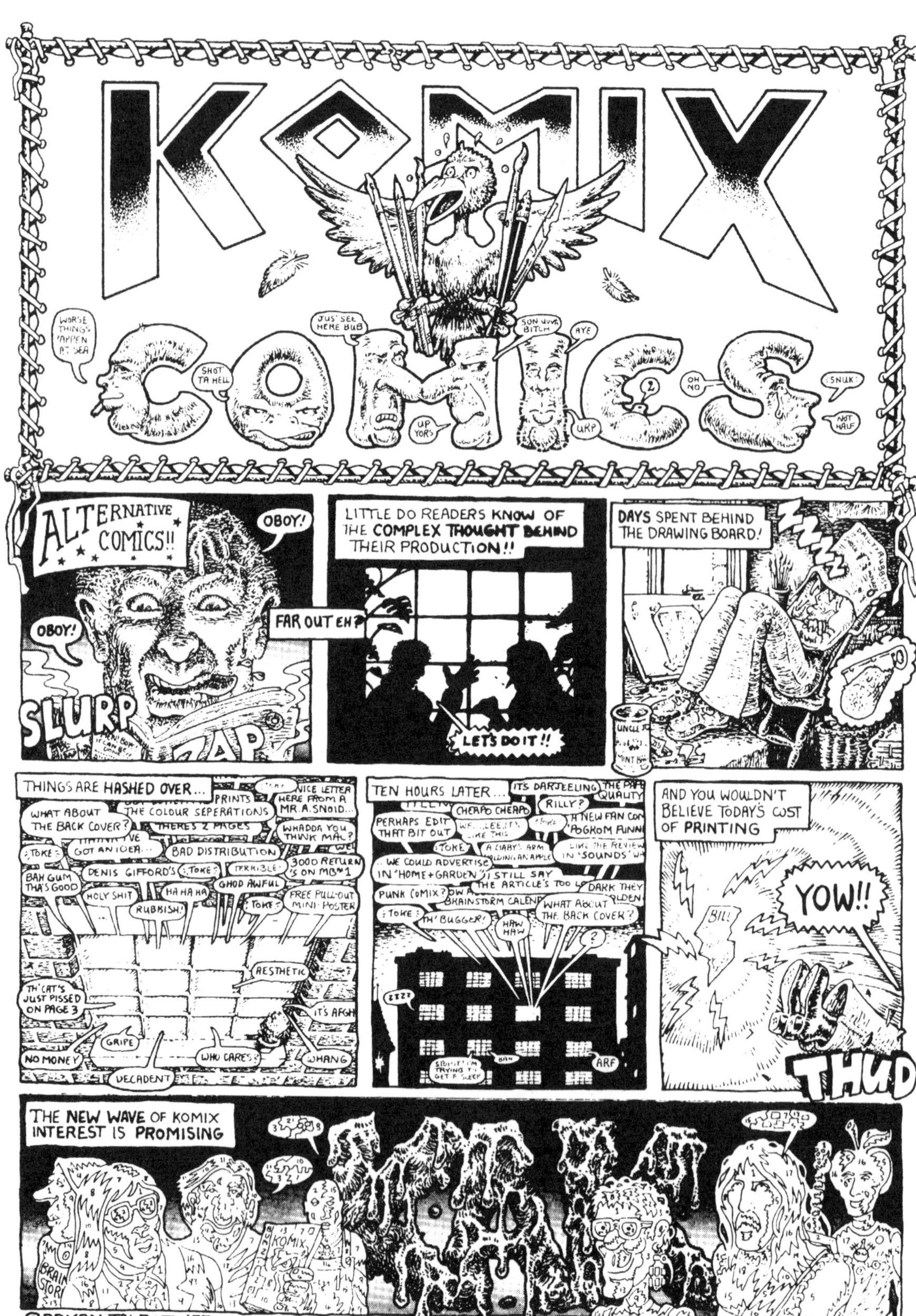
KOMIX
COMICS
WORSE THINGS 'APPEN AT SEA
SHOT TA HELL
JUS' SEE HERE BUB
UP YORS
SON UVVA BITCH
AYE
URP
OH NO
SNUK
NOT HALF
ALTERNATIVE COMICS!!
OBOY!
OBOY!
SLURP
ZAP
FAR OUT EH?
LITTLE DO READERS KNOW OF THE COMPLEX THOUGHT BEHIND THEIR PRODUCTION!!
LET'S DO IT!!
DAYS SPENT BEHIND THE DRAWING BOARD!
ZZZZ
THINGS ARE HASHED OVER...
WHAT ABOUT THE BACK COVER?
PRINTS
THE COLOUR SEPERATIONS
NICE LETTER HERE FROM A MR. A. SNOID...
THERES 2 PAGES
WHADDA YOU THINK MAC?
: TOKE :
GOT AN IDEA...
BAD DISTRIBUTION
BAH GUM THA'S GOOD
DENIS GIFFORD'S
: TOKE :
TERRIBLE
3000 RETURN'S ON MB#1
HOLY SHIT
HA HA HA
RUBBISH!
GHOD AWFUL
: TOKE :
FREE PULL-OUT MINI-POSTER
AESTHETIC
TH' CAT'S JUST PISSED ON PAGE 3
IT'S AFGH
GRIPE
NO MONEY
WHO CARES :
WHANG
DECADENT
TEN HOURS LATER...
IT'S DARJEELING
THE PAPER QUALITY
CHEAPO CHEAPO
RILLY?
A NEW FAN COM 'POGROM FINN
PERHAPS EDIT THAT BIT OUT
: TOKE :
A BABY'S ARM HOLDING AN APPLE
LIKE THE REVIEW IN 'SOUNDS'
...WE COULD ADVERTISE IN 'HOME + GARDEN'
I STILL SAY
THE ARTICLE'S TOO
DARK THEY
PUNK COMIX?
BRAINSTORM CALEND
WHAT ABOUT THE BACK COVER?
: TOKE :
TH' BUGGER!
HAW HAW
?
ZZZ
ARF
AND YOU WOULDN'T BELIEVE TODAY'S COST OF PRINTING
YOW!!
BILL
THUD
THE NEW WAVE OF KOMIX INTEREST IS PROMISING
KOMIX
BRAINSTORM
©BRYAN TALBOT - '77

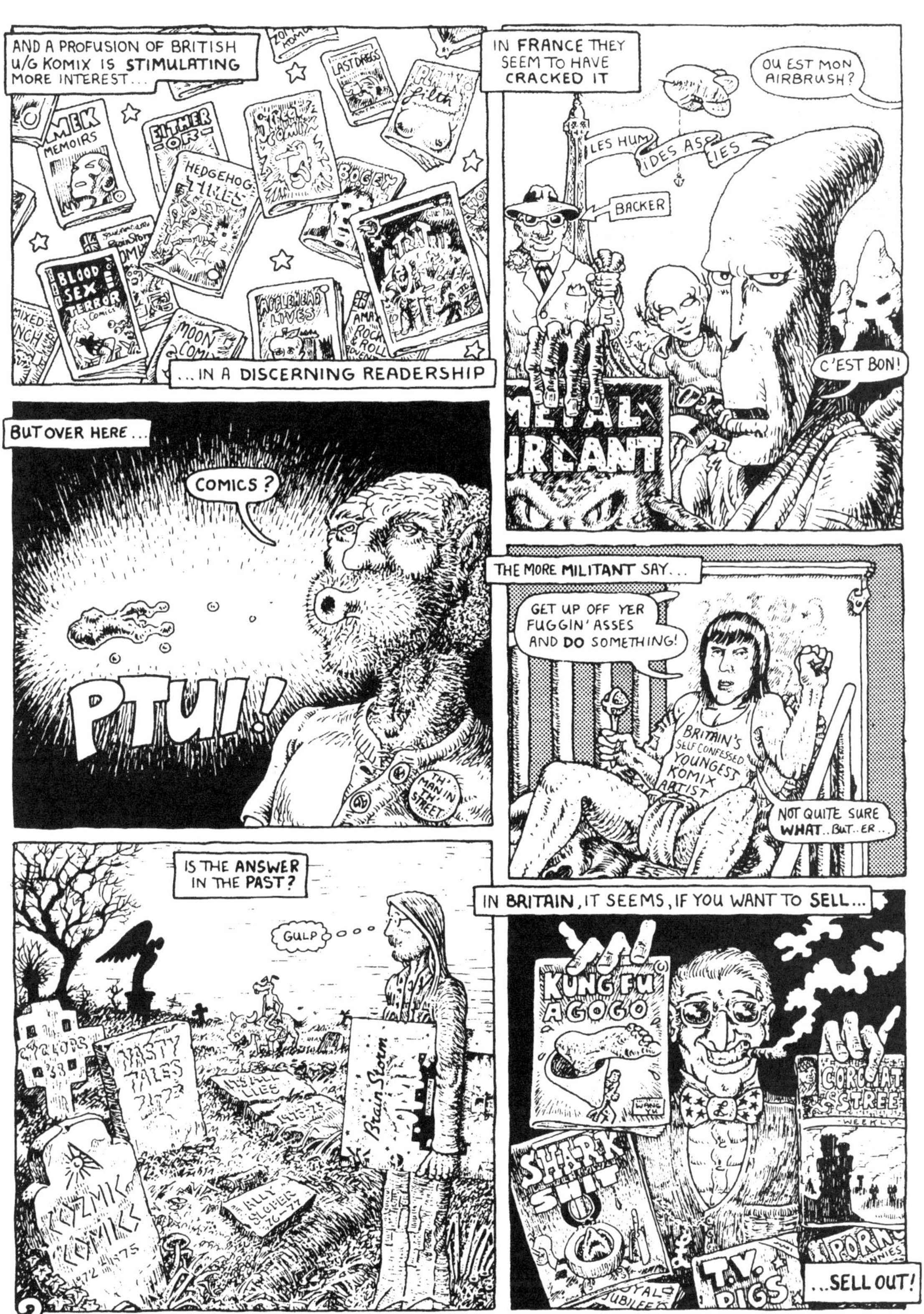
AND A PROFUSION OF BRITISH u/G KOMIX IS STIMULATING MORE INTEREST...
...IN A DISCERNING READERSHIP
IN FRANCE THEY SEEM TO HAVE CRACKED IT
OU EST MON AIRBRUSH?
LES HUMIDES ASSLIES
BACKER
C'EST BON!
METAL HURLANT
BUT OVER HERE...
COMICS?
PTUI!
TH' MAN IN TH' STREET
THE MORE MILITANT SAY...
GET UP OFF YER FUGGIN' ASSES AND DO SOMETHING!
BRITAIN'S SELF CONFESSED YOUNGEST KOMIX ARTIST
NOT QUITE SURE WHAT.. BUT.. ER...
IS THE ANSWER IN THE PAST?
GULP
NASTY TALES
BRAIN STORM
IN BRITAIN, IT SEEMS, IF YOU WANT TO SELL...
KUNG FU A GOGO
SHARK SHIT
T.V. DIGS
...SELL OUT!
2 · BRAINSTORM STUDIOS ·
WHAT A BUMMER!!

AFTERWORD

Is it really 25 years? That's a heck of a long time by any measure and, given the nature of those times, surprising that I can recall them with such clarity.

I first met Lee Harris, Brainstorm's publisher, around 30 years ago on the fringes of OZ - Britain's most notorious counterculture magazine. By 1975, I had inaugurated a publishing arm for the 'alternative' charity, Release, whilst Lee was establishing himself as the archetypical 'alternative' businessman. We were both involved with an organisation lobbying for a change in the drug laws relating to cannabis.

One day Lee appeared with a dramatic t-shirt design centred on the proclamation, 'Legalise Cannabis Now'. It had been produced for him by a young graphic designer who also happened to run a headshop in Lancashire. The designer, or maybe I should say artist, was of course Bryan Talbot.

It would have been some months later that I finally met the man. Lee knew of my enthusiasm for both comics and psychedelic art, so whilst Bryan was down in London, Lee brought him round to show me a strip he'd been working on. It was 'Out Of The Crucible' - the first Chester P Hackenbush instalment. I forget exactly what my first reaction was, but in retrospect it must have been the equivilent of somebody who in an earlier part of the century came across Winsor McCay's 'Little Nemo in Slumberland'. But, whereas McCay was content to draw exquisite and highly detailed hallucinatory panels under the auspices of his character's ever-continuing dream, Bryan was compacting a similar idea into a chemical-induced melodrama that addressed both his protagonist's mind-set and the excorcism of his inner demons. Profound stuff!

It was only after the first Brainstorm had been published that I became actively involved with the series, adding some editorial content and generally helping tidy up the production. Hackenbush returned, complete with literary and cinematic homages - not to mention my personal favourite, the chameleon-like Polly the Parrot, Chester's 'sidekick' of sorts. We also produced a couple of anthology issues which included Bryan's work and I then co-published a final Brainstorm with Lee before the reigns of such things passed to others.

This book itself came about through a series of circumstances. Lee had asked me to demonstrate some of the new technologies to him, we rapidly found ourselves discussing ways of bringing a lot of archive material together for a printed or multimedia publication that, in the style of Home Grown, would be a scapbook covering the 'high' points of five decades of counter-culture. Lee's records of this entire era are unique, as is his knowledge and experience of the times, but - despite having videotaped some prelimary interviews - the scope of this project is vast enough that it is unlikely to see the light of day before the millenium. We were looking back at the Brainstorm period when Lee remembered a fax he'd received from Bryan while he was in Amsterdam, on his 20th wedding anniversary and featuring a hand-drawm Chester asking the crypic question: "PS. When is Brainstorm going to be back in print?" After only a short discussion, Lee was convinced that, at the very least, some kind of limited edition reissue was needed.

This anniversary edition is altogether Bryan's party. A celebration of those times, repackaged and with a couple of new treats, not only for those who remember the originals but also for the ever-increasing legion of readers now seeking out Bryan's work. Indeed, only after Lee decided to publish it did we find out just how immense Bryan's popularity now is.

There are several other reasons for marking this anniversary. For Lee, proprietor of Alchemy and something of a countercultural icon, it marks the time of his first comic publishing and, by odd coincidence, married life. After the first run of Brainstorm Comix and related titles, he embarked the controversial and groundbreaking 'Home Grown' magazine, wherein Chester P Hackenbush continued his periodic adventures with the Smokey Bears in a slightly more earthbound world.

For alternative comics in Britain, Bryan's work marked the start of a small renaissance - fostering the climate in which a new breed of independent titles came into being - Hunt Emerson and friends at the Birmingham Arts Lab, Near Myths in Scotland, self-published affairs like those of Antonio Ghura, Mike Matthews and David Noon, together with a strangely titled organ called Graphixus. The mantle continues to be carried today by Knockabout Comics - also publishers of 'The X-Directory', almost a companion volume to this and collecting together many of Byran's post-Brainstorm short stories.

For me too, Brainstorm marked a departure from previous activities. The editorial role I took on the original series launched a series of career moves that kept me both involved and absorbed in the world of comics for the following decade. Graphixus magazine came first, then the creation of a minor agency for comic artists which later transformed into something more like a production company. This led to a future editorial role again following an amalgamation of sorts with Artpool and Pssst! magazine. Throughout that period I tried to promote Bryan's artwork and self-authored comics. Later, when I entered into the new field of computer and video graphics, it was knowing that the acclaimed epic of 'Luther Arkwright' was at long last nearing its hard-fought completion.

Brainstorm, although early work, remains an understated classic of its ilk and it certainly launched Bryan's career in professional illustration and comic artistry. This career even now continues its ascendancy with 'Heart of Empire' - the sequel to the scenario explored in the 'Luther Arkwright' masterpiece. For those who

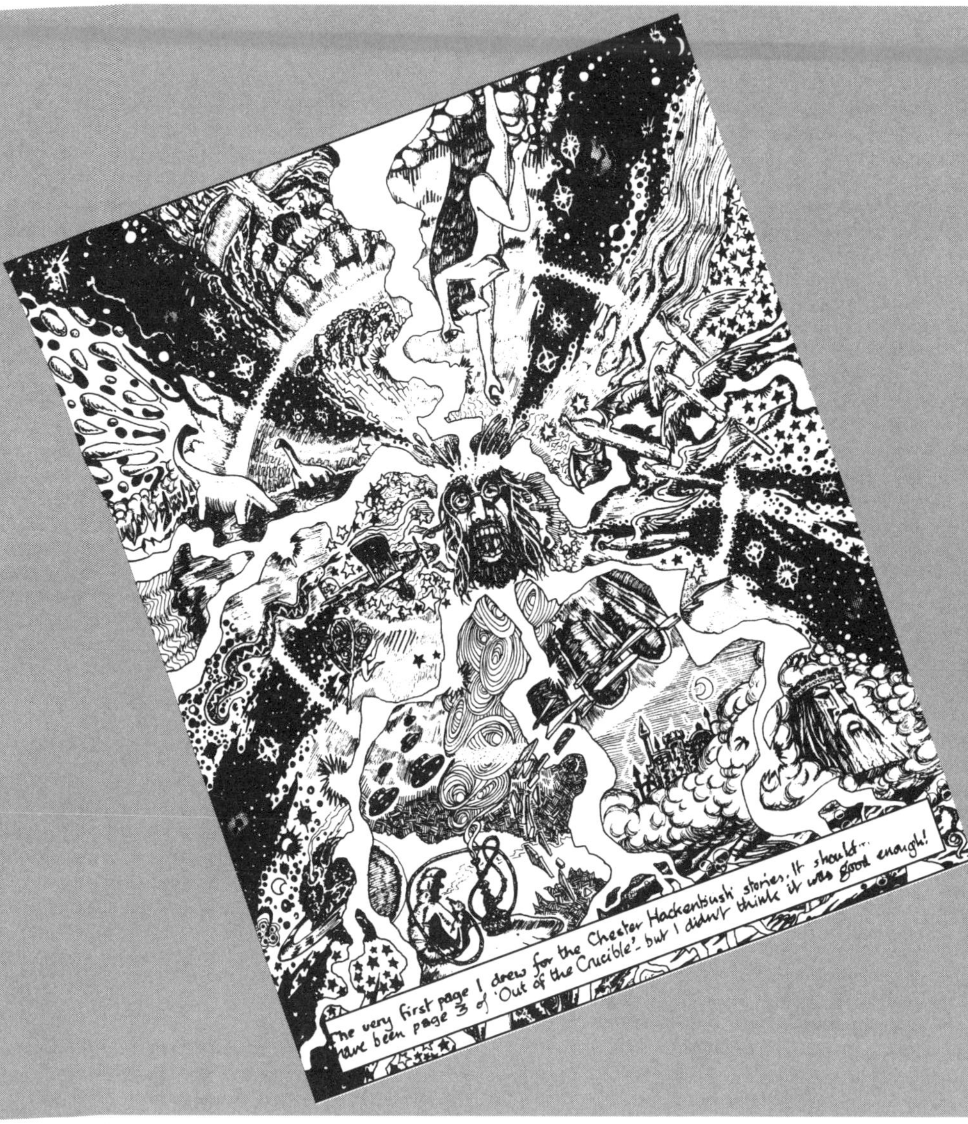

The very first page I drew for the Chester Hackenbush stories. It should... have been page 3 of 'Out of the Crucible' - but I didn't think it was good enough!

need it, we've done our best to compile a chronological summary of Bryan's work to date at the back of this book. It is a legacy of work that has attained numerous accolades, including Bryan's receipt of both the prestigious Eagle and Eisner awards.

Bryan will tell you that Chester has never really gone away. He makes cameo appearances in both Arkwright and the Omega Report and other artists have also interpreted the character. Some are shown elsewhere. The illustration above, meanwhile, is the first page ever drawn by Bryan for the Chester trilogy - it would have been page three of 'Crucible' but he rejected it as not good enough. Since this volume is all about vintage works, I thought it deserved an airing here.

As I've said, this is Bryan's party. Let's hope it's a good one and that the dance, as they say, goes on forever.

Mal Burns
London, July & October 1999.

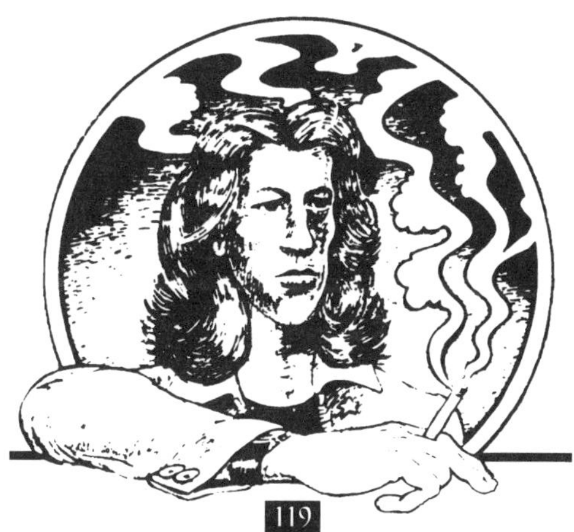

About The Artist

Bryan Talbot was born in Wigan, Lancashire in 1952 and began drawing comics for his own amusement at the age of 8. He later spent a foundation year at Wigan School of Art then obtained an LSIA in graphic design at Preston Polytechnic. In 1972, with a fellow student (Bonk!) he produced a weekly comic strip for the college newspaper. The work in this volume followed shortly after.

Following the ***BRAINSTORM*** period, Bryan created various short stories for other publications and these are collected in a companion volume, ***X-DIRECTORY: THE SECRET FILES OF BRYAN TALBOT***, published by Knockabout Comics and shown opposite.

Bryan's next major project was ***THE ADENTURES OF LUTHER ARKWRIGHT***, serialised in Near Myths and Pssst! magazines before being issued in three trade paperback volumes. It has also been re-serialised as a nine-part comic book.

Bryan has just completed a new 284 page Arkwright graphic novel, ***THE HEART OF EMPIRE*** which has been serialised by Dark Horse comics and is due for book publication in the near future.

Between the two Arkwright sagas, Bryan authored ***A TALE OF ONE BAD RAT*** which, like *Arkwright*, won him several awards. He has also illustrated episodes of '*The Batman*', '*Sandman*', '*Hellblazer*', '*Judge Dredd*' and '*Nemesis The Warlock*'. Two other complete series entirely drawn by Bryan were 'Technophage' and '*The Nazz*' with writers Rick Veitch and Tom Veitch respectively.

Bryan has held one-man exhibitions in both London and New York, besides other locations in Britain and abroad. He has also produced posters and magazine art, largely centred on the themes of rock music, superheroes and science-fiction, together with periodic advertising and teaching work.

Two long-running newspaper-style strips, '*Frank Frazakerly*' for Ad Astra magazine and '*Scumworld*' for Sounds newspaper, have yet to be republished in complete form.

In 1981, Bryan worked with science-fiction writer Bob Shaw on the Granada television arts programme, '*Celebration*' and in 1994 produced the concept illustrations for a movie adaptation the the Ramsey Campbell story '*Above The World*'.

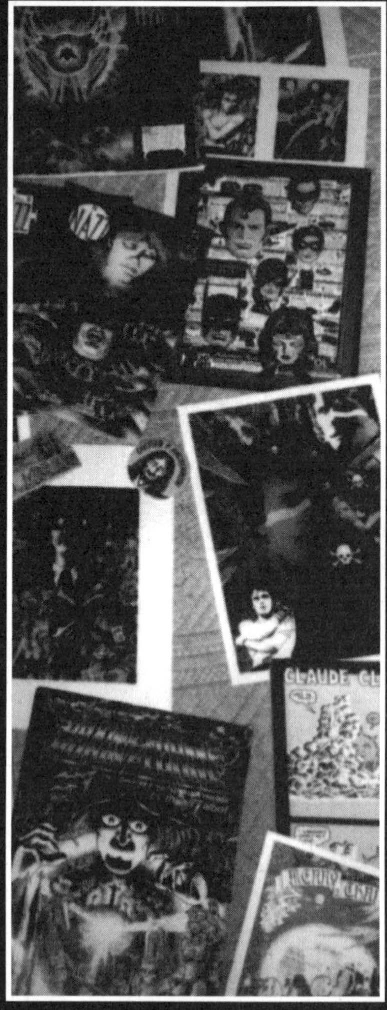